CHINESE ASTROLOGY
Plain and Simple

CHINESE ASTROLOGY
Plain and Simple

Suzanne White

Eden Grove Editions

This edition published in Great Britain, 1998 by Eden Grove Editions, 8 The Arena, Mollison Avenue, Enfield, Middlesex EN3 7NJ

Copyright © 1976, 1998 Suzanne White

Eden Grove Editions is an imprint of Axis Publishing
Distributed in the United Kingdom & Ireland by Airlift Book Company

ISBN 1 870845 31 5
A CIP catalogue record for this book is available from the British Library

Chinese Astrology Plain and Simple was first published in 1977 as
Suzanne White's Original Book of Chinese Astrology by Souvenir Press.

Printed in the United States of America.

Contents

INTRODUCTION

WHO AM I?

Far away and long ago in Paris, France, I, Suzanne White, lay me down to die. I wasn't even sick, nor maimed, nor threatened by a terminal disease. My exterior, at the age of twenty-five and a half, was actually not in bad shape at all. Yet, every time I looked into the magic looking-glass I carry inside my head, I drew a blank. "Poor little old me," said I. "Nobody loves me. Everybody hates me. I think I'll eat some worms." That would show them. That ought to cause a few indifferent people to sit up and take notice.

Obviously my objectivity meter was registering below zero. I couldn't see what was so great about being young and pretty and living in Paris. I couldn't even conceive of getting up in the morning. Eiffel Tower or no Eiffel Tower to cheer me up, I couldn't see beyond the end of my reddened nose. In my advanced state of self-sorrow, I was becoming a bore. People stopped trying to jolly me along. Why bother tickling a dead horse?

Then one day, the petulant Princess Suzanne gazed out the peephole of her self-imposed ivory tower. And what do you think she saw? An exotic pigtailed astrologer with a braided beard rising from out the Champs Elyses, brandishing a stone tablet with her name on it? Not quite. It was more pedestrian than that. I met a man.

No beard nor pigtail clouded his sunny expression. Instead of a long robe with suns and moons painted on it, this astrologer wore blue jeans and carried a Gucci book bag. His horse was a silver-gray Ferrari, his armor, a winning smile. His name was Todd.

Todd, like so many before him, listened to my sob stories with indulgent interest. Yet, somehow he was different. When I cried, he laughed. When I fumed, he giggled. Every time I insisted on being taken too seriously, Todd patted me on the head, saying, "You may as well accept yourself as you are. It is your nature to be emotional. Ups and downs are part of your lot. Why do you fight it so?"

"*Boo hoo*," I replied, "why must I be so different from everybody else? Why can't I just relax and take things as they come?"

Todd looked surprised. "Because you were born that way. It's your Chinese Chance. I looked up your sign. Conflict appeals to you. You will never take things lightly. Learn to live with it." He tossed this out as though he were passing me the salt. Todd never insisted on anything. He claimed it was not in his Goatly nature. Todd let life waft over him like the delectable scent rising from a warm plate of coq au vin. His method of resisting my skepticism about Chinese astrology was simple and painless. Todd took me to visit an exotic pigtailed astrologer with a long braided beard and a twinkle in his eye, who lived near the Champs Elysées.

That day, the wizened Vietnamese gentleman gave me his weight in golden words of true character assessment and a lifetime's worth of common-sense advice. Ever so quietly and with kindly inscrutability, the old sage said, "You are sentimental. There is much weeping in your heart. But do not trouble yourself. You are very intelligent. Words are easy for you. You are a very strong person. Do you write for a living?"

I felt like crying again. But I held the sob in check and said, "No, monsieur. I am a fashion model. I pose for a living."

The old man's piercing glance suddenly shot my way. "You must stop the modeling job. It is not difficult enough for you. Use your mind and try to write. If you do not work you will become sick in spirit."

Well, he had me there all right. I was sick in spirit and all I had ever dreamed about was becoming a writer. At that point, my literary efforts were limited to the composition of ten-page letters to friends, which most of them never bothered to answer. The concept of being paid to put words together on paper seemed no more than a little girl's dream . . . which I was certain could never come true. Not that I lacked self-esteem, brains, or talent. What was missing in my life was direction.

In short, what the Oriental astrologer had told me was something I had probably already guessed at, but could not put into focus on my own. Plainly, *I hadn't got the sense I was born with*. Rather than seeing my sensitivity as a gift, instead of rejoicing in my ability to feel things more strongly than others, I had turned it all upside down and was at that very moment living my life backward. A hyperemotional and bright young person, I was involved in a career pursuit that had nothing to offer me. Fashion modeling was not mentally challenging and gave me no other reward than an occasional glossy photo of myself to send back to the folks in Buffalo, New York.

Between intermittent consultations with my Vietnamese soothsayer and Todd's urgings to accept my fate, gradually I started to plant the positive seeds that led me to my beloved profession. The wise man's predictions were always dead right:

I would complain of lack of inspiration; he would tell me I had not yet learned to overcome my impatient nature.

I would wonder why my love life was crawling with cads and bounders; he would smile and say, "You are too warm-hearted. You help people too much. Try to help yourself. You must come first."

Despite this excellent advice, the metamorphosis of Suzanne White did not occur overnight. *Presto chango, I'm a writer.* For a time I retained my skepticism, alternately believing and disbelieving in the wisdom of my Oriental sign. So, to stay close to the fashion world and still learn about writing, I took a job as secretary to the Paris bureau chief of *Women's Wear Daily*.

Paris is not quite a small town, but nothing travels faster through its winding cobbled streets and broad avenues than chic. More and more members of the Parisian Jet Set were talking about *L'horoscope Chinois*. Chinese astrology was soon to become *très à la mode*. Along with acupuncture and new restaurants boasting a delicately spiced cuisine, the Indo-Chinese refugees (who had come to make France their home after the French troops pulled out of their ill-fated peninsula) had brought a new kind of horoscope to the European continent.

The Chinese system of fate divination had existed for thousands of years. Whatever doubts I had entertained about its authenticity were based on my own ignorance and perhaps even a tiny fear that it might be very real indeed.

In any case, nobody forced me to go back again and again to learn more and more about the subject. I was not coerced into reading all the books I could get my hands on regarding Oriental character reading. My own curiosity, the popularity of the study among people whose opinions I respected, and the precision of its judgments of human beings were my sole excuses for wanting to know all that I might about Chinese astrology.

Some years have passed since I began delving into this unusual system. In the meantime, Grace Kelly, who was born in 1929, has become aware that she is a Snake and Franqoise Sagan, the famous French authoress, discusses her Chinese horoscope sign of the Pig (for she was born in 1935) with her equally famous colleague Simone de Beauvoir (a 1907/08 Goat) in smoke-filled artist cafés. The Chinese horoscope is not only a popular topic of conversation among French and other European intellectuals, it is common knowledge among people in all walks of life. Destiny knows no social barriers. The Chinese horoscope applies to any and every one of us. And, if you don't believe me, ask any Parisian taxi driver, "*Quel est votre horoscope Chinois?*" He'll most likely fill up your cars with mellifluous phrases and predictions.

When I returned to the States in 1975 (the Year of the Cat), I thought my fellow Americans would be as tuned in to the Chinese horoscope as the French. I mistakenly thought that if I asked somebody what his Chinese sign was, he would know the answer as well as any Parisian *chauffeur de taxi*. Wrong again. Most of the people said things like, "I'm an Aries. What year is that?"

To begin to explain what I had spent so much time leaming about and living with was exhausting me. I was spending all of my free time telling people: "It's not the month, it's the year"; or "No, I don't have to know the hour of your birth"; and "Why are you so upset? It's wonderful to be a Pig. Pigs are very respected animals in China."

So I decided to write this book. It is dedicated to all of my curious compatriots who call me in the middle of the night to inquire, "If she's a Dragon and I'm a Monkey, do you think it would be all right if I asked her to play tennis on Tuesday?"

Whatever you need to know about the various signs and their compatabilities—whom to live with, where to look for your strengths and weaknesses, how to choose a business partner, or be a better parent according to your Chinese horoscope—will be found between the covers of this volume.

WHO AM I NOW?

Twenty-five years ago in Paris, I began writing books. I was a single Mom. I had no child support to help raise my two daughters. I could have taken a teaching job or become a simultaneous translator. The stability and regular salary would certainly have bought softer leather ballet slippers for Daisy, and secured a more jazzy piano teacher for little Autumn Lee. But ever since the early days of Paris in the sixties when I had met an old Vietnamese astrologer who advised me to take up writing instead of modeling designer duds, I had dreamed of actually becoming an author.

So in 1973, I wrote a novel. It sold a few copies. I was pleased. I had actually become an author. But my babies still needed new ballet slippers and fancy party shoes and school lunch tickets and math tutors and, well, you know kids. They cost money. What? I wondered to my tangle-headed middle-of-the-night insomniac self at age 33, could I write that would sell a lot of copies to a slew of people so that Baby might have new guitar strings (Autumn had changed her instrument preference) and Daisy might sport fresh pink tulle on her favorite gossamer tutu?

When I complained to her that writing was not bringing in enough to feed my family, my conservative friend and then agent, Ana Munro, suggested "Why not write non-fiction?"

"Like history and politics?" I asked. "Hardly my style."

"No, silly!" Ana laughed. "Non-fiction books are about all sorts of things. You can choose from hairdressing or cooking or decorating or astrology or religion or self-help. Non-fiction books don't tell stories. They talk about a real subject."

"You??? calling astrology a *real* subject?" I replied snidely.

"I hate astrology myself," said Ana. "But people do buy books about it."

Ana was dead correct about that. I wrote the Chinese Astrology book that very year. First, it sold thousands and thousands and thousands, in hard cover and then hundreds of thousands in paperback and then millions and millions in both hard and soft covers in every language in every country where it was ever published.

Though it continued to foster a brisk business in other countries, in the mid-nineties, this terrifically popular book went out of print in its native English language. Why? Mergers. Business complexities. I never really got it.

I was sad. But, by this time, I had other books to sell. Besides, the ballet slipper and guitar string brigade was well out of college by now. I could breathe a bit easier. I figured I'd let my first book of Chinese Astrology sit here on my office shelf forever—a monument to the olden days when I was not the High Priestess of Chinese Astrology and couldn't sell enough novels to keep the Pampers Corporation satisfied.

Then along came Jim. The guy I met on the Internet. Yes. Really. I did. After a year, Jim became my business manager (and my fiancé but that's another book). Jim takes meticulous care of my files and answers fan mail and pores over contracts and calculates royalty interests. (He also cooks but that's another book too.) In short, Jim does everything that I do badly very well. One day, not long ago, he called from his office to mine, "Hey, Suze, what is 'the little red book'?"

"Mao." I replied absentmindedly from out my inner sanctum office.

"No, Honey," he hollered back. "I mean YOUR little red book."

"Oh, it's just my first book," I said.

"Did you know that you have over a hundred letters in the Fan Mail file asking where people can buy that book?"

"Tell them it's out of print," I said and continued batting out the month's horoscopes for *Cosmopolitan* magazine in France.

"Maybe you should put it back in print," he said, walking into my office with the little red tome in his palm. "It's a good book. People love this book."

"I know. But I don't know how to sell books. I just know how to write them," said I.

"Let me handle this." said Jim.

And so he did.

Enjoy the read.

Suzanne White

P.S. And, by the time you finish reading it all, you may begin to wonder what my own sign is. Am I a jocular Monkey who strives to make you laugh so that you will forget your troubles and just get happy? Could I be a philosophical Snake who rejoices in giving out advice to the lifelorn? Or, perhaps I am a fire-breathing Dragon who takes pleasure in ranting on about herself. I might be a sensitive Pig. And, too, it is possible I was born in the Year of the critical Dog. All of these or none of these is perchance the case. But, just for fun, I don't think I'll tell you what I am. Instead, after completing this book, if you feel so inclined, drop me a note in care of my publisher and tell me what your educated guess is on the subject of my Chinese horoscope. I promise to be intrigued and flattered by any and all correspondence.

SuzanWhite@aol.com.

HOW CHINESE CHANCE WORKS

From the Year of the Rat through the Year of the Pig, there are twelve animal signs in the Oriental astrological system. To find your own sign, all you need to know is the year of your birth. Though there are no complicated rising signs nor intricate charts to reckon with, the Chinese New Year (or TET as it is called in Vietnam) falls on a different date each year. It can occur as early as mid-January or as late as mid-February. So if you were born in either of these two months, please consult the charts at the beginning of each chapter for accuracy. A person born in late January of a Snake year might not be a Snake subject, but rather will come under the influence of the preceding Dragon year.

The cycle of the Chinese zodiac renews itself every dozen years. As luck would have it, 1900 was a Rat year. Since Rat is first in the series of twelve signs and its year opened our century, we can calculate the signs of our contemporaries with ease.

Chinese legend has it that the order of the twelve animal signs was determined thousands of years ago by Buddha himself. According to an age-old tale, there came a day when Buddha felt that the Chinese nation was sadly in need of some reorganization. On the occasion of the New Year, he called all the animals in the kingdom together for a meeting. But only twelve beasts showed up for this convention.

First came the aggressive Rat, then the hard-working Ox. At their heels bounded the smiling Tiger and his crony, the cautious Cat. Soon the spiffy Dragon appeared, followed by the wise Snake. The gifted Horse came galloping after them, and up gamboled the gentle Goat. In their wake came the merry Monkey, then in strutted the proud Rooster. The last to be heard from were the faithful Dog and the scrupulous Pig.

Buddha honored them in the order of their arrival at his summit conference, and endowed each of the twelve animals with a year of its own. From that New Year forward, each successive year of the Chinese calendar bore the character of the animal that gave it a name.

Moreover, those people born in specific animal years are marked by the nature and disposition of their natal animal. Obviously, we do not take these symbolic badges altogether literally. People born in Ox years are not necessarily big-boned or muscular. But little by little, as you study the signs, you may notice some remarkable physical likenesses. Once you are familiar with the characteristics of your own sign and have examined the chapters that describe your lovers, friends, Co-workers, and family members, you might begin trying to guess at the possible signs of strangers.

FACTS ABOUT CHINESE ASTROLOGY

What you are about to discover in these pages is an ancient Oriental art of character reading and fate prediction upon which the Orient has depended for many, many centuries. Although the Chinese horoscope is different from our Western astrology, like all systems of presage, it applies the date of a subject's birth to a set or predetermined characteristics that help to predict what the basic nature of that person will be. Unlike our Western plan, the Chinese horoscope does not consider the influence of stars and planets upon the human personality. The Chinese horoscope eliminates complication. We do not have to consult with an old sage in Peking in order to read about ourselves. Our animal symbol will tell us enough to keep us going through thick and thin for many a year.

Every Oriental person about to make a great decision about marriage, family, profession, burial, or relocation will first check to see if his sign and those of the people involved indicate that any benefit will result from his prospective move. In Japan and China parents still arrange many marriages. If the family considers that a Rooster son is not well matched to a Rat woman, oftentimes the wedding is called off.

Every sixty years, there occurs a Horse year that is called the Year of the Fire Horse. The birth of a Fire Horse child, though fortunate for the child himself, is thought to be disruptive to a home and family. Since 1966 was a Fire Horse year and many Japanese women did not wish their families to come under malevolent influences, the abortion rate in Japan soared to a dizzying rate in 1965.

Certain years are not particularly productive for agriculture. Oxen subjects, who are gifted for farming, do not thrive in these years. Oxen are advised to store up provisions during the period preceding Goat and Monkey years so as not to suffer from want during these leaner times. You will find similar predictions for your own sign at the end of each chapter.

It is not unusual to see entire blocks of derelict buildings in cities like Hong Kong, awaiting demolition because sages have said the time is not right. The temporary burial of family members is not uncommon in Japan. Ancestors, according to the Oriental horoscope, must be laid to rest under auspicious conditions. Permanent grave sites are decided upon only after due consultation with augurs.

HOW TO USE YOUR CHINESE HOROSCOPE

Astrology—like psychology, religion, ESP, TM, or Yoga—is yet another way of finding out who we are and how we can be happier. Astrologers do not claim to have all the answers. As a soothsayer, I cannot (and will not) tell you if you must or must not buy a new suit on Thursday, the twenty-ninth of July, 1986. But what I can tell you is that the animal symbol that rules the year of your birth had endowed you with certain basic characteristics and helped to define your fundamental nature.

Once you are made aware of these qualities and have accepted certain of your faults, it is conceivable that you will have a better chance of making life cooperate with you. Given definite attributes to work with, you will have the possibility of molding your own life to fit your desires and ambitions. Moreover, as you examine the chapters pertaining to your friends or acquaintances, you may learn why they behave in ways hitherto incomprehensible to you.

Life is undoubtedly fuller and richer for those of us who are gifted with self-knowledge. Yet, sometimes we watch ourselves falling into negative patterns of behavior or repeating our old mistakes. Perhaps we need to be reminded of the pitfalls for which we might have watched in order to avoid the dreaded ruts we all wish we could escape from time to time. It is true that society or circumstance can prevent us from following our true natures. Poor environment or unfortunate childhood experiences have marred many a soul and thwarted more than one person from attaining desired goals. For all kinds of reasons, we sometimes repress or otherwise modify our real selves for the sake of another person, a job, or family situation.

Yet, in this day of open forum and the right to personal freedom, we should no longer be imprisoned or held back by outside restraints. Nowadays, it is more natural to "do your own thing."

For most of us, the discovery of our "own thing" is half the battle. Without the knowledge of who we are, we cannot hope to do anything but bog down in confusion or wonder, *Why me? Where have I gone wrong?* And these and other such self-pitying or deluding quicksand states of mind are the biggest inhibitors of all.

To get the most out of life, you can begin by getting the most out of this book. Read your own sign carefully. If it doesn't seem to match up with your character, perhaps you are not as self-aware as you thought you were. Let someone else read it for you. Listen to his or her comments. And read about your friends to see if you think their signs suit them.

Not only is the Chinese horoscope amusing and informative, it's my guess that this book will provide you with many a pleasant surprise. And, hopefully, you will glean enough extra knowledge of yourself to assist in casting your own future more safely and efficiently.

THE CHINESE CALENDAR

Year	Sign	Element	Year Begins	Year Ends
1925	Ox	Wood	24 Jan 1925	12 Feb 1926
1926	Tiger	Fire	13 Feb 1926	1 Feb 1927
1927	Cat	Fire	2 Feb 1927	22 Jan 1928
1928	Dragon	Earth	23 Jan 1928	9 Feb 1929
1929	Snake	Earth	10 Feb 1929	29 Jan 1930
1930	Horse	Metal	30 Jan 1930	16 Feb 1931
1931	Goat	Metal	17 Feb 1931	5 Feb 1932
1932	Monkey	Water	6 Feb 1932	25 Jan 1933
1933	Rooster	Water	26 Jan 1933	13 Feb 1934
1934	Dog	Wood	14 Feb 1934	3 Feb 1935
1935	Pig	Wood	4 Feb 1935	23 Jan 1936
1936	Rat	Fire	24 Jan 1936	10 Feb 1937
1937	Ox	Fire	11 Feb 1937	30 Jan 1938
1938	Tiger	Earth	31 Jan 1938	18 Feb 1939
1939	Cat	Earth	19 Feb 1939	7 Feb 1940
1940	Dragon	Metal	8 Feb 1940	26 Jan 1941
1941	Snake	Metal	27 Jan 1941	14 Feb 1942
1942	Horse	Water	15 Feb 1942	4 Feb 1943
1943	Goat	Water	5 Feb 1943	24 Jan 1944
1944	Monkey	Wood	25 Jan 1944	12 Feb. 1945
1945	Rooster	Wood	13 Feb 1945	1 Feb 1946
1946	Dog	Fire	2 Feb 1946	21 Jan 1947
1947	Pig	Fire	22 Jan 1947	9 Feb 1948
1948	Rat	Earth	10 Feb 1948	28 Jan 1949
1949	Ox	Earth	29 Jan 1949	16 Feb 1950

Year	Sign	Element	Year Begins	Year Ends
1950	Tiger	Metal	17 Feb 1950	5 Feb 1951
1951	Cat	Metal	6 Feb 1951	26 Jan 1952
1952	Dragon	Water	27 Jan 1952	13 Feb 1953
1953	Snake	Water	14 Feb 1953	2 Feb 1954
1954	Horse	Wood	3 Feb 19,54	23 Jan 1955
1955	Goat	Wood	24 Jan 1955	11 Feb 1956
1956	Monkey	Fire	12 Feb 1956	30 Jan 1957
1957	Rooster	Fire	31 Jan 1957	17 Feb 1958
1958	Dog	Earth	18 Feb 1958	7 Feb 1959
1959	Pig	Earth	8 Feb 1959	27 Jan 1960
1960	Rat	Metal	28 Jan 1960	14 Feb 1961
1961	Ox	Metal	15 Feb 1961	4 Feb 1962
1962	Tiger	Water	5 Feb 1962	24 Jan 1963
1963	Cat	Water	25 Jan 1963	12 Feb 1964
1964	Dragon	Wood	13 Feb 1964	1 Feb 1965
1965	Snake	Wood	2 Feb 1965	20 Jan 1966
1966	Horse	Fire	21 Jan 1966	8.Feb 1967
1967	Goat	Fire	9 Feb 1967	29 Jan 1968
1968	Monkey	Earth	30 Jan 1968	16 Feb 1969
1969	Rooster	Earth	17 Feb 1969	5 Feb 1970
1970	Dog	Metal	6 Feb 1970	26 Jan 1971
1971	Pig	Metal	27 Jan 1971	14 Feb 1972
1972	Rat	Water	15 Feb 1972	2 Feb 1973
1973	Ox	Water	3 Feb 1973	22 an 1974
1974	Tiger	Wood	23 Jan 1974	10 Feb 1975
1975	Cat	Wood	11 Feb 1975	30 Jan 1976
1976	Dragon	Fire	31 Jan 1976	17 Feb 1977
1977	Snake	Fire	18 Feb 1977	6 Feb 1978
1978	Horse	Earth	7 Feb 1978	27 Jan 1979
1979	Goat	Earth	28 Jan 1'979	15 Feb 1980
1980	Monkey	Metal	16 Feb 1980	4 Feb 1981
1981	Rooster	Metal	5 Feb 1981	24 Jan 1982
1982	Dog	Water	25 Jan 1982	12 Feb 1983
1983	Pig	Water	13 Feb 1983	1 Feb 1984
1984	Rat	Wood	2 Feb 1984	19 Feb 1985
1985	Ox	Wood	20 Feb 1985	8 Feb 1986
1986	Tiger	Fire	9 Feb 1986	28 Jan 1987
1987	Cat	Fire	29 Jan 1987	16 Feb 1988
1988	Dragon	Earth	17 Feb 1988	5 Feb 1989
1989	Snake	Earth	6 Feb 1989	26 Jan 1990
1990	Horse	Metal	27 Jan 1990	14 Feb 1991
1991	Goat	Metal	15 Feb 1991	3 Feb 1992

Year	Sign	Element	Year Begins	Year Ends
1992	Monkey	Water	4 Feb 1992	22 Jan 1993
1993	Rooster	Water	23 Jan 1993	9 Feb 1994
1994	Dog	Wood	10 Feb 1994	30 Jan 1995
1995	Pig	Wood	31 Jan 1995	18 Feb 1996
1996	Rat	Fire	19 Feb 1996	6 Feb 1997
1997	Ox	Fire	7 Feb 1997	27 Jan 1998
1998	Tiger	Earth	28 Jan 1998	15 Feb 1999
1999	Cat	Earth	16 Feb 1999	4 Feb 2000
2000	Dragon	Metal	5 Feb 2000	23 Jan 2001
2001	Snake	Metal	24 Jan 2001	1 1 Feb 2002
2002	Horse	Water	12 Feb 2002	31 Jan 2003
2003	Goat	Water	I Feb 2003	21 Jan 2004
2004	Monkey	Wood	22 Jan 2004	8 Feb 2005
2005	Rooster	Wood	9 Feb 2005	28 Jan 2006
2006	Dog	Fire	29 Jan 2006	17 Feb 2007
2007	Pig	Fire	18 Feb 2007	6 Feb 2008
2008	Rat	Earth	7 Feb 2008	25 Jan 2009
2009	Ox	Earth	26 Jan 2009	13 Feb 2010
2010	Tiger	Metal	14 Feb 2010	7 Feb 2011
2011	Cat	Metal	3 Feb 2011	22 Jan 2012
2012	Dragon	Water	23 Jan 2012	9 Feb 2013
2013	Snake	Water	10 Feb 2013	30 Jan 2014
2014	Horse	Wood	31 Jan 2014	18 Feb 2015
2015	Goat	Wood	10 Feb 2015	7 Feb 2016
2016	Monkey	Fire	8 Feb 2016	27 Jan 2017
2017	Rooster	Fire	28 Jan 2017	15 Feb 2018
2018	Dog	Earth	16 Feb 2018	4 Feb 2019
2019	Pig	Earth	5 Feb 2019	24 Jan 2020
2020	Rat	Metal	25 Jan 2020	11 Feb 2021
2021	Ox	Metal	12 Feb 2021	31 Jan 2022
2022	Tiger	Water	I Feb 2022	21 Jan 2023
2023	Cat	Water	22 Jan 2023	9 Feb 2024
2024	Dragon	Wood	10 Feb 2024	28 Jan 2025
2025	Snake	Wood	29 Jan 2025	16 Feb 2026
2026	Horse	Fire	17 Feb 2026	5 Feb 2027
2027	Goat	Fire	6 Feb 2027	25 Jan 2028
2028	Monkey	Earth	26 Jan 2028	12 Feb 2029
2029	Rooster	Earth	13 Feb 2029	1 Feb 2030
2030	Dog	Metal	2 Feb 2030	22 Jan 2031
2031	Pig	Metal	23 Jan 2031	8 Feb 2032

THE CHINESE YEARS

Rat
1900 1912 1924 1936 1948 1960 1972 1984 1996 2008

Ox
1901 1913 1925 1937 1949 1961 1973 1985 1997 2009

Tiger
1902 1914 1926 1939 1950 1962 1974 1986 1998 2010

Cat
1903 1915 1927 1939 1951 1963 1975 1987 1999 2011

Dragon
1904 1916 1928 1940 1952 1964 1976 1988 2000 2012

Snake
1905 1917 1929 1941 1953 1965 1977 1989 2001 2013

Horse
1906* 1918 1930 1942 1954 1966* 1978 1990 2002 2014

Goat
1907 1919 1931 1943 1955 1967 1979 1991 2003 2015

Monkey
1908 1920 1932 1944 1956 1968 1980 1992 2004 2016

Rooster
1909 1921 1933 1945 1957 1969 1981 1993 2005 2017

Dog
1910 1922 1934 1946 1958 1970 1982 1994 2006 2018

Pig
1911 1923 1935 1947 1959 1971 1983 1995 2007 2019

*Fire Horse Years

THE RAT

THE YEARS OF THE RAT

January 31, 1900 to February 19, 1901
February 18, 1912 to February 6, 1913
February 5, 1924 to January 25, 1925
January 24, 1936 to February 11, 1937
February 10, 1948 to January 29, 1949
January 28, 1960 to February 15, 1961
February 15, 1972 to February 2, 1973
February 2, 1984 to February 19, 1985
February 19, 1996 to February 6, 1997

RATS ARE:

Seductive • Energetic • Of good counsel • Charming • Meticulous
Sociable • Jolly • Persistent • Humorous • Intellectual • Lovable
Sentimental • Generous • Honest

BUT THEY CAN ALSO BE:

Profiteering • Manipulative • Agitated • Gamblers
Greedy • Petty • Suspicious • Disquiet • Tiresome
Destructive • Power-hungry

RATS I HAVE KNOWN AND LOVED

What one has to understand about Rat people is that once you have made it clear that you know what they are up to, they shape up very nicely . . . or else they walk right out of your life forever. Halfway measures are not their forte.

Oddly enough, according to the Chinese, the most endearing quality of Rat people is honesty. I prefer to interpret this Oriental variety of honesty as something closer to fair play, or simply a high regard for justice. Rats do not like to witness happenings in which undue partiality is exhibited—unless, of course, said Rat is the promulgator of the inequity.

The Rat person possesses a two-sided nature. Outwardly, he is generous and cheery; he seems calmly equilibriated. On the inside, Rats harbor an inordinate amount of selfishness in the form of greed and acquisitiveness. What differentiates Rat subjects from your ordinary miser is their very profound regard for the equitable sharing-out of bounty with those they feel are worthy of it.

Rat standards are high. They are not easily seduced by small talk and chitchat. If a Rat person chooses to like you, he will not hide his feelings. Once he has decided to befriend someone, both his hospitality and benefaction extend across formerly uncrossable frontiers.

In view of this stringent set of rules that the Rat usually sets up for himself, if one of his "chosen few" eventually betrays, or in any way attempts to dupe him, he is capable of both vengeance and unreasonable demands for retribution. Rats never accept to be toyed with or taken lightly. In business as well as in love partnerships, they are ruthless when crossed.

Here is a telling Rat tale. Around the corner from my house in Paris, there live two American expatriates, side by side in a pair of wooden houses. These houses were built from gardening sheds. Long ago, in the postwar forties (before the French building codes became as strict as they are today), one could still find such jewels within the city limits and with minimum investment, turn them into livable homes. Times have changed. Or, so I learned from my Rat lady neighbor, Claire Augustus (b. 1936), a few months ago.

She came over to inform me that her husband Nick wanted to convert a third small tool shack in their garden into a guesthouse. Earnestly, she recounted, "While we were in Majorca this summer, the building organization met to discuss zoning. Our request for a construction permit was refused. I am so angry, I could spit!" Claire heaved a sigh of controlled rage and went on. "From what I understand, our next-door neighbor Paul Kradlow was at that meeting. He's president of the *coproprieté* [In France all buildings are condominiums. Everyone owns his own flat.] Ordinarily what Paul says goes. I just don't understand it. We left it all in Kradlow's hands. Paul insists it is not his fault. He claims he made a very persuasive speech in our defense. That little guest house wouldn't disturb anybody. Except for Paul, nobody can even see that shack. The decision is unfair but we are legally unable to appeal it." Her eyes filled with the mist of homeowner frustration.

Two weeks after hearing Claire's diatribe against the unreasonable vote, I ran into Paul Kradlow in a Montparnasse artists' haunt. Paul is a painter. Although he has never been my favorite person, we have been neighbors for so long that we always smile and nod at each other in public places. That day, Paul uncharacteristically called me over to his table. "Sit down a minute, will you?" he said. I sat.

"Well," said Paul. "I suppose you've heard about their wild plan to turn their shed into a guesthouse?" I nodded. He blathered on, "Of course, as president of the *copropriete*, I have certain responsibilities to the building authorities. During the summer we had a meeting. The Augustuses were away, so I had to call a vote in absentia. Unluckily, most of their supporters were out of town at the time. The vote came out negative." Paul's ensuing sigh was not quite grievous enough.

"How did you vote, Paul?" He blanched, took a drink of his Bordeaux white, and winked at me as he said, "Negative." Then he smiled and winked again.

I wrenched my arm away from him. "Fine friend you are!" I railed angrily. "If I were Claire, I would—"

"She did," he murmured sadly.

"She did what?" I demanded.

"She found out from one of the people at that meeting that I had spoken out against her request for a permit." His eyes began to search mine for some small flare of neighborly indulgence. Instead I glared back. He continued, "In the middle of last night, Claire did a terrible thing to me." Paul looked perfectly sound. No scratches, cuts, or bruises. He had no family for her to threaten, so I could not imagine what Claire could have chosen to do to avenge herself of his crime against her trust. Paul took out a felt marking pen and began to write on the paper tablecloth. "Here's what she did," Paul said. "She painted these words on the side of her own shed. In enormous white letters on the dark green wood." I looked at the message he had drawn on the cloth. It said: THOU SHALT NOT BEAR FALSE WITNESS AGAINST THY NEIGHBOR! I burst into uncontrollable laughter. Only a Rat could think up such a trick. Paul's kitchen-sink view was besmirched for life with a permanent reminder of the broken commandment.

Assuming the pose of the wronged artist, Paul said meekly, "I can't even paint over it. That shed is on her property. Don't you think that's a ratty thing to do to an old friend?"

Rising to leave the table, I grinned widely and agreed. "Gotta watch out for Rats, Paul. They're all around us."

Rat people are charming. Even at their worst, they will manage to conjure up a welcoming "Hi there" or "How are you?" for a visitor or passing acquaintance. Social gatherings are their life's blood. Cloister a Rat person away from convivial companionship and he will wither and die of loneliness. Since this subject is blessed with an engaging personality and winning manner, he loves to entertain, throw parties, cook exotic dishes for the benefit of his guests, and, in general, lay on the festivities and merrymaking. If you ever get invited to a Rat bash, please accept with pleasure. You will not be disappointed. Moreover, unusual surprises may be in store, for people born under the sign of the Rat take great pride in finding new diversions for themselves as well as for their playmates.

One such astonishing fellow is my dearest male Rat friend of all, Richard Reventlow. When Richard gives a party or celebrates even the most minor of family birth dates, my curiosity barometer rises sharply.

Following his wife Sheila's most recent birthday party, she asked me, "What will he think of next? Sometimes I think Richard has really gone round the bend." Sheila was stumbling around her disaster area of a living room, righting tables and chairs, picking up specks of confetti, and wiping spilled ice cream from the carpet.

"You know, I really didn't mind the first batch of monkeys. The brown ones were kind of cute the way they rode around on tricycles and performed tricks for the trainer. My mother-in-law looked a bit frightened when that black rhesus jumped into her coffee cup, but she ought to be used to Richard by now. I guess she'll survive."

From the kitchen, Sheila had to raise her voice to a yell, "But those chimpanzees! Did you see how dirty they were? Why Richard didn't look at them before he hired them, I will never know. I mean, really, Suzanne, who ever heard of renting six wild beasts to ride around a Fifth Avenue living room on mini-motorcycles? The noise alone was terrifying."

Sheila beckoned me to her room. "Let's go into my bedroom and relax with a drink. We can watch a dumb movie on TV. Anything's better than looking at this mess."

When we had settled into our respective places in front of the television, Sheila on the bed and myself in a chaise longue, I thought of asking her what Richard had given her as a birthday gift.

"I don't know yet. He says it's going to be a surprise. Maybe he'll bring something home tonight. For all I know, it could be a pet baboon."

Sheila gave a loving laugh.

As she turned on the television set from the remote-control switch at her bedside, Sheila suddenly began to tremble all over. At first, I couldn't help but laugh. She looked so silly, just sitting there shaking like that. I was convulsed with mirth. All I heard was her vibrato cry: "That damned Richard!" she quivered aloud. "He's so loony. Do you know what he's gone and done?"

Alarming as her strange appearance was, I could not stop bubbling up with laughter every time I tried to answer her. "What is it? Are you all right?" I managed to gasp between giggles.

Just as abruptly as the quiverings had begun, they stopped. The TV set went off. Sheila, in a fit of chuckles, was reading aloud from a note she had found pinned to the pillow. "My darling wife," she read. "Hope you like this little present. It's called Magic Fingers. Remember how much you liked it when we went to that funny motel in Ohio? The medium is the massage! Love you forever. Richie."

I can assure you that Richard Reventlow is not a crazy man. He just acts like one. Last year, on the occasion of their tenth wedding anniversary, he awarded his wife a fireworks display. The year before, he gave himself a roller-skating birthday fete. He hired a rink for the evening, invited fifty friends, and followed up the skate-in with a hayride through Central Park.

Rat people have an undeniable preference for luxurious victory over the simple life. Every time I meet a new Rat, the first thing I notice is his clothing, fine jewelry, and elegant manners. Little matter the state of his bank account, background, or social standing. Rats like to look their best. They surround themselves with fine quality objects. The women of this sign have exquisite taste in both wardrobe and decorative accouterments. Their homes are often showpieces for delicate antiques or an array of jungle plants that nobody else ever seems able to grow.

This love of the good life notwithstanding, Rat people make conscientious parents. Every step of the way during a child's development captures the interest of a Rat mother or father. Be it physical or moral, if one of their own pack is hurt or feeling downhearted, the Rat will take great pains to see that the wrong is righted. Thus, Rat people can become what some of us describe as "do-gooders." They are forever being nominated president of "The Committee for Annihilation of Mental Health," or serving on the board of directors of one charity or the other.

One of our very own most famous Rats, Marlon Brando (b. 1924), has taken up the cause of the American Indian to the extent of refusing an Academy Award on television so that he could inform the public of his serious intention to help out.

Brando is a very good Rat case in point. He has always known how to put his Rat charms to excellent use. The variety of roles he has played in his life, each of them with equal facility and talent, have brought his fans much vicarious joy and heartbreak. Yet, like all Rats, Brando is not noted for his ability to compromise when dealing with directors or other actors and actresses. His on-the-set reputation is not very complimentary. Rats gripe a lot and are often dissatisfied with the efforts of others. It is difficult for them to tolerate the fact that nobody—even themselves—is perfect. This feeling of discontent sometimes results in grousing and complaints. Rats can make life very difficult for co-workers.

My mother used to talk about my Rat of an uncle this way: "Ed is an angel in the crowd. But he is a devil at home." It was true. My Uncle Ed was a misery to live with. He never came home on time for dinner. He worked long hours in his office in hopes of making that big killing in real estate (which he finally made). He snapped at his kids more often than he should have. And, according to my good mother, "Ed ran around with women."

In part, my mother's old-fashioned way of describing Uncle Ed says much about the Rat's character. But those who knew Ed understood implicitly his gift for participating in extra-household duties and charitable acts of patronage. The fact is, Ed never "ran around with women" in the way one normally thinks of that pastime. But he did organize fund-raising activities for the ladies auxiliary at his church.

And he drove piles of chattering nuns back and forth to country retreats and served on committees all his life for the betterment of conditions in a senior citizens' complex for women only. So, the Rat that he was did "run around" with women, but not in the classical sense.

Rats make a science of the art of impressing people. Nobody gets away with feeling lukewarm about a Rat. Half the time, he is hated (even feared), and the other half, he is blindly adored by those who know him. Yet, whatever the ambience surrounding him, the Rat is graceful.

Rats often deport themselves in a rather controversial manner. They are at home discussing politics with the visiting British prime minister, comfortable hobnobbing with the boys down at the local bar, and deft at convincing garage mechanics to take 20 percent off their repair bills. It is not fair to say that Rats are con artists. But they are extremely persuasive and will stop at almost nothing in order to have their way. Whether engaged in business or emotional negotiations, Rat people are never entirely free of mental calculation. Their warmest feelings and gestures of generosity are tinged with overtones of self-interest. Rarely, if ever, does a Rat person bestow love or even friendship unless he feels it will ultimately be of use to him. Their motto, "You scratch my back and I'll scratch yours," is valid. It is common knowledge among mature adults that nothing is for nothing. What is different about the Rat is his inability to deviate from that pattern except for old time's sake or because he wishes to indulge a former lover. Sentimentality of the sticky, sweet, sappy variety is very much out of the Rat's line, but he is a pushover for memories and tradition.

To gain either affection or capital, Rats will bend over backward. A Rat person, dedicated to a romance or to making a gain from a business venture, will ignore all emotional boundaries until he has reached his goal. For this reason, Rats make superlative profiteers. Sometimes, it seems as though everything they touch turns to gold. Rats are the troubleshooters of the world. They can move into a bankrupt venture, take it over on the spot, and in weeks have the whole thing in tiptop shape again. They see the loopholes, find snags, and uncover shady deals with ease and grace.

This capacity for seeing through walls and knowing just where to look for the weakest link, if used wisely, will serve to make the Rat successful at almost any undertaking. If, however, a Rat person chooses to misuse this talent, he is capable of the lowest type of indolence. If life is too easy, the Rat may become lazy.

Rats must be loved. Just because they take such enormous pleasure from social situations and are usually gifted for gab, does not mean that society's pedestrian demands on their talents are not taxing to the spirit. The Rat soul is always hungering for closer contact, more intimacy, sharing of thoughts and desires. At home, he needs to talk things through. It is almost eerie the way Rats think on their feet or calculate coups while discussing them. Deep philosophical ponderings almost never net them any benefit. Even if they spend much of their time reading or poring over documents, straightaway upon abandoning their books, they will need to discuss what they have read. If your love partner is born under the sign of the Rat, be prepared to stay up many nights rapping about the different possible strategies, deals, friendships, etc., which the Rat feels must be gone over before he sleeps.

Rat people are lovers of *la bonne table.* They almost invariably figure among those who know about wines and gourmet foods. They know how to set up beautifully appetizing spreads and they don't balk when faced with the consumption of same. Most of the Rats I know have a weight problem. They simply can't say "No" to themselves when it comes to ingesting tasty *gourmandises.* Rats are nibblers, noshers, and snackers.

Bargains and cut-rate sales leap at Rat people from shop counters, newspaper ads, and catalogs. If the A&P offered twenty jars of peanut butter for the price of ten, and you took a quick survey of the ladies who swarm in first thing in the morning, I'd be willing to bet that at least half of these "go-fers" were bom in a Rat year. Popular belief has it that Rats hoard little bits of this and that in order to be sure of something to eat when times are lean. Mind you, Rat people are not stingy about sharing their booty. They simply like to be armed for bad times. They are savers, buyers of insurance, and planners for the future. And, if by some chance, they have not thought about who will be paying that pension when they get to be old and gray, Rats will spend no small amount of their time worrying about same.

One Rat friend of mine is so preoccupied with security and getting in her stores for the duration, I often accuse her of never having had a single spontaneous buying experience. If she doesn't start collecting next year's Christmas presents in January, she fears she may not have any money left when that holiday looms on the horizon. Jayne buys her French wine, German beer, pâté de foie gras, and other nonperishables by the case or barrel. She has an extra tank of oil alongside her house in case the energy crisis takes a turn for the worse. No one is overjoyed at the thought of lacking for basics, but my Rat friend Jayne is even uneasy about the eventuality of running short of luxuries. Her home is a veritable air-raid shelter of gourmet provisions.

Much berated and attacked for not possessing the same set of priorities as other people, Rats have an unpleasant way of defending themselves. When cornered, they become most aggressive. In the midst of even a minor discussion of what should be done about a torn window shade, Rat people are capable of turning on their audience in the most offensive manner. Rat people think there is no defense like a good offense. So, when threatened (even in a small way), they strike out. Sometimes, they assume a haughty or authoritative tone and out of nowhere start snapping out platitudes of the "I'm the boss around here!" variety.

Because everybody who ever becomes involved with the malarial Rat is aware of his mercurial temper, those who know him well often avoid trouble by skirting the discussion of certain issues. Since touchy subjects can trigger the Rat to take umbrage or have one of his tantrums, a clever friend will be loath to jump in feet first and talk that point over. If the Rat realized how testy he was, he would probably be saddened by this knowledge. Rat people do enjoy debates and rap sessions, but since they are not always willing to admit their own errors or miscalculations, many people prefer not to argue with them.

Last year, I worked for a French Rat man who sold fireworks; not just caps and firecrackers, but displays, up-in-the-air high-in-the-sky showers of glorious color. Since he had decided to take the

American pyrotechnics industry by storm, and spoke not a word of English, Monsieur Lupin hired me as his interpreter. Together, we flew in to conquer the United States, but Lupin could not speak a word of English and not one prospective American fireworks client could utter a syllable of French. I didn't know what I was in for, but who could turn down a job where the product presentation at any given business meeting takes place in an open field by night under a blanket of shooting stars and Roman candle?

In retrospect, translating for Lupin would have been a snap if it had not been for his singular inability to function alone. As I have said, Rats are communicators. They have to speak in order to believe that they are alive and thinking. Can you imagine spending three full weeks (including weekends) as the seeing-ear dog of a garrulous Rat suddenly made deaf and mute by confinement in a country where you are his only means of contact with humanity? What's more, the psychology of Rats includes a hefty portion of suspicion, and this particular Rat felt very left out each time I said "Good Morning, Mr. Jones" in English. By the time he left this side of the ocean, Monsieur Lupin had a spectacular case of paranoic Americanophobia.

Every time English words escaped my lips, Lupin was sure I was trying to dupe him or take over the world's black powder supply single-handedly. He actually thought at one point that I was in cahoots with his major competition in this country. Yet, he was paying me. He had hired me in France. I had never even seen a fireworks display up close before meeting him. My work, when it only consisted of interpreting what Monsieur Lupin wished to convey to a client or manufacturer, was most enjoyable. But those long nighttime talk-ins over whiskey after whiskey in all the gloomy hotel bars across America. . . . After one week, I honestly believed I would perish from overspeak.

Life for most Rats is actually little more than an extended game of chess. Much of their time is spent maneuvering into the offensive position. The remainder of Rat lives gets gobbled up by preoccupations with projected methods of aggressively exiting from the innumerable culs-de-sac that lie in wait beyond the next move.

Basically, the Rat is a kind soul. Though his uneasiness about his own image may cause him to buffet or jostle those he fears will get the best of him, these shoves are but mild elbow jabs in the ribs of his adversaries. Rats are not the sort of tyrannical barbarians who walk over even their best friends in order to succeed. If they are somewhat promiscuous, their extracurricular escapades are only the result of self-doubt or anxiety about being attractive. When Rats lie, they sincerely believe their fibs are measures of self-defense. The whiter the lie, the more comfy the Rat.

Rats, no matter how great the scope of their success or importance, are capable of tremendous humility. No job is ever too menial for a Rat, no errand too piddling to be run for a friend.

Back a few years, when friends of mine introduced me to Rat movie star Keir Dullea (b. 1936), I learned a few facts about how lovable Rats can really be. Keir Dullea has cosmic-blue eyes the color of which varies with his mood from delft to Wedgwood. He's gorgeous, famous, talented, and still has the "lost boy" look he bore in the film *David and Lisa*. Like all Rats, he is outgoing, amusing, and energetic.

Keir, too, is a devoted friend. He is one of those people of whom we say, "He would give you the shirt off his back." He's generous and jolly, to boot.

The day I found a tiny studio in which to ply my writer's trade was a victorious one for me. The room was small and dark, typically Parisian dank and ill-decorated. But it was mine. Keir was visiting Paris at the time and offered to help me refurbish the place. Aware of my lack of talent for manual labor, I was delighted by his willingness to pound a nail and paint a wall.

Aware also that the Rat's ability to organize will always be superior to mine, I suggested that Keir plan the attack on my scruffy den on his own. I agreed to pitch in with the drudgery but admitted that I truly did not have the foggiest notion of where to begin.

First things first. Keir trundled us off to the local Parisian carpet shop where we purchased enough indoor/outdoor carpeting to cover the shoddy linoleum floor. I asked to have the rug delivered, but Keir said, "They'll never get it there on time. I'll just carry it back to your place." And, with that, he heaved the giant roll of red carpet onto his shoulder and crashed into the ceiling light fixture, breaking it into a million pieces.

After we had laughed and paid the nice shopkeeper for his lamp, Keir walked through the streets of Paris for about a kilometer, whistling as though he were one of the seven dwarfs. Parisians, unaccustomed to do-it-yourselfers, pointed and giggled as he trudged along under his weighty burden. Needless to say, French ridicule went unnoticed by our Rat hero. Keir had bagged a carpet and that was enough reason to drag it single-handedly to its destination. Besides, Rats love spectacle, especially when they create it.

In short, I am now the only living American writer in Paris who works in a studio decorated by a movie star's own hand. Keir worked for three days fixing, painting, sticking contact paper on shelves, and fitting his carpet into crannies with a bread knife. All the Rat's persistence and meticulousness went into his endeavor and the end result is both pleasing and practical.

Richard Nixon (b. 1912/13) is a Rat. Until he began to mix it up with his own brand of slick politician, Dick Nixon was considered by many Americans to be a kind of smiling nobody whom the bigwigs felt they could push around and mold into their own idea of a Presidential candidate. But I don't think the world was ready for Brother Rat's tendency to want all the power for himself. If they had read this book, Nixon's cronies would have guessed well in advance that when a Rat feels trapped or stymied by his peers, he takes one of two escape routes. Either he slinks away to become a hermit, or he turns into a dreadfully boorish bully. In the case of Richard Nixon, both avenues were employed. When aggressiveness failed, he disappeared into the woodwork.

Besides Marion Brando (b. 1924), whom we spoke of before as a prize Rat, our times have been graced by many famous Rat figures. Adlai Stevenson, Sr. was born in 1900. The year 1912 brought us playwright Eugene Ionesco. In 1924, we netted a quartet of celebrated Rat people: actress Lauren Bacall, novelists James Baldwin and Truman Capote, and Brando himself. A bumper crop arrived in 1936, among them Richard Bach of *Seagull* fame, Dick Cavett, actors Keir

Dullea and Dennis Hopper, and French couturier Yves Saint Laurent. Singer-songwriter James Taylor was born in 1948, and so was Peggy Fleming, the figure-skating champion.

Rats have a vast capacity for aggressively falling upon a task. They attack pleasure, money-making, and love affairs with equal verve. If you are lucky enough to be witness to the charming Rat's pursuit of life's rewards, you will always be assured of a great show at a very low price.

MADAME RAT

Ms. Rat is part *femme fatale* and part career woman. Between the two, she has a humdinger of a time keeping up with her desire to fill both roles. On any given day, you may catch her on the run between committee meetings and her spring cleaning, mop and bucket in hand and silk scarf camouflaging hair curlers. Upon first glimpse, you might think she is her own cleaning lady. Look a bit more closely. Lady Rat's make-up has been fastidiously applied, her fingernails freshly manicured, and underneath her smock she is wearing a tidy navy-blue skirt and blouse. Notice her feet. They are neatly stockinged and shod in go-to-business footwear. Each day of her life is a furious battle, a tussle with time and a race against the clock of Fate for the maintenance of her dual self-image.

Rat women like to be married. Idle flirtations and philanderings rarely manage to hold their interest for long. No matter how time-consuming a job she may hold, regardless of how much "coupledom" seems to take away from Ms. Rat's energy supply, for some reason she persists in wishing to live side by side with a mate. Not that the quality of marriage rapport matters to Rat women all that much. They don't seem to shrink in horror from tensions, arguments, drinking, or other types of caddish behavior in their husbands. As far as Rat women are concerned, it's all in the game.

To a Rat woman, what counts more than anything else is security. She saves her money, hoards sugar and other endangered staples, and buys the best clothes available for herself and family. (Good workmanship, you know; makes them last longer.) Yet, Rat women are also capable of enormous extravagance and from time to time are given to what appears to be wasteful spending sprees. Back and forth goes the Ratlette from extravagance to penny pinching as she buys up enormous quantities of expensive useless items only to squander them on those around her as gifts of love and emotional blackmail.

In truth, the Rat lady does not come naturally by her generosity. Albeit she wants to be noted for philanthropy, largesse (in any currency) is something she has to strive for. Oh, she may tell you that she finds waste a dreadful human failing because when she was a little girl she had to wear hand-me-downs and could never have birthday parties because her family was destitute. And she may really lend credence to that psychology as a sound reason for her reluctance to give of herself, her time, her love and affection, or her smile. Don't believe it for a minute. I (and you, too, I am sure) know scads of generous poor people who would rather give you their skimpy vittles than eat themselves.

What is further strange about the Rat woman's ambivalence toward benevolence is that most of the female Rats I know are outwardly magnanimous people. They do give fabulous dinner parties and offer to take my kids for the afternoon. But one senses that they are not very comfortable about doing so. Rat ladies worry a lot. "If I do this for so-and-so, will he do that for me?" is but one possible verbalization of their innermost thoughts.

In male/female alliances, Rat women have a tendency to lean rather heavily on their mates. The point I made before about Ms. Rat needing a husband rather than simply a companion or occasional escort or lover is based largely on this fact. Rat women, despite an enormous ability to function in social and business situations, always flee back to the nest when trouble arises. They are loath to appear to be doing any real decision-making on their own. Rat girls are forever saying, "I can't really say whether or not I will be able to come to your coffee klatsch on Sunday. I'll have to ask Ralph if he needs me at home." Could be, Ralph doesn't even care if Madame Rat attends her shindig or not. Yet, she prefers to think he does.

Because Rat women fear losing their husbands, they often

emanate vibrations of desperation vis-à-vis men. Unfortunately for Madame Rat, men feel this brand of premeditated hopelessness very strongly. It makes their skin crawl. More and more these days, strong men are attracted to their forceful female counterparts. The Rat lady's intrinsic desire to depend on a big tough male partner is likely to discourage a forceful man straightaway. As a result, Rat women often end up attracting weak men who willingly do their bidding. Once she catches such a lily-livered creepy-crawly, wily Ms. Rat makes short work of despising him for his feeble attempts to please her.

If you find yourself in love with a Rat lady, my advice to you is simple: Learn first how to corner her gently in her own petards. Try to show her in the sweetest way you can that you are willing to repay her kind attentions (and of these she has a surplus to offer) with security and tenderness so long as she can accept you for what you are. Otherwise, if you fail to warn the future Madame Rat of your intention to remain at least partially independent of her, she will destroy your love by smothering your spirit. She will feel duty-bound to try and change you. Every Rat woman has an idea of what her Prince Charming ought to be like. If you do not cooperate and refuse to measure up to her draconian standards of masculinity and flair, in the long run she will let you down.

Elizabeth, my best female Rat friend, is English. She lives in London. Liz is married to a very handsome actor who drinks, beats her up regularly, and consorts madly with other women.

On the rare occasions when they are on speaking terms, Liz treats Tony like a child. "Here, darling, let me straighten your tie. Don't be late to the theater, precious. We wouldn't want you to miss your cue," she flutters.

After Antony had left that evening, Liz confided to me, "I'd be willing to bet he goes out drinking after the show. He's nothing but a gin-sop. He never even makes love to me any more. It's a good job he doesn't try, either. He repulses me."

One day in a weak moment, I asked her about it. "Why do you two stay together? Is it for the sake of the children?"

"Mercy, no!" Liz replied as though shocked at the very mention of her offspring. "They are away at school. What possible difference could it make to them?" She crossed her silken legs and loaded an ivory cigarette holder.

I gaped at her. "Well, then???" said I.

With a shrug and a glare, Liz wheeled about to snap, "You Americans do ask the most indiscreet questions. I suppose I stay married to Antony Granville because he is my husband. Isn't that reason enough?"

Yes, Liz. Your marriage is reason enough in itself. What a Rat woman needs most is an attractive framework from which she may go out into the world and exercise her charm and winning ways. She is a superb house-holder, a superior hostess, and never less than fascinating company.

MONSIEUR RAT

In his own head, the Rat male is never wrong, unattractive, or selfish. The world is a terrible place, people are no damned good, and he has too many responsibilities and not enough support from loved ones. Indeed, Rats feel they were born with the short end of the stick tightly locked between their sharp teeth. So sue, Brother Rat. Write a letter to God. Phone the Pope. Put Scotland Yard on the case.

The other day, while prowling about my mother's attic, I came upon a wooden box containing the personal effects and correspondence of my Rat Uncle Ed. The stacks of papers, letters, and documents inside intrigued my snooping eye, among them a yellowed folder containing a series of handwritten dated lists. Each was entitled "Sacrifices." They were notes to my uncle from himself and constituted a kind of diary of what he had felt about life from early adulthood through old age.

So typically Ratlike is this data, I feel I ought to share some of it with you. The April 18, 1935, sacrifices are my favorite. The faded penciled list read: "(1) Today, I lost my good fountain pen. (2) The dog ran away on Sunday. (3) Shirley tells me I have halitosis. (That's bad breath.) (4) I dug up my grandfather's watch from the old homestead. It's broken. (5) Tomorrow is my birthday and Shirley is not going to give me a party. No money. (6) My auto is irreparable. The throttle sticks. (7) I haven't sold a property in four weeks."

Poor Rats. Nobody understands them—nobody, that is, except themselves. Because Rat men feel a lack of comprehension from others, at times they can be dreary company. They are never satisfied with the moment in which they live and hence spend enormous sums of time and money in attempts to improve same. Rather than blame themselves for any single error in judgment or timing, they prefer to waste their energies mulling it about or talking it over with a willing audience.

Should Fortune nominate you to one of these voluntary Rat listening posts, permit me to give you a tip. Do not, under any circumstances, suppose for one second that you can reason with a male Rat. Let him do the talking. He needs to work things out in words before he can act on them. Nod, smile, grunt, shake your head from side to side, and *tsk* a lot. In short, lend your ear if you will, but keep your credence for yourself. Getting involved in his maze of Rat peregrinations may indeed serve to cleanse and purge his troubled soul, but you in turn may have to spend three days at a shrink or at least in the shower so as to wash that man out of your hair.

Rats make excellent lovers. Sexually, they are imaginative and go about their business with hearty appetite. Rat men are usually not guilty of self-indulgence in bed. There is a tinge of self-interest in their desire to please, but then nobody's perfect.

Mr. Rat is a very presentable figure at social gatherings. He may not always be cheerful to waiters or servants, but he does treat guests and companions in a charming fashion. And, for the most part, Rat manners are impeccable.

When a Rat man takes up with a woman, often she is in some state of need or under weighty psychological pressure. Rat men like to feel they are being helpful. The danger here, of course, is that once the subject of his seduction shows signs of standing on her own two feet and is no longer needful of his attentions and aid, the Rat swain may either try to bully her into resubmission or else he will leave her in the lurch.

Rat men are the kind who pride themselves on how many times

they have made you cry or laugh or in some way amused your emotions and titillated your nervous system. Soggy, routinized relationships do not interest Rat males. They love romance, revere passion, and seek tenderness with exaggerated zeal.

In a way, when you ponder this for a moment, just about everybody owes a natural human debt to someone who is clever enough to cause him to weep a single tear of emotion or choke on a hearty guffaw. There is something about the Rat's poignancy that makes him a man to be reckoned with by friends and foes alike.

CO-SIGNS

RAT/Aries (March 21—April 20)

The sign of the Rat is ruled by the element of water. Aries goes under the influence of fire. Together, they ought to be able to produce much hot air. Charging through life, bombasting pronouncement upon pronouncement, this Rat is an effective business person and a self-righteous know-it-all. Is there no area where the Rat/Aries will allow himself to be undercut, taught a lesson, or pried loose from his outdated ways? This person may be arrogant, but that same haughtiness is the result of fear of failure or rejection. He lives off the fat of the land . . . and complains when the spoils don't live up to his greedy appetites. Generous and charitable when properly admired, the Rat/Aries is a benefactor who prefers not to remain anonymous.

RAT/Taurus (April 21—May 21)

Taurus will have a calming influence upon the Rat's nervous nature. But, when crossed, rather than being merely benignly volatile, this Rat may become violent. A sensualist, a hedonistic lover of life, the Taurean Rat will be a fine host and cheerful company. Slower to react to early pressures than many of his kind, the person born under these two signs may wait until rather late in life before he succeeds. Give him a chance to work out his ponderous problems in young adulthood. The rewards will be worth it. Rat/Taurus people resent authority. The arts will attract them. This subject is at his best when surrounded by plenty of love and indulgent applause. Sensitive and tender-hearted, he will be a kindly provider.

RAT/Gemini *(May 22—June 21)*

Inconstant to a fault, this Rat cannot keep his mind off the possibility that somewhere beyond his four walls is yet another challenging set of circumstances in which he can shine. Gemini, an air sign, lends supplementary gusts that stir the Rat's watery personality to unheard-of heights of slapdash. Nothing, is ever finished, tasks remain shabbily bungled, and moreover, it is always someone else's influence that causes the Rat/Gemini to botch jobs. Endearing though these folks may be, they are not to be taken very seriously. Acting, showmanship, jobs that require movement and travel will appeal to this subject.

RAT/Cancer *(June 22—July 23)*

A prestige sign for Rats to be born under, Cancer cools them. With the Rat's imagination and Cancer's plodding good sense, there should be no obstacle to progress. Limpid of soul, kind of heart, the good Cancerian Rat will toddle along most aptly when engaged in business or the arts. Watch out for symptoms of eternal inner dissatisfaction, anxiety, and unexpressible anger. Hedonism is one thing. Self-destruction through excess is far more perilous. The Rat/Cancer is a home-maker, a nest builder, a potterer around the grounds. If he is bringing home the bacon, you had best know how to cook it with style. Rat/Cancers need to entertain. It's in their blood.

RAT/Leo *(July 24—August 23)*

Full steam ahead! Here fire and water combine again to produce uncommon energy. If you think your Rat/Leo is about to have a heart attack any minute, relax. Activity is the only thing that soothes his driven spirit. Power-hungry and critical of others, this Leo both needs and deserves that position of strength he has gained. With all the fervor, a grain of instability lurks menacingly over the head of this Rat. He does have to talk things out and purge his inner turmoils through blustery displays of rhetoric. Let him rant on. When he quiets down, this subject can be a fine teacher. He knows a lot and can impart knowledge with unusual flair.

RAT/Virgo *(August 24—September 23)*

Odd, isn't it, that Rats can be born in the sign of the virgin? Somehow purity and naïve good will don't seem to suit them. Surprisingly enough, this earth/water duo is remarkably compatible. Somewhat more finicky than even the normally fastidious Virgo person, the Rat/Virgo will pay quick and critical lip service to any deviation from the normal placement of his personal belongings. Dressed in discriminatingly subtle good taste, this person is generally most attractive to the opposite sex. He may not appear interested by such dawdlings. Don't be fooled. Underneath all that false propriety, Rat/Virgos are sensualists. Inside of every stiff and well-bred human being in this sign lives a lusty gobbler of goodies, just dying to be released.

RAT/Libra *(September 24—October 23)*

All that talk? I honestly don't know if I could handle it. Libra love, don't you ever get a jaw-sore from it all? If this person does not find a career where the gift of gab is a prerequisite, I will never invite him to my party again. Rat people must work out solutions to problems through wordy examinations of parameters. Libra subjects, because they seek a balance in every aspect of life, are wont to commit gobs of time to verbose examinations of every side of every story. There ought to be less of that rat volatility here. Certainly, we can expect enormous devotion to the finer things of life. Luxury not only appeals to this Rat, it suits him. If I were on a desert island with this person, I would daydream about boxes of Band-Aids washing up on the beach, two for my ears and one to stick on my Rat/Libra's mouth.

RAT/Scorpio *(October 24—November 22)*

If there ever is a Nobel Prize for cleverness and astute judgment of the inner workings of the human mind, the Rat/Scorpio should get it. A delver into the occult, a digger-up of clues and reasons why, a sharp wit, and a terrible temper are all embodied in this one beastly character. All day long (and some nights, too) the Rat/Scorpio creates won-drously imaginative patterns and directly swirls round and destroys them . . . *Bam*! Like that. The Rat/Scorpio is a soothsayer. He tells the truth about almost everything he sees. And, since nobody much wants to hear the truth, he is sometimes discouraged and sorry he ever said anything. Next day, he's at it again. "Perhaps," thinks the Rat/Scorpio, "this time they will listen." And, once again, *Kersplat*! Some powerful liar or other whacks him in the teeth. If such a person exists in your entourage, listen and heed his counsel. Nothing he says should be taken lightly, even though he is sometimes exceptionally joc-ular; he means every word of that warning or prediction. He knows the best and the worst about life. Give him your full attention.

RAT/Sagitarius *(November 23—December 21)*

Tact is not the primary quality of Rat people born in the sign of Sagit-tarius. "The truth and nothing but" drives the pistons of this subject's energy vector. Privately, he will be idealistic and intellectual. In public, this Rat is expansive. He knows how to make a silk purse from a grain of salt, or a mountain surge up from a hill of beans. You will marvel at this Rat's ability to charge at obstacles larger than himself and top-ple them with his charm. Sagittarians are aggressive. Rats are persis-tent. This is an energetic combination that guarantees success, provided that the environment is free of constraint. Good humor will reign supreme, so long as this heady Rat subject is applauded and cared for in the style to which he would like to become accustomed.

RAT/Capricorn *(December 22—January 20)*

Capricorn is hard-rock sureness of foot. Nothing new is ever under-taken unless its merits have been proven many times before. Rats, too, are adulators of tradition and fear change. The subject promises to be rather more long-suffering than necessary, self-deprecatory, and hard to please. To loosen up the gear works of this finely tuned, watchful soul often requires much urging, or maybe a truth drug would help to draw him out of himself. Once you have taken steps to ease him into a situation, the Rat/Capricorn will suddenly appear more brilliantly adept at functioning within a set of boundaries than any other Rat. It was all his idea in the first place to take up skiing, he may tell you, as he schusses down that treacherous slope, passing each obstacle with finesse and style. A dependent type, this Rat will not enjoy bachelorhood. There must be someone close by at all times off whom the Rat/Capricorn can bounce his thoughts, fears, desires, and successes.

RAT/Aquarius *(January 21—February 19)*

Far and away the maddest of all the Rats, the Aquarian Rat leads a life apparently full of heedless and carefree exploits that he claims are trailblazings toward a better world. He, like many other Rats, can see around corners and pass through walls, unscathed. Trouble is, those closest to him rarely benefit from his victories over the inevitable. He can be extremely neglectful of family and friends. Rat/Aquarians always feel there are more important things to accomplish than fireside chats and home-cooked meals. What security could be more important than that of the starving masses? Individuals matter less than underdeveloped nations. Personal offspring can only rank second in emotional importance while there are still hungry children in Africa. Lovers can hurry up and wait until this Rat decides to cease his scoutings for causes, crosses to bear, and burdens to take up. The way the Rat/Aquarian sees it, there will always be more intimacy around than he cares to handle.

RAT/Pisces *(February 20—March 20)*

Without a strong backbone and a level head upon which to lean his multifarious notions, this murky combination of variables may never get off the ground at all. Above all, the Rat/Pisces wants to depend. Of the gleaners of this earth, he is the heavyweight champion. Whether off the fat of the land or out of another's pocket, this Rat will always try to assure himself a comfortable living out of the least possible physical and mental effort. His charm is undeniable. His wit and love of nature appeal to those stronger than himself. Unfortunately, all the selfless love he seems to be showering on someone else is often calculated to bring him gain. Be it metaphysical or pecuniary, the Rat/Pisces wants quite a bit of his associates' fortunes for his own. The strength of this subject is his capacity for surviving intermittent poverties whilst planning his next coup. Rat/Pisces people can earn acclaim in either arts or letters. Business is better left up to more sensible types whose feet don't leave the ground every two seconds.

PRESCRIPTION FOR THE FUTURE

Rapacious Rat, you are among the strongest influences in the Chinese zodiac. When Buddha called all the animals together, you got there first. From way back then, the honor of lucidity and clairvoyance has been bestowed upon you. Why, since you are endowed with special powers of vision, must you so taunt yourself with reiteration? Why do you cling so fervently to the past? Moreover, we wonder for what reason you insist on aggressiveness as the path to sorting out your differences with the present.

Mainly, I suppose, the gift of perspicacity weighs heavily on your soul. Truly, you feel (and may actually be) superior to those with whom you are forced to deal. Yet, without communication you feel we will never recognize you for what you know yourself to be. How, you wonder, can those of us who do not ply our various life styles with charm and push ever grasp what you are all about? Do you ever hear yourself speaking? If so, I would be willing to barter my left pinkie finger against the odds you are not always comfortable as your own audience.

You want your ideas to bounce off an intelligent ear, and you don't always trust your own opinions enough to allow them uncontested forum inside your head. Yet, you know full well that you are a capable and sensitive soul. Why do you nag at yourself so? We all find you charming and witty. But you doubt yourself and need us for repeated confirmation of your plans and projects.

"But," you may exclaim, "I do not wish to be left alone. I want you to listen to me. Exchange ideas with me. I can't hole up in some baseboard and gnaw my way through life's ordeals without an audience!"

Your point is well taken. I think you are probably correct in thinking that you are not a loner. You need a presence (or six) in your life that can soak up all the extra flak you ceaselessly conjure for yourself. But people, even those of us who adore the very ground you rampage, do get weary. We may even (God forbid!) have our own lives to live.

You are more ambitious than most. You accomplish many worthy tasks. You are clever and wily and do much to earn the respect of your public. But you worry too much. Your sweet-natured self is repeatedly disappointed in those of us whose energy level is not up to yours.

Try to accept us for what we are. And then set about telling yourself how terrific you really are for us onlookers. Assume the role of greatness, indulgence, and repose and soon you may see that it comes naturally to you.

COMPATIBILITIES

Affairs of the Heart

You, restive Rat, will be happiest with a partner born under the sign of the distinguished Dragon. Rats sometimes worry unduly and gnaw away at themselves from within. Dragons let their anxieties show, trot them out, and let off steam at each new upset. Let a daring Dragon do some of that fidgeting for you. Dragons are not only exciting, they are wise. You will have your work cut out for you all the days of your life. Applauding, admiring, and encouraging the Dragon is an easy task for a generous, garrulous Rat.

Possible, too, are Ox people. Oxen are plodders. When you flag, they are always there to bail you out of quagmires of emotional depths. The Ox lover will want to wear the pants, but will endeavor to smooth out life's wrinkles for a beloved Rat.

Rats simply adore Monkeys. Providing the Monkey knows how to limit his trickery, this duo will be blissfully happy. Rats give up much for love. The busy Monkey must respect that fidelity clause.

Other choices are Dog and Pig. The Dog shares a love of sentiment and romance with the Rat. As long as the Rat remembers to bring home presents from those long trips, the Dog can stay put and mind their community stores. If the Rat can adapt himself to the Pig's delicate nature and be slightly more gentle, a Rat/Pig match could work well. Both are *bons vivants*, enjoy a good joke or new best seller, and are sensual in the extreme.

A hypersensitive Rat should avoid protracted love affairs or marriages with Horses. The double dose of egocentricity that the Horse inflicts on his Rat love could serve to confuse and hurt those born in Rat years. In another way, the Cat, being housebound and reclusive, may find the Rat's socializing disruptive to his preference for quiet. Besides, the clever Cat has all he can do to resist trying to annihilate some of that Rat aggressiveness. Unless the passion is overwhelming, Rats should avoid Horses and Cats, and never should a Rat take up with a Fire Horse. Disaster is certain to follow.

Social Affairs

Rats like people. Sociable and generous, they give themselves easily to comradeship. But not everybody is capable of being a good friend to the agitated Rat. Two Rats, comfortable because they are at home with their mutual foibles, can make a fine pair. But twin Rats will tend to pick on each other. A Pig will make an excellent chum for a jolly Rat. They can expect much frolicking and laughter from their union. The Rat will think up lovely schemes. The pleasant Pig pal will not mind carrying out the Rat's amusing plans. Snakes also have a lot in common with Rats. Snakes give sound advice. Rats can take all the reassurance they can find. Dragons, as well, make good company for the Rat. The Rat is impressed with the Dragon's dash and pizazz. The Dragon delights in Rat applause. Monkeys, of course, make fascinating company for the Rat, who admires Monkey agility of spirit. Rats wish they had that easy Monkey grace of contact with fellows. Malicious Monkeys can dupe any earnest Rat, so that unavoidable emotional strain will eventually be put on the sentimental Rat. Rats and Roosters get along in a flashy, superficial manner. The amity will be short-lived. The Rooster's braggadocio gets on Rat nerves.

Rats should steer clear of the idealistic Tiger or Dog. They misunderstand each other from the word "Go." And Cats should be avoided. They really don't respect Rats. The relationship will be little more than civil.

Business Affairs

Rats are often active independents who flourish in small businesses where they are called upon to meet the public and exercise their redoubtable charm on customers. The Rat might open his own bar or restaurant. Too, Rats enjoy the prestige of executive positions. They must not, however, be given desk jobs as they are not at their best when sedentary. Sales-managing positions involving travel, meeting clients, lunching with prospective buyers, and holding meetings for crews of personnel will amuse and delight the Rat. He will keep meticulous accountings of his generous business expenses.

If a Rat person does choose to enter a business partnership, he is advised to do so with a dominant Dragon, a lucky Pig, or even a Monkey. With this last accord, however, there may be sparks. Monkeys are tricky and intelligent in commerce. Rats idolize Monkeys, almost too blindly at times. The Monkey may turn on the adoring Rat partner and finish him before they share in any profits. As in love and friendship, the ego drives of the haughty Horse are usually too strong for the amenable and pleasant Rat to withstand. Rats might try a venture with Oxen. As long as the Rat rushes about selling and sniffing out new contacts, the Ox will be satisfied to hold down the fort back at the office.

Family Affairs

As a parent, the Rat is protective and authoritarian. Rats like their children to show signs of intelligence early. They will spend much time with little ones, teaching, inventing games, and encouraging creativity. For these reasons, Rats get along well with malleable, sweet-natured kids. Babies born under Ox, Goat, or Pig should bring much happiness to his Rat parent. Complicity will be found in the favorite Monkey child, who astonishes his indulgent Rat parent with his wit and wile. Horse children will exasperate the Rat parent. "Why?" asks the Rat mother or father. "Must he/she be so selfish?" If the Horse child does not quit the Rat's nest at a young age, the Rat may find a way to forcibly urge him to go out and seek his own fortune.

Since the Rat is a sociable type and enjoys company, whatever signs his kids are born under, he will try to befriend, advise, and provide amply for their needs. Tiger, Dragon, and Dog offspring may consider themselves to be one cut above their striving Rat parents. With these, the Rat will be obliged to exercise his aggression, his only way to prove that he deserves respect.

THE OX

The Years of the Ox

February 19, 1901 to February 8, 1902
February 6, 1913 to January 26, 1914
January 25, 1925 to February 13, 1926
February 11, 1937 to January 31, 1938
January 29, 1949 to February 17, 1950
February 15, 1961 to February 5, 1962
February 3, 1973 to January 22, 1974
February 20, 1985 to February 8, 1986
February 7, 1997 to January 27, 1998

Oxen are:

Patient • Hard-working • Familial • Methodical • Loners • Leaders • Proud
Equilibriated • Reserved • Precise • Confidence-inspiring • Eloquent
Self-sacrificing • Original • Silent • Long-suffering • Strong • Tenacious

But they can also be:

Slow • Loutish • Stubborn • Sore losers • Authoritarian
Conventional • Resistant to change • Misunderstood
Rigid • Vindictive • Jealous

45

OXEN I HAVE KNOWN AND LOVED

The ox is stability personified. Viewed from either end of the telescope, Oxen will stand fast in the face of most kinds of calamity. Though they may intone great sighs of despair, fling their hands to the skies with exasperation, and rant endlessly on about how frivolous the rest of us are, they always come through. You can count on an Ox.

Generally speaking, the Ox is not a dabbler. Rarely is he a jack-of-all-trades and master of none. Finding a career, making enough money, or having friends enough to assist him in times of struggle are the least of his worries. Oxen are achievers. Not merely boasting blowers of their own horns, Oxen are steady plodders. They eschew such frivolities as charm, aggressiveness, brilliance and heartiness. When they speak, they have something to say. Their natural eloquence affords them a guarded, carefully delivered (and often witty) rhetoric that just about nobody can deny.

There are so many examples of Oxen who have succeeded in this rat race of life, it is difficult to know where to begin telling you about them. At any level of society, among friend and foe, when you discover someone was born in the Ox year . . . he is usually anything but a loser. Even though he may seem to you slow and mirthless, regardless of how cloddish he appears on the surface, the Ox subject is usually able to control his own destiny—and he often regulates the fates of a few more of us besides.

As I examined the birth charts of the past hundred years, the number of famous contemporary Oxen I came up with nearly bowled me over. If I tried to detail accounts of all of their lives, this chapter would take an inordinate amount of space. I propose, instead, a short list of their names for your consideration. Oddly enough, most of them are men. More about the possible reasons for that later.

Primarily interesting to me is the fact that our twentieth-century enemy of enemies, Adolf Schickelgruber Hitler (Ox/Taurus b. 1889) heads up the list of Oxen we have known and hated. I am not a historian, so the reasons for this Ox's horrid behavior and ultimate demise forever remain unclear to me. Suffice it to guess he was part genius (misguided, of course) and mostly madman.

To get to the more pleasant side of things, Charlie Chaplin was born in the same year as Adolf Hitler. His fortunate genius has turned up more mouth corners and elicited more belly laughs than the world can count. As a performer, a family man, and solid citizen, Chaplin has done a bang-up job.

The year 1901 marked the arrival of Gary Cooper and Walt Disney. Unforgettables such as these two greats of our time are nothing to be sneezed at. When a talented Ox sets out to accomplish something, he forgets the meaning of the word "can't." He pushes on through despite resistance or massive struggle. The yield in 1913 was no less fabulous. Under the sign of the Ox for that year, we find Burt Lancaster, Vivien Leigh, famous dress designer Oleg Cassini, and that giant of existential literature, Albert Camus. See what I mean? The charts for Ox years rarely, if ever, come up with ethereal flighty types who make their marks overnight. Oxen types are powerful, long-standing shapers of images and souls.

The harvest of Oxen for 1925 is a-clutter with giants. In the twenty-fifth year of this century, there arrived on this planet Malcolm X, William Styron, Gore Vidal, Richard Burton, Art Buchwald, Russell Baker, Howard Baker, Johnny Carson, Sammy Davis, Jr., Jack Lemmon, Peter Sellers, Jonathan Winters, William Buckley, and Velvet

Fog Mel Torme. That's a heavy bevy of Oxen. Like bulls in a china shop, most of the above members of the Ox race have either left or are still in the process of leaving indelible marks on our society. When it comes to getting down to business, Oxen do not fool around.

Look at the list of thirty-eight-year-olds who already plodded their ways to the surface by 1975: Bill Cosby, Dustin Hoffman, Robert Redford. And Eric Segal's teeny-weeny monolith of a book still tugs persistently at the heartstrings of most of America.

And how about Oxen Jane Fonda and Dory Previn? I wouldn't be so bold as to imagine these ladies were, by virtue of their associations, merely lucky. Both of them have records of solid hard work behind them. Regardless of their fortuitous births or marriages, Oxen are tenacious and methodical. When they decide to make it, they usually do. Or, they die trying.

Jack Nicholson is certainly no accidental genius. This screen-star may seem to all of us to have arrived at his success naturally. He is, after all, such a talented actor. How could such a gifted man miss? Well, folks, I knew Jack Nicholson in France back in 1965. That year, he was missing on just about all cylinders. We were in Cannes for the film festival. Jack Nicholson was a thinnish pale version of his present handsome self. I was a pregnant public relations girl who carried enormous red balloons along the beach to promote a ghastly film nobody wanted to see. Jack was in Cannes that year as the agent for a couple of Roger Corman Westerns nobody wanted to buy. He was wearing torn and faded blue jeans. Faded blue jeans were not the rage that year. Jack wore them because that was all he had. He was not, to anyone's knowledge, an actor. For that matter, none of us knew he even wanted to be an actor. He was then what some people might term a hustler.

During the festival, Jack managed to take up with a crony of mine. Pam was an unpregnant, lively, balloon-carrying English girl. After the festivities, the couple split to London. Then, together, they went to California. Finally, they broke up. I saw my friend Pam some two years later in Harrod's gourmet food department and asked her, "Whatever happened to that cute hippie chap you met at Cannes?"

"Oh, him. I saw quite a bit of him for a while. But he is not my type. Not very romantic, really. I even went to California with him at one point. But he was always working so hard. I came back here alone. There was no hope." Pam is not the type who lets much moss grow under her stones.

"What's he doing now?" I inquired.

"He's an actor. He's in that new Peter Fonda thing. It's called *Easy Rider*. Jack's the best thing about that film." She smiled the proud grin of a celebrity lover.

"I didn't know he could act." It was a pleasant surprise.

"Neither did I. But I know one thing for sure. When Nicholson wants something, he goes after it. He's an exceptional talent. You'll be knocked out."

Pam was right. Along with millions of other cinema fans that year, I flipped for Jack Nicholson. He turned out to be an extraordinary talent. Who could have known?

A few years later, as I loitered in the doorway of the chic dress shop I managed in Paris's Latin Quarter, who should happen along but old Jack Nicholson.

"Hi!" he gaped. "What the hell are you doing here?"

"And you?" I kissed him on both cheeks and demanded, "What does a famous hipster movie star want in a Parisian couture house? Or, aren't you speaking to me any more now that you're so important?"

Jack reddened visibly. "I came to France to plug my new film. I have a lady friend with me. Have you got anything that might fit her? She's about your size." Jack seemed uneasy in the plush surroundings, but he accepted my invitation to sit down while I showed him a few frocks. His co-star, Dennis Hopper, stood solemnly by, unnerved by the posh of it all. Jack asked me what I was doing running a shop. He evidently remembered my period of glory in Cannes, complete with Rolls Royce and long colorful drinks on the terrace of the elegant Carleton Hotel.

"Hard times, old boy. I'm raising my kids alone now. Trying to do some writing on the side. Keeping ends together," said I, as I trotted out our loveliest line for his consideration.

The hearty Ox altered his attitude in a flash. "Hey, I didn't know about that. So you broke up with your old man, huh? Good for you, baby." He patted the seat next to him. "Sit down for a minute. I don't really care about that dress. I'll send her in tomorrow. She can choose something she likes. I'm hopeless at romance, anyway."

I sat there and chatted with Jack for about ten minutes. He wanted to let me know a few things about what he called "making it." He warned me that I would be discouraged. That people would put me down and reject my efforts more often than they accepted them. He said it was a hard game. And—typical Ox remark—he offered to help me in any way he could. If I wanted to send him a script or a bit of my novel, he would try to show it to a publisher friend of his. Did I need any money? Were the kids okay? Etc., etc.

Being a star had not changed Jack Nicholson's basically practical nature one iota. I count him among the few people one ever watches climb to fame unscathed by the superficiality of the milieu. Down-to-earth, good, strong, and willing to help—that's the Ox character. I hardly knew him, yet he admired my industry and ability to make it on my own. Even though I had "known him when," I confess I was slightly cowed by his show of friendship in my regard.

As he and his famous pal made their way to the door, Jack called over his shoulder, "Don't hesitate to send me your stories. I'll try to help you." All I could think was *Now he didn't have to say that.*

I never had occasion to take Jack Nicholson up on his generous offer to assist me. And I don't know for sure if he could have or even would have given my stories more than a chuck into the wastebasket. But, as I perused the astrological records of my past acquaintances and came upon Nicholson's 1937 birth date, it did not surprise me to discover he is an Ox.

As I attempted to point out in the introduction, nothing about anyone's life is ever quite perfect. Oxen are no exception to this rule. Appearances, in the Ox's case, are always deceiving. Many of them are at times deeply unhappy, troubled, jealous, and angry people. What is different about them is this: Whereas the slog and drudge of day-to-day routine and downright grind can deter a lesser soul, the Ox is born with more room and time in his head and heart for personal suffering. Setbacks that topple even the more imaginative tough Tiger or the driven Horse cannot hope to touch the taciturn Ox. Adversity almost seems to please him. The more trouble, the better. It is only grist for his mill.

Meanwhile, back at the "White House" in Paris, France, I had been saving up an Ox person for your entertainment for over eight years. Madame Anne-Marie (b. 1913) is an undiscovered saint of a woman whose unsung miracles should perhaps remain incognito. I would hate to lose her to the heavy-duty public eye incumbent upon recognized sainthood. She is my children's nanny, my long-time friend and mother substitute in a foreign land, my angel of mercy, a credit to the French Cordon Bleu, and the darling of the Fourteenth Arrondissement. There are in fact about three and a half books inside of this magical plumpish fairy godmother. Trouble is, her parents were too poor to send her to school. She cannot write very well. Not that she ever allowed a minor thing such as illiteracy to stand in her way. She taught herself the alphabet and set to reading along with the fifty children she has raised in her life. She is a master of any piece of knowledge up to and including the fifth grade. At the age of ten or eleven, her charges usually go off to boarding school and she must begin all over again with new ones, at the first-grade level. Her mind is awhirl with misinformation. Her spirit is alive with keen instinct. She could win a debate with Charles de Gaulle with one brain lobe tied behind her head.

Anne-Marie was born in 1913, in a tiny hamlet in what was then backward and inaccessible Brittany. Until the age of four she spoke only the Celtic language of her country. (Bretons still resist the fact that they ever became part of France.) At five, this middle child among eight siblings, was "farmed out." I never understood that expression until I met Anne-Marie. Farming somebody out indicates simply that long ago (yet not all that long ago) when poor parents had too many children to feed, the kids, once toilet-trained, were hired out as shepherdesses, baby-sitters, manure pitchers, cooks, and bottle-washers to rich farmers in the region. The girls took most of the brunt of this. Boys stayed home and worked on their parents' farms.

At any rate, at age five, Anne-Marie was a shepherdess. For her toils, this tiny child received comfortable lodgings (a haystack), one apron (per year), a pair of wooden clogs (every two years), gratuitous beatings and thrashings, and the handsome annual sum of one hundred old francs (about five dollars pro rata 1918). This salary went directly to the parents.

At the age of ten, Anne-Marie escaped from this enslavement to her uncle's café on the Breton coast. Her uncle was a kindly man. He took little Anne-Marie in as his waitress. By the time the farmer dared to ask her parents if they had seen her (he was afraid they would sue him for beating her), almost a year had elapsed. Anne-Marie was allowed to stay with her aunt and uncle. At twelve, Anne-Marie was cooking and waiting table in the seaside café. She tells marvelous colorful stories of picking up burly rude customers by the scruff of the neck and hurling them into the street. Of course, child labor was against the law in 1925 France. But her uncle had friends in the gendarmes.

At fifteen, Anne-Marie went to Paris in order to make her fortune. As any well-informed French person will tell you, peasant girls who made their way to Paris in those days were quickly snapped up as either housemaids or prostitutes (or, a little of each, depending on the lasciviousness of the masters of the house). Anne-Marie went to work as an upstairs maid in the home of a rich nobleman. All the men of the family, from the indolent father on down to the idiot son, came rapping on the door of her unheated attic room at night (*noblesse oblige* or something like that). A good religious girl, Anne-Marie spent the next ten years of her life devising new methods of barricading doors, and learning to avoid lurid glances, fanny-pinchings, and smart remarks. At the age of twenty-five she married. She was a pretty young bride; she wore white.

Her husband, a dashing young type from the langorous south of France, was never what you would call a pillar of strength. But that was all right with Anne-Marie. She preferred to run things her way. During the Second World War (also Anne-Marie's second Great War) she gave birth to two children. So that they might grow up among the fine people she had come to admire in the ritzier neighborhoods where she had worked as a maid, cook, and nanny, Anne-Marie took a job as concierge in a fine old building in the Sixteenth District of Paris. Even though she held a menial position as quasi-servant and door watcher in this chic edifice, Anne-Marie's children would go to school with well-heeled youngsters. She was determined to make their lot superior to hers. Her kids were as good as anybody else's. They would go to college. Of course, they might not have their own rooms or desks to study at or often enough money to buy books. They themselves were not even all that concerned if they did go to school, but Anne-Marie is not the kind of person one contradicts. She would have walked ten miles in the snow to go to school, and she did not hesitate to remind them of this fact.

By the time I met Anne-Marie, her two girls had married one engineer and one doctor respectively, each drove her own car, and one of them spoke English. And Anne-Marie had told Papa that he would stop drinking or his walking papers were right handy. Today, he's a teetotaler.

The reason I wanted to tell some of Anne-Marie's grueling story is that before I knew her I had no idea what tenacity was. I was ignorant of what integrity might really mean to a human being. Hard work was a concept I had certainly heard bandied about enough. But, before the appearance on my scene of this Ox of a woman, I was a babe-in-arms where labor was concerned. And I did not know all that much about stubbornness or rigidity of thought either. Was I in for a shock!

When my babies were very small, I went back to work. At first, Anne-Marie watched them for me during the day. Then, little by little, as time went by and she fell in love with the two infants, she would tell me, "Why don't you just leave them with me overnight? Go out and see a movie. You look tired. You need some amusement."

Like a liberated teenager, I would dash off to some fun-filled sidewalk café, at ease in the knowledge that my kids were safe and warm in their little beds at Nanny's house. She still lived in the same two rooms with her husband, together with two folding cribs, a playpen, a jolly-jumper swing, a huge double French baby carriage, plus enough diapers, romper suits, and bottle sterilizers to sink a battleship.

At three in the morning, when I would come trailing back home, the light would be on in Anne-Marie's pocket-hankie kitchenette. She was in the habit of staying awake well after everyone was securely bedded down for the night. After the TV went off at eleven P.M., she would set about her household chores. She washed all the diapers by hand (boiled the water on the stove), and by the same hand ironed the ones from the day before. She cooked up great pots full of carrots, peas, and beans and ran them through a hand sieve to make baby food. (She wouldn't let them eat commercially prepared stuff.) She scrubbed her floors so the kidlets could crawl around without getting germs. About the only thing she did not do was bake her own bread. At about four A.M. she would turn off her light. Her husband had to be awakened at five. She did require some sleep.

By the time the children were a year old (they were born in the same year and are not twins), Anne-Marie was keeping them full-time at her place. She claimed it was easier for her that way. At first, this solution was most unsatisfactory for me. I wanted to take my kids back to my apartment in the evenings. "But you are tired. They will waken you in the night," she protested. I told her that in my country even working mothers took their children home at night. She announced in no uncertain terms that such a modern practice was total nonsense. "Young women need their rest," she chided. "Take them on weekends. Otherwise you will not be able to do your work."

Each evening when I came home from the office, she would be waiting for me with a chubby smiling baby under each arm and my cup of steaming fresh coffee on her oilclothed table top. I played with the kids until their bedtime. Sometimes, I helped her feed them, too. But mostly I didn't do it as well as she did, so she would take them in turns. She did everything better than I did. And I learned more common sense from her than I did in fourteen years of schooling.

I learned that scolding children didn't give them complexes. I understood after a while that bundling them up really did prevent colds. I accepted the fact that if one fed them only fresh farm produce and non-chemical foods they would not need expensive vitamin supplements. She taught me that if you proceed gently enough a baby can be toilet-trained at eighteen months without trauma. In short, Anne-Marie gave me more free down-to-the-ground practical advice than

any battalion of child psychiatrists could have hoped to. In addition,
' she loved me and my children with a fervent ardor and passion which
made me comprehend straight off that I had better not commit too
many errors in judgment or she would have my head.

There is a bit of the old shrink in her, too. Anne-Marie is *au
courant* of almost everything about human nature there is to know. I
laugh when I hear people complain about their Jewish mothers'
minute attentions to them. I suppose they have never allowed a Breton
peasant lady/sophisticate/Parisienne/tough guy into their lives.

What I am saying about Anne-Marie adheres so strictly to the
Oxen behavior pattern that I probably could stop right here and let you
fend them off for yourselves. Like all the other Oxen, Anne-Marie is
plodding and safe. She is an excellent provider. But she is not without
fancy. Anne-Marie tells a funny story with grace and incisive wit. She is
slow. Oh, is she slow! When I want to take the kids to the two o'clock
movie, I tell her I will pick them up at noon. They are always ready,
clean, scrubbed, skirted, and sweatered to kill—at one forty-five.

She is tenacious and rigid about her old ways. For Christmas last
year, I bought Anne-Marie a washing machine. She didn't use it until
Easter, when spring cleaning was under way. She washed some cur-
tains. I asked her if perhaps she was not using it regularly because she
didn't know how to run the machine. I offered to help her.

"I can read," she told me. "I just don't want to ruin my good
sheets by putting them in that wringer. It spins them around and
scrambles them something awful." So there.

It is safe to say that all the Oxen I know are angels in lout's
clothing. There is nothing mild or particularly philanthropic in their
demeanor, yet they all enjoy the reputation of being benevolent friends
who nevertheless drive a hard bargain. Their manner is, in fact, sometimes a deterrent to getting to know them easily. They often seem
gruff, even stand-offish. Yet, they will put everything they have behind
a person who shows himself to be worthy of their affections and assistance. If you examine the charts for people you know who were born
in Ox years, I suspect you will agree with me. They will buy you dinner, watch your children, or write you a check—if the returns from

their efforts are in line with a pre-set standard of excellence and toil that they themselves adhere to. Woe unto the money-borrower who claims to the Ox that he needs a certain sum for his wife's operation, or an advance to see him through hard times, and in reality uses the loan for a holiday or drinking spree. Oxen, like elephants, never forget. They like to be helpful, but they do not tolerate being made fools of. Their rages—though few and far between—are memorable, sometimes even dangerous. Forewarned is forearmed. If you intend to con anyone out of anything, make certain it isn't an Ox.

Oxen are among the best human beings around. And they are often limitlessly talented in some area which requires enormous concentration and application to detail. A writer buddy of mine, that scion of the contemporary American literary scene, William Styron, is an Ox. A truer example of the southern gentleman novelist does not exist among us today. Bill Styron's breadth of field in the discipline he has chosen for himself is not even slightly apparent when first you meet him. In fact, a lot of uninformed people imagine him to be a "high liver," a hearty drinking man, and rather more light-hearted than his weighty books belie. Perhaps he does it on purpose, but sometimes he seems to carry a glint around in his eye that causes one to suppose he might even be a bit on the simple side. Knowing him as I now do, as my guru and friend, whatever reservations I may have had when, as a budding young writer, I first tremblingly encountered him in his own living-room cocktail-party setting (holding a stiff whiskey and smiling rather more bovinely than I thought worthy of such a giant of American prose) have been dispersed. William Styron may be a lot of things. But he is not simple. For him, the most significant areas of life are his work and his home. Any conversation with Styron regarding writing, whether it lasts two minutes or three hours, is tantamount to four years of degree-earning creative-writing courses at a leading university. The urgency with which he discusses his own work and that of others is an education in itself.

Like so many Oxen I have had the luck to know, William Styron is an arch example of what my mother used to refer to as "still waters running deep." There is a hesitancy in his social speech pattern that causes one to imagine he may be shy or afraid of saying the wrong thing. He is not one for small talk. With this Ox, life is all pith. Without substance, there can be no life. Chitchat bores him.

Oxen are some of the world's most accomplished patient listeners to prattle. But, faced with the time, the situation, and the right audience, the Ox is transformed. He will talk, in detail, of any experience you are willing to follow from beginning to end.

Styron once told me the most captivatingly intricate tale of an ear operation in childhood I have ever lent my own ear to. He gave me background on the doctor and the doctor's family, his own parents' attitudes, his dreams and doubts about the pain of the intervention; his boyhood fear of catching cold lest the procedure would have to be repeated. The story took what seemed to be hours. Actually, it lasted fifteen minutes. When it was over, I felt as though I had read a best-selling novel. Architecturally, the story stood on its own. Every picayune point fit where it belonged. The Ox's mind works with remarkable wit and incisiveness. Befriend one and you will never be bored.

So you will not think this ability is attributable to the fact that Styron is a writer, I must add here that our own Anne-Marie, back in Paris, is also a marvelous raconteuse. She has no training in plot development or character formation. But can she spin a yarn! After a good listen to one of her stories about life in the old days in Brittany, one feels cleansed, relaxed, and sated. She makes you think you have known her cousin André all your life. She outlines him from hair color to shoe size. She conveys his accent to perfection and spices or embroiders on each account so that even if you have heard that one before, you enjoy it more each time she tells it. Eloquence is an Ox gift. They almost never prattle on about nothing. They deliver their words with ease. They seek to intrigue and amuse their audience. And they succeed.

What is probably the paramount characteristic of Oxen is perseverance. There are not enough strong sticks in Christendom to break the wheel spokes of any Ox's cart. Cast an obstacle in his path, step on his toes, or insult him—he will only take it as a challenge. Provoke him or do him wrong too many times, and you may be very sorry you did. His vindictiveness can be deadly. And, should you try playing around with the integrity of an Ox just to test your own strength, and should he not react as vehemently as I have warned you, make no mistake. His indifference is not a compliment to your own forceful personality. He is not afraid of you. You have not cowed him. Over the long run, his powers of indifference toward those he no longer esteems are the most deadly weapons of all.

One last thud may prove useful on the subject of Oxen. Who's the bulliest bull of them all? No, not Captain Hook! Try again. Who's the daringest dread in the world? No, not even Mao Tse-tung can hold a candle to this one. The Pope? Nope. The grand and glorious grandpa of all the Oxen, ladies and gentlemen is—trumpets, please— Napoleon Bonaparte (b. 1769).

I never knew him personally, but I hear tell he never shrank from taking the bull by the horns.

MADAME OX

If a French person calls somebody a *vache*, which translates literally as "cow," it is a minor declaration of war. *Vache* is a strong word. Children are not allowed to say it unless they are actually describing the animal in a lesson on farming. Even at that, *la vache* is sure to elicit a smirk or two among classmates. If someone (male or female) is said to be *vache*, it means he is downright nasty. A swear word one commonly hears among the French if a finger is pinched or when the hammer slips is *Olh, la vache!* In France's basically agricultural culture, the language has no doubt retained so earthy a curse as *vache* because so many people deal closely with these cantankerous female creatures every day. I would not enjoy having to announce to a French woman that she was born under the sign of the female Ox. She might think I was calling her a *vache*.

What I am getting at by this winding rural route is that if I did not have the luck to speak French, it would be more difficult for me to feel as I do about Ox women with such conviction. The lady of this species is not someone I would recommend to just any unsuspecting rake. Ox women are what some may describe as tough customers.

Sentimental drivel bores them. Tear-jerking movies may annoy them. Weakness of will in a mate may attract Ox ladies. But after a time, the milk of human kindness can curdle and convert a contented cow into a shrewish Bossy.

If the truth be told, Ox women don't really need a helpmate in the traditional sense of the word. A shoulder to cry on, a warm body to reach out for in the night, or a comforting tower of strength to which she can turn in times of trouble would probably only symbolize weakness of character. Although many Ox ladies may be loath to acknowledge this in view of the popularity of liberation and runaway wives, the majority of Ox women prefer to stay at home and run the show from the wings rather than go out and become world-beaters. That way, they never have to be subservient to anyone.

Women born in the year of the Ox are vulnerable. At home, they may impart dictums and order ultimata with the severity of high-ranking S.S. officers. Within the domestic realm, they seem to manage those around them with tremendous courage. It almost seems they sense that their own limits do not extend beyond the family threshold. When Ox women set foot into the big, bad world, they almost always take care to clothe themselves in a tough armor of grim self-assuredness. They do not know how to smile ingratiatingly, nor do they ever convey the kind of whimsy that outsiders often seek to identify with femininity. Ox women are the salt of the earth. They are the breeders and the motherers of small helpless things, children, stray animals, and drunks. When they try to deny this instinct for procreation (as the more foolish among them do from time to time), they often end up embittered and cynical. The best place for an Ox woman is in the home. From out her hearth, she will send us some of the world's most well-behaved children, hard-working husbands, and delicious baked hams or batches of scrumptious cookies for the church bazaar.

When I mentioned earlier that an astounding number of Ox men had succeeded in making the grade in this life, I promised to discuss the reasons for this overwhelming edge that male Oxen enjoy. Frankly, I cannot blatantly say that ladies born in Ox years are never gifted for commerce or the arts. Acting, after all, was never unbecoming to the beautiful Jane Fonda. And Dory Previn writes a searingly poignant song for herself. Can you feel the hard edge in the work of both of these women? Do you sense, as I do, the almost rancorous cutting quality in the creations of these two women?

Sentiment and duty, to the Ox woman, are one and the same. She is most always a model of marital fidelity. If her husband strays, our Ox lady is the sort of wife who will blame herself first. After she regains his attentions, she may never let him live down his peccadillo. She may remind him of it for the rest of his life. No, she is not doubtful of her ability to get and hold her man, that is not actually her problem. But women born under the sign of the Ox, not unlike their male counterparts, deplore insubordination of any kind. What they give, they feel they have a right to demand in return—for honor's sake.

Above all, the Ox woman adores her family. She reveres her past and dawdles lovingly over the present. The loss of a loved one, a broken promise, or any of life's inevitable wounds to the soul will be sure to pierce her pure and trusting heart. If you love this tenacious rock of Gibraltar, you must promise me you will never let her down. She deserves the best because she gives the most she can.

MONSIEUR OX

An Ox man is happy when he finds some way of venting his talent for bossing others around. The Ox does not make a contented subordinate. Although he is usually worthy of the executive role in whatever he undertakes, laboring under this taskmaster's dictates is not fun and games. When he gives an order, inherent in his very tone is the tip-off that "this is no drill." It's his show and he intends to run it his way.

Our beloved Johnny Carson (b. 1925), the insomniac's nanny, is a model Ox. Nobody—but nobody—upstages our man John when it's his turn to speak. My guess is that Johnny Carson appeals to many of us largely because we all wish we had the guts to say half as many outrageous things as he does (and get paid for it, to boot). Carson has the market cornered on what a lot of people call chutzpah, or gall. He doesn't mince his words. He tells it like it is. And he wins the hearts of millions of viewers from coast to coast because despite all that nerve and spunk Johnny Carson remains a likable chap. No matter how blasé he may seem on any given subject, he always maintains a cheery twinkle in his eye. Underneath his apparent sophistication and TV slickness, we just know he is a simple nice guy from Nebraska. We can sit there and watch him night after night as he spars with some of the wittiest minds of the nation (often hitting well below the belt), and somehow— no matter how biting the remarks, no matter how many times he verbally punches a starlet in her pretty little tummy—when anyone dares to deliver him a punch in the ribs, our hearts still skip a beat. Will he win this one? Can he stand up to the jabs? The answer? . . . Always.

Friends, Oxen do not bruise easily. Least of all, hard-working men like our friend Johnny Carson. One doesn't think of it much any more, but Monsieur Carson did not shoot to stardom overnight. He began his career in show business as a stand-up comedian. Telling lame jokes to rooms full of drunk and disinterested Midwestern supper club patrons, who would sooner throw their soggy expensive dinners in your face than bother to laugh at you, is not my idea of the bedroom path to success. People who have the kind of courage it takes to stand up there alone and talk above the din in such places deserve a special vote of encouragement from all of us less brave than themselves. Talent is one thing, intestinal fortitude is another.

It is interesting to note here that, in my opinion, the one replacement for Carson on his own show who might ever be real competition for our hero is Bill Cosby (Ox 1937). Cosby has that same intangible force of presence that typifies a great talk-show host. He looks so easygoing and calm. He handles everyone with aplomb and grace. But watch him sometime when the chips are down. He can smooth out a ruffled ego, do a fast commercial, and tell a good joke in the same breath. Rattled?. . . Never. Cosby acts like he invented cool.

Ox men are all tough-minded. Although they are often hailed publicly, in their private lives they are rarely understood. Because they mean so well and are sincerely trying to do their best in whatever job they choose, their home lives may suffer from neglect. They feel it, too. When Johnny Carson gets a divorce, the entire country feels the throes. I have never heard Dick Cavett (Rat 1936) so much as mention his wife's existence. Have you? Incidentally, Mike Douglas and Merv Griffin are also Oxen subjects. That year, 1925, was a big one for network talents.

As I was saying, the private lives of male Oxen are not always smooth sailing. Women have difficulty accepting how Ox partners may very well be profoundly in love, but nevertheless are unable to play Romeo, Lothario, or even the obedient Dagwood Bumstead. The Ox is incapable of taking a back seat in any major decision-making effort. He may be proud of a pretty wife, a good provider for his lovely children, and even be able to give the family dog an occasional pat on the head. But, basically, he doesn't need to be looked after or fawned over or bolstered up in times of need. He is a loner. With or without a wife, he will make it. Regrettably perhaps, he can go it alone, spend those dreary nights away from home in dingy hotel rooms, eat that roadhouse food, and thrive. I am not suggesting that he enjoys these empty pastimes. I am only reminding those of you who have trouble dealing with an Ox male, that even though his family is greatly important to him, in the final analysis he is strong enough to live without it. If you feel he is inattentive, if you resent all the time he puts into his work, if you wish he would spend more time wooing both yourself and the children, don't harp at him. It will do you no good. Find interesting outside activities that will distract you and help fill in the gaps you feel. Even though your man sometimes enjoys a pipe, his comfy slippers, and a fireside sit, this repose does not necessarily include paying attention to you.

Your Ox man will not be a dandy. He doesn't care much about fancy dress affairs or public images. He usually likes the country, is enthralled by leafy bowers, and soothed by the sunset over a hillside. He should not be expected to don kid gloves when he explains his position in this or that situation. He's a down-to-the-ground, solitary self-starter—and a hell of a finisher in the bargain.

CO-SIGNS

OX/Aries *(March 21—April 20)*

The Chinese sign of the Ox is symbolized by "little water"; no interpreter has yet been able to make a more coherent translation for us. This small cold shower ought to put a minor damper on the fire of an Aries person born in an Ox year. You can't keep a good man down. And Aries people are considerably more adept at the pursuit of goodness than most. Aries are quicker than Oxen. They are also more vigorous. An alliance of the two signs ought to enliven the Ox. He may be more of an introvert than you would like, but take heart. He is thinking. He's probably cooking up a new scheme for taking over the world. Riding on this robust person's coattails will require a hardy resistance to the elements. Grit your teeth. It may be a rough ride.

OX/Taurus *(April 21—May 21)*

A little water on the earth's surface may in this case be expected to encompass an ocean of power. As you may have noticed, this program is a double bull, featuring first our Western hero, El Toro himself, and his Eastern carbon copy, El Inscrutable. It is no mean match. Obstinate to a fault, once this person has a notion in his head, he will take himself resolutely by the horns and barrel on through until the project, plan, or enterprise is accomplished. Taurean Oxen will make good friends and willing beasts of your worst burdens. If you need a strong shoulder to cry on, do not hesitate to call on this Ox. I'm warning you, he will not indulge you in any trite self-pity, but he will probably give you a good stiff drink and some dry clothing to wear. This Ox is a lusty liver of the good life. Nature, in all of its glories, delights him. The sexual appetite is hearty. Though somewhat perfunctory in technique, the ground is fertile and there is lots more where that came from. Watch out for that evil temper. The dam doesn't burst often, but there's a lot of water behind those gates. Hold your nose and jump.

OX/Gemini *(May 22—June 21)*

It is auspicious for a Gemini subject to find himself born in an Ox year. These mercurial people can use all the stolidity they can find to keep themselves from flying away. Since Geminis are usually gifted for talk, you can be sure that an Ox bom in June will spin you a fine yarn on those long winter nights. He ought to be witty beyond belief, rather more nervous than other Oxen, and compelled to speak more wantonly as well. If any Ox can be expected to serve as a charming and loquacious dinner partner, it will be this one. I predict lots of laughs and very few tears will cloud the horizon of this subject's life.

OX/Cancer *(June 22—July 23)*

Great pools of Cancer water meet what the Chinese call the "little water" of the zodiac. There's an uncommon amount of stodginess in this person. Power, force, integrity, and clout will be his missions. He ought to be able to stick to any undertaking through thick and thin. If he wants something (even you) badly enough, wild horses would be but a drop in the bucket as an impediment. He probably will not resort to trickery or ruse in order to make it in life. This Ox prefers the most direct route between two points, and if anyone can walk the straight and narrow, our Cancerian Ox can. He is more sensitive than the majority of Oxen, and I would not advise the light-hearted approach when dealing with his emotions. Cancers tend toward rancor, anyway; it would not be advisable to toy with this veritable water buffalo's nerve endings. Rages? . . . You wouldn't believe he was the sweet Dr. Jekyll you knew only yesterday.

OX/Leo *(July 24—August 23)*

Tempered somewhat by the influence of the Ox's water element, Leos born in the Year of the Ox will probably not take themselves as seriously as Leos are wont to do. This person can offer tremendous succour to those less fortunate than himself. I do not suggest you approach him for charity, however, unless you intend to return his philanthropy in kind. Leo Oxen are born leaders. Quieter and less flamboyant than usual, they nonetheless wield a mighty big stick when power is accorded them. This plodding human dynamo ought not to push his luck in the authority department. His ego might get in the way of his common sense and the walls of his fortress could come tumbling down. Napoleon, poor chap, even though he was born reasonable enough and ascended to the throne through a series of imposingly well-designed strategies, did allow all that *gloire* to muddle his lucidity once too often. If things look very rosy for this subject, he is advised to remember that Waterloo may lurk menacingly close to the end of that starry scepter.

OX/Virgo *(August 24—September 23)*

I almost wish I were an Ox/Virgo. They are such genuinely clear puddles of virtue in this murky mire we contend with every day. But, in truth, I think I would be afraid to step into the shoes of such a good guy. Virgos make excellent friends. So do Oxen. Virgos work hard. Oxen are industrious as well. Virgos pay their bills and cultivate their own gardens and stay out of trouble and keep their noses and their nests neat and clean. So do Oxen. It's a marriage made in heaven. Slog, Grind, and Drudge could be the names of the children. This person can do great things with his life. Count on him when you need sound counsel. Don't ask him to teach you how to cheat on your taxes. Virgo Oxen are among the most honest of souls. They couldn't recognize a subterfuge if they ate it for dinner. What's bad about them? Not much really, except they suffer more than they should because even if they protect themselves with asbestos gloves, they soon discover to their dismay that this bed of roses they are living in is covered with tough and thorny prickers that can penetrate the most pristine of souls.

OX/Libra *(September 24—October 23)*

Libra is an air sign. The Ox's still waters run deep enough that Libra's slight breeze will probably not even rumple the surface. One thing that Libra will surely do for this Ox character is endow it with some flair. Oxen lumber and plod. Libras seem to walk on air. Our solid Ox is decisive and controlled. He has not much time for frippery, luxurious décors, and the like. Libra will highlight up the Oxen side of this person with a ray or two of sunshine and *lux*. You can expect to find this Ox firmly ensconced in an artistic career requiring hard work and glib. Both Libran and Oxen subjects are noted for their talent for pleasing an audience. Don't expect him, as one often does of a Libra, to take a middle-ground position in important matters. Although he may seem to strike a happy medium when dealing with testy subjects, he is rather more one-sided than he appears.

OX/Scorpio *(October 24—November 22)*

The double water sign of Ox/Scorpio is a redoubtable combination indeed. Having one of these venerable personages for a friend is like owning the controlling stock in a greased-lightning mine. Having an Ox/Scorpio for an enemy, I should imagine, would be similar, except that this time you are inside the mine when it caves in on your head. A lode of sympathetic things can be said for this type. Oxen born under the sign of the Scorpion will be all muscle and sinew. Their spirits promise to be both resistant and resilient. Dauntless in the face of danger, fearless when confronted with ill health, enemy opposition, or plain old bad luck. Scorpio Oxen are classic examples of those champions among us who function in disaster and finish in style. So much for the good news. All Scorpios are vindictive and vengeful. So are Oxen. Scorpios like to have their own way. Oxen are not famous for their malleability. Scorpios can have viperous tongues. When they happen to be Oxen as well, watch out for sparks. They mince not a word, but get straight to their work. And they can make short shrift of anyone who gets in the way of their progress.

OX/Sagittarius *(November 23—December 21)*

This ponderous rabble-rouser's fire is not quelled by a little Ox spritz of water. Sagittarian Oxen are fighters. And they are winners. High ideals and hard work combine in this subject to form an invincible nature. Remember what your mother told you about never judging a book by its cover? She was probably talking about this toiling behind-the-scenes struggler against injustice, famine, ill-treatment of minority groups, and whatever various horrors contribute to the misery of mankind. On the surface, he may seem docile. Underneath his serene exterior there burns an eternal torch of benevolence toward his fellow man. If you are wondering who is addressing the envelopes for Planned Parenthood, or if you cannot imagine who sent you that gruesome pamphlet about the starving masses in Biafra, think about all the Oxen you know and find out if any of them were born in December. For the good of the order or the furthering of a good cause, a Sagittarian Ox will lay down his life. And he will do so discreetly, quietly, and with the utmost of good intention.

OX/Capricorn *(December 22—January 20)*

If you happen to meet up with one of these vital souls, please take heed. Capricorn Oxen are world-beaters. They are also rigid, difficult to live with, and strong of will and conviction. Personally, I wouldn't wish this union of hard-nosed souls on my worst enemy. But some people enjoy uphill struggles. Who am I to argue? Oxen born under the sign of the goat are prone to spend long periods of time on their own. They do not seem to need either company or support. Once they set their minds on an objective, there is no stopping them. You may, in fact, never see them again until they have reached their goal, triumphant. In this case, there are about 650 notes of caution. Capricorn/Oxen study too hard, work inordinately long hours, push that old Sisyphean rock up whatever hill seems the hardest to climb; and, with it all, they never seem to get anywhere. Is the pleasure in the struggle itself? Frankly, I can't tell you. All I know is that of all the successful Oxen I have mentioned, not one of them is Capricorn. Maybe, with all that push and pull, they dry up their resources before they can apply them to real life.

OX/Aquarius *(January 21—February 19)*

The water-bearer, of whom the ruling element is air, herein carries water to water. It is a desirable alliance. The main ingredient is elbow grease, the condiment is fancy. Aquarians are imaginative. They have a kind of extravagant world view, which permits them to see beyond the vicissitudes at hand. The Aquarian subject who is lucky enough to be born an Ox should be more level-headed than many of his

Aquarian brothers and sisters. This visionary person would do well to engage in political activities or social work. No less despotic than other Oxen, his majesty will at least be enlightened by truth. Don't expect your Aquarian Ox to be home-loving or acquisitive. If he hankers after anything, it will probably be power.

OX/Pisces *(February 20—March 20)*

Good for you, Pisces! You have chosen to come into this world under propitious auspices. The fusty old Ox with his intractable ways will give you the extra character strength you so need to keep your own head above water. Early in your life, you will feel the twinges of Oxen force stirring in your loins. Take the blessing by the horns and use it well. With your imagination and the Oxen's brutishness, you two should go far together. Choose a career that demands patience and artistic flair. You are among the more fortunate among us who are gifted with both. Something akin to procrastination or foot-dragging may try and get in your way from time to time. Don't let yourself be duped into thinking that life's treasures will come your way automatically. Be active. Keep moving. If anybody can do it, you can.

PRESCRIPTION FOR THE FUTURE

Ominous Ox, even as you read this to yourself, I can hear the rumblings of denial in your head and heart. *Balderdash! Hogwash! Nonsense!* and such churn about within you. I am aware that you consider such pseudo-sciences as astrology and other mysticisms that are not recognized by the A.M.A., the F.D.A., and the Bureau of Motor Vehicles to be mere drivel. Relax. This time, like it or not, you are on my show.

What gnaws at thee? Why indeed must you exhibit all that conservatism day after tedious day? Is there a little voice in the back of your brain that tells you, *Watch out, Oxie baby. If you crack too many smiles, let down your guard once too often, the goblins'll get you!?* Come on now, cheer up. We know you are a serious type and that you like to get things done your own way in your own time. But aren't you ever going to have any fun?

It isn't fair to tease an Ox. They say it only makes you worse. But you do make it awkward for those of us who are more jolly. When you decide to introvert yourself, resist a new idea, or take a stodgy stand on some subject you tell us is outrageous or too far-out, the Great Wall of China has nothing on you.

On the other hand, Ox orator, if you are the one making the fun, if you tell us one of your gorgeous stories and we sit transfixed by your glibness for hours on end, it suddenly becomes perfectly all right for everybody to roll about in the aisles. Dost thine ego not wax a mite too puffy?

What I am suggesting to you (nobody can "tell" an Ox anything) is that the longer you allow yourself to stand fast in the face of frolic and frisk, the older you get and the harder it is for you to change your ways. Young or old, rich or poor, your nature prods you to stay close to the conventional. The orthodox is always a more comfortable path for you to follow.

But what about the rest of us? Where do we come in? Are we forever condemned to tiptoe by your armchair, turn down the stereo, and look busy? Maybe we just want to think our thoughts or loll about the carpet reading a comic book. Perhaps we like make-up and mini-skirts. Is there any role for us in your life other than that of frivolous dependent?

All right, I concede the fact that it is often you who pays the rent. You are probably the legal king of your castle. But if you hate it so much and it makes you grumpy, why don't you stop it? We will all go out and get jobs and stop playing patsy to your every command. You can quit your odious position as chief. The braves and papooses will smoke the pipe of peace with you. We will sign a treaty to take over all the hard parts so that you can learn to dance the boogaloo and write poetry.

How does that sound to you? Life would be beautiful. Time on your hands. Leisure. I'll bet your mouth isn't even watering a bit. The whole idea offends you. If you couldn't be the boss, you think the whole world would come tumbling down around us. Wrong again, my dear Ox. It may surprise you, but there are entire families of human beings on this planet who live in pretty houses with picket fences and shipshape gardens—and they haven't even one single Ox person among them.

The reason I propose this impracticable scheme to you at all is that I know you won't take me up on it. You are too proud of what you are capable of doing. You have a remarkable ability for achievement and a healthy drive to succeed. It is what we like about you most. It may even be what you like most about yourself.

However, you are prone, by virtue of this competency, to judge the acts of others rather more severely than you should. Take stock of those you love. Is it not true that they bring sunshine into your otherwise stuffy existence? Is it not patently so that without their loud stereos and guitar strummings, you would remain forever ignorant of modern trends? Why, if you didn't have that hippie daughter of yours or that idiot ne'er-do-well of a nephew to argue with, you would never have any fun.

If you still wish to sacrifice yourself to hard work and providing, should your desire to rule the barnyard remain uppermost in your heart, then continue to do so. Nobody's going to stop you. But please, good Ox, leave the rest of us to our levity without all that harumphing accompaniment.

Nature has invested you with power. You are stronger and more able to cope than most. It is your lot. But is it a reason to preach at us? Must we forever sneak around avoiding your wrath when we feel like enjoying ourselves? We are not like you. There is little chance we will be able to measure up to your stringent standards. No matter how hard we try, our idea of fun will always seem to you untoward.

To you, we look for strength in our need. For you, we make the effort to reach the highest peaks. We want to please you. In turn, could you please let us choose our own aims? May we fight our own cherished battles and reach for the kinds of skies that make us feel most comfortable? We may trip and fall. We may not always succeed as you have. And, in our hour of failure, we may come crying on your doorstep. And you will bid us enter—so that you can bawl us out.

You have a streak of self-righteousness in you. You adore being able to tell a weaker soul, "I told you so," or, "Don't say I didn't warn you." Those are the cruelest words in the English language. A good Samaritan is not a finger-wagging mother-in-law. Do you think you can keep that in mind?

COMPATIBILITIES

Affairs of the Heart

The patient Ox will be proudest of a Rooster mate. While the Rooster is out in the world strutting his stuff, the tenacious Ox will tend to home fires. The Rooster, though sometimes flashy in appearance, is deeply conservative. The authoritarian Ox must be allowed to rule the Rooster. Oxen are reserved and stick close to the rules, as well. A good second choice for Oxen would be the charming Rat person. A Rat in the home of an Ox will infuse the erstwhile heavy atmosphere with gai ety and sociability. Too, the loving Rat will remain faithful to an Ox partner for the sake of long-term respectability.

Snakes are possible partners for Oxen. Since the Ox is most content when working at keeping house and home together, there will be room for the Snake to slither out from under the yoke of family. The Ox will dominate at home. The Snake will bring home booty. If Snakes can ever be faithful, Oxen have a better chance than most of keeping them so. Snakes know a good thing when they see one. The Ox's example of industry makes this rapport a productive one for both parties.

Nor is a team of Oxen anything to be sneezed at. Their mutual life will be sedentary, quiet, and blessed with peaceful homely pursuits. Oxen, because they are family oriented and original thinkers, will establish good partnerships with Cats (who do not mind taking orders from the bull), Monkeys (who will benefit from the security offered by an Ox mate), and Dogs (as long as they don't see too much of each other).

We must take into consideration the fact that passion is relatively unimportant to the Ox person. Romantic idealism sometimes seems to them mere ornament. Oxen have no time for frip-frap. Goats, for example, cannot be expected to render an Ox happy. People born under the sign of the Goat need time to ruminate artistry and muse on poetical ways and means. The hard-driving Ox is impatient with Goat caprice. The Ox will not lift the Goat from his bed of roses, but instead will sneer at what be considers lassitude and inertia. Both would get hurt in the ensuing struggle.

Oxen must resist the temptation to become involved with Tigers. Though the Ox's seriousness and equilibrium may settle some of the Tiger's inner disputes for a time, eventually the stronger Ox will crush any spontaneity the Tiger has left and will drive him away in shame.

Social Affairs

Though it seems strange, Tigers make durable friends for Oxen. When the Tiger lacks in perseverance, the Ox takes up the slack and endures routine tasks. But Oxen must never agree to share quarters with a Tiger. Their combined wills are strong and inviolately stubborn. Though the Ox will always win out, neither subject will find growth within such a mutely tension-charged atmosphere.

Roosters and Oxen are well-matched friends. The Rooster is busy, busy, busy; the Ox, too, is occupied all the time. The Banty brings his enthusiasms home to roost, where the Ox diligently shines and polishes them to be put to good use. There is much concurrent activity and progress in such a couple.

Although Cats and Snakes have more refined tastes than Oxen, they intrigue one another. Monkeys also fascinate Oxen, but they find devious ways of upsetting the Ox's conservatism. The Ox attracted to a Monkey should be wary of ruse. Oxen should have as little as possible to do with Dragons or Horses. Their senses of morality do not mesh. Since both Dragons and Horses are proud to a fault, the self-sacrificing Ox will lose in any bargain he makes with these arrogant fellows.

Business Affairs

Oxen make excellent comrades-in-arms for Rats. They are sure of foot and put their work before almost any other pursuit. A not-so-nice Rat could take advantage of the Ox, but likely will not since he respects the security that Oxen have to offer.

Though Oxen can love and like Roosters, they should not try going into business together. The Ox does esteem the Rooster's ability to make-do in a crisis, but he cannot tolerate those long periods of famine that Roosters are so famous for. Two Oxen could buy a farm and make a go of it together. Their lives would not be a bowl of cherries every day, but then Oxen don't mind hard labor. Over the long run, the Horse's air of superiority, strangely enough, raises the hair on the Ox's thick neck. The working atmosphere will be positive as long as these two keep out of each other's way. Oxen never demean hard work, and we all know that Horses can pull those plows when they must.

Above all, Oxen must not enter a business where a Dragon or Tiger is in charge. Oxen do not take kindly to the authority of others, particularly when it is unconditional. The high-flown notions that Dragons or Tigers sometimes entertain only get under the conservative Ox's skin and grind axes that are soon used in pitched battles.

Finally, the Ox does well on his own. Whether at home or in the world, the Ox prefers to go it alone. Just about nobody is more capable of organizing a sound commercial endeavor. The Ox can use some assistance in meeting the public, but for whatever slog and drudge is involved, he is better off counting on himself. He will find almost everyone is less frugal and lazier than his mirror image.

Family Affairs

Oxen—as we have noted—are parents who want their children to toe the mark, sit up straight, and pay attention to business. In return for obedience, no parent showers more love, affection, and self-sacrifice on progeny than the good Ox mother or dad. It is within the family that the sometimes rigidly nonromantic Ox will find a vent for his emotions. Male/female love is often disappointingly half-baked for the reticent Ox lover. Parental obligations inject his spirit with hopeful sentiments. The Ox is sometimes so taken up with his kids that he forgets about his mate. Duty first. Trivial dalliance with adult love takes second place. The main hitch with Oxen parents is that redoubtable authority of theirs. It can get in the way of understanding. A Goat child will cower under the draconian regulations imposed by an Ox mommy or daddy. Goats were made for smaller things than their rigid Ox patrons can accept. Dragon, Horse, or Tiger children will have to uncurl their hair before going to bed each night. The Ox rules with an iron will, setting example after example of his pride in work. The latter three signs are self-starters, capable of hard work and application, but the Ox does not agree to anyone's sense of priorities but his own. Dragons and Tigers will resist authority with strength and valor, but the poor Horse child may be driven away at a young age. He cannot comprehend the necessity for blind sublimation of his ego. No amount of comfort or reneging on the part of a saddened Ox parent who loses his Horse to the big, bad world will bring the headstrong Horse home in a hurry. He simply will no longer hear the voice of the wounded Ox.

Snake children know how to feign passivity and kittens use their charms to wheedle favors from an Ox parent. Monkey kids gad about amusing their stern Ox parents; even the tenacious Ox cannot withstand the wiles of a cute little monkey-faced son or daughter. Pigs, though generally tractable people, are also remarkably intelligent. If the Ox parent thinks his Pig child is complying with a given rule, he may be surprised to find out that as soon as the Pig is big enough, he will strike out on his own and content himself to drop mom or dad Ox an occasional postal card from Timbuktu.

Needless to say, the secret of getting on with an Ox parent is apparent acquiescence. Nodding in agreement and yessing the Ox is better than any vain effort at rebellion. A rebellious child is a pariah for the Ox parent. He might even be capable of disowning such an ingrate. If you have an autocratic Ox parent, smile and agree with what he says and pursue your choice of radical behavior as discreetly as possible. Though you may find it hard to believe, that rigid disciplinarian who is your parent wants only the best for you. Try to remember that they ask as much of themselves as they do of others. Oxen really do mean well.

THE TIGER

THE YEARS OF THE TIGER

February 8, 1902 to January 29, 1903
January 26, 1914 to February 14, 1915
February 13, 1926 to February 2, 1927
January 31, 1938 to February 19, 1939
February 17, 1950 to February 6, 1951
February 5, 1962 to January 25, 1963
January 23, 1974 to February 10, 1975
February 9, 1986 to January 28, 1987
January 28, 1998 to February 15, 1999

TIGER ARE:

Hugely generous • Well-mannered • Courageous •Self-assured • Leaders
Protectors • Honorable • Noble • Active • Liberal-minded • Magnetic • Lucky
Strong • Authoritative • Sensitive • Deep-thinking • Passionate • Venerable

BUT THEY CAN ALSO BE:

Undisciplined • Uncompromising • Vain
Rash • In constant danger • Disobedient • Hasty • Hotheaded
Stubborn • Disrespectful of rules • Quarrelsome

TIGERS I HAVE KNOWN AND LOVED

Have you ever known a person fairly brimming with gifts, talent, beauty, intelligence, and fun who un-dauntedly and confidently changes jobs with the same nonchalance with which seven-year-olds take leave of their teeth? "There's more where that came from" is the unflinching motto of people born in the Tiger years. A Tiger never feels the need to lay in stores for the long cold winter ahead. Money in the bank seems to him the lazy man's way to security. Marriage strikes the Tiger as little more than encumbering compromise. The Tiger, man, woman, or child, is what my mother used to call "a handful."

Several such characters have at one time or another peppered my entourage. As lovable as they are slippery, Tigers have more magnetism in one whisker than other beasts can boast in a full beard.

Take my old school chum, Gloria, for example—that is, if you can locate her. Gloria is one of those people who is everywhere and nowhere at the same time. She's a fashion model. No, I'm wrong. This year she's actually a public relations director for a computer firm. Modeling was last year's occupation. The year before that she was running the admissions department of a small coed college in Indiana.

Four years ago, when she lived in Paris, Gloria was a cracker-jack journalists. One day I accompanied her to a press conference where she was interviewing Katharine Hepburn. Or, rather, Ms. Hepburn (1909 Rooster) was doing her level best to politely skirt Gloria's adamantly posed queries about her private life. "What precisely was your relationship with Mr. Tracy?" she did not hesitate to ask Katharine the Great. "Would you call it a marriage?"

"If I could find a phone, I would call you a taxi," came the elegant reply.

Gloria didn't bat an eye. "His long illness must have been very hard on you. You seem a bit testy on the subject," she piped back.

"Miss Hepburn would prefer not to discuss the subject of Mr. Tracy's illness," said Hepburn's loyal secretary firmly. "She has come to Paris to promote her new film."

"Why is it you never wear dresses?" Gloria obligingly changed the subject to one even less discreet. Ms. Hepburn, ignoring the question, turned toward a silver tray of petits fours. "Is it because you are ashamed of your legs?"

As I watched Gloria perform open heart surgery on Katharine Hepburn in the palatial public rooms of the Bristol Hotel that day, a sandy-forelocked movie idol named Alain Delon (1935 Pig) leaned over me. Before my knees buckled at the prospect of Delon speaking to me, I heard him whisper, "Who is that journalist woman? She's a real tigress."

I gathered my senses long enough to explain that she was my pal Gloria. "What is her phone, please?" he asked. Thinking maybe he wanted to be interviewed, I gave him Gloria's office telephone number.

As we passed through the star-studded receiving line on the way out, Gloria's hand seemed somehow mysteriously entangled with Alain Delon's for a few seconds too long. She disengaged herself finally and went on to bid *au revoir* to Ms. Hepburn. My turn to cling a bit, I extended a trembling paw. Delon took it limply in his, leaned his expensive mouth to my right ear, and beseeched, "Give me please her home phone number."

By the time I caught up with Gloria she was being affectionately embraced by Katharine Hepburn. "You must understand," said Kate to Gloria. "It is difficult for me to discuss my personal life with the press. Please don't be hurt by my reaction to your questions. You are such a sweet girl. . . ." And on and on.

Gloria had dinner that evening with Alain Delon, lunch the next day with Katharine Hepburn, and tea with Vicomtesse de Ribes. I entertained my Aunt Mildred from Topeka who was in Paris having plastic surgery done on her hammer toe.

Tigers are the most preposterously beguiling people going. The more outrageous things they do, the more people are drawn to them. Their capacity for achievement, however, never seems to follow along classic lines. From out of nowhere, they leap into a spotlight. Without what we think of as the necessary education, training, background, or hard work, they often come up smelling like a rose. Let's just say they are doomed to success.

Why doomed? Mainly because they really do not have much control over their destinies. Even though she may never have hankered after the throne, Queen Elizabeth of England (a 1926 Tiger) had that scepter thrust at her by the freak abdication of her uncle and the subsequent death of her father at an early age. Her daughter Anne (a 1950 Tiger) may herself be in for some surprises.

What was less likely to happen to France in 1958 than Charles de Gaulle (an 1890 Tiger)? Yet, there he was, straight and tall, characteristically godlike and imbued with such a sense of himself as to disallow just about anybody who might have dared try to tell him the truth about how silly it all looked. Oh, certainly some quarters of the press and public opinion attempted to make fun of de Gaulle. There are all manner of protest newspapers in France that scathe the very skin off politicians with what they write. But Tigers, like de Gaulle, don't read them and weep. Tigers are more likely to read them and rejoice in the challenge, redouble efforts to rule, distribute propaganda for themselves in larger quantities, and in short, meet every affront head-on, nose in the air and sinewy muscles poised for the kill.

For all their irresistible pluck, Tigers are not always the kinds of people one should follow blindly. Although they usually look like they know what they are about and where they are headed, if you plan to pursue a Tiger through this jungle we call life, I suggest you take along more than a pocketful of bread crumbs. Leaders they are; winners often, too—but not invariably. Sometimes Tigers are too headstrong for their own good. They'll be capable of the kind of self-pride with which Louis XIV (a 1638 Tiger) reigned over France. In his case, surrounded as he was by wise lieutenants and advisers, a long monarchy full of prosperity (for the court, of course) and parties at Versailles were a sure thing. Of course, those were the good old days. Louis' modem-day counterpart, Hugh Hefner (a 1926 Tiger) has not fared so well of late. Unexpected glories befell him for a while, but somewhere along the way his lieutenants must have failed him. The same is probably true of H.R. Haldemann (a 1926 Tiger) who obviously fell into bad company.

Not all our famous Tigers have been so foolish. Germaine Greer (a 1938 Tiger), the coolest of all feminists, has borne the strain of her own notoriety very intelligently. So far, at least she has not appeared as the star of her own blue movie or publicly disrobed in the House of Commons.

Tigers are often legendary heroes rather than real ones. It all seems to be done with mirrors. And it works. Does Evel Knievel (a 1938 Tiger) actually perform those stunts, risk his life every other Thursday in front of thousands of panting fans, for real? Is Elaine Kaufmann (a 1938/9 Tiger), famed New York literary crying towel, really the brains of her own operation? Recent competition from her miffed ex-headwaiter who has opened his own concurrent joint around the block is cause for some wonderment.

I am convinced that Miles Davis (a 1926 Tiger) is an accomplished horn player, perhaps the best in his field. But let me recount an incident that may give us a hint about why he's so "tops," so untouchable, and so devastatingly adorable.

Once upon a time in Paris, when free-lance writing was but a gleam in my own impoverished eye and I was earning my living by managing a high fashion "couture" house, many Americans of no little means and snoot passed through our busy fingers during that year. One of them was Mrs. Miles Davis.

Pert, young, and beautiful, Mrs. D. tried on every gown we showed her, decided on two or three she couldn't live without, and asked us to put them aside until her husband could come in and pass judgment with his American Express card.

Just before closing time (seven P.M. in Paris), I looked up from my desk to see lurching toward me a wispy, arm-dragging apparition I shall never, ever forget. I may have missed the details because the over-all impression of scarlet leather breeches and waistcoat, complete with matching boots, was so terrifyingly delicious, I almost didn't notice the enormous ermine-trimmed sheepskin cloak Mr. Davis was wearing as insurance against Paris' nine-month rainy season.

My boss, Vicky Tiel, co-owner of the business with Elizabeth Taylor, does all the designing. Davis made short work of her with this remark, "Hey, baaaaabeeee, you are the MOST." Calculated stop, throaty voice guaranteed to seduce even the most reluctant subject and a smile that was indescribably sexy. As I watched in mitigated admiration, Davis curled his arms around the petite Miss Tiel. From without the sheepskin, I swear I could hear Vicky melting drip by drip into a puddle of delight.

"Oooh, Miles, cut that out!" she squealed without meaning a word.

"You look egggszackly like my first wife. Mmmmmm hmmmm!" continued the virtuoso.

Ordinarily, Vicky doesn't allow herself the luxury of fraternization with customers. But Miles Davis was obviously an exception. "You gon' make meee a beeeyooteeful shirt!" Miles fetchingly commanded.

"What color?" swooned my desk-mate. Then, gathering her business acumen and courage, in a neat little inoffensive gesture, she pushed him away, saying, "I'll have to take your measurements. Take off your coat."

I swear to you, folks, Vicky Tiel is so otherwise occupied with designing and paper work she doesn't even take the measurements of Madame Giscard d'Estaing by herself, with her own tape measure on her own time. Ordinarily, there are people to handle that sort of trifle for her. Nor does she make and sell shirts for men.

But, in the exceptional case of Miles the Tiger, Vicky would have taken his temperature, pulse, and heartbeat in the bargain.

Miles heaved his narrow shoulders imperceptibly underneath the engulfing garment, shrugged off his coat, and threw it on top of my head. Yes, that's correct, I suddenly found myself emitting muffled groans of smother in an overheated room. And do you know what he said as I emerged gasping for breath, fighting like a mad racoon? He glared soothingly in my direction and smirked, "You jes tell youah grandchildern, baby, you wore Miles Davis's coat." Then he chuckled a lot.

I probably ought to have been furious, uncontrollably enraged and humiliated. I wasn't. The magnetic field surrounding Miles Davis (and many other Tigers as you may note when you start hunting down the signs of your friends) was so full of sunshine, it confounded even viper-tongued old me. All I could think up to retort—and this under my breath since the customer is, after all, always right—was, "I hope you live long enough to tell your grandchildren that Suzanne White wore your coat."

Mrs. Davis got herself a couple of smashing frocks that day. Two weeks later we sent a dozen ruffled chemises off to a post office box number in New York for Big Miles. I wrapped the package myself—lovingly.

Adventures like that one are always occurring when Tigers are lurking about. Tigers love risk. Bravura is their middle name. How about Rudolf Nureyev? It isn't just every Iron Curtain ballet dancer who pirouettes off an airplane in London and decides to become the best-loved darling of the dance in the entire free world. It takes a Tiger to pull stunts like that one.

I mislead you perhaps by all these stories of top-level Tiger talents who prowl our earth. Tigers are not always famous celebrities or jet setters who cozy up to movie stars and throw cloaks at ladies. Most Tigers who roam among us are average citizens trying to fight their ways out of this paper bag like the rest of us.

But there is always something a bit special about Tigers. The Chinese claim it is innate luck that makes Tigers able to slide into home plate just when everything looks blackest. Call it luck or call it guile, the Tiger in your tank will probably be at least unique, his own person, not easily influenced, fighting the system, courageous to a fault, and even if you can't stand the sight of him, venerable.

What I mean by this is that ordinarily one does not feel lukewarm about Tiger people. They are often beloved chums and cohorts. They are also frequently objects of extreme enmity. But, friend or foe, it is the rare human being who does not respect the Tiger for his grip on life. His generosity where others are concerned as well as his natural authority and resilience guarantee him no end of veneration.

For Chinese astrologers, the Year of the Tiger is symbolized by wood. They say he "stirs wood" or "mixes it up." The lay interpretation of this exotic symbolism is that the Tiger represents the awakening of life. He makes things grow and protects against natural disaster. As the third sign on the list of animals, the Tiger falls in even-numbered Yang years. Yang means action, force, drive, and determination. Although he may appear relaxed, the Tiger is never at rest. Always on the lookout for a cause, he knows how to wait before making a decision, the right moment to pounce. Yet, Tigers are stronger in the ultimate execution of tasks than in the judgment department. They would do well to listen to counsel from the wiser, more passive Yin signs from time to time, or to take a tip from the sage Dragon who can take up the slack by worrying about the Tiger's leaping before he looks.

One more Tiger tale to illustrate this hasty precipitousness from which the Tiger suffers. In the south of France, there are many beautiful tourists who spoil the many beautiful beaches with their too many beautiful bodies all summer long. In order to get in a little unpolluted swimming, the alert vacationer on the Riviera will often drive to the mountains behind Nice and Cannes for a dip in one of the many crystal pools and streams they offer.

While baking one day last summer in the reflected rays of thousands of stacked oiled bodies, I overheard my neighbor planning just such an expedition for the next weekend. When asked, he agreed I might go along with him. His instructions were clear. I would meet him in town on the café terrace at the port at ten o'clock Sunday morning. It was a long hike he warned, and I should not bring heavy packs, just a lunch and some sneakers for climbing over rocks.

My light lunch and I were on time as were my handsome Tiger guide and two other adventurous souls who had brought their three small children along for the walk. We drove ten miles up into the foothills of the Alps on dirt tracks and dusty cow paths, excited at the prospect of cooling off before a pastoral brook before sharing a lovely alfresco spread together in the unspoiled nature that lay before us. Roger, our hero, spent the harrowing drive extolling the virtues of this primeval site he had heard about from some very *au courant* residents in Saint Paul de Vence. He stopped the car finally and got out, saying, "It's only another half-hour from here by foot."

There were footpaths everywhere, into the woods, around the woods, downhill and up. Roger embarked on one of these and beckoned us to follow him. The parents of the children went directly behind Roger, then came the kids. I brought up the rear.

A half-hour passed more or less uneventfully. That is, we had so far seen no river, heard no babbling brook, seen no water other than the droplets of perspiration in front of our squinted eyes. Roger encouraged, "It's just a bit farther." And he galloped along, veering left and then right, politely holding back branches for the person behind, dragging child after child up little precipices, warning us of the odd slippery or loose rock we shouldn't step on. A more delightful host or confident captain of our fate we could not have desired.

Three hours later, as I exchanged portage of the kid with the sprained ankle for the one who wouldn't stop crying because he was hungry, I heard (through the buzzing of the heatstroke I had become host to), "That's very strange. Very strange, indeed. They must have moved it."

Our chorus of groans and moans echoed in the hills. Roger had failed us. It was like waking up from a bad dream only to find out that real life was a worse nightmare. Now the kids were really shrieking. They thought we were lost. They were right. Roger had not only failed to find the stream, he had walked us round in circles.

We sat down under the shade of a blade of dry grass and sweated out lunch. One of the kids stopped crying and reduced his complaints to a whimper/sob cadence. The parents were pale with fright. Roger was smiling and joking about what a shame we had missed the best hours of sun around that glorious pool we had heard so much about. He played with the children, collected the rubbish from our lunch, and somehow not a cross word was heard from any of us. It was impossible to dislike this nice man who had led us to our death.

After lunch, we all looked at Roger for some sign that indicated he might be ready to lead our descent. He looked indulgently back at us. "You know, we are really terribly lucky we didn't find that place. It's crowded on Sundays. Full of tourists. Come on. I've got a better idea."

Why nobody questioned Roger in the first place, I will never quite grasp. But the fact is nobody did so in the second place, either. It was as though he just had to know what he was doing. A leader born. We got up and followed him again, this time down the mountainside. The going was less rough. About fifteen minutes after we had embarked on our supposed re-entry to civilization, Roger stopped dead, shaded his eyes with his right hand, and peered into the distance. "That must be it," he noted casually.

"What???" we wondered in unison.

"Beatrice de Campenon's house. She lives all alone up here since the old count passed away. She'll be delighted to see us. She has a fabulous pool, too. She'll probably ask us for dinner. I hope you all like caviar. It'll be such fun to stay the night. She'll let the children sleep in the tower. It's such a lark for kids up there. I used to stay entire summers with her when I was small. My mother was her husband's mistress, you know."

It was all true. The charming Madame de Campenon did exist. Her hospitality was faultless. Her pool was perfect and the children played pirates in the tower until well after dark. The Armagnac and the beds weren't bad, either. I slept right through Roger's unmerciful snorings.

Tigers are foolhardy, but they are lucky. Give them an insurmountable problem and they revel in overcoming it. One way or the other, it can be said it is difficult to keep a good Tiger down.

Tigers are not particularly well-known for their happy marriages. Prolonged monogamy distresses the Tiger. He thrives on passion, fresh ideas, adventure, and intense activity.

Should your Tiger be born at night, the aspects are less perilous. A Tiger born between sunrise and noontime is in constant jeopardy. The sensitivities run deeper in the day Tiger. It will be difficult for him to escape from himself when the going gets rough. Unpleasant though the subject may be, I feel obliged to mention that violent death, accidental demise, and the like can do in the unwary Tiger. Marilyn Monroe was a Tiger (b. 1926) as was Isadora Duncan (b. 1878). The Tiger must guard against excessive self-destructive behavioral patterns, but more about that at the end of this chapter.

As for career choices, it's safe to say that Tigers can do almost any job that requires leadership and calls upon him to exercise authority. A Tiger would be comfortable as a corporation president, a high-ranking military officer, or even a Mafia chief. Because of his distaste for hierarchies, unless of course he is at the top, it would be unwise for the Tiger to seek to remain in a lifelong position of subordinate in a complex business or academic structure. As a means to the end of becoming boss of such an enterprise, subordination will serve the Tiger well. But, if he feels no advancement, no challenge, he will become bored. Better he should go to a bank and borrow the money to set up his own hot dog stand, school, or political party. He cannot suffer boredom and remain content for long. Besides, his aptitude for leadership and his love of the human race in general makes the Tiger an excellent and benevolent commander. Better a cheerful despot than a dissatisfied office boy.

MADAME TIGER

Has it ever occurred to you that the expression "man-eating tiger" might not have been invented by members of the British Raj whilst drinking gin and tonic and discussing wildlife on some jungle outpost club veranda? It's just a thought, but I wonder if maybe it was something they overheard an Indian maharajah say about his Tiger wife.

Tiger women are alluring beyond belief, captivating, amusing, and sexy. They are neither materialistic nor are they grasping and possessive. Quite the contrary, Tiger women are intangibly, exasperatingly independent. Not always beautiful in the classic sense, Tiger women nonetheless rarely have problems attracting men. Swains flock to their sides, camp on their doorsteps, put up with untold amounts of hair-raising competition, and all this because once or twice a week Ms. Tiger deigns to favor them with a stroke or caress.

To set out to catch a Tiger woman is a job for a willingly patient man. Her seeming disdain for security, her dashings here and there in search of adventure, and her natural gift for controlling others require that she unceasingly be understood and redefined. She is not much on explaining herself or her actions. If you are after a Tiger lady, there is a lot of guesswork in store for you. A hundred times at least, you will ask yourself why she walked out of the house in the middle of the night, where she might have gone, whom she is with, what she is thinking; and—most of all—does she need your help, has she been in an accident, or is she depressed and feeling lonely?

You may try to solve some of these mysteries by merely asking a civil question such as, "What's wrong, honey?"

"Not a thing. I'm busy. I'm thinking. I have a lot on my mind. Etcetera, etcetera," she will usually reply. She is Miss Cool and Collected. But underneath that veneer of self-assurance may seethe a raging storm. She's thinking, all right. And she is probably very, very busy, as well. Her eyes may be practically swollen shut from crying, but she will ride out her own secret storm. She will find it exceedingly difficult to allow herself the luxury of sharing her woes with you. It might look like dependency. Dame Tiger is absolutely terrified of becoming dependent on anything or anybody besides herself.

Sounds awful, doesn't it? Not to worry. There are enormous compensations for your patience. Her strokes and caresses, no matter how few and far between, are sheer delight. When a Tiger girl is your girl, the rewards are not few. In bed, when you finally get her there, she is truly worthy of the title "Tigress." Before you know it, she'll have you eating out of her hand with words of love and passion beyond your wildest dreams. Her personal enjoyment of the act of love is certain to pleasure and flatter the man who loves her well.

Tigresses are generally faithful, not constant but faithful. Because of this inconstancy, her life is often a sketchy patchwork of torrid affairs interspersed with long fallow periods wherein she devotes herself entirely to her work or her children. Under the best of conditions, however, the Tiger woman can flourish on monogamy. Tigers do everything they do in blitzes. They gobble joy as voraciously as they raze obstacles along the way. They believe in spending blocks of quality time with their mates and have little or no truck with small talk or common politesse.

If you give your Tiger love enough rope, she will hang onto you. Allow her great periods of rumination and deep thought without interruption. Let her go on that separate vacation. And don't ask her any indiscreet questions when she comes home. She wants to feel that her life is her own. If you don't find her home when you get there and she has left no note saying she went to a convention in Cleveland, then she has probably simply gone on a three-week jaunt to Europe because somebody called her on the phone to ask her to speak to a group of women factory workers in Brussels. Maintain control of yourself and don't act like you might die without her at your side. If you can do this and not blow your own brains out from worry and despair, your Tigress will come home switching her tail behind her, full of news and fun, impassioned about one thing or another and laden with glorious presents for you and the kids.

You see, deep down inside, Tiger ladies are harboring a giant supply of marshmallow fluff. It's the sleek skin and sure-footed gait that makes her took so damed invincible. Scratch a Tiger and you'll find a pussycat, a voluptuating feline who needs you to seduce her away from herself. She gets little relief from her own thoughts and projects, plans, and schemes unless an outside force wheedles her into it.

I am not inferring that this seduction routine I am advising is a simple one. Not for a moment. You will have to cajole, wine, dine, tickle, and chat her up endlessly and repeatedly. As I said, it takes a lot of patience. She'll begin by waving you away with the bat of a paw.

Then she'll hide herself in the bathroom for two hours. After that she may bury herself in a book for another hour. Unless you have the spunk and inventiveness to draw her away from these seemingly empty solitary pastimes without getting severely mauled in the process, Madame Tiger will barrel right on through on her own, never knowing you were in the room or in the mood.

So, gentlemen, if you set your traps enticingly enough, if you are willing to share the life of a super-occupied dynamo whose feelings are entombed in a cement vault and very easily hurt when the lid is pried open, go right ahead. But don't say I didn't warn you.

MONSIEUR TIGER

These chaps are fiercely interesting. Tiger men always make me think of the kind of man I dreamed about when I was a little girl. The man I would marry would have to be as strong and as tough as an infantry. The man I call my own would have money and power and call on the phone. I'm sure you know what I mean. In the olden days, girls were resigned to the image of the husband fighter, hunter, chairman of the board, and soldier who went out in the world to seek his fortune while wifey-poo sat at home and waited for him to ring up from Peoria.

In these troubled modern times, however, it is not so easy for Tiger men to find a homebody who is at the same time an intelligent conversationalist, a good mother, an excellent cook and hostess, and a stay-at-home who hovers longingly over a hot telephone. What to do? Well, Tiger men will have to do a lot of prey-stalking on the run.

My kid brother is an excellent example of the Tiger man. His steady girl friend has moved in and out of his London apartment about five times in the past two years. "We love each other," Brother John admits to me periodically, "but I can't stand having her around all the time. She's underfoot."

"Why, John!" say I. "That's a terrible thing to say about Carole. She's a darling girl, so willing and helpful and kind to you. I really can't fathom why you say such wicked things."

"I don't see what's so wicked about wanting to be alone. I can make my own breakfast perfectly well, clean up after myself, and take my clothes to the laundry. I don't need Carole here all the time. What's more, Suzanne, I honestly have to admit I don't like to share my toys." John is so dashing, it about breaks your heart to imagine how saddened Carole must be to rent her own flat again, pack her belongings, and split every time John gets to feeling hemmed in.

But with Tiger men, ladies, that is just the way the cookie crumbles. They cannot put up with too much attention. And they sincerely do not like to share their toys. If you love a Tiger man, ask him for money, presents, trips; to find you a job or help you keep the one you have. But don't touch his record player! Don't meddle with his well-arranged (although maybe messy) housekeeping. And, above all, don't cling!

Carole's side of the cohabitation saga I just sketched is this: "I don't see why it bothers him to have me around. I am at work all day while he paints at home and at night when I get home he's usually out, anyway. We scarcely see each other in the house. In fact, I see him more when we don't live together."

And therein lies the secret of handling this handful. In the first place, don't ever move in. Let him come to you, and even if you really don't mean it, ask him if he minds terribly if you didn't see each other on Wednesday because you have a group therapy session. This kind of display of independence intrigues the Tiger. He is not necessarily jealous of your outside pursuits, but he will be all the more attracted to you if you seem to be doing something on your own. You don't have to attend a meeting or go to that session at all. You can just stay at home and twiddle your thumbs, if you wish. But don't answer your phone or your doorbell even after midnight when he thinks you are home and maybe he could come over for a nightcap. Be unavailable to him in a consistent and slightly secretive manner. Tweak his imagination and he'll follow you anywhere.

Your Tiger mate will seem bossy sometimes. Relax. Try to remember that he is laboring under the impression that it is his job to be naturally superior to you. If I were you, instead of getting angry at him, I would giggle a lot each time he tried to remind me how much I needed his help. Tigers have a finely honed sense of humor. They can laugh at themselves with impunity since underneath they are so sure they are better than most people.

Whatever happens (and plenty will) between you and a Tiger man, I hope much of it occurs between the sheets. Tiger lovers are well worth the many detours you may have to take to keep their interest up. They are not much on foreplay, but tend rather to get down to the business of lovemaking and stay at it for veritable hours. If you can, take the phone off the hook, hide his shoes, and entice him with long involved conversations during which you ask his advice about every three minutes

Tigers like their women to appear weak. But they cannot put up with real lily-liveredness in anybody. The ideal mate for a Tiger would wear green-smelling perfumes, dress in exotic gauze fabrics, and carry a knife between her breasts. He wants the outside all gooey and the inside hard as nails (probably because he is just the opposite).

CO-SIGNS

TIGER/Aries *(March 21—April 20)*

The elements of fire and wood unite here to create a rare blaze. The ego is paramount in the case of both signs. Aries are sprinters, strong beginners, project undertakers, and persistent forgers ahead. What better combination than these two dauntless soldiers? Something a bit less energetic and vehement? Hugh Hefner is a Tiger/Aries. Have they no shame, these Tiger rams? Not very much, I'm afraid. If it gets out of hand, throw water on it.

TIGER/Taurus *(April 21—May 21)*

Here we have wood and earth together. Solid Taureans gain something valuable if they are born in the Year of the Tiger. Power and money come easily to Tigers. Taureans cannot be happy unless they have lots of both. If the Tiger bull can learn not to be so stubborn, he might be able to sit back and enjoy the applause. Give daily gaiety injections and more love and affection than anybody deserves.

TIGER/Gemini *(May 22—June 21)*

I shudder to think. All that air and wood? It's positively eerie. Tiger/ Geminis will need two sets of disk brakes on all four wheels to keep them from going into zany business ventures, marrying the wrong partner five or six times in a row, or rushing off to the big city with ten cents in their pockets to take Broadway by storm. Lots of education and hard work in childhood will assure this person a solid future. Without a sound structure, he could fail at almost anything. With a firm basis to fall back on, a brilliant career is assured. Keep a cool washcloth handy and apply to forehead frequently.

TIGER/Cancer *(June 22—July 23)*

Does wood plus water sound a bit soggy to you? Could be you don't appreciate the stay-at-home silent type we have here. The slower the pace, the warmer the home fire, the more sedentary your Tiger/ Cancer could become. All that Tiger deep thinking and sensitivity will be compounded by the Cancer's need for a warm haven to call his own. The Tiger side of this character will want to rush about making things happen only to be met head-on by the homebody side of the coin on the other shoulder. Hypersensitive to criticism and less willing than most to listen to advice (which he so desperately needs), this crabby Tiger may also be just that from time to time. Jolly the old crab along. Cancers love to be in positions of authority. Out of curiosity, take a survey in your office. Note the many executive Cancers. And don't be surprised if many of them were born in the Tiger years. The coalition of the two signs is a power match made in heaven.

TIGER/Leo *(July 24—August 23)*

Fire and wood again. Shining brightly, the Tiger/Leo ought to be the happiest of beasts. The indisputable king of the jungle hasn't a worry in the world. For once, his arch rival is on his side. Nothing short of an excess of pride and preening vanity should daunt him. His ego might just get in the way of his brain from time to time. If you deal with this creature, keep your sense of humor. His roar is worse than his bite.

TIGER/Virgo *(August 24—September 23)*

What with earth and wood rooting for them, these people should expect the best from life. What the Tiger may lack in ability to stay on the straight and narrow, Virgo should make up for a hundredfold. Virgos are discriminating persons whose good taste and gift for living graciously are undeniable. The Tiger will bring strength and courage to the easily swayed Virgo. Tigers are honorable, virtuous even, but they are not gullible and naïve the way Virgos tend to be. In his turn, the Virgo will give the Tiger a sense of charity and taste for perfection. The alliance of these two signs is full of noble promise.

TIGER/Libra *(September 24—October 23)*

Hot air and balsa wood. Will it ever fly? Yes, and gracefully. This duo portends safety for Tiger subjects. Libras spend lifetimes seeking harmony. Tigers spend most of their time hunting down conflict. I would say the Tiger gains here from the well-balanced Libra side of his character. The uncompromising nature of the Tiger will be tempered by Libra's all-powerful desire for equanimity. The Libran Tiger may talk too much. Don't shush him. Talking is his security blanket, his safety valve. As long as he doesn't suck his thumb after the age of thirty, you can rest assured he's making out just fine.

TIGER/Scorpio *(October 24—November 22)*

This time the wood is floating rapaciously across the water. Scorpios and Tigers are so alike that such a person could be said to expect to either leap off a bridge before he's old enough to swim, or burn a very respectable amount of them behind him throughout his hectic life. All the aspects of the Tiger/Scorpio combination are not positive. But they are all strong. Those gangsters I was speaking of earlier might readily be found among this lusty group of Tiger people. The manner of this person may be gruff and put you off. Don't be alarmed. The reason for this is simple. Scorpio/Tigers are off-putting gruff people. Don't forget to look for the marshmallow fluff. It's in there somewhere.

TIGER/Sagitarius *(November 23—December 21)*

This time fire and wood can burn their brains out for the same wasteful cause. I think of Sagittarians as noisy idealists. Tigers run a close second. Neither of these two signs is eminently marriageable. The pullings on the reins will be many. The sense of satire should be acute. An excess of profound thought may shadow the Sagittarian Tiger's eyes. Buy him some sunglasses.

TIGER/Capricorn *(December 22—January 20)*

From this earth/wood alliance, one can count on plenty of grass-roots growth in a hurry. Capricorn dependability and ability to fight for what he believes in despite setbacks will give a steely toughness to the foolhardy Tiger. He will be a fast friend or redoubtable enemy, if you are willing to listen to the constant dronings on about political causes, humanitarian movements, and social reforms. Self-doubt is a notorious Capricorn trait. The bold Tiger's self-assuredness and belief in his natural superiority should benefit his Capricorn side. Conflict will arise with regard to security. Tigers don't care about it. Capricorns give their lives for it. This person will need scads of money in order to have a suitably safe homestead and still afford all those airplane tickets.

TIGER/Aquarius *(January 21—February 19)*

Wood with many little air holes punched in it can float unless the holes grow too big and it sinks from lack of substance. Aquarians think mostly about brotherhood, desegregation, starving millions, and great causes. Tigers do their share of this type of grandeur-inducing for themselves, as well. The ensemble might play some very earthshaking social music, providing they keep their feet on the ground. The Tiger, in this instance, will provide protection for the Aquarian. Since it is difficult for Aquarians to think about today and what is close at hand when they have so many obligations to greater causes, the match may only add to the problem. Tigers are not exactly homebodies under the best of circumstances. But Aquarians are straight thinkers. Tiger/Aquarians should take advice from wiser than they before embarking on their noble missions. Open-mindedness is a quality with which both are gifted. They can do the world much good. Provide a soapbox.

TIGER/Pisces *(February 20—March 20)*

Wood swims this time underneath the water, mitigating its effectiveness. Pisces people are artistic and sensitive. Tigers are sensitive and a little crazy. Tiger/Pisceans would do well to secure their careers before the age of thirty. Child prodigies and young geniuses should fare well under this auspice. But a Tiger/Piscean must guard against putting himself in a position of susceptibility. Remember that the Tiger is in constant danger. It doesn't look so good for the sensitive Pisces, either. Girded by a sound career early in life, this person should suffer less— but not all that much less.

PRESCRIPTION FOR THE FUTURE

Tiger dear, have you noticed that your emotional life tends to be more stormy than most? Has it come to your attention that you are impossible to live with? Do people criticize you for your apparent selfishness? Your answers to one or all of these questions is likely to be: "Oh, yes, all the time."

If it is of any interest to you (and stop me if you have heard this before) there are remedies for what's ailing you. Cures? . . . Not really. But at least temporary relief does exist that may help you render life a bit more livable for yourself and those who love you.

Psychiatrists and counselors of all varieties are always advising rebellious souls like yourselves to learn how to compromise and to accept the inevitable—not to fight city hall, as it were. You probably feel very strongly that such counsel is all right for other people but simply does not work for you. Or, if you acquiesce and make an attempt to look as though you are going along within the so-called normal boundaries of everyday life, you are undoubtedly aware that this outward acceptance you display is only sham.

I am not insinuating that you are blameless. You are a hothead, a warrior, a self-starter, and a free spirit. Trouble is, not everybody else in this world can accept that about you. You know very well how magnetic you are. People are drawn to you. They enjoy living in your aura of self-assuredness and spunk. It makes them feel protected and safe. Even though you know underneath all that bravura that you are scared to death, others somehow never seem to suspect that you are anything but totally sure of yourself.

Maybe you feel sometimes that you wish there were somebody in this world who would be able to understand you. You, after all, understand them and listen to their problems and sort them out of scrape after scrape. But who will ever get you out of your hassles? The answer? Right again. Only yourself. Self-reliance is a gift. Learn how to use it. Take the responsibility of being on your own more and try not to conform just for the sake of conformning.

Maybe you long to be "one of the gang." If so, that is perfectly fine. But, to be simply a member of a group or a participant in an activity, you will have to swallow your tongue and put your ego in your pocket at least fifty times a day. Remember, you like to have things your way. It is not the Tiger nature to sit back and let himself be guided. There is the rub. You want to boss but you are too nice a person to revel in the grovelings of your subjects. Weak people who never challenge you or your opinions serve only to annoy you.

My advice then to Tiger men and women is this. Steer clear of compromising situations. Stay out of community activities unless they vote you chairman of the steering committee straight off. Be your own person. But don't play around with the emotions of other people unless you want them to give it right back to you. Basically, you are a kind soul, a noble type who means well. But you are also stronger than most of us. In the long run, you do not need the company of a cheering section in order to survive. So go it on your own. Create your personal avant-garde. Much good work is ahead of you. Choose your lieutenants well and get out there and fight.

COMPATIBILITIES

Affairs of the Heart

Rash and inconstant, the Tiger lover is rarely anywhere he is supposed to be at that precise time he is needed. The intrepid Tiger has no patience with fools. Nor does he like to sustain love relationships with those weaker than himself. The Tiger engaged in a marriage or love affair in which he has to chide or cheer his limping partner will lose interest and try elsewhere. Tigers are not cruel people. They simply cannot waste their idea of precious time on anyone who does not measure up to their high standards of courage and endurance.

In protracted emotional situations, Tigers who choose Horse people as partners are in luck. The Horse enjoys an honest, diligent, dignified image to which the Tiger can look up. The Horse will stand by the Tiger in his revolutionary efforts, yet he will not lose any skin from his nose through becoming too deeply involved. The Tiger who is fortunate enough to afford himself a Horse mate will find his rainbow's end right at home where it belongs. Horses are noted for their selfishness in every area of life but love. For the sake of a passionate Tiger, a Horse might give up every vestige of his ego in favor of a good sex life.

Dragons bring both wisdom and love to the terrible Tiger. The strength of Dragon people is enhanced by the addition of Tiger temerity and spunk. Tigers, who usually will not listen to anybody, take advice from the Dragon. Though this union will not be all sweetness and light, Tigers and Dragons make progress together. Each in his own way can expect growth and learning to emanate from their alliance.

Tigers get on with Dogs, too. The Dog will surely take up the Tiger's cause and be content to live in his shadow. In turn, the Tiger will ennoble the diffident Dog and bestow honors on him that the Dog might never have dreamed of requesting from any other quarter. Loyalty is essential to the Tiger. He must feel his love partner is on his side. No tiny treasons will be tolerated. Happily, devotion is easy for the diligent Dog.

Some Tigers like to take wily Monkey partners on as lieutenants. But the Monkey is so unpredictably mercurial, that such a union can amount to sheer beguilement of the venerable Tiger by his Monkey mate. Silent Snakes and careful Cats will be far too well-behaved to amuse the danger-loving Tiger for long. Besides, Cat people are of the same race as Tigers. They know just where to meow for attention and love, and just how to hit below the belt for that crushing blow to the intemperate Tiger's ego.

Possible partnerships can be found between Tigers and Pigs. The Pig is amused, and the Tiger often takes advantage of the Pig's good nature. Rats, too, can get along with Tigers, but only if the Rat is out of town one week and the Tiger is away on a speaking tour the next. If they must see too much of each other, Rats and Tigers may try to interfere in each other's social lives.

Oxen will try to destroy a Tiger. They cannot put up with such undisciplined behavior for long. And other Tigers, though they will get on like two neighboring houses afire, will exercise a nefarious power on each other. Such mutual destruction through excess is to be avoided like the plague.

Social Affairs

Tigers make enduring friends among Dragons, Cats, and Pigs. The Dragon pal will boost the Tiger's sometimes flagging morale. The Cat will offer him refinements he doesn't know how to get for himself. And the Pig will keep the Tiger in stitches with his bawdy stories.

A Tiger can befriend a Goat or Rooster, but he probably will not take this comradeship very seriously. The Tiger will have to realize all the projects, run the show, and keep things together for the Goat. The Rooster, for some reason, doesn't tempt the lucky Tiger. Perhaps he is afraid some of those Rooster hard times will rub off on him.

Horses make jolly friends for Tiger people. Tigers respect them for their dash and drive. Horses like praise and Tigers can applaud with all four paws. Though the Horse and the Tiger must beware of argument over details in which one or the other prefers to wield an upper hand, in general they make a positive pair.

Above all the others stand the Tiger and his Dog chum. Dogs take nothing but strength from these friendships. Tigers admire the idealism of Dog people and share in their liberal attitudes. Their mutual devotion is admirable.

Business Affairs

Tigers usually do not choose to associate themselves for less than 75 percent of any profit-seeking venture. However, if they do succumb to the temptation of association or corporate effort, certain signs conform more aptly to the Tiger's needs.

The sign best capable of handling the Tiger's temerity is the Dragon. Dragons are wiser than Tigers. They are equally strong and courageous, but Dragons are not foolhardy. Tigers are. Second choice for Tiger's co-worker should be the Horse. The complications and tiffs over who really gets the glory will be many. But, in the end, the Tiger will always give up money for power. Horses are not so nonmaterialistic as all that.

A business partnership or even office relationship between the Monkey and the Tiger is ill-advised. Monkeys are crafty. Tigers are straight-up honest. The Tiger prefers to use force; the monkey, guile. And the Monkey, unhappily, is finally no match for the venerable Tiger. The angry Tiger will eat a traitorous Monkey for breakfast.

Goat people also manage to exhaust the Tiger's resources after a time. Goats have the kind of longevity in passive resistance that exasperates the hasty Tiger. Though the Tiger can understand the Goat and even likes him immensely, he cannot help deciding finally to pick up that shovel and dig his own garden.

Obviously, Dogs make fine allies for Tigers. But they may be mutually blinded by ideals. Political or artistic ventures could work well. But never should a Dog and a Tiger go into business together. They can't tell the difference between red and black columns on a ledger. Pigs make impatient partners for Tigers. Pigs are good at business and lucky in finance. Tigers are so enormously spendthrift and generous that they are likely to donate all the Pig's profits to the poor.

Family Affairs

As a parent, there is no question in the Tiger mind that the house, the furniture, and the very soap in the bathtub belong exclusively to him. No, no, Tigers are not selfish or stingy. They are foolishly giving and open-handed. But Tigers are born with natural authority. Everybody respects the tawny terrific Tiger. Because of this innate venerability, a weak, forgetful, or distracted child may suffer. The Tiger's tot may know he is not obeying or pleasing his enviably eminent parent. But perhaps he cannot live up to such a standard. Tiger rages are ominous; their deep regrets, just as impressive.

For the terrible Tiger to deal with a Snake, Goat, or another Tiger with any kind of realistic gentility will be enormously challenging. A Snake child will make every attempt to obey and venerate a Tiger parent. The Tiger will be aware of his efforts, but these two sorts just don't understand each other. Tigers are quick, Snakes are slow. Tigers are passionate. Snakes are logical. Unless the Tiger mollifies his authoritative air while the child is still young enough to recover from the wounds inflicted by the Tiger's volatility, the Goat child could be permanently damaged by Tiger tyranny.

Horses, Dragons, and Pigs can get along well with a Tiger parent. Nobody can really tell a Horse what to do. If he feels like submitting to his Tiger mom or dad's request, the Horse child will do so with alacrity and good will. If not, he will simply ignore the Tiger's voice. Arguing will be status quo, but much understanding can come from the mutual respect these two signs feel. Dauntless Dragons can take care of themselves in the face of the Tiger parent's high standards. And Pigs? Well, Pigs do not love being bossed around, but they love their Tiger parent for his magnanimity and ability to see his own faults. The indulgent Pig child will excuse his Tiger parent any transgressions. The Ox, on the other hand, will not put up with Tiger oppression for a second. From age one, he will set out to prove that fact. If the Tiger can adjust his gun sights a bit, the rapport will improve. Compromise is tough on both subjects.

THE CAT

THE YEARS OF THE CAT

January 29, 1903 to February 16, 1904
February 14, 1915 to February 3, 1916
February 2, 1927 to January 23, 1928
February 19, 1939 to February 8, 1940
February 6, 1951 to January 27, 1952
January 25, 1963 to February 13, 1964
February 11, 1975 to January 30, 1976
January 29, 1987 to February 16, 1988
February 16, 1999 to February 4, 2000

CATS ARE:

Discreet • Refined • Virtuous • Social • Tactful
Unflappable • Sensitive • Companionable • Solicitous • Ambitious
Gifted • Forgiving • Prudent • Traditional • Hospitable • Clever

BUT THEY CAN ALSO BE:

Old-fashioned • Pedantic • Thin-skinned
Devious • Aloof • Private • Dilettantish • Fainthearted
Squeamish • Hypochondriacal

CATS I HAVE KNOWN AND LOVED

Japanese and Chinese astrologers usually refer to this symbol as The Rabbit, so my American friends who know a bit about Chinese astrology were surprised that I refer to it as The Cat. In Paris, though—where *l'horoscope Chinois* came to us via Vietnam—we always say "le Chat."

A Cat friend is indeed one of the few affordable luxuries of our day. More than a fly-by-night companion, a Cat associate actively participates in the lives of his bosom acquaintances. Never a burden to respected members of his entourage, the Cat contributes willingly, discreetly, and diplomatically to his chosen relationships. Neither cloyingly possessive nor shruggingly blasé, Cat gestures of generosity know how to curl up patiently in front of the fire and wait until they are summoned.

Satisfied to function independently, Cat people rarely fall victim to serious emotional trauma. Nervous breakdowns do not present much of a threat to those bom in Cat years. Though scarcely what one might call hardy or courageous in the face of upheaval, Cats maintain stability by wisely skirting issues that might devastate their psyches.

You may protest that by avoiding problems one does not solve them. You are right. But Cats prefer walking away from an unwieldy situation to pouncing feetfirst into a basket of crabs, where they may risk facing dissension. Cat people are forever informing us that such and such a marriage didn't work out, or "William and I just couldn't get along," or "I am sincerely happier on my own. Cohabitation doesn't suit my nature." Be it marriage, business partnership, or mutual creative endeavor, Cat people are not given to vain perseverance for the sake of maintaining a failing relationship.

In fact, I only know single, divorced, or remarried Cats. Not one of the Cat people in my acquaintance is the other half of an enduring marriage on the verge of its golden anniversary. Cats are not exactly sissies. They are sometimes 'fraidy Cats. Declared wars or convoluted struggles that seriously threaten their equilibrium can send Cats scampering up tree trunks. And it is not really necessary to call the fire department. Cats are remarkably able to retrieve themselves from their safe perches on high branches. They enjoy finding their own routes out of hiding. Cats have nine lives, remember? And so would you if you fled the scene every time an emotional boogeyman reared his ugly head.

What makes them so adaptable? Well, the fact is that Cat people really never open their emotional doors wide enough to risk defeat. Love attachments are not their *raisons d'être*. Though Cats may be romantic, sympathetic, responsive, and even at times overly indulgent with their mates, they are definitely more devoted to harmony and peace of mind than to relationships of record-breaking duration.

Cats appear to be thin-skinned bleeding hearts. Turmoil upsets them. They retreat from the military, steer clear of open hostility, and tread lightly in aggression-charged circumstances. Whatever Cats produce in their lives, be it artistic, financial, or domestic, the tone will be conservative, tasteful, and traditional. If a Cat sculptor carves what he intends to sell as the portrait of an eagle, you can be fairly sure that his statue will look exactly like an eagle. You will not have to walk embarrassedly around and around the work, squinting and raising your thumb to decode his abstractions. Cats like things very much as they are. They are neither revolutionary nor hotheaded. Even when Cats devote their skills to social reform, they go about their mission in a peaceable manner.

Years ago, in my early Paris days, I met a talented young songwriter named James Friedman. Jim was born in 1927. When I ran into him, it was 1962 and Jim had already had four years of the Parisian gourmet starvation diet. He was hankering to return to New York in order to sell some ballads he had written to popular singers whose protests and ranklings had begun to filter across the Atlantic. I had been in Paris only about two years by that time. The city was so beautiful, I decided to stick it out for as long as it took to die of loveliness. Jim took a charter flight home. I did not see him again until this year in New York.

Jim now writes songs for people who appreciate and want to sing them publicly. Words and music, Cat Friedman's ballads are goosebump-in-spiring messages of love, longing, loss, and finally, the refusal to suffer any of it. Even a protest song, when composed by Jim Friedman, is devoid of militance or threats of revenge.

Though obsessed by human suffering, Jim does not urge us to go out and burn bras, buildings, or buses in order to vindicate misery. Though applicable to a universal audience, Friedman's work does not propose practical solutions to poverty, racism, or acts of God. He states facts—touching, incisive, tragic realities that can shatter even the most stolid listener. Jim, in true Cat fashion, writes of the emotions and experiences that modern life has forced so many of us to leave behind. Concepts such as "true love" and "Christmas in the snow" or "my playground pals" run through all of his lyrics. His tunes are of the good old-fashioned ballad school. The one most positive fact about people of this sign is that their clinging to tradition and respect for the past make me sure that we need Cats. America, the world, the universe, and you and I need more Cat people.

Cats round the edges of our brittled souls and carry us back to root levels, which our drivings for accumulation of wealth force us to forget and leave behind. Cats, you see, don't usually enter the race in the same way that others choose. In order to avoid confrontation, they leap from crowded subways in rush hour and walk home in the rain. They travel on weekdays to avoid crushing crowds of tourists and only enjoy living in atmospheres that seclude their tender-hearted spirits from ugliness.

All Cat houses are homes. People born in Cat years cannot tolerate transiency. Travel, they will—but only when certain of comfortable accommodation. Dislocation of goods or misplacement of cherished possessions will demoralize even the sturdiest breed of Cat. He likes things where he can find them, in place, ready to use, and decorative in the bargain.

Cats, though domesticated, are not particularly family oriented. Parents, children, and mates take a back seat to friends in the lives of Cat subjects. Contact with kin may be dutiful, even perfunctory. What Cats want out of life does not come in the shape of giant sprawling barns full of noisy, disruptive children who incessantly howl for attention and distract their Cat parents from the more urgently important job of receiving four or five close friends for dinner. No, Cats don't love interruption or confusion about the house.

I do not wish to imply that Cat people are not responsible to their offspring. Sometimes they are overly indulgent, too lenient, and even negligent in disciplining their kids. Since they themselves resist involvement in the normal hectic pace of social patterns, Cats can readily understand why a child would not enjoy obeying rules or joining a team only to undergo rigorous herding in and out of buildings or buses. The wiser of the parent Cats I know are generally clever enough to have spouses who don't mind handling workaday kiddie care. And those who can afford it, though they do lend their time to counseling sons and daughters about studies and behavior, will often send their progeny to boarding schools.

For Cat people to be able to function at full efficiency, all exterior obstacles must be removed from their paths. A messy studio, unwashed dishes, or a pile of accumulated laundry leering from out a brimming hamper will nip any creative effort in the bud. Cats hate disorder. Mental harmony, for them, is engendered by congruous surroundings in which they can work productively and seek to build even more perfection. Transfer the brushes of a Cat painter from one side of his easel to the other and it may throw off his whole day.

The presence of architectural permanence was so important to one of my Cat friends that when his fourteenth-century French château self-destructed in a fire some years ago, he simply could not tolerate it. Though Edgar (b. 1927) Plissé lives in Paris, where he plies his trade as a successful psychiatrist, he always considered his true home to be the family castle. He had spent many moons there as a child. Lost in the blaze were generations of antique furniture, the ancient beams of the big country kitchen where Edgar had passed so many happy hours joking with servants as a boy, the Aubusson tapestries, and a collection of fine paintings.

I had heard the disastrous news through a mutual acquaintance and hastened to call Edgar's office immediately to offer my sympathies. His secretary said that Edgar had left that morning for La Creuse, a sumptuous rural region south of Orléans, to survey the damage. "He is desolate," she told me confidentially. "I don't know what he will do."

After hanging up, I immediately dialed through to the regional operator in La Creuse. The village is so tiny, I asked the local operator if she had heard the terrible news about Monsieur Edgar Plissé's house. She had. It was a miracle, she told me, but somehow the phone at the chateau was still operational. She rang the number for me. Another miracle, Edgar answered. "*Allo, oui.*" His formerly strong voice seemed diminished by half.

"Edgar, my poor duck," I said. "It's me, Suzanne."

I could envision Edgar standing plunk in the middle of a stone-walled room, full of the charred rubble of his memories. In his hand was, of all things, a half-melted telephone. The image was both surrealistic and sad. He managed a not-too-tragic answer: "How nice of you to call. I'm right in the middle of trying to decide which of the living-room beams is still strong enough to hold a noose. I think I'll hang myself."

I knew he was joking. But, in such drastic circumstances, Edgar's suicide did not seem a far-fetched solution. According to the telephone operator, there was nothing left of the interior except the sculpted fireplaces. The walls, she had said, were still standing. All I could say was, "Now, Edgar, don't do that. There must be a better way." (Not that I could think one up right quick.)

He laughed limply. "I'm not about to do myself in. Don't you fret. It's pretty horrible here. But I still have my six-hundred-year-old walls. Old stones don't melt." He paused. "But jewels do," he informed me. "My grandmother's gems were hidden upstairs in a secret coffer. They are all melted and squishy. You wouldn't want them. I guess I'm not the good catch I was last week."

Glad to hear he was not on the brink of mental ruin, I dared to ask, "Edgar, whatever will you do?

The voice brightened. He sounded almost his normal self. "Why, rebuild, of course."

And rebuild is precisely what my Cat friend Edgar did.

In the proper environment, Cats function at peak performance level. And, should their homes for any reason crumble, they will find ingenious ways to rehouse themselves in the style to which they have become accustomed. Because Cats so love their homes, they also enjoy entertaining, fixing drinks, cooking, setting a pretty table, and in general, socializing. Hordes of strangers repel Cats. Small clusterings of convivial guests delight them. Cats can hold forth on almost any subject. Though often they must be prodded to open up to an audience, once a Cat is on his feet in a gathering of companions, he relishes every word of a funny story as it passes his lips. Cats are neither shy nor timid, but are nevertheless independent entertainers. The Cat esteems "One Show Nightly" more than he does full-time life-of-the-party gregariousness.

In finance, as in creative pursuits, the Cat is often a winner. Innovative and open-minded, he always finds ways to apply his talents and earn enough income to keep the wolf from the door. (Usually, the absence of predators will suffice.) Cats, although they thrive in luxurious settings, are usually able to stop at the first million, retire, and make-do with a medium-sized revenue from investments. Never driven by extremes such as fear of poverty or a desire for showy yachts with which to impress their competitors, Cats, from earliest adulthood, are placid investors of their time and cash. They go about money problems with quiet professionalism. Ambition, for a Cat, is relative to how much money he thinks he will need to assure a pleasant life style through old age.

On this side of the ocean, I know a Cat lady (b. 1939) who married a very wealthy man. It is Sandra's third marriage and her new husband Jeffrey's second. One of the first things Sandra told me when she explained her situation is why she had not asked for any alimony from either of her previous rich husbands. "I'm not greedy," the elegant Sandy said. "Jeffrey has plenty of money for both of us. My first husband kindly agreed to a settlement which permitted me to buy a couple of income properties in Florida. The second gentleman had given me so much jewelry that I thought his parting gift of fifty thousand dollars cash more than adequate. I'll always get by. Even if Jeff leaves me, I'll manage."

Now, people who have income property in Palm Beach and receive fifty thousand in cash upon quitting no-children marriages are not what I call poverty-stricken. But there was a certain modesty about Sandra's remarks that at least set her apart from those shrieking bleached and childless harpies who crowd the courtrooms of our country with demands for unreasonable and unwarranted lifetime pension plans from rejected husbands, so that they can spend the rest of their useless days occupying deck chairs somewhere in the South Atlantic. Sandy is a reasonable rich lady.

However, Sandra is not an idle rich lady. Far from it. Shortly after marriage, Sandra and her new husband Jeff bought a rickety picturesque old country store in Massachusetts and set about turning it into a business. Because real country stores are gone forever from their village and everybody shops in supermarkets nowadays, the couple decided against becoming grocers. Instead, since Sandra knew a lot about French cuisine and had always been interested in arts and crafts, they brought in a clever architect and turned the old store into a combination restaurant, gift shop, and art gallery.

Jeff administrates the business. Sandra does the buying and arranges for artists to show in the gallery.

No matter how affluent Cat people become, they always remain industrious and involved in some work project or other. In Sandra's case, this personal endeavor took the form of organizing artistic objects to buy and sell. In the case of other Cats, this self-motivated ambition ranges anywhere from raising green plants to earnest volunteering for ecological programs or finding funds for starving painters. Even the richest of Cat subjects can rarely be found idle, slothful, or dissipated.

Cat people are sometimes accused of being snobbish or snooty. They do tend to spoil themselves materially and they are also very conscious of their own and others' degree or lack of sophistication. Because of their penchant for the arts and nature in its loveliest forms, Cats do cultivate a more effete crowd of people than either you or I might choose. Their manners and speech can sound affected. No matter what their social backgrounds, Cats are believers in upward social mobility. They seek out refinement the way Rats seek out listening posts, with cheerful determination and pluck.

You will never find a Cat who refuses to help a friend. No matter how "down" you are or how "up" they may seem by comparison, you can always call on a Cat in times of trouble or illness. Though they may drive up to your shanty in a Rolls Royce, luxury will not prevent them from rolling up the bouffant sleeves of a hand-tailored shirt and digging right in. First we change the sheets; then we wash the house from top to bottom; after that we prepare a nice vegetable soup and feed the patient from a silver spoon we keep in our Christian Dior alligator bag, just for that purpose.

Cats do not faint at the sight of their friends' blood. Your illness or worry is their own. Their house is yours to use; their bed, their kitchen, their whiskey, their cheerings, their comforting smiles, and jokes are all yours. Mind you, after they have you safely tucked under a satin eiderdown, a warming glass of grog at your bedside, Cats will pad silently about cleaning up the mess your intrusion has created. They never say anything. They just go about the business of righting misplaced items, wiping off table tops, and rinsing out glasses. Then, they will return to the room where you lie luxuriating in their hospitality to sit at the bedside and hold your feverish hand through the night.

Naturally, like all human beings, Cats live under a certain amount of inner strain and sometimes feel a definite lack of mental quietude. Notwithstanding, Cat people are born with a measure of discretion that permits them to keep their turmoils to themselves. They may discuss or even complain of mild head- or heartaches. But Cats almost never employ the modern "getting to know you" tactic of baring their souls to strangers in order to favorably color whatever they say with preconceived, preimposed ideas of either real or imagined handicaps. A Cat's perception of his own stability is not predicated on pity, empathy, or sympathy from a third party.

Physically, Cats are basically hardy folks. Yet, not all of them would agree to this assessment of their state of health. Hardly the sniveling type who ceaselessly whines or gripes when ill, the Cat is nonetheless very much aware of his every ache and pain. Usually he "doctors" more than he should. A Cat person may run to the dermatologist immediately upon sighting the tiniest wart or mole. He favors specialists. Partly due to his meticulous nature, and also because he truly believes that an ounce of prevention is worth a pound of cure, the Cat is one who plans to die healthy. As I mentioned earlier, rather than appear humbling or out of control, Cats turn away from situations that they instinctively feel may lead to their demise. Gossip, intrigue, involvement in skullduggeries and thickening plots only moderately interest Cat people. To lend an ear or an hour of time over coffee and cake is one thing, but to be forced to actually testify in favor of a friend who is accused of a crime would not please even the most faithful Cat companions.

Please do not misconstrue this Cat quality as cowardice. As long as they know they can handle drama or strife, Cat people will not shy away. When faced with a cantankerous person who is riled by frustration or anger, Cat subjects neither duck behind a chair to avoid confrontation nor rush up and swat the declared enemy in the nose. Instead, Cats will try to reason with him, to soothe his ire with common sense and diplomacy. Violence, unless the Cat is absolutely obliged to straitjacket an opponent by force, ranks as a taboo in the feline code.

Cats make excellent organizers of their fellows. Any orders they issue are usually underscored with purr rather than power. To avoid creating undue resentment, Commander Cats like to set the example for their subordinates by showing that they, too, can perform menial tasks and keep a desk orderly or a wastebasket empty. Though this may seem hypocritical to executives who snap out directives and lay down the law with an iron hand, again I remind you that Cats, not gifted for meeting opposition with aggression or hostility, prefer to rule with a velvet glove.

Even Cat people who have risen to positions of extreme power and are famed for their ability to rule entire countries manage somehow to gain the respect of their subjects through example. Obviously, no dictator or monarch ever escapes the historical responsibility for unpleasantnesses. The reign of Fidel Castro (b. 1927), like that of Queen Victoria (b. 1819) of England, has been marked by unsavory incidents. Powerful Cats use their executioners as Cat's paws. These less squeamish brutes willingly carry out imprisonments, beatings, or the odd hanging. The Cats can handle diplomacy, summit conferences, and the establishment of behavior codes for their peoples.

Though the inclusion of the above two names in our Cat chapter may surprise you, remember, if you will, that Castro, dressed as a mountain guerilla, smoking Havanas and looking so tough, is very much alive today. No one actually saw him lead a platoon of scraggly soldiers over a hill and risk his life for them. No, sir. Castro "looked like" his troops. He be-costumed himself in order to convince his rebels that he was one of them. In Cuba's feudal, pre revolution society, Castro was an attorney. He was obliged to prove to a countryside full of peasants that he, too, was but an ordinary man. Simple people fear and mistrust professional men who sweep into their villages in big limousines, suited and tied in the ritzy trappings of government officialdom. So Castro had his tailor alter some old army fatigues and went into the mountains uniformed as a common solider. When you think about it, that kind of pussyfooting makes infinite sense.

Queen Victoria, whose royal birthright it was to rule England, set a rigorous example of prudish domesticity in her personal life. For over fifty years, Victoria's metaphor of smothering motherhood and puritanical uprightness extended itself throughout her country. Her spirit forged an entire empire with the dogmatic belief that stiff upper English rule could save the world. Victoria Regina was hardly a public person. She stayed very much sequestered within her own homely circle. Political in-fighting was left to members of Parliament, whose job it was to perform the "dirty work" of lawmaking and execution. Tle precepts by which Victoria ruled have become a household word for all English-speaking peoples. Certain forbidding furniture is Victorian, old-fashioned rules and regulations are termed Victorian, and strict parents who sit on their children like hens on eggs are dubbed Victorian. Good Queen Vicky was extremely powerful but, rather than merely dominate her subjects, she preferred predominating their life styles from the palace wings.

There are other celebrated Cats among us whose exploits show how they have managed to put their talents to good use. The year 1903 gave us food critic James Beard, who so deliciously exemplifies the Cat's tastes for refinement and delicacy. Edgar Bergen, the famed ventriloquist/inventor of Charlie McCarthy, was also born that year.

In 1915, novelist Saul Bellow, whose style and ability won him the 1975 Nobel Prize nomination, came into the world. The next Cat year was 1927. Singer Harry Belafonte, playwright Neil Simon, actors Peter Falk and George C. Scott, and writer/playboy George Plimpton surfaced that season. In 1939, movie directors Francis Ford Coppola and Peter Fonda came into the picture. With them arrived singer Judy Collins and actress Ali McGraw. TV personality David Frost is also a 1939 Cat. You will note that among these renowned figures, there are no generals, presidents, or military heros. George C. Scott came closest to the top-brass image when he played tough General Patton in a biographical film. You may recall, too, that Scott turned down an Oscar because he considered the whole business rigged, or simply not worth the trouble of donning a tuxedo.

Usually Cat people do not much care for applause and public acclaim. They enjoy their work and go about it calmly and with much self-discipline. Though they are perfectly delighted if that same work appeals to audiences, kudos are not their sole objective when they set about a task. I don't recall ever having seen either Albert Einstein (b. 1879) nor subsequent Cat Henry Miller (b. 1891) on masses of TV shows. Do you? Cat geniuses are quiet geniuses.

What menaces the equilibrium of Cats is intensive exposure to affliction. They, of course, always prefer to divert disaster or simply ignore its presence. But sometimes life, circumstances, moralities, or duty can forbid turning one's back on strife. Wars, enemy occupations, world financial crises, and other such entrenched hardships place demands on human beings that might be termed "inhuman." In these junctures, Cats do not always perform well. The Cat is a beast that hates to be trapped, confined, or cornered. A person born under the sign of the Cat, rather than spring viciously at the throat of his adversary, will attempt first to duck out underneath his foe's feet; he may whine, hiss, and growl, but will finally give in to an indomitable force. It is with much regret that the Cat succumbs, but surrender he will. The front lines are no place for such a refined soul to set foot. Adversity in large doses confuses and frightens him.

He is capable of enormous displays of compassion. The Cat cares deeply for those he loves. But he hesitates to give himself over to total commitment for fear one day the emotional tide may turn against him. The Cat needs security and mistrusts what he perceives as an unkind world full of not-so-generous people. He invariably prefers to count only on himself for safe harbor.

Cats are steeped in virtue, devoted to refinement, and cautious about change. They make independent, aloof, and not very-demanding comrades. As long as they are comfortable and cared for in small ways, the Cats will take care of the larger problems on their own. Life with a Cat, though not always a full-time three-ring circus, is a curious affair.

MADAME CAT

Feline females require less personal attention than many of the ladies we encounter in this furry world. They are good managers, fine householders, and deft dealers with destiny. However, Cat ladies do require scads of the less intimate manifestations of affection. They need money, a home to call their own, and unlimited time in which to dabble, read, and unwind. The Cat woman left on her own for days on end rarely complains of loneliness. Solitude, though perhaps not a lifetime's worth, suits her.

Women born in Cat years are preeners. They spend much of their time preparing themselves to face the outside world before so much as stepping out for an errand. Fat or thin, tall or short, the Cat female is generally sleek and well-dressed. Not as aware of the last touch of accessory or added bauble as, say, the tantalizing Snake woman or the fabulous Horse, Madame Cat takes a broader view of her appearance. She favors clinging garments of soft wools and simple basic dresses that enhance her figure.

Whatever she wears, my Krazy Kat friend Ellen Saint Charles (born 1939) is always perfectly attired. I sometimes wonder how she does it. Even her jeans seem hand-tailored.

Ellen is one friend whom I do not often get to see. She lives in Hollywood, travels in Mexico to hunt artifacts, and only comes to Paris once or twice a year to buy clothes for her dress shop in Beverly Hills. Whenever she is in town, Ellen rings me. Since ready-to-wear fashion collections are shown at approximately the same times each year, I usually know about when to expect Ellen's call.

It must have been three or four years ago when she came unseasonally into town during the month of November. Her unanticipated trip had something to do with a French actor boyfriend she had uncovered in Mexico and was longing to see. Knowing Ellen's penchant for effete young men of futile bent, I had a private chuckle when she said, "Suzanne, wait until you meet Pierre. He is simply the best man I have ever met. He's tall and handsome with deep-set eyes full of sadness. You will absolutely love him!"

I made a date to rendezvous with Ellen for lunch at the Plaza. Before ringing off, she said, "Bring along a change of clothes. We can have our hair done and sneak in a facial and a manicure before Pierre comes round at six for drinks in the bar. I do want you to meet him."

Gulping, I reminded her that I was not in particularly solvent monetary form those days. Her response was typical Ellen. "Whatever do you mean?"

I said, "Well, the hairdresser and I are on the financial outs. If you see what I mean. . . ."

Ellen snickered. "Silly goose! You know we can charge it here. What are you worrying about? Just get in your car and come over."

Rich people are forever misunderstanding me. "I don't have a car." (I had sold it to buy dancing lessons for my kids.)

Ellen was abrupt this time. "Then take a cab. I'll leave the fare with the doorman. And forget about the clothes. We'll find some around here. Please hurry. I have so much to tell you."

By the time I arrived at the Plaza, Ellen had made us twin appointments at the hotel's chic beauty establishment, guaranteeing an afternoon of kink and wrinkle reparations. My guilt regarding the exorbitance of the treatment's price, I must admit, flew conveniently out the window into the Avenue Monlatgne. And, later, when I viewed the result in the Dior dressing-room mirror across the street, I figured a little larceny among friends was better than looking like a hag when I met Ellen's critical Pierre.

By five-thirty P.M., I resembled what I had always imagined I might, should ever a good witch remove the spell of eternal "bluejeandom" from off my scruffy literary soul. I felt terribly special sitting there in the Plaza lounge, awaiting the arrival of a French movie star. Even though he wasn't my movie star, I can dream, can't I?

Six-thirty winked at me from the clock above the bar. Six forty-five leapt to my eyes from the waiter's watch as he served our third drinks. Pierre had been expected for six o'clock sharp. By seven, when the big hand hopped on the twelve's back, I suggested to Ellen, "Maybe he's been held up. Movies are an unpredictable business. Or, perhaps he's caught in traffic."

Ellen, cool as the emerald she wore on her finger, said, "I may as well face it. He isn't coming."

Placing a reassuring hand on her arm, I placatingly offered, "Now, now. We mustn't jump to conclusions. Can't you phone him?" Ellen set her decorously emptied glass on the table and said, "I don't like to push people. If Pierre doesn't love me, I won't pressure him." She signed the check and left a message with the bartender, saying, "Madame Saint

Charles has gone out for the evening." Ellen glanced conspiratorially in my direction. "Just in case Pierre comes snooping around."

Instead of passing the soirée with the man she had come across an ocean to woo, Ellen invited me to dine with her at Jean Castel's famous discotheque/restaurant, have a dance or two before it got too crowded, and maybe find somebody else to enchant with her feline wiles. I accepted. During dinner, Ellen removed a small velours box from her bag and handed it to me. On it was stamped "Van Cleef and Arpel." On my face was written "Is this some kind of a joke?"

Ellen explained, "I was going to give this to Pierre. It's his birthday today. I came over to help him celebrate. You might as well have it. I think it's pretty." I opened the box and peeked. "Don't you?" she asked worriedly. Inside the tiny velvet coffin was an amber-colored stone mounted in gold and attached to a fine chain of that same precious metal. It was exquisite. I almost wept, but instead swallowed hard and thanked Ellen for the consolation prize. I really admired how Ellen had surrendered herself so easily to the loss of Pierre. But, more than that, I felt desolate for old Pierre himself. He had not only missed out on a liaison with a charming Cat lady, but he had also missed out on the birthday present that Ellen had destined for his ungrateful neck.

Irresistibly lovable, Cat women are the kinds of ladies who make having lady friends worthwhile. They are easy company, full of fun, and capable of standing on their own little Cat feet. As lovers, they are gentle and caring; but they don't cotton to adversity, nor do they hang about watching marriages disintegrate into hostile battles of will. Cat women are usually willing to pay any price for peace of mind and solidarity of self.

MONSIEUR CAT

Tom Cats are good to their wives, sweet to their children, and adorable to their friends. They proffer a ready helping hand to anyone who deserves their loyalty. Male Cats can be counted on to participate in role-sharing within a household or family. Although they are not parents who hover and wring their hands over babies, they do like

their kids. Cat fathers treat their children more as friends than possessions or symbols of achievement. In one way, Cat men are even
vaguely competitive with the athletic son who beats them at tennis or
that daughter who out-skis her dad on a tough slope.

The intelligence of Cat men is often put to best use in situations
that a require the transformation of abstract concepts into ordered
thought or a possible course of action. The Cat man, despite this ability to render fuzzy ideas coherent, is not likely to enjoy being nominated the executor of his own plan. He will gladly sit back and watch
more pragmatic people struggle with snags and hassle workmen, while
he himself commences to formulate yet another project.

Though he generally appears well-groomed and adequately
attired for all occasions, Monsieur Cat is not overly preoccupied with
fashion. He usually exhibits natural talent for "the studied casual" in
his mode of dress. Loose-fitting, comfortable garments that do not
constrict his lithe form please him more than stiffly starched shirts that
simply serve to please his host, hostess, or boss.

By necessity, all the male Cats in my life are engaged in some
form of business. One practices law, another medicine. There are
among them a marketing expert, an art organizer, and even one Cat
who vends his own songs. No matter how efficient these Cats are at
commerce, they all dream of relief from the burdensome intricate con-
volutions that automatically accompany deals and negotiations for
salary, fees, royalties, and the like. Though all Cat men are eminently
capable of earning good incomes, ideally they would rather not be
obliged to consider such banalities.

My lawyer friend wishes to be a writer; the marketing researcher
spends his life dreaming of the day he can give up business and
become a full-time sculptor; the psychiatrist longs to single-handedly
eradicate mental illness so that he can retire and become a gentleman
farmer; and the songwriter racks his creative brain for a solution to
the "agent problem." I always hesitate to remind these worried Cats
that no matter how esoteric a métier one pursues, business will still be
business. In truth, they probably do not need my chidings to be aware
of that fact. Cats are pretty smart Cats.

Because of the Cat man's inherent desire to remove himself from the rigors of the rat race, he sometimes appears distant or preoccupied. *Shhhhh!* Don't disturb him. He's ruminating. Cat men love to think. They take long walks alone, drive around for hours in search of solutions to problems, hole up unattainably behind telephone-answering machines for days on end, and may just up and disappear to Europe for a few months to get their heads together. This vanishing act ought not to be taken personally by the women in the lives of Cat men. It is not you whom these Cats are trying to escape. What they do try to get away from is "it all." Cat men seek oblivion virtually anywhere they suspect it might be hiding (which is often merely elsewhere).

One brief Cat man profile may illustrate how adroit Cat men can be at dodging reality.

Omar Lerman (b. 1927) is a free-lance art organizer. Yes, I know that such a job description smacks of the vague. But obviously, art organizers do accomplish something. Omar has not yet starved to death. Suffice it, for our purposes, to say that Omar Lerman is extremely talented and knows how to put artistic concepts to work for people who pay him to design exhibitions, put together fireworks displays, and travel a lot.

Omar looks like all four of his own pet Siamese cats, with a pinch of teddy bear thrown in for cuddle. (If men can be called huggable, Cat men surely meet the physical requirements.) Like all Cats, Omar enjoys the privileged position of being pursued at all times by lots of women. I have always thought that one of the most attractive male qualities (which only a small percentage of men learn while still young enough to do anything about it) is unavailability. Because they are independent and able to function alone, Cat men attract curious women who keep wondering why they never stick around long enough to become entrapped. In any case, Omar has this concept firmly etched on his brain. He is literally never home.

The last time I got to see Omar the Cat was about a year ago. We had some business dealings. During my fireworks period, I was selling, Omar was designing, and some more important people than either of us were buying bombs and Roman candles. On one of said rare occasions, we were invited to Washington, D.C., for a pre-bicentennial meeting.

It is almost too popular a neurosis to admit these days, but I'll tell you, anyway . . . I get the heebie-jeebies in airplanes. For our Washington visit, we (Omar and I) had to take Eastern Airlines' hourly shuttle flight from New York. Omar said the ride would be smooth and quick, "nothing to fear." I was still scared.

In short, about five minutes after takeoff, our plane began to shake apart. Beneath my securely fastened seat belt, I characteristically commenced to turn into a catatonic. My fright, as it turned out, was Omar's cue to transform himself into "Doctor Feelgood," your friendly airborne psychiatrist. The whiter I waned, the funnier Omar waxed.

His first counterproposal to my advanced acrophobia was, "How you like to have a nice little drink?" Through clenched teeth, as the fuselage rattled and rolled about in thunderclouds, I forced out half an answer: "Don't serve drinks this flight. Too early."

Omar took my clammy hand in his and purred, "Oh, really? Well, then, how about if I sing you a song?"

Leaning back in the upright seat, all my mental hatches battened against inevitable crash, I shook my pale face from side to side, begging, "Please leave me alone. I'm scared."

From some distant, yet very real place in the out-of-control airplane wafted a familiar voice singing to the tune of "Wells Fargo Wagon," "Oh, the Eastern shuttle is a dandy shuttle and I ride it just to while the hours away." It was Omar, performing a song and dance routine in the middle aisle of a shuddering giant bird in which we both were preparing to perish. Paroxysmal with fear and unable to speak, I gestured wildly for Omar to be seated before the hostess scolded him for standing up in a crisis. But my gesticulations were to no avail. He kept it up.

Now Omar sang to the tune of "Stormy Weather." "Don't know why. We are up here in the sky." I wanted to scream. But the Cat had my tongue, my attention, and my giggle meter squarely in his paw. I began to laugh uncontrollably.

Omar the Cat continued his soft-shoe. Through a couple more

thunderstorms and three deep atmospheric plummets, Omar spontaneously rewrote a few more old standards. After another ten minutes, my resistance to his routines had broken down entirely. The plane's dips and dives had ceased to frighten me.

Then Omar kneeled at my feet and started singing to the tune of "Carolina in the Morning." "Nothing could be finer than to be in this airliner in the mawning. Nothing could be worser than a hostess and a purser who are yawning. Pilot's really sorry, doesn't have much news. This flight is oh so gory, I wish we had some booze."

Talk about captive audiences. The petrified passengers and crew did nothing but sit gaping at Omar's bizarre comedy.

By this time, I felt miles better. The turbulence could have kept up all night. I wanted to have a good time, or die trying. So I got up and stumbled along with my friend. We moved ahead in order to reach our entire public, and both of us continued Omar's song: "Eastern has a service that can really make you nervous in the mawning." Etc., etc. We were positively unchained! Any stupid lyric would fit our tunes.

We did not die. We finally landed at some Godforsaken Pennsylvanian Jerry-built cornfield landing strip. Omar admitted, "You were so damn scared. You weren't about to get any reassurance from that terrified crew. What else could I do? I had to sing."

I'd really been thinking that Omar had gone air-crazy up there in the jostling heavens. Then I realized, Cats take care of people. When they can't get out of a tight spot, they avert disaster in the most exotic ways. I don't know what would have happened if the pilot had stalked from the cabin to lower the curtain on Omar's act. I expect my friend would have obliged. Cat men like to help out a pal, but they are not stupid enough to be mistaken for hijackers and get shot over a little turbulence.

CO-SIGNS

CAT/Aries *(March 21—April 20)*
Vital to the "negative wood" by which the Chinese symbolize Cat people is Aries' feisty fire. Boundless energy endows this Cat subject

with the spunk he needs to leap hurdles that most members of his sign would rather escape. Art and all of its trappings will ensnare him while the Cat/Aries is still young. Though he may be successful in business, he would prefer to avoid commerce and to pounce repeatedly upon the various metaphysical careers that so entice him. Superficially, this Cat may seem hyperactive. But he can be slowed to a compassionate crawl by the intrusion of someone who needs his help. Appeal to his sense of altruism and the driving Cat/Aries can be transformed into a lap-sitting pussycat.

CAT/Taurus *(April 21—May 21)*

The nature-loving Cat is abetted by the earth element in the sign of his birthmate Taurus. He is *unbudgeably* home-loving. I fear you may have to acquire an electrified gold-plated cattle prod in order to get this luxurious Cat to go out at night. Taurean Cats prefer the hearth to more sophisticated haunts, and of an evening, can generally be found luxuriating 'neath a source of warmth, be it human or hot water bottle. Sensual and epicurean, this subject is also a good provider. He is unlikely to shy away from work. Too, he will probably be of good cheer, an excellent host, and a gentle parent. The Cat/Taurus resists adversity by ignoring its existence. This Cat figures that what he doesn't know will not hurt him. Acquisitive, artistic, and cuddly, this kitty has a heart of gold and a mind like a steel trap. Give him a collection of thick books, musical instruments, plush carpets, and a cord of wood for his birthday; he may never come out to play again.

CAT/Gemini *(May 22—June 21)*

A soaring biplane of a person is the Cat/Gemini. Combining the forces of wood and air, this subject flits from pillar to post, rapidly and without forethought. A bit of an alley Cat, the Gemini is less timorous than other felines. He may not wish to expose himself to real danger, but because he is able to whistle such a happy tune, he can divert his enemies' attention. Nervous as a Cat in pursuit of some sordid adventure, this person may appear perpetually on the prowl. It might not be possible to hie him off to the veterinarian for an "operation," but perhaps it would be wise to limit his field of activity by house-training him at an early age. Jolly and full of the devil, this Cat subject needs an indulgent firm hand to stroke him into settling down to one project at a time.

CAT/Cancer *(June 22—July 23)*

Mollified by Cancer's watery depths, the Cat who is born a moon child should be less skittish than others. Immersed in his own depths, the Cat/Cancer will not enjoy the company of people whom he considers shallow or superficial. If life deals him some low blows and he has to suffer as a result, this Cat person may prefer introversion to dependence on friends. He is not your "jolly good fellow" of easy confidences and one-night stands. The Cancerian Cat takes himself (and others) seriously. In early years, he may find upheaval almost too much to tolerate. As he grows older, wiser, and more sure of himself, what was once introspection and ponderousness may shift its focus. The Cat born in Cancer may improve with age. He is a late bloomer.

CAT/Leo *(July 24—August 23)*

For a Leo, this person is calm. For a Cat, he is aggressive. Summer's fire shines from within this creature's lemony coat. Leo Cats will probably not be as outgoing and demanding of attention as other Leos. But, even though he appears to take a back seat, when trouble arises or chips are down, you can count on him to rally to the cause. Leos are often self-centered. The Cat's influence on this leonine subject will be positive. When he desires a position or spotlight, he will (unlike other Leos) probably know how to "cool it" and wait his turn to be noticed. There is something regal about this haughty Cat person. One is tempted to endow him with leadership qualities he may not really have. That air of superiority is perchance only the result of a healthy diet that has perked up his sleek coat. Soft and gentle when things go his way, he will expose his claws in a tight spot.

CAT/Virgo *(August 24—September 23)*

Solid citizens like these don't exactly swarm in our midst any more.

The Cat/Virgo is like a four-hundred-year-old building that has withstood the rigors of as many hard winters, yet can still welcome us to its cozy fire. All purity and refinement, the Cat/Virgo will see to the needs of others with charm and aplomb. Beneath that pristine glare lies a sensuous beast who wishes he could communicate more easily. Small talk not only bores the Cat/Virgo subject, it frightens him a bit. He nervously wonders, *Why are we not building something? Where are the workmen? What time is it? Have we made any progress today?* The Cat born in Virgo is a veritable construction engineer of progress. He stalks the prizes of prosperity with a determination and a will to succeed uncommon in Cat subjects. Trouble is, our Cat is a Virgo virgin, naïve and easily duped. He must watch where he places his pawprints. Enemies may be in hot pursuit.

CAT/Libra *(September 24—October 23)*

This air-ruled feline personifies the pedestrian notion of femininity as it used to be. Libran Cats are jolly good talkers. They waver, vacillate, and balance themselves on an eternal hot tin roof. Garbed in finery fit for royalty or better, these Cat/Libras are intangibly lovable. Though they seem weaker than others, there is tremendous strength in so feeble an appearance. People talk to them. Who could be afraid of this gentle creature? Couched behind that ready smile, ready to spring into reverse, is a wily tabby who spends gobs of time feeling people out and discovering their foibles. Neither aggressive nor harmful, Libran Cats are elusive to the nth degree. When they seem to be in one place, they suddenly are not there any longer. Then they pop up elsewhere. A Libran Cat's a mighty wary beast. This Cat's hiss, though not to be taken as lightly as we think, is much worse than his scratch.

CAT/Scorpio *(October 24—November 22)*

This Cat may impress you as nothing more than a lovely old wooden bridge spanning the treacherous Scorpio waters. Go ahead, try to cross him. The tolls will be exorbitant. Crouching under that sweet little foot-bridge is a grumpy old troll to be reckoned with. Never underestimate the occult powers of a Cat/Scorpio. If one of these subjects walks in front of you at a cocktail party, you need not rush to the kitchen for garlic or a crucifix, but you had best step lightly on those little Cat feet. All that sleek and swagger is fascinating, those tender glances so alluring, that sexy outfit so becoming. If you find yourself clutched in the Cat/Scorpio's paw, make nice. Don't pull away immediately or shriek. It encourages him to dig his claws in a bit deeper. Pet this Cat into submission. And, while you're at it, enjoy yourself. But keep your eye on the EXIT signs. They may prove invaluable when the moon is full.

CAT/Sagittarius (November 23—December 21)

Spurred by the Sagittarian's fiery optimism, this Cat will be less fearful, hesitant, and squeamish about change. Sagittarians are known for their ability to confront demons, face the music, and clout whomsoever gets in the way of their instinctive idealism. Cat people born under the sign of the archer benefit from such pluck. Ordinarily it is difficult for Cats to bear the consequences of disaster, but here his spirit is infused with courage. Even though the Sagittarius's bravery is sometimes merely blind faith, this marriage should be a happy one. Sagittarians endure adversity. Cats go about their business warily. The match is solid and positive. This Cat is the pick of the litter.

CAT/Capricorn (December 22—January 20)

Reserved and more aloof than any of his brothers, the Cat/Capricorn is predictably cool-headed and severe. This combination of earth and wood is unfortunately so ingrained with tradition, that sometimes Cat/Capricorns cannot see beyond the end of the last century. Here is a Cat who prefers splendor to sloth, rigor to fun, and success to love. Unapproachably disdainful, if this Cat is confronted with unseemliness, he probably will not even notice. He lives cautiously, surrounding himself with luxury and bastions of subordinates who protect him from the facts of life. One cannot argue with this Cat. He has it together, as they say. But what he misses by never poking his whiskers into the fires of life may be something he will only reckon with well after it is too late.

CAT/Aqaurius *(January 21—February 19)*

So gifted is this combination of fixed air and wood that he sometimes seems a million miles away from earth. Aquarians are other-oriented. They think more of those they pity than of those close to them. Cats, altruistic in the extreme, are sometimes guilty of neglecting their families for less personal causes or companions to whom they may owe loyalty. This alliance of signs may tend toward the esoteric, the effete, and the metaphysical. Bringing home mice and chipmunks to lay at the feet of mistresses and masters will be their last consideration. Though hardly the conquering hero on a white charger, the Cat born in Aquarius will be cerebral and involved in larger-than-life projects. If I were to give advice on their care and feeding, I would tell you to leave them alone. They're not about to come home wagging their tails behind them. But, if you give them enough rope, they may agree to take you along on their next foray into the nether regions of the bizarre.

CAT/Pisces *(February 20—March 20)*

Agreeable, but not particularly social, the Piscean Cat may well incur your exasperation long before he wins your affections. Indecisive, adaptable, and without guile, the Cat born under the sign of the fish is hatched with an attitude of *je ne sais quoi* that can drive a more determined person to the SPCA, where it is hoped they will find him a good home. But, if they can't. . . . Well, let's not jump to conclusions. The Cat/Pisces is a dreamer, an explorer, and an artist. He wants to know how everything works before he places a single paw on it. He is, in fact, Catlike in the extreme. He watches his step through half-opened eyes, and when tired of one subject, he leaps to another or lies down to sleep off the one he just exhausted. This Cat is a darling. He needs love, affection, tenderness, and nurturing. Lavish it. He will not harm you. The Cat/Pisces may intrigue you with his delvings into first one and then the other area of study, but I promise that you will never be bored.

PRESCRIPTION FOR THE FUTURE

Considerate Cat, little need be said further regarding your qualities of self-reliance and privacy. Your inner strength of character is admirable. Though you are not the life of the party, those who know you are entertained by your winning ways. You are much admired for your altruism and charitable acts of selflessness.

One does not fear for your safety. Public opinion has it that Cats can take care of themselves. Yet, maybe this is a partial mistake. The truth is, you function well as long as you are not obliged to tangle with beasts or situations that are out of your self-imposed shallow end of the pool. When we see you run in front of a truck, we still want to dash into the road and scoop you into our arms. Though for the most part you cleverly avert danger and skirt the borders of treachery, some perils inevitably crop up in the course of your nine lives.

As long as you play that game of Cat and Mouse within familiar realms of acquaintance and endeavor, there is no doubt you will survive. But what of natural catastrophe? How can you be certain of remaining immune to social instabilities or pandemonious cultural changes? The fact is, cautious Cat, no one is ever completely sheltered from cataclysm.

In order to assure yourself of real safety in the face of ominous strife, I suggest you begin your apprenticeship in sorcery at a very young age. Possibly, it will always be beyond your means to charge at enemies, claws drawn for battle. In any case, such aggressive behavior certainly rubs your fur the wrong way. Conflict sets your nerves on edge. You arch your back and hiss. But, rarely, if ever, do you choose to leap at the threat of a foe. When challenged, your personal policy is isolationist. Cats keep their enemies at bay by holding them at paw's length. The stories of your cunning fake-outs of opponents are legion.

I do not wish to transform you, cool Cat, into a terrible Tiger or belligerent bull. But perhaps you should be advised to sharpen your claws on minor conflict, while you still have time to learn a new trick or two. You know how uncomfortable you feel when the environment is laden with confusion and charged with discord?

Well, instead of turning your face away from such scenes, may I suggest you stick around for a bit and watch the action? You will be surprised how much can be learned from even the most minor victory over fear of confrontation.

Risk-taking is not your forte. You sidestep involvement, evade everything from taxes to trauma, shun strange places where you don't feel at home and take it on the lam when the heat's on. My assessment of your situation may be unfair, but somehow, with all of your talents and superb qualities, you remain in the shadow of those more boldly courageous and sanely selfish than yourselves. I sometimes hear regret subtly couched in your own self-effacing comments: "Last year I missed my chance to go to Europe. The house needed a new roof, the insurance wasn't paid, and the car needed a trade-in. Even though the flight cost practically nothing in view of all my unpaid bills, I couldn't just take off like that."

Conscientious Cat, spoil yourself. Jeopardize that mortgage, miss that dental appointment, hold on to your crumbling car for another year. Go ahead, take a chance. The wages of daring may be the bricks of an inventive future where formerly ominous obstacles topple at a single swat of the paw.

COMPATIBILITIES

Affairs of the Heart

Cat folks are both capable and ambitious enough to handle marriage with Goat subjects. Goats are peace-loving and artistic. Cats prefer not to have their boats rocked by the raucous intrusion of boisterous beasts. Gentle lotus-eating Goats will suit the calm Cat down to the last hair of his whiskers. Goats are fantasy people who long for security. Cats adore taking care of their loved ones. The arrangement is a good one. This couple will share a life of refined surroundings, if the Cat can afford to foot the bills.

Second best for Cats are people born in the unlikely sign of the Dog. Protection from mundane pressures should be sought by both.

The world is not always a kind place for this pair of tender souls. Within the proper context of hard work in a peaceful atmosphere, prosperity should follow them throughout their union.

A good third choice is available to the Cat person in the form of the scrupulous Pig. Pigs don't take to *sturm*, *drang*, or upheaval in their daily existence. The Cat will bring much of the necessary refinement to the intelligent, cultured Pig. They instinctively like each other. And why not? They are both so gentle and silently strong.

Snakes, Horses, and Monkeys make good companions for Cats. Both Snakes and Horses may find their Cat friends a bit on the pipe-and-slippers side for their sophisticated tastes, but the Cat is malleable when in love. He may learn to love concerts and galas for the sake of his partner's well-being. With the Monkey, the Cat will find complicity. Cats can be fairly tricky when they set their minds to averting disaster. Monkeys give them courage to face adversity. Cats are not wild about kids. The Monkey will have to settle for fewer children.

Without an extra measure of self-denial, the Cat will not be able to tolerate the dash of Dragons. If, however, the Dragon is the bread-winner, the relationship between a Cat and himself might be interesting. As for Cats and Roosters, the Cat should be wary of trying to endure such cohabitation. The boasting ways of Roosters unnerve cool Cats and no Cat person is placid enough to withstand the Rooster's ups and downs. The same is true of Cat/Tiger rapport. Although the Cat will be intrigued by his Tiger mate, he may eventually find all those Tigerish highs and lows a bit much to bear.

Cats can get on with their Cat counterparts. Double Cat alliances are adorned with a love of beauty and gracious living. These two might open a candy or gift shop together.

Social Affairs

The Cat makes a superior companion for almost anyone whose Chinese Chance it is to be admired by him. Because Cats are so sociable and solicitous of friends, it is possible for them to get along with just about everybody else. With the exception of the Rat and the Rooster, all signs are compatible with Cats. The Rat, for obvious reasons, is a Cat's too-easy prey. And Roosters have too much noisy enthusiasm to appeal to the peaceful Cat's sense of discretion.

Cats do have their preferences. They rejoice in the company of Snakes, Goats, Horses, Monkeys, and Dogs. The sometimes bawdy Pig shocks the Cat's puritanical side, but they do get on well despite this limiting factor.

Monkeys are the most durable friends for Cats. There is something about this mutually admiring couple that makes even the most infrequent meeting seem as though it were only yesterday the two chatted together about books, movies, people, and life in all of its various conditions. Cats, too, make lasting friends among members of their own race. So much is to be discussed and agreed upon around the cozy Cat hearth.

Tigers bewitch Cats with their magnetism. But Cats sometimes end up disliking themselves and their Tiger pals for having surrendered to the Tiger sorcery.

Business Affairs

In business, as in friendship, the Cat gets on with almost everyone. Cats do adapt themselves to circumstances in order to avoid conflict. This quality is invaluable when Cats must deal in commercial or financial areas. It serves him particularly well in negotiations with testy Tigers, dreadful Dragons, and high-minded Horses.

No task is too demeaning for the Cat. He goes to great lengths to set a fine example for his employers or employees. With this in mind, we can well imagine why Cats are among the only creatures who are capable of extruding hard work from gracious Goats and sagacious Snakes.

You might not think so but the Tiger and the Cat go well together in work situations. Cats are careful, Tigers are bold. The match is a sound one. Pigs also get along with Cat co-workers. Pigs have great luck in business. Cats are skillful investors. They might make oodles of money if they are not careful.

Two Cats might open a group medical practice or run a refined hair-dressing salon. The Ox may slow the already too-prudent Cat.

Finally, the Dog is a fine partner for a busy Cat. Dogs take up the burdens of others. They respect the Cat's diligence and discretion in his professional life. They get along like Cats and Dogs extremely well.

Family Affairs

Cats, as parents, are usually rather reserved and vaguely indifferent. This attitude does not stem from the fact that Cats don't like kids. But disruptive influences throw Cats off the beaten track. I suppose we have to agree that children, though rewarding in many ways, do not have the reputation for contributing to family harmony. In any case, Cats take a while to get used to being easy with their own and other people's off-spring.

If there is a choice to be made, Cat people would do well to plan their children's birth years wisely. They get on famously with those born in Cat years. They toddle on nicely with Goats and Snakes and Pigs. Monkeys do not displease Cat parents. Instead, they amuse and fascinate their Cat moms and dads. Ox children confuse the Cat parent. They seem so strong and blustery by comparison to themselves. Dragons parade their good manners just a bit more than the Cat enjoys. But Cats do find Dragon children astonishingly competent at what they do.

Even a Tiger child is not a bad bet for the good Cat. With a pair of well-honed senses of humor, these two may learn to live together. But Rat children baffle the Cat. Cats don't trust Rats and find it hard to believe that the most well-behaved of Rat children are not pulling stunts behind their parents' backs.

THE DRAGON

THE YEARS OF THE DRAGON

February 16, 1904 to February 4, 1905
February 3, 1916 to January 23, 1917
January 23, 1928 to February 10, 1929
February 8, 1940 to January 27, 1941
January 27, 1952 to February 14, 1953
February 13, 1964 to February 2, 1965
January 31, 1976 to February 17, 1977
February 17, 1988 to February 5, 1989

DRAGONS ARE:

Scrupulous • Sentimental • Enthusiastic • Intuitive
Shrewd • Tenacious • Healthy • Influential • Vital • Generous
Spirited • Captivating • Artistic • Admirable • Lucky
Successful • Autonomous

BUT THEY CAN ALSO BE:

Disquiet • Stubborn • Willful • Demanding
Irritable • Loud-mouthed • Malcontent • Other-worldly
Impetuous • Infatuate • Judgmental

——— ——— ———— ⬥ ———— ———

DRAGONS I HAVE KNOWN AND LOVED

When I was a child, I thought quite a bit about Dragons. Many was the time I wondered how it must feel to be one. There were songs about "Puff, the Magic Dragon," and somebody called "The Reluctant Dragon," who complained that he would have preferred another role than that of professional boogeyman. As I grew up, I developed a special tenderness for those scaly illusions of grandeur. I liked the idea of a Dragon who wanted to come down from his mountaintop and mingle with people. I wished very hard that one day I might meet a real, live monstrosity and perhaps take him in as a pet.

Some five or six Parisian years ago, this childish dream came true. I happened, one day in a sidewalk café, on a thoroughbred Dragon of a man, who graciously deigned to transform himself into a human being in order to fall hopelessly in love with little old me. The feeling was, for about two years, devastatingly mutual.

From this distance and time lapse, my objectivity quotient is operating at maximum efficiency. The romance has been over for many years. I am ready to discuss it frankly, because I want very much to convince you that my experience with the above gentleman left me with no doubt in my mind. Folks, Dragons really do exist.

Now, for your information, falling in love with a Dragon person is a common ailment. Members of the opposite sex hardly ever leave them alone for long enough to breathe a little gratuitous fire of their own. They are pursued relentlessly for their favors. Dragon women have more suitors than they can take the phone off the hook to avoid. The love lives of Dragon people make soap operas look like they were written about the inner workings of a Carmelite convent.

To begin to describe Dragons is about as challenging as attempting to explain the functions of an electronic brain to a tribe of uneducated Zulus. One of the reasons for this problem is Dragonary elusiveness. Just when you think you have your finger on any given Dragon quality or peevish fault, up comes a glaring fact that turns the whole idea round and makes it appear ridiculous.

Dragons are so forcefully selfish and strong-willed that often their self-centeredness walks right up to their good sense and pops it in the eye so it can't see what it was saying. Yet, there is no use imagining that Dragons don't have weighty good sense. They are among the most sensible, straight-thinking people in the universe. And they always land on their feet.

What Dragon people have a great deal of difficulty grasping is the concept of sharing even a corner of their spoils with others. They work, sometimes from morning till night, hurling ultimata at everyone in sight in an effort to keep things the way they (and only they) want them to be kept. Unfortunately for those who try to love them, Dragons affect an attitude of "like it or lump it" when their protracted love relationships settle into routine. Without the spice of a hurdle to conquer or an indifferent partner to convince, Dragons may become bored with an ongoing affair or marriage and seek distraction elsewhere.

I have to confess, I do not know a single Dragon husband or wife who does not have a mistress or lover or two. Outside Dragon circles, such extramarital devices upset many a family applecart, cause pain to the spouse, insecurity for the children, and gossip among the neighbors. Yet, in the several cases of Dragon mates I have in mind, not one of the partners even vaguely suspects that husband or wife has strayed.

For a long time, I had trouble liking these people who commit adultery and leave their mates to hearth and home. Then I began to analyze their characters. What I discovered is that Dragons honestly consider themselves superior to the norm. They are almost other-worldly. All the people I have in mind here have achieved remarkable success in business (or, in one case, in the theater). Dragons are not noted for letting grass grow under their feet. They tumble obstacle after obstacle in an effort to blast their way to the top in a hurry. Their means are not always the most orthodox. Dragon people don't like to sit behind desks. They hate to take orders and enjoy giving them.

The foregoing sounds like an advertisement for the perfect tyrant. It is. Dragons are despotic. They want what they want when they want it and not tomorrow. Yet, in every single case, when that clause in the marriage contract that refers to "for worse" rears its nasty face, the Dragon comes to the fore. He/she comforts, holds hands, makes tea, serves, and waits in all manner of crisis situations. In sickness, Dragons are the original whiz kids. But, in health, they do tend to leave the cave rather more often than they ought.

Is it that Dragons feel best when faced with catastrophe? Do they like their mates to create bedlam in order to remain interesting? I don't think so. My experience with Dragons tells me they are not quite that dumb or insensitive. This quality that they exhibit is more like "any time you need me, just whistle." Otherwise, they have more important things to accomplish than hanging about the house mooning over a breakfast table and being "in love."

Remember, I was once beloved by a Dragon prince. His name was Paulo. The time was many years ago in a quiet Parisian summer month of August. In the eighth month of the year, Paris empties itself of all but a skeleton of the population. French city dwellers take their one-month (by law) vacations in August. They leave town in droves on the first of the month and return tanned and tired at month's end. Holiday time for the French has somewhat replaced religion in their modern lives. My Dragon prince was no exception.

As an outsider and hence mere observer of this annual madness, I long ago decided that the best month in which to partake of Paris's gratuitous delights—museums, parks, food, walks along the Seine, etc.—must be the old month of August. It is at precisely that time of year that anyone who needs me can most assuredly find me "at home." If I do take vacations, there is always June or September in the Mediterranean or January and February at winter sports meccas in the Alps. Who needs crowded beaches in August? Paulo, that's who.

It was the prince's legendary habit to "make the scene" at Deauville during August. Deauville is a windswept resort burg on the North Atlantic coast where Europeans imagine themselves more chic and "in" than anybody alive, during what they call "the Season" (August). For the summer, expensive hairdressers open seasonal salons there. Parisian discotheque owners set up two months shop therein. Dior, Hermes, Cardin, and the gang open their summer boutiques in Deauville. The gambling casino lights up every night like a mini Times Square and people flock in full dress to play roulette and be seen by other people who flock there to see them. It's a nice arrangement for those who get their kicks that way, but it was never my favorite summer pastime. Deauville is the Saint Tropez of the north—only colder.

This particular month of August, when I was in Paris and Paulo was hobnobbing in Deauville, I came down with hepatitis. There were many other sensible souls like myself who had stayed in town to relax during their vacations, and my friends were around to take care of me while I was sick. One of these, a Greek-American girl called Nadia, came to stay with me.

Paulo was not the hovering type of lover who calls every day to remind you to keep on the straight and narrow. Once a week was about all he could muster. I never worried. I knew he had about fourteen other girl friends besides me. When you know a thing like that, the best thing to do is ignore it and hope it will go away.

True to form, Paulo phoned on Friday at midnight. Nadia answered. She told him that I was sick in bed and couldn't talk. Paulo ordered her to put me on the phone. Nadia countered with, "She's upstairs asleep," which I overheard because she had to raise her voice to make herself understood. (French phones don't always work very well.) The cackling sound that came back through the receiver was unintelligible, but very, very loud. Nadia went on, "Suzanne has hepatitis. She's in bed. Please call tomorrow between two and four in the afternoon. She hung up and went back to bed.

It must have been three o'clock when the familiar *rap-rap-a-rap-rap* came wafting over the wavelengths to my sleep-filled ears. I assured myself I was dreaming, until I heard the whispered exchange going on down in my living room.

"Paulo! What are you doing here?" Nadia shushed at him.

"Where is Suzanne?" was his accusatory inquiry. "I told you over the phone. She has jaundice. She is very sick. Has to stay in bed." Exasperatedly, she bade him sit down.

"I didn't come here to chat. I came to see Suzanne." Paulo spoke in a perfectly normal modulated bark. Then I heard his footsteps on the stairs, *clomp, clomp, clomp*. The comforting pad of the well-worn Gucci loafer. He shook me awake. "What's wrong with you?" There was concern between the lines, but sick as I was, I was also damned annoyed at him.

I dragged myself awake and felt in vain for the light. "Oh, Paulo, it's you. Didn't Nadia tell you I was sick? I can't talk to you now. Have to sleep—" As I said this, I felt myself sinking back under the covers in a near faint. I was not supposed to exert myself. Doctor's orders. And simple to adhere to, since I could not have exerted myself if I'd tried. At that point, breathing was an effort.

Paulo sat down on the edge of the bed and took my dampish limp palm in his hand. As I oozed back into dreamland, I felt his lips on my forehead and a gentle stroking back of my bangs.

That's all I remember until about nine o'clock the next morning. I awoke, vaguely aware of another presence in my room. Somebody was touching my hand. At first I was alarmed. "Nadia!" I called out.

"It's all right, chérie. I'm here now. Everything's going to be all right." When my eyes finally agreed to focus on the intruder, I saw a bolt-upright Paulo, sitting exactly in the position he had assumed in the middle of the night. He had been watching me from his perch on the side of the bed all night long.

"Where's Nadia?" I wondered in a sickly moan.

"Nadia's gone home now. I'll be staying with you until you are better." Paulo plumped my pillows and assisted me tenderly to a sitting position.

Mandatory home nursing service was all I could think of. I did not want Paulo to take care of me while I was sick. In the first place, I hate to be seen by men when I'm not pulled together and in command of all my faculties. When people offer to hold my vomiting head over a toilet bowl, I reject them angrily. Besides, Paulo hated to read aloud and despised the game of scrabble so fervently that he had once tried to throw mine into the fireplace. I was in a helpless panic at the thought of Nadia leaving me alone with this male nurse.

What was I supposed to do? I couldn't even go downstairs to call the police. Besides, they were probably on vacation, too. *No,* I told myself. *You must not freak out. Be calm. He will soon tire of the confinement of being cooped up with an invalid. By that time, you will be well enough to use the phone and you can call Nadia and get her back.* I knew full well that Nadia wasn't leaving town, because she had no money to go anywhere.

I relaxed and played the Camille role that Paulo demanded of me. All day, while he sat in a chair smoking Havana cigars, I lay abed seething because I wanted to read or write or play botticelli with Nadia. When I asked for a magazine or a book, Paulo told me to get some rest. In truth, he was a very apt attendant. When the doctor came to see me on the following Tuesday, he nodded a lot and said Paulo was doing a fine job. I had no bruises from the shots. Paulo had been careful to use different veins each time he gave me an antibiotic injection. His shots hurt less than Nadia's, too. He cooked very tasty applesauce. But, most important, the doctor said, "You must force her to rest." Well, Paulo deserved an A+ for compulsory repose. He wouldn't even let me daydream for fear I might tax my struggling spirit. Mind you, I was very definitely "in love" with this man. But I hated his guts for clamping down on me in this time of need.

But why? you may be asking yourself. Why didn't she just tell Paulo to go away?

Well, folks, if you know any Dragon people, imagine yourself operating at half-tilt in their company. Think of what it would be like to be bedridden and in the loving hands of a hard-nosed, spiny-backed fire-breather. I don't care if you are King Kong . . . there is no use fighting a Dragon.

The kind of authority that Dragons exhibit is neither conjured nor feigned. With them, domination is a divine right. When a Dragon friend has coerced you into seeing just the film you never wanted to see in your whole life on an evening when the last thing you wanted to do was go to a movie, there is no cause for surprise. In lieu of pitched battles, almost anyone in his or her right mind will choose submission. If, however, you are not in control of your senses and do perchance opt to cross the Dragon's willful path with drawn sword, there will be no need for you to seek further foe.

Dragons make the most complete enemies anyone could hope for. They are vindictive, resentful, rancourous, and strong. Like our friend, the elephant, a wounded Dragon never forgets. The best thing to do if they decide not to like you is avoid them. Sidestep, take your phone off the hook, and get yourself an unlisted address. Better still, move to Topeka and change your name.

The names of some of the Dragons of Dragondom we all know and love (or hate) might serve to point up what I am saying. To begin with, there was that kindly old gent, Hermann Göring, Nazi official and darling of the S.S. Hermann was born in 1893/4. The other notable Dragon born that year was Charles Atlas. I don't know if he was as strong as he looked in those brochures he sent out, but he was at the least a powerful hustler. After them came the famous Dragons of 1904, James Cagney, Judge John Sirica, and movie producer Sam Spiegel.

The ranks of Dragons are full of tough-guy types like Che Guevara (b. 1928) and James Coburn (b. 1928). No-slouch Jimmy Connors of the tennis set came into the world in 1952, and Cannonball Adderley in 1928. After hatching Bernardo Bertolucci, who directed Last Tango in Paris, 1940 gave us John Lennon, Al Pacino, and Ringo Starr. Tango's female lead star, Maria Schneider, was born in 1952, no slouch in the female-lead department herself.

It is a brilliant group. Rife with pizazz and replete with spectacle, Dragons thrive on glitter, splash, pageantry, and majestic ostentation. They either like to dress up in gaudy regalia or make it a point to "dress down" in well-tailored jeans and/or Salvation Army-type garb. Whichever vestmental affectations they adopt, you can be certain it is indeed an affectation. Dragons are never the kinds of people who roll out of bed in yesterday's rumpled clothing—unless, of course, they have decided on a hippie posture and want their costume to be completely authentic. Then they may sleep in the same outfit for a week running, in order to be sure every slovenly detail is attended to.

Salvador Dali (b. 1904) lives his farcical life in three very separate places. Summers, he and his wife reside in the seaside village of Cadaques on Spain's Costa Brava. In the fall, Dali usually comes to New York City for a few months. They spend some of the spring in Paris at the Hotel Murice. Idyllic, *n'est-ce pas?*

With all of this gadding about, Dali still manages to spend much of each year painting and drawing. He works extremely long hours in his Spanish studio by the sea, rising at dawn and laboring through the day until sundown, when pink champagne flows and friends and neighbors are allowed to visit the Cadaques house for consultations or chats with El Maestro. Dali's wife, (ex-wife of French poet Paul Eluard) is a Russian woman of uncertain age who long ago undertook to run Dali's life in an orderly way so that he would accomplish the maximum of work. A small and wiry woman, Gala Dali seems the perfect Dragon's mate. She has devoted her life to his brilliant career. It is rumored, Dali might have amounted to very little had it not been for Gala's early intervention.

The scrape-of-the-shoulder episode I am about to recount strikes me as indicative of Dragon love for ceremony and ritual. From what I have seen of Dali, he may well be a grade A painter, but he is also a showman of the first order. With Dali, every word and phrase is calculated to enchant his audience. He moves across a room as gracefully as his pet ocelot, swashbuckling and swiping at the air around him with his gold-headed walking stick. Fact is, even if Dali were a terrible painter (which I do not think he is), his magnificent presence would be a masterpiece in itself.

Back in the old days, when I was but a shy young mother of one six-month-old girl baby, I had occasion to visit the gilded suite of rooms that the Dalis occupy during their Paris sojourns. At that time, I was busy trying to promote a film that my child's daddy has directed but could not sell. Since the movie was called *Who's Crazy?* and we knew Dali was, Salvador was the logical choice to endorse the film for publicity purposes. Through his secretary, we requested an audience with the master. It was all arranged, two o'clock in the afternoon on a Wednesday, just the day I could never get a baby-sitter. Mine was a dandy fix. There I was, invited by Salvador Dali to his very own salon and nobody to watch my baby. I decided to take her along.

Carefully, I dressed little April Daisy in flowing lace and garments fit for a princess. Good thing I did. Dali chose that very afternoon to perform his first baptism—on my baby!

Meandering into Dali's living room as I did that day, babe in arms, both of us dressed to kill, I cannot say I felt as though I owned the place. In fact, I was scared to death. The first thing I laid eyes on was that sinuous beast of an ocelot, who stalked about on a silken settee located in front of a carved marble fireplace. Dali's secretary dashed over to me warning, "Stay right where you are. I don't think the ocelot likes children. We've had some bad experiences recently." While the gentleman led the wildcat away on a sterling silver leash, I stood dumbly by, clutching my bundle on the threshold of the vaulted doorway of a veritable church of a room.

Suddenly, the master looked my way. Until then, he had been engaged in demonstrating a golden spoonlike antiquity, which he held firmly in his right hand. A circle of sycophantic art dealers and amateurs was assembled around him, smiles pasted on their faces. They nodded incessantly and muttered, "*Oui, maître,*" "*Bien sûr, maître,*" or "*Formidable, maître!*" To tease them, Dali had been asking what they thought this shiny *object d'art* was used for in the Middle Ages. Like eager schoolchildren, they responded by raising their hands and shouting out inanities. "It's a key!" said a lady in a yellow bonnet. "*Non, non.* It is a ladle for soup. I have seen one like it in Rome many years ago," cried a wizened little man in a pin-striped watch fob. Dali shook his head and smiled cat/canary-like at all of them. All at once he whirled about, his velvet cloak swooshing through the air, and said in a very loud voice, "Dees objet, ladeez and gentlemen, eez an earrrleee deevice for cleeening up zee caca!"

As faces reddened and obsequious titters filled the air, Dali turned his back on them and glided toward me. Taking my hand, the master demanded to be allowed to hold my baby in his arms. I thought perhaps I might keel over right there. Was I proud? Or, was I worried he might feed April Daisy to the ocelot? Before I knew what was happening, Dali was carrying on, "kootchy-kooing" the drooling blond infant and chucking her under the chin like a senile grandpa.

Perhaps it was just a show. I still don't know for sure. But out of the blue moirée-filled nowhere, I heard him command, "Call to the rrroom serrveece for one bottle of finest water!" Said Dali, "I am about to perforrm baptismo of zees beeeyoooteefool niña!"

My knees shook so hard I could hear them above the din. The baby was chirruping and smiling as though she had spent most of her life in the arms of famous madmen. I prayed that she wouldn't spit up her lunch and spoil the effect. She didn't.

When the tuxedoed waiter brought in a bottle of Evian mineral water, atop a silver tea tray, Dali told him, "Poot eet on zee center table!" He called everybody over to the middle of the salon and began chanting some Spanish mixed with Latin (or vice versa, I couldn't make it out) and drawing crisscrosses all over April Daisy's forehead. The ritual only took about five minutes. At its end, Dali handed the baby back to me with a hearty "*Merci, madame*" (for the use of my baby). Then, Dali himself in person ushered me to the door and walked me down to the elevator. I got in a quick plug for our film. He agreed to stand behind anything with "crazy" in the title, shook my hand, kissed April Daisy on the nose, and said, "Always in her life she will be famous! She has the blessing of the master." Why he had less accent when he spoke to me privately, is anybody's guess.

Years later, when Daisy (as we now call her) had grown some three feet and found her girlish voice, she one day, in that almost-whine of curious children, asked, "Mommy, who is that funny-looking man on TV who advertises the Lanvin chocolate? The ugly one with the mustache?" (These days, Dali does commercials on French television.)

When I told her the story of her ceremonious baptism, she reacted by shivering all over. "He's so icky. How could you let him touch me?"

What could I tell her? The only way to explain such weird behavior to an eight-year-old kid was to hug her and say, "He's a very fine old Dragon painter. You know what I told you about Dragons. They can't keep their hands off any chance for a show."

Daisy looked up at me innocently and replied, "Oh, yeah. He looks a little bit like a Dragon, too. Doesn't he, Mom?"

Dragons take care of themselves. Rarely will you see a Dragon person who is out of shape or pot-bellied. They are likely instead to be among those of us who trot faithfully every week to the gym, jog around parks every morning, inhale great handfuls of vitamins, and drink gallons of water to keep their plumbing systems from rusting. I know one Dragon man who, because it is to his liking, attends splashy elegant dinner parties where the hostess cooks fabulously rich plates of gourmet foods. He politely fills himself to the brim at each sitting. Then off he goes to the men's room, where he claims that he discreetly sticks his finger down his throat and gets rid of the beautiful repasts. I suppose there is more than one diet method in the world. But that one would not be my choice, even though I have to agree it is an eminently Dragonlike thing to do. As the Dragon prince used to say, "When you're ahead, keep your head!"

The Chinese tell us that contact with Dragons is lucky. From my experience it is also extremely exhausting. Dragon people just about never stop moving. They dart from target to target all day long (and sometimes far into the night) hustling deals and making contacts, chatting with people who need their advice, calling others on the phone, and perhaps even stopping once in a while to drop in on a loved one or family member. Although they often pretend to deplore the very existence of a sickly grandmother or ailing father, Dragon people are exceptionally solicitous of their parents. Even if they only visit or call them in order to rehash old quarrels or pick over old bones, Dragons are dutiful where family is concerned.

I have a Dragon-lady friend who lives outside Paris in a large country house that she runs most indubitably alone. Oh, she is married. But her husband's work takes him away for months at a time. Nicole (or Nini, as we call her) is one of those country dwellers whose home is so gorgeously pastoral and at the same time so close to the city that every Parisian who finds out that she exists wants to spend every weekend as her houseguest.

If you are one of the lucky people whom Nini invites to her lair for an overnight stay, your memory of her home, her food, her beauty, and her bad temper will live forever, rubber-stamped on your brain cells. She is the perfect Dragon hostess. Breakfast is whisked away from the heavy wooden refectory table by eight-thirty A.M.. If you don't get up early enough for coffee and warm bread, you have to wait until lunch for the merest smidgeon of food to pass your lips.

Lunch preparation starts at nine A.M. with shopping for and/or collecting of vegetables from the garden. If you want to eat at noon, you participate in the luncheon arrangements. Nini may not require your cooking or marketing services, but if you appear the least idle or shiftless, she will find a job for you. Take your pick: You can weed the rows of beans she planted last week or maybe you feel like doing a little ironing or mending? And, if you are not so good at household tasks like washing up the breakfast dishes, you can always groom the dogs or horses, play with some of the other guests' children to keep them occupied, or address envelopes for Nini's favorite charity.

In Nini's house, it is best never to pick up a magazine or book unless you have a good hiding place under a bush in the woods where you plan on sitting out the morning while reading it. Not that this Dragon lady doesn't keep an ample supply of news and fashion periodicals around the living room, there are tomes of them. But they are to be read after the lunch dishes are finished or before you go to bed at night. At all other times of day, including four o'clock teatime, loafing about is off limits. And Nini does not hesitate to let you know that. "What are you doing sitting on your butt?" one can hear her explode at an unsuspecting gentleman caller.

"I'm reading," he might dare reply timidly. "Well, there are better things to be done around here right now! Do you have a car?" She snaps her questions like a cap pistol.

"Yes. It's that yellow Volkswagen with the sun roof. Do you want to use it?" he may offer gently.

"Get in it and go to the market in the next town. Buy me three dozen eggs from the farmer. The one with the beret. He's in the left-hand corner of the market center. He yells a lot. You'll recognize him without any trouble." She shells out the necessary francs for the eggs and huffs out of the room. Nobody ever says "Go yourself!" or "Who do you think you are?" or even "Do I have to?" The natural authority with which Nini gives commands is uncontestable. She's a Dragon par excellence.

Prudishness is a Dragon specialty. I have never known a Dragon person who was comfortable in frank discussions about anything smacking of the off-color. In fact, heavy discussions of any sort may put them off. You see, Dragon people are glib, silver-tongued at times, clever at making scintillating comments, and giving wise counsel. But they are not deep thinkers. Dragons are anything but philosophers. Rather, they think quickly and make adept and rash judgments that tend often to be correct. Their instincts are good. But they are short on erudition.

As far as family obligations go, my friend Nini takes the blue ribbon. Her mother, who lives comfortably in a villa on the French Riviera, is a notorious hag, complainer, griper, and grump. Yet, every month, Nini packs herself off for at least a three-day visit with the old marquise. Even Nini's father doesn't go home any more. He has moved to North Africa for so-called "business purposes." Her siblings (she has two) live in Mexico and New York City respectively and only make reluctant yearly pilgrimages to visit the old bag. Each time Nini returns from Cap d'Antibes, she is pale and haggard from days of arguing about nothing. Even in good weather, when Nini returns with a lovely tan from lying out on her mother's seaside terrace, one can tell by her gravelly voice that she has been yelling at top shriek more than usual. Once I asked her, "Why do you go there? It wears you to a frazzle."

"Oh, her. She's a harmless old grouch. I feel sorry for her. I don't suppose I was an easy child to raise. My father was no prize husband. Even though they always had lots of money, her marriage must have been a drag." Nini shrugged and went back to stirring up a cake batter for teatime consumption. I sensed it would not have been diplomatic to pursue the subject.

Dragon people, as soon as you broach an area that they have previously decided is out of bounds for discussion, will draw an invisible lead curtain to let you know that it's a no-no. If you so much as hint that you want information beyond their established taboo frontier, they will not hesitate to request your immediate departure from their sight. Most Dragons I know have a close circle of very good friends who understand and tolerate their idiosyncrasies. Newcomers are regarded with suspicion and grilled carefully before they are allowed to take their place in the cherished inner sanctum of Dragon trust.

Indiscreet questions such as "What did your father do?" or "Why are you wearing that ridiculous red rag around your neck?" pop out of Dragon mouths as though they were molten morsels of baked potato that defy swallowing. Dragons are plainly not meant for careers where diplomacy or word-mincing are prerequisites. Their comments can bite deeply into the hearts of anyone who is not prepared for them. Perhaps it is their instinct for the flaw in any given situation or personality that endows Dragons with their sometimes evil-tongued commentary. But, whatever it is, a remark like "Why don't you get on the stick and discipline your rotten kid?" or "I met your husband last week and I think I might as well tell you, he's a certified jerk!" can do much to discourage budding friendships.

Whether on his own or surrounded by a bevy of faithful intimates, the Dragon will be a basically dissatisfied human being. His personal superiority and native efficiency weigh heavily on his mind at all times. Nobody or nothing can ever quite come up to his Dragonian standards. Life itself is a perpetual halfway measure, a struggle for perfection in all things. Since we all know that little if anything is ever even close to total excellence, his Excellency the Dragon is destined to remain eternally discontent.

According to experts in Chinese philosophy, the Dragon is sure to bring four blessings with him when he steps into this life. He can be sure of wealth, virtue, harmony, and longevity. Yet, they say Dragons are made of paper. Each dawning is a rebirth for our Dragon fellows. Like the phoenix bird, the Dragon may die each time he falls asleep, only to be reborn the next morning, spawned of his own ashes. Man will never be certain whether or not he invented the Dragon. He is neither mythical nor human nor animal nor spirit. He is all of those things. And then some.

MADAME DRAGON

Much in demand for her vitality and shining appurtenances, the Dragon Lady is a living duality. By her very existence, she is a contradiction in terms. She may seem sophisticated, worldly-wise, strong-minded, and prudent in the extreme. At the same time, she can be brutally down-to-earth, warm-hearted, generous, and lovingly understanding.

To the uninstructed observer, her persona may appear to be that of a slick or even slightly lunatic gadabout who seems not to care a whit for other people's feelings. On the other hand, if you are among those fortunates to whom this lady deigns to show her true character, you will probably see her as a kindly earth-mother type who would give you the shirt off her back in return for a smile or a compliment.

Most Dragon women I know who are mothers of small children give one the snap impression of personifying the strict disciplinarian parent, one who never lets her offspring out of her sight for fear he or she will commit some heinous crime against social behavior patterns. Dragon mommies are forever telling their kids off: "Sit up to the table!" "How many times do I have to tell you to wash your hands before eating?" "What's wrong with you, Johnny?" "Can't you see I'm busy?" They do not exude indulgence.

Lady Dragon may very well be able to command an army, move a mountain single-handedly, or drive twelve solitary hours through fog and rain to attend a business meeting. Nor will a Dragoness budge on opinions or causes she has decided to champion. But, like their male facsimiles, Dragon women (though they hotly deny this) are attainable via one route—sentimentality. Dragon ladies are as broadly romantic

as the most maudlin grade B movie you ever saw. Hard to believe?
Well, sometime, just for fun, watch a Dragon woman react to a falter-
ing old man attempting to cross the street by himself. Take a gander at
her when she meets an unhappy child whose ice cream cone has
dropped on the sidewalk. Follow her steps carefully as she takes that
old man's hand and see how fast she digs up change from her purse in
order to replace that sorrowful kid's ice cream. No. Dragon ladies are
not really all sinew and muscle. They just look that way.

Household chores and routine will stultify even the most old-
fashioned of Dragon women. They like to keep a clean house and have
things in order, but hate the workaday aspect of it all. Most Dragon
women I know have household help, or at the very least enforce rigid
rules whereby each family member must pitch in and help out.
Dragons like to decorate their homes in rather outrageous taste. They
are not known for muted tones of beige and off-white. Walls will
almost always reveal touches of vivid shades of yellow or green. To
the Dragon lady, brightness counts.

As I pointed out earlier in this chapter, fidelity is not the major
Dragon virtue. Though she flirts wildly and appeals sexually to even
the most stolid of old fogeys, her obvious flirtings about are usually
not very serious. If she does take a lover, her illicit activities will be so
well hidden that even her best friends will never know. In this one
respect, Dragon women are models of discretion.

Conversely, however, should you bring the boss home for dinner
and your Dragon lady doesn't take an immediate shine to him, put her
in a closet or send her to her room. Nothing keeps Dragon women
quiet when they feel like talking.

A grisly experience with just such nondiplomacy was visited
upon me one evening in Paris by a Dragon wife, who will for obvious
reasons remain anonymous. At the time, I was seeing a rather famous
movie star gentleman who was genuinely important to Madame
Dragon's husband. Said husband is a film director. Because my
boyfriend's signature was needed on a contract, the director rashly
invited us to his home. We arrived to find a houseful of guests having
pre-dinner drinks.

As we walked through the door of the couple's posh flat in the chic residential Sixteenth Arrondissement of Paris, I was smiling gaily. I shook hands all around and kept my nose very high. I had been told of the wife's penchant for driving away untitled dinner guests. Reputedly, she only liked snobby people. So as not to rock the boat, I tried to act as charmingly uppity as I could.

I don't think I was in the apartment for three minutes before my hostess, a dynamo in bright fuchsia silk, came barreling toward me with blood in her eye. Perfunctorily, she extended her hand and said in a mellifluous growl, "Who are you?"

"How do you do? My name is Suzanne White." Her presence was so threatening, I almost panicked and curtsied my best dancing school dip.

"I don't care about your name!" she added. "I just want to know who you are. What do you do? Why are you here?"

Gulping, my voice sounding thin and frightened away up over my head, I uttered these words, "I'm with him." I pointed in the direction of my escort.

"Then stand over there!" said the Dragoness. Dutifully, I complied and went to hang about where my date was discussing the film contract with the Dragon's spouse. Soon, I had almost forgotten my brush with death and was chatting away with the two men. Out of nowhere, she re-appeared. "What are you laughing at?" she poked me to demand.

"Oh, Mrs. Blah-blah, your husband is sooo funny," said I, wiping away my tears of glee. "Can you tell me where the ladies' room is?" I then whispered conspiratorily to my hostess.

"We only have a men's room," she snapped. She grabbed her husband's arm and asked sharply, "Isn't that right, darling? The powder room is reserved for grown-up lady guests."

Her husband looked alarmed. My swain took me gently about the shoulders to keep me from fainting. I swear she had fangs. I kept having an argument with myself about whether or not she was drunk. She wasn't. She was soberly offensive. Her husband prodded me away from the cheery group and walked me toward the lavatory, saying, "Pay no attention to Margaret. She has a thing about young people."

I splashed some cold water on my face and returned to the living room. By this time everybody was in the dining room. I felt like a fool bursting in after the meal had begun, but figured perhaps she would have too much to do with serving and organizing things to notice. On tiptoe, I entered the clattering and looked for my place at the table. My date was gabbling away with his neighbor and did not notice me. Suddenly, a clanging noise went up from Margaret's end of the table. She was tapping on a crystal goblet with her butter knife. Silence ensued. "Friends, I am terribly sorry but there seems to be a mistake here. We have one guest too many. Do you think she would mind if we asked her to leave?"

The host quickly rose and led me from the room. As we went through the archway, I heard him state in a very firm voice, "If Margaret does not behave herself this evening, I am afraid we shall have to send her away from the table!" In hot pursuit, my gentleman friend emerged from the assembled guests to comfort me. I asked to be taken home. He took me out to dinner.

Now, all Dragon women are not Margarets. Not by a long shot. But, given half a chance, they do try their luck at intimidating people until they have tested them out for a while.

My advice to any man who is intrigued by such a complex woman as the Dragon lady is to take the reins from the beginning, wear the pants at all times, and when in doubt, put up your dukes. Although they don't enjoy being dominated, the only real way to tame a Dragon woman is by ascending to the top of the mountain with her and giving her a friendly shove from time to time so she won't think she owns the place.

MONSIEUR DRAGON

Men born under the Dragon sign are tough nuts to crack. Their entire existence is predicated on the supposition that earthly preoccupations such as who gets to carry out the garbage or drive the children to piano lessons are well beneath their dignity. Faced with banalities such as these, the average Dragon will balk. But, if he doesn't back off from the task, he will accomplish it with a hint of superiority as though to say, "Any idiot can do this menial chore. Why should I have to dirty my clever hands touching all this filth?"

To those of you who have Dragon men in your lives, or are considering taking one on for more than dalliance purposes, I am driven to say, *Beware of the green-eyed monster!* On both sides, this relationship will provoke jealousies. In sexual, professional, or social affairs, Dragon men are unable to accept female supremacy at anything but householding and child-rearing. Partly for this reason, Dragon men do not always enter into long-term affairs or full-time marriages. At any rate, they often rebuff women who appear to want them to "pop the question" or "get hitched."

If you still feel you might wish to attach yourself to that dashing Dragon man with whom you are so desperately enamored, start off on the proper footing. Let him know right from the beginning that you are a no-nonsense lady who can fend for herself. Otherwise, though he may wine and dine you, cover you in furs, and set you up in the home of your dreams, before too long your Dragon will err and stray like a lost lounge lizard. Since what he is after is a challenge, give him all the flack you can without causing a riot. Make him aware that you have every intention of keeping your job or pursuing your studies after marriage. Without this premarital toughness on your part, your Dragon man may eat you alive.

There are loads of good things about Dragon men. They are usually successful and lucky in finance. They are healthy and tend to take excellent care of themselves. They are presentable and well-dressed. Also, Dragons are sentimental to a fault. If you feel all communications have broken down, you can always rely on his feelings of tenderness toward you to draw him out of any funk he may choose to enter.

Moreover, Dragon men make fine mates for women who need to be taken care of and do not mind staying mildly in the background. Whatever is happening in his life is usually his "trip." If you and a medley of fine children happen to like to be the occasional focus of his attentions, then perhaps that is sufficient for you. If any of you falls ill or needs advice or money, he will always be there in a jiffy. His loyalty to family does come first.

To make him happy, you will be required to shower attentions on him, giggle a lot, and constantly remind him how fantastic he is. To keep him happy, you will almost surely have to threaten his masculinity about ten times a week by doing your own thing your way and proving your strength repeatedly. Dragons are easy to infatuate, but difficult to interest over long periods of time. In the final analysis, Dragons do not respect weaklings and will always be drawn away from them by someone more forceful. So, if you are intent on catching him, please do me the favor of planning your bow-to-hold-on-to-him strategy well in advance.

CO-SIGNS

DRAGON/Aries *(March 22—April 20)*

Dragons born under the sign of Aries will be somewhat more sensitive than most. The needs of their fellow human beings will be important to them. Headlong, the Aries ram will charge, full of vitality and life giving energy. There is a lot of warmth emanating from this healthy blaze of wood/fire combination. Cozy? . . . Well, not exactly. But the Aries who has the luck to be born a Dragon will plow on through, no matter what. Adversity and setbacks mean nothing to him. They only provide fuel for his fiery will. Somewhat more abrupt than he ought to be, this Dragon may have difficulty keeping his friends. The best advice I can give is control and temperance in all aspects of life.

DRAGON/Taurus *(April 21—May 21)*

Stubborn? Headstrong? Willful? You haven't seen anything until you have witnessed the power behind this bulldozer of a person. Nature study is in order here. The calming action of forests, streams, and seasonal change are essential to the Taurean Dragon's mental stability.

He should never be asked to live in a torrid jungle clime or transferred to Arizona where the static environment may clamp down on his already too-harried nature. This Dragon will tend toward the arts. He needs stimulation in order to apply himself to his chosen field. Given half a chance and the right surroundings, the Taurus Dragon will win every battle. His force is indomitable.

DRAGON/Gemini *(May 22—June 21)*

The sign of the twins augurs a sketchy future for the Dragon born under its influence. Hopping first on one foot, then the other, this subject will spend much of his time pawing the earth and wishing he were more directed. I call this type of person a sprinter. Many a fine start on this project or that will end up in disaster. Women of this sign sometimes acquire the bad habit of impulse buying. They never know what they want for longer than it takes for them to become infatuated with it. But Dragon/Geminis are generous and warm-hearted. Just as they have a hard time saying "no" to a bargain, they will never refuse the chance to give of their tenderness or loving care. Mercurial in the extreme, these subjects will keep anyone involved with them on tenterhooks most of the time. Sit back and enjoy the show.

DRAGON/Cancer *(June 22—July 23)*

Quiet strength personifies the Dragon/Cancer, who is a raft of power floating on a limpid sea. In times of need or sorrow, you will always be able to count on the Dragon/Cancer. He loves to give advice and is apt at choosing the right path out of many for both himself and his friends. Rather more ponderous than other Dragons, the Cancerian will attack goals slowly and with great deliberation. If I might suggest marrying any Dragon at all, it would certainly be more safe to hitch your wagon to a Cancerian Dragon than to those born in any other sign.

DRAGON/Leo *(July 24—August 23)*

Look before you leap into this searing bonfire. Leos reek of power. Dragons spew great flames of that commodity. There will be a dearth of homey nights around the fireside with this character. Why should a

Dragon/Leo stay at home if he/she can go out and rule the world? If you don't find this subject at the head of some giant organization or leading an army, please call me immediately. Your discovery will be a first in history. Dragon/Leos are gloriously rich in all the necessary leadership qualities. They direct films and build empires, they conduct orchestras, and inspire poetics. At maximum production level, they should be doing the work of at least two human beings. If you find Dragon/Leos in subordinate positions, they are probably very unhappy Dragons indeed.

DRAGON/Virgo *(August 24—September 23)*

Here's an interesting duo, fastidious, hard-driving, and driven at the same time. The combination of mineral and wood, two vital energy sources, give this subject a personal conscientiousness unequalled in all other signs. If a Dragon/Virgo should decide to achieve a goal, the plodding will be no obstacle, the years of training no trouble at all. Such an alliance will make for sure success. Application of early training should result in highest honors when it comes to recognition in a field or career of the person's choice. Talent is not lacking. The will is pure and strong. There is much goodness in the hearts of these people.

DRAGON/Libra *(September 24—October 23)*

Best suited for home and family, the women of this combination sign will be likely to spend much time entertaining. If given half a chance, they may even do a bit of old-fashioned social climbing. Dragon/Libras ought to be flexible and chatty people. To identify them in a crowd, look for those people who are talking much and listening less. Much of the hyperbole is designed to soothe an unwitting audience. There may be some domestic hankypanky afoot. Turn the other ear. Whatever they are about, it is usually handled artistically.

DRAGON/Scorpio *(October 24—November 22)*

Step aside . . . Here comes the Dragon's Dragon. Until now, who had control of all the burning passions in the world? Who could inspire more rages and offend more people at one blow than our friend, the viper-tongued Scorpio? Fact is, there are not many competitors for the title—except perhaps the Dragon/Scorpio. He fights so often, and with such verve and pizazz, that he often forgets to succeed at what he set out to accomplish in the first place. At the least, this subject will be of stormy temperament. At best, he may prosper at law, or even turn out to be a famous general who takes pleasure in wiping out enemies by sheer force. Not an easy sign to live with, this Scorpio would do well to take a rain check on marriage until he has reached at least one of his professional goals.

DRAGON/Sagittarius *(November 23—December 21)*

An idealist, a flag waver, and banner carrier. This subject combines fire and wood with gusto. Add some fuel in the form of money, and he is off and running toward more windmills than you can shake a stick at. Too much optimism can be a dangerous thing. This person suffers from over-belief in himself. His projects will often turn out to be empty schemes. His hopes may be dashed more than once by reality's fickle finger. Excessive and overly ambitious, Sagittatians born in Dragon years must be taught while still very young to be patient and cool their heels in learning situations before they rush out to beat the devil.

DRAGON/Capricorn *(December 22—January 20)*

Work, work, work. And impatience. Rigorous attention to detail is this subject's byword. Few people have more difficulty expressing their innermost thoughts than Dragon/Capricorns. On the other hand, their outermost thoughts will come bursting from their lips (sometimes maliciously), as though they had all been planted in careful rows on the tips of their tongues at birth. Slower to achieve objectives than other Dragons, the Capricorns born under this sign will always succeed if given time to actively pursue what they go after. When pressed or rushed, they tend to panic and slow down. This subject is angular and rigid in his viewpoints as well as in his judgments of both himself and others. Life for the Dragon/Capricorn is not simple. He needs an abundance of tender love and trust from his friends.

DRAGON/Aquarius *(January 21—Februaty 19)*

Soaring free spirits make up the large majority of the subjects born under these two signs. For some strange reason, Aquarian Dragons possess more intuition than other people. They can readily see beyond the moment in which they live. As a result, their long-range advice is valued by friends and acquaintances. As far as home life goes, there would have to be flood, famine, or an act of God to remind them that somebody might be waiting up for them, fending off the bill collectors or holding a birthday party for a child. These people sincerely feel they are not part of the normal world. Humor them. And insist on a joint checking account. Not that they are stingy or small with money. They just have a way of forgetting about such niggling details as unpaid bills, rent, and school fees.

DRAGON/Pisces *(February 20—March 20)*

A Pisces who manages to get himself born under the sign of the Dragon is indeed a lucky fellow. All the Piscean sensitivity and artistry can be easily put to work when coupled with Dragon toughness and spirited application. Art, in all of its forms, will be a passion with this subject. Whether or not he puts this passion to good use will be a question of mind over matter. Pisceans are often distracted by emotionality. Dragons can be drawn away from serious pursuits by answering the call of their own sentimentality. A Dragon born in the sign of the fish would be well advised to surround himself with people wiser and more diligent than he. They will show him the path to success. Once he is on that path, he ought to be invincible.

PRESCRIPTION FOR THE FUTURE

Dauntless Dragon, "As you go through life, make this your goal. Keep your eye upon the doughnut and not upon the hole." I read that somewhere on a luncheonette menu when I was twelve. Until now, I had never found a way to use it. Dragon dear, your vertiginous virtues inspired me. *Merci beaucoup.*

Why is it that people hesitate to come right out and defy you?

What makes you so forbidding? Is it your wry smile of *savoir-faire*? Perhaps it is your magnificent manners. Or, it could be that undeniable snap in your very voice and step that puts others on the instant defensive.

Not that innate superiority such as yours is a bad habit or even some character trait that you might strive to erase. You truly are a very special person. And it sticks out all over you like extra chrome on a Cadillac. That air of grandeur may, in itself, be responsible for what you sometimes tell us is the inability of your cohorts to understand you.

Nobody, not even the delightful Dragon, enjoys feeling misunderstood. It just isn't all that much fun to sit out one's day on a windy mountaintop without a friend in the world. What you really want is someone to whom you feel close, don't you?

You are a preponderant human being. You do emanate vibrations of prosperity. And most of the time you have the situation very much in hand. Your Dragonly demeanor and sharp wits keep you very much at the summit of all the heaps you encounter in life.

Too, you daring Dragon, there is a part of you that would prefer to be simply normal, weak from time to time, depressed and out of sorts on the odd Wednesday, or so ill that people would not expect you to perform your stunts and help them as they muddle through. But, like everything else, there is an onerous price to pay for being so naturally forceful. That tax on your happiness does not please you.

If you wish to change into a sniveling squirrel or meek mouse so that people will feel more cozy around you, put that absurd notion out of your head immediately. It would be impossible. Yet, there are some easy remedies for certain appeal that you may want to swallow.

Since your charm and pizazz are so imposing, why don't you try to temper them a bit? Slow down to what you think is a veritable snail's pace. That will be the normal cadence of most anyone else you meet. Keep some of your pithy comments and apt advice in reserve. Don't give away your hand from the outset of any game. Make an effort not to judge those whom you meet by your own draconian Dragon standards. Everyone is not as gifted, healthy, and perspicacious as you. They may have many other fine qualities, which, if given half a chance, they will be willing to impart to you.

You are a sentimentalist. Underneath the prodigious airs you seem to exude, there is a tender, warm-hearted soul. If you are after the acquisition of friends or a lover, tone down your grandeur to a dull roar. Otherwise, no one will be able to see just what a nice guy you really are. Show your adoration of babies and tiny helpless creatures. Gush a bit over the attributes of others. It will make them happy. It will help them understand who you really are, and all the truest affections will be returned to you in kind.

COMPATIBILITIES

Affairs of the Heart

The Dragon is a much-pursued figure. Not only is he sought after for his wisdom and good counsel, but Dragons are jolly attractive love objects as well. It could be all that snappy artistry or even the Dragon's vitality that others find so appealing. But, whatever it is, many suitors always want to get into the Dragon's act. Dragon women are often demanded in marriage.

The Dragon himself is not all that involved with emotional dalliances. Whether he means it or not, at times he gives the impression that he just doesn't care. Though not aloof and distant, like the Cat, the Dragon gives off vibrations of such autonomy of spirit that we frequently imagine he doesn't need the support of enduring love to survive.

With this in mind, it is easy to see why Dragons get on with Monkeys. The average Monkey person is as enthusiastic as a Dragon, equally gifted for business, affable, inventive, and very independent. Dragons, however, are guileless in love. Monkeys, who are never without wile, gain the Dragon's respect. The two complement each other well. But, don't forget, Monkeys are the only people who can fool the doubting Dragon.

Rats, too, can hang onto a Dragon lover or mistress. Warm-hearted and indulgent, Rats generate much verve for love. When a Rat finds a Dragon to adore, he goes at the affair with enough tenderness for both of them. And Dragons can always use a bit of softening up. The Rat will be proud of his Dragon, sing his praises, and applaud Dragon successes resoundingly.

A Rooster is a good alternate choice for a Dragon. One thing is sure. With a Rooster, the Dragon will find no competition in his professional life. Instead, the Rooster will take pleasure in scratching leftover crumbs from his Dragon's wake. Roosters are satisfied to use their own cleverness to help Dragons survive whatever setbacks they may experience.

If they could make the necessary mutual concessions, the Dragon and the Tiger would be an indomitable team. The Tiger's noble ideals are admired by the Dragon, who will advise him wisely and give him an extra portion of force to add to his character. The alliance will not be all roses, but with a bit of diplomacy much can be accomplished by these two willful creatures.

Dragons can also get much out of attachments involving Snakes, who are themselves attractive and whose appearance makes the proud Dragon even prouder. And Horses are hugely admired by Dragons for their grip on hard work and taste for fine clothing.

Cat women can get on well with Dragon men. The Cat's good manners appeal to the Dragon's sense of what is proper.

Dragon people, without much effort on their own parts to prove credibility, will not have an easy time with either Oxen or Dogs. Members of both of these signs do not particularly respect the Dragon's ceremonious ways.

Social Affairs

The Dragon is an influential bigwig in the cycle of Chinese Chance. Companionship is a natural outgrowth of his ability to meet the public. But real friends about whom he cares and feels deeply are a far more rare commodity in the life of a Dragon. Remember, the good Dragon is a sentimentalist. The only way to his head is through his heart.

Snakes make superlative friends for Dragons. They are both gifted with special sagacity and wisdom. Both are intuitive and shrewd. Snakes enjoy the Dragon's showiness. They also help him to put the brakes on his ostentation through subtlety and skillful accessorizing.

His closest friends may be found among Monkey subjects. Dragons find the Monkey's cheerful agility relaxing. For once, the Dragon can trust somebody—but should he? That part of the bargain is entirely up to the Monkey's discretion.

Rats and Tigers please the Dragon as friends. They form jolly friendships. The cheerful Rat is never a threat to the Dragon's pride. The Tiger, though he argues with him from time to time, never holds the Dragon's vanity against him.

For successful friendships to evolve out of relations with Dogs, Roosters, or Pigs, the Dragon will be obliged to slow his enthusiasms somewhat. People of these signs are, like everybody else, attracted by the Dragon. But they find it difficult to trust his gift of gab.

Business Affairs

In commerce, the Dragon is advised to seek partners who match his strength, rather than those less forceful than himself. Tigers and Monkeys can handle the Dragon's vitality and will work by his side without fear of eclipse.

With Rats, Roosters, or Dogs, the Dragon may encounter problems of ego conflict. Unless the Dragon is the unmitigated boss, the financial end of these businesses could take a sharp dip in no time.

The artistic Goat constitutes a good possibility for Dragons. The Dragon can undertake to serve as his Goat friend's agent or manager. Their combined talents may earn them much money. The Goat never minds being commanded so long as he is comfortably well-off.

The surest road to a gold mine would be a venture with a person bom in the Year of the Pig. Pigs are uncannily lucky in money matters and Dragons know how to dress up a product or process. These people complement each other in business, and the scrupulous Pig is neither greedy nor dishonest.

Monkeys, I repeat, are top-dollar good for Dragon business-people. But they also know how to manipulate the blustery Dragon. Much attention must be paid to the details of bookkeeping.

Family Affairs

Since Dragons do not love to be challenged and are giving of themselves in emotional circumstances, they make compassionate yet sternly authoritarian parents. A Dragon dad or mom understands how hard it is to be a child. But they do not put up with any nonsense from kids. The child should behave in the manner that his Dragon parent sees fit. And that, my friends, is that!

Due to this autocratic but still sensitive approach, the Dragon parent will automatically find it easier to get along with either a respectfully strong-willed child or one who is so malleable and loving that he will not challenge rules. Tigers, Horses, and Monkeys find hand-in-hand living with Dragons a delight. Rats and Snakes are dutifully respectful. The Dragon is generous and asks a great deal in return for handouts. Roosters and Dogs, both wary and needy of extra attention, find the Dragon parent too strict and inflexible.

Most members of other signs will accept being putty in the hands of a Dragon parent. They trust he will set them on the right road.

Dragons who give birth to other Dragons can expect fiery times ahead. Whose authority will be adhered to? That is a moot, yet intriguing question.

THE SNAKE

The Years of the Snake

February 4, 1905 to January 25, 1906
January 23, 1917 to February 11, 1918
February 10, 1929 to January 30, 1930
January 27, 1941 to February 15, 1942
February 14, 1953 to February 3, 1954
February 21, 1965 to January 21, 1966
February 18, 1977 to February 6, 1978
February 6, 1989 to January 26, 1990

Snakes are:

Wise • Cultivated • Cerebral • Accommodating
Intuitive • Attractive • Amusing • Lucky • Sympathetic
Elegant • Soft-spoken • Well-bred • Compassionate
Philosophical • Calm • Decisive

But they can aslo be:

Ostentatious • Sore losers • Tight-fisted
Extravagant • Presumptuous • Possessive • Vengeful
Self-critical • Phlegmatic • Lazy • Fickle

SNAKES I HAVE KNOWN AND LOVED

Out there somewhere slithering through rich grasses, dawdling now and again for a chance to strike it rich, is the darling of the Oriental signs. . .the alluring Snake. Seductive beyond belief, restful and sage, people born in the Snake years emit their particular form of magnetism in what I like to think of as a kind of pleasant ooze. Absent from their repertoire are such characteristics as belligerence or swagger. Snakes are neither aggressive nor blatant. They are masters of reptilian grace. Rarely are they ruffled or upset. Snake people give everybody, including themselves, the impression that they really "have it all together."

Way back in Sunday school, we were warned about snakes. If you recall Eve's undoing in any detail, you may be able to recapture the eerie feeling that Satan's disguise elicited in your clean slate of a tousled six-year-old head. That serpent in Adam's grape arbor must have been an attractive item. Otherwise, why would a perfectly intelligent grown-up lady like Eve fall for his routine? I mean, she had a decent, hard-working husband, enough to eat and a bottomless wardrobe supply. Yet, we know full well that one day she just up and announced, "Adam, if you were the only man on earth, I would have nothing more to do with you." That snake had her head turned around so far she couldn't see the forest or the trees. She blew an idyllic marriage, traumatized one of her sons into becoming the first murderer on earth, and managed to smear the family's name all over the papers in the bargain. Scandalous, *n'est-ce pas?*

So we have it on good advice that Snakes are among the world's most irresistible creatures. Certainly some of you will protest, "I hate snakes. They're so ugly. Oooooh. Slimy icky yechhy snakes. Ugh!" and all that. With you, it is certain snakes wouldn't have a chance in hell. You are too virtuous and well-adjusted to ever fall prey to the wiles of a snake. Don't be so sure of yourself. These beasts have an act unparalleled by all others. For the most part, they are uncommonly beautiful, somewhat forbidding, and helplessly sexy.

A heady little side trip into the golden jet set crowd may help me to illustrate my point.

Riddle: Who is the only woman you can think of who favors *haute couture* T-shirts, sumptuous Mediterranean holidays, expensive Parisian abodes chock-full of servants, dark glasses, and similarly shaded husbands? Who sends her children to the best private schools in the world, is accompanied to the powder room by two burly bodyguards everywhere she goes, sets the pace for oodles of fashion-conscious women all over the world, and doesn't know how to open a can of tuna fish?

Is it Grace Kelly Rainier (b. 1929)? Or, perhaps you were thinking of Jacqueline Kennedy Onassis (b. 1929)? The answer? . . . Both are correct. One and one make two of them born in Snake years.

Beyond the obvious luxury of their life styles, there is something else that strikes me as common to the above-mentioned women. Why did Prince Rainier ride into Philadelphia on a white horse and carry off an Irish parvenu's daughter? Why did Jack Kennedy choose Jackie to be his first lady? And what in the name of Zeus was Onassis thinking of when he married her? In a word, what these titans of the twentieth century were after in all three cases was beauty. Snake women often—not always but frequently—succeed through their beauty.

And what were the ladies after? Well, we take it they weren't lusting after just any old vine-covered cottage in Paducah. And I would find it hard to believe they merely wanted to have their names on the society page. Don't try to tell me that they were both members of a sun-worshipers' club and so decided to marry into the Mediterranean millionaire's clique to be sure of lifetime beach rights. It's too coincidental. Snakes like money. They hate vain work. They are among the planet's most comely creatures, and moreover, they are exasperatingly lucky. If it weren't that Snakes don't have any limbs to speak of, I would be tempted to say that Snakes like to start off their lives on a firm footing—and keep them there forever.

The daughter of an actress friend of mine is a Snake. A high-fashion model of the first order who makes all the magazines every month in Paris, Daffodil Du Roy was ten years old last week. Françoise, her mother, has been chasing Daffy in and out of the lime-light since the child was one and a half. Early on, before I really knew Françoise very well, I chanced to comment one day that I wondered if it wasn't dangerous for Daffy to spend so much time in front of the cameras. Wouldn't her schoolwork suffer? Was it not risky for a little girl to be prancing about the streets carrying her portfolio in and out of taxis and making calls on photographers? Secretly, I accused Françoise of being one of those dreadful stage mothers who push their kids to follow in their footsteps.

"She has always been that way," Françoise told me. "Daffy has never stopped acting since she was old enough to watch the expressions on faces hanging over her cradle."

"Could it be," I offered walrily, "that because you are in the theater you were a mite too encouraging of her antics?"

"So many people have accused me of that, Suzanne. For a long time I worried about it, too. I even made Daffy stop working when her grades went down in school two years ago. I was sure it was all my fault for allowing her to do so much modeling." Françoise has a winning smile. She is also a very down-to-earth no-nonsense mother. Her kids have to eat everything on their plates and help with dishes. They are polite and far from spoiled. Still, I wasn't convinced.

"And what happened then?" I hoped she would say something reassuring.

"Her marks stayed down. I wheedled and scolded and hired

tutors. I spent hours with her over homework. It didn't do any good. She claimed she didn't like school." Françoise poured me a glass of port.

I grinned her a knowing grin. "Come on now, Françoise. Daffy is not a stupid child. How could she not like school? She's so bright."

"You are right. Daffy is in the top ten percentile. I only know that because I had her tested. Her IQ is 140. She should have been a real achiever in school. But every time she looked at a book she went all pale and limp. She didn't listen in class, her mind wandered. She was daydreaming." The dutiful mother, Françoise, had tried almost everything.

"So what did you do? I know she's working again because I saw her photo in last week's *Elle.*"

"I took her to a child psychiatrist. She wasn't sick. I was. Sick with guilt. I imagined it was all my fault for letting her flaunt her face all over Paris photo studios. I tell you, I was a wreck." Françoise pulled her pretty stockinged feet up under her on the velvet couch.

As it turned out, the doctor had several talks with Daffy and discovered her mother had committed a grave mistake. Apparently, before the marks began to go down, Daffy had been naughty one day and said something cheeky to Françoise in anger. Françoise had warned her then, "If you aren't more respectful of me, I will make you stop working. You think because you can act smart with those photographers you can get away with answering me back. I am your mother. Remember that!" Typical child/parent dialogue.

The problem, as the doctor described it to Françoise, was that the very idea of having to stop the work she loved so much had caused Daffy to begin fretting over the possibility long before the bad report card had come home. It was not modeling that was causing the daydreams. It was the fear of having to stop it. After that summer, Daffy went back to work and to school. Both pursuits improved immensely. She's saving her earnings to study theater when she grows up. And she almost never sasses her mother any more.

Soon after I heard this story, in my usual fashion, I looked up the 1965 Chinese horoscope table. Sure enough, right there next to Jackie-o and Grace was the birth year of little Daffy Du Roy.

In the case of the Snake, beauty is not only skin deep. Coupled with the serpent's good looks is an enormous amount of innate wisdom. Snakes have a judiciousness about them that borders on the supernatural. One imagines sometimes they enjoy the gift of inner light or clairvoyance. By this, I am not implying that all Snake people are mystics. Far from it. Their kind of sagacity is instead almost a sixth sense. They have excellent judgment.

Take Bob Dylan, for example. Back in 1963, when I was first living in Montparnasse, there existed in that artist neighborhood an aura of being "on the scene" in a big city during what we all considered to be protest time. As expatriates, we were not all aware of just how vehement the movement was back in the States. But we were young and American and we listened to the new music and we all knew who Bobby Zimmerman was. I was so into Dylan's "Blowing in the Wind" record, I could hardly remember my own name. I had memorized all the songs. I was a fan.

All variety of celebrated and not-so-celebrated souls used to err and stray about Paris on their way from London to Ibiza or Morocco and back. Lots of them crashed at my house, mostly because the house next door where all the groovy parties were held was usually full. I got the overflow.

Whether because nobody was quite sure who he was or because he was so quiet and unassuming, one Sunday night I was awarded Bob Dylan as a houseguest. Don't misread me, please. I said a houseguest and I meant a houseguest. There were already four or five musicians wandering about the place looking spaced and acting important. One of them was my future ex-husband. Besides, I was already too old to be a groupie. Dylan, for me, was simply somebody formidably talented. He was so in I was delighted to put him up during his European tour.

Admittedly, it was exotic having this star sitting against the wall of my living room strumming tuneless cacophonies to accompany his grainy voice. I was impressed. So impressed, as a matter of fact, that I could hardly sit still. I wanted Mr. Dylan to remember his visit to Paris. I pleaded with my fiancé to take us all out to some wonderful discotheque where Dylan could enjoy the music and be seen by *le tout Paris*.

Timidly (I used to be shy), I threaded my way through the lounging bodies on my floor, knelt down beside the slouching minstrel, and said, "We'd like to take you out to some gassy places. We know where all the best music is. We can really show you the town." To my astonishment, he deigned to look up at me. "Huh?" was all he muttered. Then he returned to his strings. I repeated to myself—panting.

"Oh yeah, sure." Bob Dylan had uttered three words to me. I was beside myself with juvenile ecstasy.

Militantly, I shooed everyone else out of the house. I went in to put on my make-up while the two "cats" sat plunking in the salon. I was going out with Bobby Dylan. Okay, so he wasn't my date. But he was in my house. I wanted to call my mother in Milwaukee but the transatlantic time difference made it unfeasible. Anyway, she wouldn't have known whom I was talking about until 1966.

We got into the car. Three of us in a Ferrari 2 + 2. I was driving. Sports cars have a way of turning me into Sterling Moss. I threw the car in first—and stalled out. The nervous laughter on my part didn't hide the mortification. But I forged ahead. "How about Castel's?" I said gaily.

"What's Castal's?" Bobby queried politely.

"It's this great private club, all red velvet and plush. It's where all the beautiful people hang out. The music is out of sight." We all talked like that then. Can I help it that it sounds old-fashioned now? I can't believe I was such a nit.

Anyway, guess what he said. He looked me straight in the eye and requested ever so calmly, "Could we just buy a bottle of cheap red wine and drive around the city? I'm performing tomorrow night in London and I haven't even seen the Eiffel Tower. Would you mind terribly? Loud music gives me a headache." Tell me, whose mother would believe that statement? Then he added, "The night before a concert I always tuck in early." And I thought he was a star. Was I ever disappointed!

The reason I told that story (besides enjoying the brag about Dylan sleeping on my floor) is that after thinking it through and discovering that he was born in 1941, I remembered that getting to the top of any profession takes lots of hard work, rest, careful planning, and self-discipline. Of those wares, Snakes have more than their share.

Give a Snake his druthers and he'll often find a calling he wants to follow to the bitter end. Ordinary tasks and certain of the more banal school subjects may be expected to bore him. Unless a job is directly related to what he feels compelled to do with his life, it seems to him superfluous.

The brand of exhibitionism with which Snake people are vested is not to be confused with showing-off. Snakes are not usually horn blowers or back-slapping belly laughers. Theirs is a pristine ostentation. Their presence is a display. Picasso (b. 1881) was a Snake. Although he was no slouch in front of a camera and enjoyed trotting out paintings for his favorite photographers, his image was one of powerful dignity: Piercing black eyeballs in a perfectly shaped bald head topped a body dressed only in well-tailored French mariners' T-shirts and tight pants. The outfit was definitely not *recherché* in the fashionable sense, but it had his trademark on it. Nobody else could have hoped to pull it off with such quiet flourish.

Snakes can always be counted on to come across with sympathy and wise advice when dealing with friends or family. Money? . . . Never. Presents? . . . Perhaps. But Snake people do not part with their booty gracefully—unless it is for their own extravagances. And despite the fact that they are most always lucky in finance, when they find themselves short of money, they become apprehensive and short-tempered. I daresay none of us would enjoy being in the position of having absconded with any meager smidgeon of the fortunes of Howard Hughes (Snake, 1905), Aristotle Onassis (Snake, 1905-'06), or our own Jack Kennedy (b. 1917). Where money is concerned, none of these three gentlemen were ever noted for slapdash generosity.

One reason that I enjoyed a good laugh over the strained tone of the recent Onassis/Jackie fortune division is that here we saw the professionally refined approach on the parts of two hungry Snakes at full tilt. Not that Jackie got off too badly in the final sharing, but it is my guess she had imagined things would tip more in her favor. She would have done well to insist that more buildings be put in her name when love was in first bloom. Snakes don't like to be taken for sugar daddies, even by other Snakes.

A TV producer friend of mine in Paris is a classic example of Snakery in action. Paul (Snake, 1929) fills the serpent role so well I ought to include his picture here as a guide to recognizing Snake people. Their heights, good bones, finely shaped features, and graceful carriage are certain to attract the eye. I met Paul in the London living room of a plush mutual friend. Over crystal goblets of amber-colored sherry, Paul told me his story. He was in London shooting a cosmetics commercial but straight-away would be moving his home base from New York to Paris. I know that Paris is a magnificent place to live, but it has rarely been noted for its excellent TV productions. I wondered aloud, "What will you be doing in Paris? How will you work there?"

Paul had it all figured out. He had arranged a deal with one of our leading beauty product companies to do all of their TV spots from French TV studios. They liked the idea since production costs were slightly lower and more exotic models were available at lower rates in Europe. If a model is established in New York City, it usually means she has spent her apprenticeship abroad earning much less money. At any rate, Paul was content with his arrangement. It would allow him nine months in Paris per year. The other three would be spent back in New York writing scripts, editing, and soaking up the New York scene he so loved.

Still, Paul did not speak French. He had so few connections in the French film world. He was going cold. I wondered aloud, "But why?"

Paul tried to clarify: "I truly love New York City. When I came there from Michigan as a young kid, they gave me my start. I adore the cultural ambience of New York. I'm a ballet fanatic. There is very little good dance in Paris. I shall have to accept cramming in all my culture-vulturing in three months. I have no other choice."

I suspected perhaps there was some personal story behind all this wanton emigration, an ex-wife or girl friend Paul wished to escape. Soon, I understood. He looked saddened as he said, "I have to get away from New York. I have too many friends there who depend on me for emotional stability. If I have to stay one more week, I shall go mad."

To me, this seemed a plausible notion. Yet, it also seemed to me that if one had too many friends leaning on one for succor in times of need, one might be able to plainly tell them to "go away." Not Paul. He loved them too much. There was Maureen, the failed ballerina, and Harvey, the ex-singing star. He could never say "no" to Martha, the struggling poetess, or shut his door in the face of Niko, the forty-year-old model whose hair had begun failing out after her disastrous marriage broke up. Even though none of these people were costing him money, their problems took up all of his leisure time. His equilibrium was failing.

Emotional cripples were littering Paul's doorstep. He would simply have to move out of his beautiful East Side town house and flee to Paris in order to stave them off. Too, in France he hoped to be able to complete his book. It was to be called *Victims: A Study in the Care and Feeding of Losers*. At least his sense of humor was intact.

So it had not been an ex-wife or girl friend, after all. Paul was, in fact, never married. He explained he would not have time for a family. He was too busy making money and consoling the sad sacks of the world. What wife could have put up with it? I confess I cannot imagine.

This dispensing of free wisdom and sympathy is common among Snake people. They take in strays. Paul has four cats, all of them too fat and all of them found in New York gutters.

And do you know what happened to Paul after he moved to Paris in hopes of getting away from his moral responsibilities? The second year he was there he bought a huge old apartment, fixed it up in his inimitably refined taste, and began taking in new patients. There is Gilles, the mixed-up son of Paul's concierge. Poor Gilles can't hold a job. Or, we are greeted by Marie-France, the confused young painter whose one-woman show is always about to open somewhere soon. The phone is often answered by Charles, the rakish hairdresser friend of Marie who lost his job because he wasn't homosexual. Borderline cases—not real crazies—dapple the landscape of my dear friend Paul's life.

Five years have passed since I met him in that London drawing room. His latest scheme is to buy a house in the French countryside so that he can stage yet another retreat from the ambulatory nut cases he collects. They need him too much. Besides, he told me recently, "It's time they stood on their own two feet."

I brightened. Paul was maybe getting some sense into his head? Not on your life. He is going to transform this famous country house he is considering the purchase of into a small orphanage for children of broken homes who need a good rest. I give up. He's wonderful and charitable and kind. His sanity seems to remain relatively whole as long as he is surrounded by these loonies. Who am I to judge?

Yet, I admit it crossed my mind one day that perhaps Paul thinks of me as one of his cases. I do call him a lot for advice on what to wear when I am interviewed by a publisher. I did ask him how to write a good piece of ad copy when my own chips were down so far that I was reduced to jingles and jangles. He has helped me, too. One day, when I was presenting a novel idea to Maurice Girodias (Goat, 1919), the noted porno publisher, Paul told me to wear my "Suzanne White costume." Not twigging immediately to what that could be, I asked him, "What in the name of God is that supposed to mean?"

"You know very well, Suzanne. Ex-Vassar, ex-hippie, ex-housewife, chic Parisian ladylike journalist. See what I mean?"

"Not a clue," I told him. "It sounds mighty eclectic to me. Wigwam socks, Weejun loafers, embroidered torn jeans, and the jacket to my pink Chanel suit?"

Paul giggled. "Oh, Suzanne, you are dense sometimes. Just wear your plaid kilt and comb your hair."

What a plaid kilt has to do with all those images he described, I still do not know. I went to the interview looking for all the world like an aging English schoolgirl. It worked. Girodias thought I was a genius. Ah! The magic of Snakes.

This doubt I mentioned earlier did however somewhat cloud my friendship with Paul of late. Was I one of his cases? Did he think of me as vaguely dependent? The answer? . . . Yes. And here is how I found out.

A while ago, I began having some bang-up successes with my writing. Since I was in New York and Paul was over there scouring La Touraine for an orphanage site, I had not asked his advice for any of the dealings this side of the Atlantic. When I got home to Paris, I phoned him. "Hey Guess what? I sold two books, got a contract for another, fell in love, and got my hair cut." I was so pleased not to be calling for moral support. I thought Paul would be enraptured. Finally, somebody who calls to tell him something positive has occurred in his life.

Do you know what he said to me? I still can't get over it. I was crushed. Paul, my mentor and guru who had taught me so much, said, "That's nice, Suzanne. You will call me if you need anything." And hung up.

Later on, I discussed this weird reaction with another ex-friend of Paul who fell out of favor with him when she married a swanky millionaire and settled down to being a happy wife and mother. "He doesn't want you to be successful on your own," she informed me. "He likes to play God. "

That, my friends, is a typical Snake story. And, if it isn't, can you tell me why Mao Tse-tung is a Snake (b. 1893)?

Snake people sometimes tend to hinder their own progress. Until they find that single pursuit that they need for survival in what they consider an otherwise colorless world, they can be the world's most annoying dabblers. Often, they don't come to self-realization early in life. So they spend miles of time picking on themselves and at others during the pre-career period. The "What shall I do? I am bored" syndrome is rampant among Snakes. They are nervous people, anxious even. They don't enjoy inactivity, but seem to need to have the script written for them by other people. They feed, in fact, off the souls of others. Not maliciously, mind you. Snakes are not your garden-variety parasite. It's the stimulation of the needs of others that prods their imagination. Send a Snake packing and he will die before sundown. He needs human contact. Snakes are cold-blooded, remember? Animation around him invigorates the Snake. It gives him cause to believe there is something out there he can do that will eventually satisfy him.

Just as my friend Paul is possessive about his hangers-on, Snake people are jealous of their mates. Oftentimes they will have large families. This proliferation is not necessarily due to the fact that Snake people love staying home and changing diapers. More likely, it is a ploy on their parts to immobilize a spouse. Theirs is a double standard. It is quite all right for them to go sniffing about the globe in search of flirtations or even more serious affairs. But they don't particularly cotton to the idea of their helpmate following suit. A truly wise Snake would discourage this fickleness in his character. Daily lectures from within his own head should assist him in keeping his tongue in his mouth.

Considering the boundless insight with which most Snakes are gifted, they have to pay close attention to career choice. Slowed somewhat by a nitpicking attention to detail, once they have found their path in life they are quick to plunge in and take over the market. Another famous Snake, Carole King (1941), was long a clever and prolific writer of songs for other singers. Aritha Franklin (Horse, 1942) used to do a lot of Carole's songs. Who but real pop buffs knew their source? Little by little, with a good deal of prodding and encouragement from her entourage, Carole was deciding to become a singer of her own works. Finally, one day, she made a record. She called it "Tapestry." It outsold all other recordings that year and is still one of the all-time greats. The songs are magical, Carole's piano accompaniments are brilliant, and her voice is pure pleasure to the ear. She's a natural. But she had to come to that realization in her own time.

Carole King's house, too, is crawling with adoring near-misses. Just this summer I attended a party there. There was Sara, Carole's old school friend whose husband had left her penniless with two small kids to support. She lives in the garage. Then there is Mark, the singer who never made it and never lets you forget it. You will meet Rick, the guitarist who is drying out after a long bout with alcoholism. Charming people, one an all, but ever so sycophantic. Interesting to me was the fact that Ms. King was nowhere to be found at this vast shebang. "She doesn't spend much time in Connecticut," I was told. She stays out in California most of the time whilst this crowd of fans utilize her New England estate as a halfway house. They keep things clean and vacuum the pool on the odd chance Carole might visit. The house is lovely on the outside. The inside looks like a comfy motel. Only one room has any character. That is Carole's studio/bedroom cum brass-bed, fireplace, hurricane lamps, and Victorian piano. Evidence of somebody who cares about her surroundings and needs to house about twenty people in as many bedrooms to make it all worthwhile.

But I digress. Careers? Ah yes. Snakes are not trivial people. They should enter careers that call upon their patience with detail. Writing, decorating, film-making, and other such artistic professions will suit the average Snake. But there are not really very many average Snakes, so they are often to be found at the top of their vocations. Silent leaders.

MADAME SNAKE

First off, I must tell you that the superlative compliment a Japanese man can make a lady of that same national persuasion is this: "You are a veritable snake of a woman." Sounds awful, doesn't it? But there you have it. Oriental families who give birth to a girl child in the Snake year are considered eminently lucky. Snake daughters, thought to be guaranteed beauty and wisdom, are easily married off. That, in the Orient, is no small consideration.

It is true about women born in Snake years. Even though sometimes they have not been endowed with the perfect features of someone like Grace Kelly, they usually have a spark of something so profoundly female about them as to assure their attractiveness. Julie Christie (b. 1940), the British movie star, although she isn't what I would call ravishingly beautiful, possesses quality good looks. And she knows how to get herself together. That is more like it. Snake women are always well turned out. From the small gold earrings right down to the classy alligator pumps, their accessories are always just right. No Snake woman would ever wear white shoes after Labor Day unless she happened to be a nurse. They follow the fashions and are usually aware of what ought to be done about hemlines for next season.

The stylishness is ever so appealing to the mate-seeking male. All right, we jokingly think of men as being attracted to Raquel Welch (a 1942 Horse) or Marilyn Monroe (Tiger, 1926) types. But most men do not marry center foldouts. They are turned on by the sex symbols but they usually are not prepared for lifetime "hot" breakfasts. The Snake woman is the marrying kind. She is not comfortable living out of a suitcase. She needs her own boudoir, an ample dressing room lined with closets, a cupboard or four in which to keep her battery of cosmetics, a home base where she can put her minks in storage, and a good library full of leather-bound classics. The kitchen is the least of your worries. She won't go in there much, anyway. She will not be likely to balk at a house in the country with an indoor swimming pool, either. Just so she can have duplicates of her wardrobe in the city. Snake women are not cheap dates

How to please them? Besides opening a bank account and filling their Christian Dior bags with plenty of plastic fantastic credit cards, you will have to remember not to harp on the fact that she hasn't got out of bed in three days. Snake women like their privacy. They need time to think, and read, and file their toenails. Don't call in a staff of shrinks. Your Snake will rise up as soon as it is time to go to the hairdresser.

Any gentleman interested in bagging himself a Snake lady would be ill-advised to seem too available. Snake ladies like a challenge. Seduction is their department. You don't have to arrange for much more than a white horse or a limousine for the elopement scene. Keep the presents rolling in and act busy. Invent board meetings that keep you occupied some evenings, then go bowling with your cronies. Send her poems, hand carried by messenger, written on parchment. The more hearts and flowers, the better. These efforts do not necessarily have to be your own. But watch where you plagiarize. Snake ladies are usually well-informed students of romantic literature.

Too, you might try to escort her to as many posh events to which you can finagle entry. Snakes like society. And I don't mean having a bunch of pals over for pizza. I'm talking about premier performances of plays, dress-up nights at the opera, and the inaugural ball in Washington. Ms. Snake loves to be seen coming down that Cinderella stairway in full regalia. It's part of her trip.

Among all this serpentine and splash, you will have to contend with the fact that Snake women are as jealous as cobras. They hate to be made fools of. Go ahead, be unfaithful. See what she gets up to in her quiet seething way. Snakes are masters of the double-cross. Don't have your first heart attack if you find your valises on the sidewalk and your ex-best friend in your favorite Barcolounger reading your newspaper with your martini in his hand.

Snake ladies are the sorest of losers. They do not abide chicanery unless they commit it themselves.

What you have to gain by taking up with a Snake woman is a gentle partner, in or out of crime. Snakes do stand by their cohorts. They like to help out. Their advice is always good. Even if they seem to be nagging a bit, intruding in your business life, and making too many inroads into your privacy, they are only doing it for your own good. Courage! They are great in bed.

MONSIEUR SNAKE

Now, here's a challenge for the woman made of steel. Give a Snake an inch and he'll take four kilometers and ten years off your life. "But he is sooooo handsome," you will protest. "I can't take my eyes off him."

If I were you, I wouldn't let it bother me. He is not very expert at taking his own eyes off himself, either. Snake men are exquisitely dressed in a way that, although it may seem casual, is studied down to the last herringbone.

I mentioned my friend Paul who lives in Paris and takes care of loonies. But one thing I forgot to tell you is that Paul would murder for a Saint Laurent suit, with patch pockets and matching raincoat. Yet, he is not a garish dandy. His dress is anything but effeminate. It's what people used to call foppish. Paul has taken advantage of the fact that these days men are urged to dress up. Billowing bow ties, satin shirts, velvet dressing gown, smoking jackets—the lot! What is strange about the getups Paul sports is that he never looks out of place. He just looks better than everybody else.

What makes the Snake man so alluring, on top of all this fancy-dress business, is his apparent grip on life. Snake men are not often unstable. They don't whine a lot about how they can't make it to the top because so-and-so is standing in their way. Instead of wallowing in self-pity, they find ways to sting their competition on the jugular and hide the handy, dandy snakebite kit.

Walking over cadavers is one of the Snake man's specialties. That weakened body in the fancy coffin could be yours. Yet, if you are strong and willing to take on the role of standby organizer par excellence in his home, the Snake man can make an excellent mate.

After you have read all this, if you still think you want a Snake, here's how. First off, don't give him time to think about other women. How can you do that? . . . Simple. Be sure to involve him in every thought you have. Talk to him about details that you know full well you could handle alone. Let him think you are weaker. He likes to take care of people, remember? It is not uncommon for Snake men to marry women with four children and provide for them. If you don't have a ready-made family to offer him, tell him you have a sick mother in Peoria whom you think you really ought to invite to spend a few months. He'll be delighted. For one thing, it will keep you out of his hair. For another, he will take great pride in giving of his hospitality.

Be prepared to dine out a lot. Don't appear sloppily arrayed for a fancy restaurant date. Never overdress for a picnic. Snake men like their women to be intelligent, talented, vaguely helpless, and supremely decorative.

It's no secret to me why the John Cassavetes/Gena Rowlands marriage has held up so well. John, the director (Snake, 1929), comes off as the brains behind their mutual film projects. Gena (a 1936 Rat) is the vehicle for John's genius. She's a brilliant actress. But she isn't the flashy Hollywood babe one thinks of as a star. My guess is he likes her that way—intelligently malleable.

Or, ponder André Previn's (Snake, 1929) bust-up with his first wife, Dory (a 1937 Ox). She wrote about it, either before or after her nervous collapse, in a song. "Beware of young girls who admire your sheets, bring you bouquets of daisies, and praise your husband." Or, something like that. Anyway, she was talking about you-know-whom. Mia Farrow (a 1946 Dog), the "young girl" in question, was obviously always hanging about Dory's husband, admiring his work, and lauding both Previns for their successful marriage. Then, Bingo! No more André. No more marriage. Somehow Dory must have forgotten to keep the praise quotient up. Or, perhaps she was pursuing her own career just a bit too openly? At any rate, it's pretty sure André was not being kept sufficiently amused by his songwriting partner and wife.

So, I caution you Snake admirers. Serpent gentlemen are full of surprises. They don't flaunt their dissatisfaction. They would prefer to just up and disappear overnight. You will have to do a lot of second-guessing in order to fathom your Snake mate. And I am afraid that if you have any real self-seeking mission of your own, he will not stand by in the wings while you go out and lick the world.

I spoke of this quality earlier. While the fire is being built in your heart, you can count on the Snake man to kindle it, feed it, and even buy the wood. But, once you have your strength in shape, when you feel you can really get out there and fight your own battles, he is liable to slink right over you in a crowd. He doesn't like to be one-upped by his woman.

CO-SIGNS

SNAKE/Aries *(March 21—April 20)*

In this head-on collision of a person, fire meets fire. All the best qualities of Snakes, however, may be thwarted by the soldier-line Aries' intrusion. Snakes are slow-moving, philosophical, luxuriating creatures. Aries never stop pushing at fate. The hefty dose of dual personality here, well-handled, might permit the subject to wax creative in the best sense. If the Aries side of this character ever stops long enough to consider how much the deeper-thinking side of himself has to offer, he could produce loads of fine work. The Snake does not adore action for action's sake. To achieve happiness, in this case, he may have to put up with his share of what he considers wasted motion.

SNAKE/Taurus *(April 21-May 21)*

What? . . . A fire raging inside the earth? Call the fire department! Mobilize the National Guard! But take your time. We've got all day.

Snakes born under the sign of the bull will procrastinate, hesitate, fret, and fume for years before they erupt. Volatility, however controlled, is still volatility. Step lightly around these people. Artistic in the extreme, the Snake/Taurus may lie about for a while before he decides to strike. A determined Snake who probably has some gold coins under his mattress in preparation for that rainy day. Don't ask him to hurry. He'll only slough you off . . . or bite your head off.

SNAKE/Gemini *(May 22—June 21)*

Air feeds the fire of our Snake/Gemini. Everybody gets a piece of the action. A dedication to self-discipline would help. Too much fire, after all, can be destructive. One thing is sure, where Gemini flies off too easily in all directions at once, the Snake looks before he leaps. It is a sound match, providing for enormous versatility. Words, elocution, writing, high-mindedness, and diplomacy are suggested careers. Every possibility for blazing the trail to the top of the charts.

SNAKE/Cancer *(June 22—July 23)*

This is one Snake who might be counted on to stay home and attend to business. Cancer spritzes the fiery Snake with some good old-fashioned H_2O. A smolder with powerful grudges and a streak of possessiveness as long as a boa constrictor, this Snake could zap you from out of nowhere if you lift the wrong rock. He will not be the kind to let go, chalk it up to experience, and start all over again. A good provider with truckloads of affection to dote, the Snake/Cancer makes a Jewish mother look like a monkey. If you enjoy having a pillow held over your face, marry one of these people. They are adorable as long as they are happy. Crossed, they will become moody and even dangerous.

SNAKE/Leo *(July 24—August 23)*

Double fire signs are less livable for those who own them than they are for the rest of us to tolerate. Life for the Snake/Leo person, despite the way it may seem to outsiders, will not be pure easy street. There is a great possibility for much personal suffering. These subjects are strong-willed and tough-minded. Adversity will not take the upper hand. Snake luck and Leo pluck will ultimately see them through. But the going won't be smooth. A surprising brand of Leo, soft-spoken and outwardly calm. The fire rages inside. There's nothing wrong with this Leo that a million dollars couldn't cure.

SNAKE/Virgo (August 24—September 23)

Earth warmed by the fires of Indian summer, these two signs share many common traits. Compatibility of spirit should make for a stable being. He may, however, be a trifle too meticulous—picky even. If he seems to be intruding, waiting on you hand and foot, organizing your life against your will, it is because he must be allowed to be of service to those he loves or perish of the frustration. There is a lot of basic good in this person. Boost his morale. He could be seriously lacking in confidence.

SNAKE/Libra (September 24—October 23)

The fire waxes, blown by great gusts of heady airiness. What with the Snake's craving for beauty and Libra's dire need for same, one can expect to find an aura of unparalleled loveliness surrounding this subject. If not, you can be certain the Snake Libran is searching for that idyllic atmosphere in which to balance his emotional budget. His quest will be a languid one. Yet, it is very real to him. A highly female overtone shades the character. He must be encouraged to do away with the small talk, take off some of that extra garb, and settle down to some earnest work.

SNAKE/Scorpio (October 24—November 22)

Tidal waves of Scorpio water will tend to dampen the already slow burn of the Snake. Hesitation, self-doubt, and even self-destruction could result. Within one soul, both elements will be at odds to overcome the other. So much emotion and deep thinking may blacken the horizon. Detailed nightmares, somber daydreams, and the like do not necessarily have to be put to bad use. Instead, they must be channeled, nurtured, and force-fed into creative activities. Water, remember, will appear to burn quite brightly, providing you throw enough oil on its surface. Lubricate this subject's life with a healthy dose of laughter. He is nature's cynic.

SNAKE/Sagittarius *(November 23—December 21)*

Two energetic flames, side by side, licking at each other from time to time, make this combination a brilliant one. With ease and grace, this person will manage his own life in his individual way. He likes a clean house, a well-filled bank account, healthy pursuits such as sports, and long country walks. One slight hitch, the Sagittarian Snake may be as stubborn as a mule. Unbudgeable and opinionated, in his own silent way he always wins. Why? Because he really believes he knows better. His way is best for him. If you cannot conform, he'll search elsewhere for his ideal.

SNAKE/Capricorn *(December 22—January 20)*

Allow me to mention once more the names of some famous Snakes. Can it be sheer coincidence that Mao Tse-tung, Howard Hughes, Aristotle Onassis, and Mohammed Ali are all Capricorn Snakes? Fire and earth in harmony make them diehards, tough nuts to crack, nononsense pushers, and shovers aside of obstacles. They have the necessary wisdom and strength to lick the world, and their Capricorn side gives them the wherewithal to accomplish great deeds. Mind you, they may be insufferable to live with. Personal and insistent to a fault, they simply do not give up easily. A winner!

SNAKE/Aquarius *(January 21—February 19)*

These Snakes will have to be on their guard against being extinguished by the air of Aquarius. A tendency to depression, perhaps even madness, haunts their lives. This very creative combination, given discipline and a good education, will overcome the rough edges. Each new situation will require they bring solid training with them. The tendency is to be flighty and irresponsible. They seem thoughtless. In reality, they are preoccupied. Hold their hands—if you can catch them.

SNAKE/Pisces *(February 20—March 20)*

This is a sensitive soul, indeed. There is more water than fire. Some way must be found to spur or warm or even jolly along. Pisceans have about all they can do to keep from drowning their sorrows, anyway.

Snakes are strong but they lack self-confidence. Both signs tend to slowness. The serpent hesitates. So does the fish. My advice is to buy a cattle prod and urge this subject along through his early life into a well-chosen career by the age of twenty-five. Otherwise, he may never be able to rise from the depths of his wallowing. Early push is recommended. Or else it may be too late.

PRESCRIPTION FOR THE FUTURE

Slender Snake, you are a wise and individualistic human being. Your talents are many. Most important for your survival is that you find a vehicle through which you can express your wealth of gifts. It will usually not be discovered in another's soul. You are not really a dependent type. So don't ever be foolish enough to think that this marriage or that partnership is just exactly what you need to stabilize yourself. Looking for equilibrium in another, even if they have it to offer, will never quite satisfy your own needs.

The reason, of course, that I insist upon warning you away from relying on others for your security is that, more than most other people, you are tempted by this solution. Forget it. That rich man who proposes to buy you all those goodies, although he may improve your surroundings, will not be able to provide the personal achievement you so demand of yourself to be happy. Make yourself comfortable. Go to work on your inhibitions about joining the daily slog right away. You are too smart to put up with your own character weaknesses for long. Find a career or make a good home for your family. Devote yourself to it. Or else, self-hate and disappointment await you later in life.

Dorothy Parker (b. 1893), the famous writer of the twenties and thirties, was a Snake. She was one of our wittiest cynics. Her name is well-known to all, yet her works fill only one book. In all the time she lived, she struggled against her inability to put her nose to the grindstone and keep it there. She fell in love with weak men whom she foolishly thought would save her from drinking, dissipation, and sloth. Glibly, I daresay Dorothy Parker had mountains of talent and very little backbone. She dallied over details. She doubted her ability to really be funny. She spent wildly on clothes. Yet, she never had enough money to take a taxi. She indulged herself in every dodge from alcoholism to attempted suicide, searching always for that stability she so longed for and dreamed was to be found on the outside. Because this mythical perfect atmosphere was never anywhere she looked, Dorothy Parker died a lonely and impoverished woman.

Get down to business. Stop clinging to traditions that are no longer useful. Don't procrastinate. If you try, you will find that you are capable of quick decision-making. What worries you is that your decision might be the wrong one. That is where your judgment must come in, put its foot down, and say, "I am responsible for my own survival. If I have made a foolish move, I must swallow my pride and take the consequences." You can always pick yourself up and start all over again. But you are not always quite certain that you will, so you hesitate. But you shouldn't. Everyone makes mistakes. We all get our clothes mussed from time to time. Looking ridiculous never hurt anybody. Remaining that way is dangerous. If you make a small fool of yourself, go home, put on a pot of coffee, and make a list of all the qualities you know you have. A second list should include all the possible solutions to your problem. And, instead of making a third list, set yourself to attacking each day as it comes.

You can be happy. Because you want to find your salvation in others, and if those people you call upon for help don't give you what you need, you incline to blame them. You are vengeful. You'll show them. And you pout. Or, you refuse to answer the phone. You are not about to let them see you ruffled. You almost never make brash scenes. Instead you seethe with rage, anxiety, and grump-ishness.

Overcoming this streak of revenge in yourself could be more deftly handled as follows. Go to a splendid flower shop, buy a bouquet of gaiety (preferably one that costs you more than you want to pay), and have it sent over to your latest scapegoat's house. Humble yourself once in a while. It does wonders for the soul, especially when you have paid for the peace-making gift out of your own pocket. Do not shudder and wriggle about so. You know very well I'm right.

Basically, you are a kind person. You deplore hurting others. But you can't tolerate any show of indifference on their part. So you strike out at them, and you often hit below the belt.

You are endowed with natural superiority. Most people recognize this in you. But woe be unto him who doesn't. Cataclysmic things sometimes occur in the Year of the Snake. Stock markets come crashing down. Wars break out. It's no surprise when you realize how much self-righteousness is in the air during those years.

Relax, lovely Snake. Take yourself and others a bit less seriously. There is no doubt the world is a disappointingly imperfect place. With a little more mental elbow grease from wise people like yourselves, it could improve. Write that book. Take those lessons. Practice. Stay with it. The rewards, because you are very good at whatever you undertake, cannot help but come back a thousandfold.

COMPATIBILITIES

Affairs of the Heart

Snake love partners have a preference for arrangements wherein the object of their affections grants his or her exclusivity to his beloved. What belongs to Snakes is very much theirs and theirs alone. Any deviation from the straight and narrow on the part of a person involved with a Snake may cause some very unappealing jealous reactions.

Mind you, Snakes themselves are not noted for their undying devotion and permanent fidelity to mates. But let's just say they like it better if they can always come home to the same faithful spouse or lover. Loyalty in love is not a Snake forte. To avoid emotional ruin, Snakes must make every effort to resist the temptation to flirt. Two can always play that dangerous game called love.

Now, in the case of the Snake who is enamored of an Ox person, the problem of infidelity rarely arises. For a start, Oxen are rigorously capable of maintaining their helpmate's interest in the conjugal rites. And, secondly, because the Ox is basically home-loving and less passionate than sensible, he will be able to find sufficient emotional outlet with children and domesticity to forestall any woes he may feel about the Snake's slitherings out at night. Too, the Snake really does not mind conceding the role of boss in the house. The Ox can rule unhindered.

Snakes and Roosters are well-matched. Though they bicker, this couple always muddles through. The first few years may be stormy but in the long run, Snakes and Roosters learn from their disputes and the storm abates. If they do not iron out their differences, the Rooster is capable of turning on the Snake just for spite.

Dragons are a fine choice for Snake subjects. The Dragon is the only partner who can be certain to keep the Snake interested forever. There is much admiration and mutual understanding between these two people. And the Dragon is a fascinating fellow.

The Snake will be allowed his cherished freedom of movement by both the Dog and the Pig. But their motives may be decidedly different. Whereas the devoted Dog will lie by the fire and wait for his mate to come home, the exasperated Pig partner may be trying to give the Snake enough rope to hang himself. Pigs do not mind being toyed with, but they do not enjoy strangulation.

Tigers are too much for the quiet Snake to handle. The Snake, unless he can force himself to be more open and forthright, will come to a sorrowful reckoning at the hand of the noble Tiger.

Social Affairs

Snakes are amusing and well-bred enough to attract companionship from almost any quarter. Besides, they are reputed for their beauty and fine taste. Snake conversation is often intellectual and smacks of the cultivated.

But, beyond the first chat with a Snake, not just everyone remains intrigued. There is in Snakes a certain veneer of sophistication that such rustic creatures as the Pig, the Dog, or the Ox find "snooty." Moreover, the calm decisive Snake does not always take to other people rapidly. His intuition tells him when he is not meeting the mind of his interlocutor.

Precisely that perceptivity captivates those who do become friends with Snake people. The anxious Dragon is calmed by the

Snake's philosophical attitudes. The Cat shares the Snake's interest in the arts. The Rooster is intrigued by the Snake's wisdom and earnest compassion. The Horse's rages do not outrage the composed Snake. Snakes find Horses excellent company and faithful friends.

The Monkey is not awed by the Snake and the feeling is mutual. Perhaps the Snake finds the Monkey too terrestrial and overly nervous for his placid nature. Other Snake persons are of interest to Snakes. They may keep each other at arm's length, but Snakes enjoy observing their counterparts.

Tigers and Snakes do not usually fall in love with each other, yet they can be fast friends. A mutual concern for the fate of their fellow-mer will keep many a midnight oil alive. Both Tigers and Snakes, even if they disagree, revel in a good gab session.

Business Affairs

The decisive Snake may find solitary work the most profitable. A Snake can study or write long treatises almost better than anyone else. Snakes are patient with detail, slow to react to turmoil, and almost too accommodating. These qualities make it clear that Snakes are often more successful in pursuits that require reclusive and cerebral application. Commercial ventures so often involve sales work and quick thinking on one's feet. Snakes find such goings-on hazardous to their repose.

If, however, Snakes do intend to engage in business rather than philosophical inquiry, they will do well to consider the birth years of associates. Goats, Cats, Roosters, and other Snakes will probably not fare well as co-owners and operators of commercial enterprises. Though the Snake is wise and possesses much intuition regarding speculation, there may be more talk than work when any or all of these subjects band together in a work effort.

The Monkey will be tempted to outmaneuver the sympathetic Snake. The Tiger and the Snake will never agree on where to invest or from whom to buy supplies.

Since Snake strategy is generally good, he should team up with the diligent Horse or the hard-driving Dragon. Both of these will manage to keep the Snake's energy level up. Rats and Cats are also good for Snakes in business. The Rat will lend sociability to any mutual undertaking. And the enterprising Cat will delight the Snake by agreeing with most of his intellectual schemes.

Family Affairs

The sagacious and sober Snake proves a good parent. His wisdom serves him well when dealing with children who have problems or fears. One small worry, however, is that the Snake is absent from home more than he might be and may lose track of some of the more pressing issues that occur there. Because Snakes are exclusive and jealous at times, they may assume too much guilt for their kids' mistakes and worry themselves unduly over details. In a father, this trait is not so troublesome as in a mother, who might invade her child's privacy through wanting to know too much about his inner thoughts.

Children born in Pig years may be victimized by the proprietary streak present in a Snake parent. Pigs never enjoy lying, even by omission. They will find themselves dodging indiscreet questions and wishing they did not have to.

The Goat or Cat child should be happy to find himself under the roof of a Snake mother or dad. Providing the surroundings are comfortable and refined, both Goats and Cats will be content to share them with the elegant Snake. Monkey children, too, will find their niche in the Snake's ambience of calm. The Monkey is adaptable and concerned for his own welfare. He will make concessions. And the pleasant-natured Rat will be blissful with a Snake parent to guide and listen to him.

If hitches there are (and hitches there may be), we can expect to find them in households where children are born in Tiger or Ox years. The Snake will be called upon to exercise much patience and comprehension when dealing with either of these two children.

THE HORSE

THE YEARS OF THE HORSE

January 25, 1906 to February 13, 1907*
February 11, 1918 to February 1, 1919
January 30, 1930 to February 17, 1931
February 15, 1942 to February 5, 1943
February 3, 1954 to January 24, 1955
January 21, 1966 to February 9, 1967*
February 7, 1978 to January 27, 1979
January 27, 1990 to February 14, 1991
*Fire Horse Years

HORSES ARE :

Amiable • Eloquent • Skillful • Self-possessed
Quick-witted • Athletic • Entertaining • Charming • Independent
Powerful • Hard-working • Jolly • Sentimental • Frank • Sensual

BUT THEY CAN ALSO BE:

Selfish • Weak • Hotheaded • Ruthless
Rebellious • Pragmatic • Foppish • Tactless
Impatient • Unfeeling • Predatory

189

HORSES I HAVE KNOWN AND LOVED

Horses—be they mythical winged stallions, racing models, plow pullers, gallant hurdle jumpers, studs, mares, foals, ponies, wild broncos, or plodding wagon draggers—are extremely popular animals. Likewise, people born in Horse years, no matter what their trade or talents, are amiable, pleasant, and likable creatures. In one way, like their animal counterpart, Horses symbolize achievement, success, hard work, and independence. However, when winning has eluded them once too often, the image of a Horse person bespeaks bitterness. A failed Horse is a hotheaded simperer who resents having been put out to pasture.

Knowledge of when to forge ahead, to feel when he must stay "neck and neck" and choose just the right moment to pass that finish line in a blaze of glory, is an unknown quantity with which every Horse person is born to struggle. With all his gifts and boundless energies, the Horse can never be completely sure of winning. And who really ever knows in advance where to tread, how to ingratiate himself, and upon whom to paste that compliment he has been mulling over for the past few weeks?

Throughout their lives, Horse people are instinctively aware of their innate superiority. From childhood on, they prance and gallop along as though nobody existed except themselves. When challenged to obey an order, Horses do so at their whim. If what you request seems reasonable, often the Horse will carry it out with grace and flair. If he has neither time nor respect for your idea, he simply will not do it. No excuse or explanation seems necessary. He merely does as he sees fit.

The world, for Horse people, is their oyster and theirs alone. Should you be fortunate enough to be chosen to share their lot, Horses will be generous, productive, and affectionate within the boundaries placed on the situation at hand. Those limits are rarely of your design. The Horse creates the environment in which he circulates. Either you adhere to his conditions, or you get out. Nothing could be simpler.

Nothing, that is, except to tell him to get lost, threaten to move his things out of the house, and be so kind as to pack them for him. Horses cannot tolerate being one-upped on the home front. If chucking you into the snow is his idea, you may think he means it and prepare to leave. Don't worry, he will stop you. However, scenes like these can be side-stepped. With the aid of a little psychology, handling Horses is as easy as raising weeds in your vegetable garden.

Outmaneuvering Horses can be an amusing game. For a start, argument is useless. Horses can outdebate just about anybody but another Horse. Call it Horse-sense, if you will. Horse people have a kind of nose for guessing what your next line of attack will be. They see it coming. They sniff at it for a second, then use your words on you before you have had a chance to articulate them. If you like the feeling of having someone take the words out of your mouth, hang around with some Horses. It may cure you of that masochistic pleasure forever.

Generally speaking, the best way to tackle a recalcitrant or difficult Horse crony or colleague is that old favorite—the silent treatment. Mute presences, walls of nonspeaking, grunts of assent, and polite nods of disinterest will drive an angry Horse to distraction. You see, the Horse has a streak of the con artist in him. If he can cajole you into a position of exchange, where your ideas and words are inevitably pitted against his, the Horse is almost sure to be able to talk you into a plan or scheme.

But, if despite his prancings, pawings, flattery, and flip, you coldly ignore him and go about your business in your own manner and time, the Horse loses by default. Every step of the way, dealings with Horses require quick thinking and clever manipulation. That fact may strike you as disagreeable. It may indeed be preferable to sink into a torpor of letting him have his own way. But Horse people do not tolerate inertia. If you sit back and take it on the chin, Horses get bored and grumpy.

Always drumming up new methods of reaching whichever goal he has set for himself, the Horse seems incapable of relaxation or rest. To a Horse, vacation from work means time away from the office for scheming, building, fixing, planning, puttering, and exhausting rounds of outings. You will not find many Horse people sunning themselves placidly on beaches, unless of course there are thirty-five other people clustered round with whom he can commune, rap, chat, banter and converse. On the move from dawn until dusk, the Horse is too busy fulfilling objectives to sit through even a mildly dull movie. As long as no important people are offended, he will get up and walk out after five minutes. Even when he is at his most inactive, the Horse never idles. He can amuse himself with pieces of string or find a new way to stick bottle caps on cardboard in an attractive pattern.

Horse people are fine travelers. Even on lengthy airplane journeys, when passengers seem restive and squirm in their seats after five hours of coffee, tea, and milk, the Horse will be busily engaged in anything from a chat with his seat mate to fashioning paper models from safety-regulation folders. Although Horses adore voyaging, they are not mad about arrivals. Waiting around airports, packing and unpacking cars or valises, finding taxis, and scouring parking lots for rented cars seem but vain busywork for Horses.

The everyday job of shoveling sand from out one's life is the worst task a Horse person can be forced into. Be it cleaning his desk surface, picking up his clothes, washing dishes, or dusting table tops, the Horse will always try to find a way out of chorelike tasks. Often lucky in finance, the Horse can usually hire someone to accomplish such humdrum piddlings. But, without funds to pay domestic help, the

Horse will either leave his personal effects in a shambles or con some-body else into doing it.

Horses are dandies. The women and men alike always dress in a rather dashing manner. Workaday though it may seem to some of us, the acts of shaving or primping before mirrors never seem to discour-age a Horse from sallying forth well-groomed. This preoccupation with personal appearance is no minor consideration. Horses take their outward image very seriously. A Horse, for example, would never dream of trotting to the supermarket in a mismatched tie or unironed skirt. Nor would a Horse appear at a cocktail party in what he consid-ers proper hayride regalia. Whether he be hippie or sophisticate, the Horse cuts a figure exactly suited to the occasion.

Clifford Irving (b. 1930), now renowned as the failed Howard Hughes swindler who got his just desserts, is a Horse's Horse.

I have known Clifford for many years. His former home base was the Spanish Island of Ibiza. I have been vacationing there for some twelve years. Cliff's nickname, among island habitués, is Sheriff Deadwood Tree. It has something to do with a defunct scrubby shrub that sits as if painted on his front lawn and a bit more to do with Clifford's Horsey preoccupation with the law.

The kinds of scrapes that Clifford Irving managed to get himself into during his long sojourn as an expatriate island dweller are classic examples of how Horses sometimes view the world as though it were a giant rose garden for schemers, surrounded by a fence to keep out honest Horse people. Horses sometimes find the successes of others exasperating, especially when those same others have earned easy money doing nothing. The Horse may take one of two tacks in dealing with his envy of tycoons or gangsters who earn their fortunes riding bareback over the cadavers of the poor. Either the Horse will take up the cause against such ne'er-do-wells or else he will attempt some chi-canery of his own.

In Cliff's case, as we all know, he opted finally for the latter solu-tion. But not before he had tried out innumerable more virtuous efforts at improving his image and income around Ibiza and the world.

For years, Deadwood Tree Irving was most respected as an

author of books and accumulator of subscribed-to *Time* magazines
that everyone wanted to borrow because *Time* costs twice as much in
Spain. On his off-time, Cliff protected people from harm. He staged a
fisticuffs bar room brawl for the salvation of someone's house key. He
drew up a petition against a French film star he thought was cheating
at poker. He lent money to struggling novelists who couldn't sell their
work. He took care of strays and in general held a respected position
in the expatriate community.

But all the while something was gnawing away inside of
Clifford's Horsey soul. While others were making it big by painting
fake masterpieces and selling them to Texans, Cliff was still only an
unrecognized, underpaid writer. So he cooked up his intriguing plot to
strike it rich by authoring a biography of a man who never came out
of hiding. It seemed a dandy plan. But it didn't work.

Horse people should never attempt to get rich quick through ille-
gitimate means. If they have an idea or a project they will always have
to put their whole force behind same, exhaust themselves, and shed
gallons of sweat before achieving that goal of real wealth.

Work comes naturally to the Horse. Just as in the case of
Clifford Irving, now that he is out of prison and back on the job, he is
once again writing and striving in the proper Horse fashion. Enticed
by the prospect of an easy buck, Cliff (like many a Horse I have
known) went all megalomaniac and began building castles in the air.
He convinced himself that his design would work, but Horses should
take heed of his experience. Never underestimate the powers of international gangbusters, espcially if you are an honest Horse.

Though I have given much space herein to the foibles and pitfalls
of the Horse, I feel duty-bound to remind you that Horse people are neither evil, nor small-minded, nor ungenerous. Horses are the most hospi-
tality-conscious people in the entire Chinese zodiac. They thrive on
social events, concerts, openings, theater dates, small or large dinner
parties, and group functions of all types. As host, hostess, or guest, you
can be certain any Horse will be a jolly addition to a social function.

Horses not only enjoy entertaining, they very often like to cook.
Deeply involved in the preparation of a fifty-ingredient fruitcake, my

Horse chum Shiela Reventlow (the woman whose Rat husband gives all those exotic parties) said to me the other day, "When I'm busy with my cooking, the whole world could tumble down around me. I am oblivious to anyone or anything."

That's a standard Horse remark. Oblivion through perpetual motion is the Horse's key to mental health. Horses keep busy. They fix things, make their own Christmas cards, knit sweaters for their loved ones, design extravagantly complex bathrooms, appliqué tablecloths, shorten the sleeves of their shirts, build elegant wooden trees for their cats to climb on, and make intricate patchwork upholstery for an old retired couch. Equally gifted with their hands as with their agile tongues and spirits, Horses are more intellectually skillful than academic.

Because Horses are so dextrous in thought, word, and deed, they can succeed at any métier that involves politics. The public at large gives them no cause for trepidation. You may find them in every field, almost always good at what they do and ever ready to begin untried projects. It is perhaps because of this firm self-belief and grip on their egos that we notice so many Horses among famous people. To say there are "many" celebrities among Horses is a glaring understatement. Beginning way back in 1894 with the births of Jack Benny, the Duke of Windsor, and poet e.e. cummings, the list is long and rich with both fame and fortune.

The year 1906 was a Fire Horse Year. This phenomenon will be discussed later in more detail. Suffice it to say that every sixty years constitutes a type of Chinese century. And this particular Fire Horse Year, 1906, produced New York City's Mayor Abraham Beame, Samuel Beckett, and Adolf Eichmann.

In 1918, Spiro Agnew was brought into the world, as were Pearl Bailey, Rita Hayworth, conductor/composer Leonard Bernstein, and writer Alexander Solzhenitsyn. Then 1930 brought us Anthony Armstrong-Jones, jazz musician Ornette Coleman, writers Jimmy Breslin, John Barth, and Clifford Irving. It was a good year for Horses with special aptitudes. Astronauts Buzz Aldrin, Neil Armstrong, and Charles Conrad also joined us in 1930.

The year 1942 was, for some mystical reason, either an extremely lucky or a disaster-tainted year for its subjects. Among the more fortunate members of this team of Horses figure actresses Karen Black and Madeleine Kahn, novelist/poet Erica Jong, and three of the top singer/songwriters of today, Paul Simon, Harry Nilsson, and Beatle Paul McCartney. Those people born in 1942 who never made it much past their own roaring twenties were singers Jim Croce, Janis Joplin, and Jimi Hendrix. Untimely death also came to actress Sharon Tate, who was a 1942 Horse. Even more enigmatic than the fact that they died young is the reality that all of these people were born between December of 1942 and February of 1943. I have no data to suggest that those two birth months were particularly ill-fated, but would be intrigued by any communication from readers regarding others who were born during this time. We may shed some light on the tragedies.

In a happier vein, 1954 sent us tennis player Chris Evert. In one less pleasant, Patty Hearst also arrived in 1954. The year 1966 was again a Fire Horse Year. Surely, there are many of you who had children in 1966. Whichever way they choose to assert their talents, you are hereby advised that your Fire Horse children will be exceptional.

There is something of the noble in Horse people. No matter whence they spring, proud Horses retain the attentions of audiences. They inspire confidence and earn respect in the community. Practical in the extreme and capable of extraordinary leaps at adventure, Horses constantly surprise the members of their entourages.

Horses are anything but freaky. They rarely appear out of line in wardrobe, hairstyle, or other vestmental accessories. Ostentation in dress does not fulfill their need for popular acceptance. Horses prefer not be offend anyone by wearing embroidered flowing djellabahs, shaving their heads, or creating wild make-ups that might rub others the wrong way. Clothes-Horses they are, but if you look hard, you will always find that added touch of status quo.

Due to their desire and drive to communicate with others, Horse subjects sometimes tend toward telephonomania. Two Horse men friends I have, one in Paris and one in New York, must donate enough money yearly to the intercontinental phone systems to pay all their employee health benefits for eternity. In Paris, my chum John

Larimore (b. 1930) makes phone calls the way other folks abuse the family bathroom. Trying to get through to John by telephone is like attempting to rouse a tenacious bathtub sitter from a tubful of bubbles and books. What's more, not only is reaching John by telephone a test of patience of Sisyphean stature, this Horse also calls me at least twice (if not ten times) to be sure he has the hour of a dinner engagement correct, to ask if my watch shows the exact same time as his; to wonder, "Are you washing your hair?" or "Are you too busy to talk?"

To tease a Horse about his "Phonia" doesn't seem to discourage his zeal. With John, who is a close pal, I have tried almost everything from insults to leaving my receiver off its hook. When I once committed the latter crime against the communications industry, John nagged the entire operational staff of the Paris office for hours trying to make them ring my number. What he didn't know was that not only had I removed my speaking device from its cradle, but I had also yanked a tiny fuse from the connection box on the wall. No sound could have emanated from my telephone no matter how it tried. So John blitz-phoned all of my neighbors until one of them agreed to come to my house and fetch me.

Calls relayed through third parties always scare me. I thought one of the children had broken a leg at school. Expecting the principal's voice when I picked up my neighbor's apparatus, I politely said, "*Allo, oui.*" To the urgent tone of John's "Are you okay?" I replied, "I'm busy writing a book! G'bye!" and hung up. My non-English-speaking neighbor must have though I had gone mad. I thanked her for her time and vacated the premises without explanation.

The second of the marauding callers is another 1930 Horse. Writer Jimmy Breslin rings certain victims every day and sometimes both day and night. When I first had the misfortune of answering the telephone of one of the people on Breslin's permanent call list, I almost slammed the phone back down. As a houseguest, I had not been warned of the imminent danger under which the nervous system lives when the host's number has come up and he or she is absent from the apartment.

Breslin's calls are worth reporting in detail.

The phone rings. Gently, quietly, no reason to suspect this call will be different from all other calls, I pick it up and politely say, "Hello."

A strident boom cracks at me, "Where's Don Forst?"

At first, I am so rattled by the request I forget the name of the person whose phone I answered. "Don who?" I wonder courteously.

"Forst! Where is he?" More boom and stride.

"Who's calling, please?" My request for information is lilting feminine charin itself. I think perhaps this caller suspects me of being an idiot child or burgling intruder. I am trying to reassure him.

"Breslin!" Jimmy explodes in my eardrum. "Where's Forst?"

Now to me, part-time New Yorker in the extreme, Breslin could have been the piano tuner or even the caller's first name. I had no reason to think James Breslin, the famous best-selling author, would be calling my friend's home. So I asked, "Breslin who?"

"Jimmy Breslin! Where's Forst?" The tone was persnickety.

"Ooooh. *That* Breslin." Fearing I would lose the rhythm of my cheery charm, I quickly added, "I'm sorry, sir, but Mr. Forst isn't here right now. May I take a message?"

"Where is he?" came the terse reply. This time I obliged. "He left for the office some fifteen minutes ago. He ought to be—"

"Then he's on the train!" was Breslin's final word. He hung up.

Eventually I called my friend's office to warn his secretary that a man named Jimmy Breslin might call her in the very near future and scare her half to death. But first I just sat in front of the antique secretary that bears the phone in the Forst household and shook for about five minutes. I felt as though I had just hung up from talking to the CIA, the FBI, the state and storm troopers, all neatly molded into one harsh gent.

At dinner that evening, I recounted the experience in detail. My host who has known and loved Breslin for years, ranks about fourth on the Breslin phonomania list. After recovering from a hearty laugh over my story, Mr. Forst told me, "Listen, Suzanne. You couldn't have been expected to know, but you went about Breslin all wrong. Jimmy is a kind-hearted man. He doesn't mean to be gruff with people. It's just his manner. Underneath that brusque bark, he is really quite gentle."

"Well, you couldn't prove anything about his gentility by me," I said. "He tried to bully me. And he succeeded. I was petrified."

My host gave me a tip on his Horse friend. "If you met Jimmy, you'd see that he isn't really ill-mannered at all. He just doesn't know you yet. Once he does, he'll be a bit more friendly."

Next day, the same challenge presented itself. But I had meanwhile looked up Breslin's Chinese sign. The worst thing to do in Horse crises is reason with the beasts. Second-guessing them is useless. One must either ignore them altogether or blast them right back with their own brand of hoof and mouth.

Phone rings. I answer, "Hello."

Right on cue, "Where's Forst?" It was "Bully" Breslin all right. I blammed him one good. "Who is this? Whaddayou want?"

"And who is this, may I ask?" came a somewhat less surly question.

"My name is Suzanne. Is this Breslin?"

"Yes. This is Jimmy Breslin. Do you know where Don Forst is?" Breslin was polite. Not sweet or gentle. But at least courteous.

"He's on the train!" I said and hung up.

That time I only shook for about three minutes. It is not customary for me to behave like a menopausal Catherine the Great when I speak over the telephone. But it was my only defense. And it worked.

These days, I can laugh with Breslin about those terrible early days. My friend was right. Jimmy Breslin is a very gentle and kind person. Being a gifted Horse, he is also very bright and skillful and eminently pragmatic. But he does have phonomania. If the phone ever rings at three in the morning and a double-barreled bazooka on the other end coldly demands the whereabouts of someone you know, could be you are not in contact with the NKVD or Interpol, it might just be a skittish colt disguised as the Big Bad Wolf.

Horse-laughs are not really attributable to people born under the sign of the Horse. Dragons and Tigers and Rats might be guilty of guffawing great gusts of laughter, but not Horses. They are either too discreet or too sensitive to criticism for such undecorous transgressions to pass their lips. Someone once told me that her mother used to say of her Horse father, "Herbert is the kind of person who goes down to the basement to laugh." Amused Horses either titter politely with their hands clasped over their mouths or else settle for flashing a knowing smile.

In fame or infamy, Horses are usually caricatures of themselves. They are well-meaning, agreeable, industrious, and content inside their own skins. All the abilities that Horses possess are applicable to life. They work things through on their own. Horses don't really enjoy asking other people for help or leaning on anyone's shoulder to cry. From time to time, when they are reminded that assistance from outsiders is imperative, people born in Horse years are hard put to accept that fact. When they do engage you as their assistant, co-worker, or helpmate, do not be alarmed when you find out that whatever your official capacity, the Horse has agreed to your presence only as a necessary evil. In all cases, Horses prefer to handle everything their way. You must either learn how to take orders gracefully or abandon the assignment as quickly as you can. The Horse is a missionary unto himself. No matter who helps him earn that victory, our Man O' War wants top billing in the winner headline.

THE FIRE HORSE

This unusual cyclical phenomenon occurs only once every sixty years. Any Fire Horses you find in your acquaintance will either already have made their mark, or surely will have begun to exhibit their various talents in astonishing ways.

The person born under the influence of this thirteenth sign of the Chinese cycle of twelve animal symbols will bear basic Horse characteristics. But, endowed with superior wisdom, he will put them to use in unique ways. Interestingly, Oriental popular belief has it that in the event of a Fire Horse birth, the parent family will suffer division or at least excessive strife following the birth of this child.

Because Fire Horse people are exactly like ordinary Horses—only more so—they are sure to face lives full of controversy and hard work. If regular Horses are self-centered, these rare subjects are egomaniacal. Should, for some reason, the sun not choose to shine upon his esteemed person for a daring moment, the Fire Horse will win back its favors in multifarious and surprising ways. He knows how to turn the misfortunes of others to his own advantage, and does not hesitate to practice the art of persuasion through confidence.

Cunningly, with a well-placed compliment, pithy remark, or pleasant smile, the Fire Horse can subtly trample an unwitting adversary into the turf. Proud and headstrong, the Fire Horse is anything but a loser. And, because he is so intrinsically powerful, the Fire Horse will probably consider himself indomitable.

Herein lies the danger of exaggerated egocentricity. Whereas his career may pose little or no problem, love can send the Fire Horse round the bend. When this rarified beast falls in love, his innate guard automatically descends. Affairs of the heart place his self-assurance in a dangerously vulnerable position. Underneath the almost supernatural temerity of the Fire Horse hides a gooey soft center made of sugar and spice and everything nice.

In love, as in all other facets of his life, the Fire Horse charges ahead valiantly, shrugging off self-doubt as though it had never existed. Rejection or rebuff never even enters his haughty head. Of course, we all know that the bigger they are, the harder they fall. The cry of a wounded Fire Horse lover will pierce the air with questions: "Why, oh, why doesn't so-and-so love me? How could he let me down? I would do anything to have her back."

Well, perhaps not just anything, fair Fire Horse. It is not always a good idea to allow yourself to carry a torch for a cruel and indifferent master. There are other races to be run, lots of fish in the sea, and more worthy people out there who can return your affections in a manner worthy of your unflinching devotion.

Within the shank of this hell-bent creature exist myriad magical gifts. There is nothing he cannot do well. Capable of much concentrated effort, the Fire Horse directs his energies exclusively at those goals that he passionately desires to achieve.

Even if it is true that the appearance of a Fire Horse on a family scene is not fortuitous and the blessing of his birth must inevitably be mitigated by some household rift, there are compensations. Though his presence may disturb parental peace of mind, the Fire Horse invariably replaces this loss with a monumental contribution to his environment. His public life can be expected to reward a proud parent and heal any wounds his unintentional intrusion on the planet may cause.

The Fire Horse is a scarce and wondrous benediction indeed.

MADAME HORSE

Horse women are less lucky in love than in other domains. Strong, willful, selfish, and practical to a fault, women born under the sign of the Horse can expect to succeed at business, technical, or artistic endeavors. They are talented in areas that require application of design and calculation. Horse ladies both enjoy and excel at careers or pursuits that allow them room to plan.

Since love and its related subjects can scarcely be expected to follow rigorous patterns or respond to sets of Horse-drawn rules, these women often find themselves short of breath and patience when dealing with unknown quantities incumbent upon amorous delight. Horses are stubborn and like to have their own way. Successful love relationships are by definition nothing more than series of compromises. Horse women resist going Dutch in alliances where the only regard for their concession is affection or tenderness.

The one happily married Horse woman I know is a friend I have mentioned before, Shiela Reventlow (b. 1942) of New York City, Paris, London, and wherever else she follows her own and her Rat husband's relentlessly restless footsteps. Shiela, before she became the contented wife of her busy husband, was that very same spouse's uncompromising and confused wife. As she tells it, "I was trying to make Richard my mission in life. All I thought about for the first two years of our marriage was whether or not Richard was comfortable, happy, still in love with me, and sufficiently pleased with the way I behaved. Neither of us was comfortable with that arrangement. But I didn't know it at the time. I was driving Richard away from me. I insisted that he lovingly accept my constant hoverings and attentions. Even while he was at work, I would call him three and four times a day. I used to beg him to come home for lunch so he would get enough vitamins. I wasn't a wife. I was a pest."

Laughingly, I pressed Shiela for the recipe she had used to change the flavor of their conjugal bliss. She was very open about it. "We went to a marriage counselor. At first, I didn't want to go. I thought, my marriage was perfect. All I ever talked about was 'Us,' what we were going to do, where we would travel, how many kids we would have. It's true, Suzanne, I had turned my marriage into a planned mission. And a very selfish mission it was. Richard finally convinced me that I was an unhappy mother hen."

"How did he do that?" I was interested to know.

"He said he was going to leave me," smiled Shiela pertly. "That made me sit up and take notice. The counselor had to make me understand why."

Horse people are capable of great frankness. They usually have a lot of Horse sense. Shiela is no exception to the rule. Once she had conquered her unwillingness to seek help, she was not so foolish as to turn a deaf ear to advice. What she found out from the gentleman who served as her mentor was what she might have eventually figured out for herself—too late. All the talents she was born with had driven her to strive for success in everything she did. In school, sports, and art, play production, and eventually in her premarriage career as a fabric designer, Shiela wanted to be the best. And she usually was.

When marriage came along, Shiela did not see the bond she had committed herself to as merely a state in which she would live for the rest of her life while engaged in other enterprises. Marriage (her marriage) for Shiela Reventlow, was it. She confronted each connubial day as though she had been elected to lead a nation into prosperity. Richard was her prime minister. She expected him to cooperate with a master plan to create the perfect marriage. All Richard wanted to do was resign his ministerial function. He could not bear his wife's cloying possessiveness and enforced complicity. He would have liked it if Shiela had kept her job, but since they didn't really need the extra income, Richard felt that asking her to work would be unfair. He suggested she have her own friends or maybe do some part-time design work from home, but Shiela wanted none of that. She needed no one or nothing more than Richard.

Once the counselor explained all of this to Shiela, she came to realize that she had misunderstood what marriage was supposed to mean. For her, a project had always been just that, something into which you throw your energies full tilt and gallop toward a successful end. As time went by, she accepted luncheon dates with some of the girls, and found that none of those ladies were inhibited from having interests outside their homes. One girl was a painter, another gave dancing lessons, still a third ran a decorating business. As she loved to cook, Shiela finally approached her husband for a loan to start a small cooking service for bachelors who wanted to give dinner parties but had neither time nor inclination for food preparation. Today she's off and running one of the most successful catering companies in the city of New York.

What Shiela Reventlow's story shows is that Horse stubbornness and drive in women, though essential in almost any professional undertaking, can be disastrous to a love affair or marriage. Love cannot be planned. It doesn't comply with norms or averages. The ingredients are not calculable by grams and tablespoonfuls. The oven temperatures and cooking times are not found in books full of recipes. Timing love is not like timing a breakfast egg. There is no formula but good will and experience. This can be learned, but Horses are not always able to grasp subtleties.

If Patty Hearst had been anything but a Horse, she might not have plunged headfirst into disaster by choosing terrorism as her personal mission. I pity the poor attorney elected to talk her out of it. You can lead a Horse to court but you can't always make her think.

MONSIEUR HORSE

Selfishness and lack of whimsy are the two highest hurdles a male Horse has to confront when trying to avoid personal disaster in love. All Horse people are in a perpetual inner quibble over practicality versus what they fear might be only trivial dalliance or futile fun. Horse men resist the sorcery of love almost as much as they need it.

Profoundly pragmatic and hard-working, the Horse man who is uncertain of his footing in sentimental situations can stumble and become unable to effectively pursue the multiple schemes he devises to keep himself occupied. Most times, he is not willing to take romantic risks. Love affairs and other emotional hanky-panky are rarely long-lasting and secure. The Horse man wants none of those suffering part-time sweet-hearts who phone him in the middle of business conferences to snivel their woes into a telephone. What he usually seeks in marriage is an able wife who can champion his cause, bear his children, cook his meals, see that his pants are pressed, and share his bed in the bargain.

Horse men are supremely self-oriented and egotistical. Though they can share parts of their lives with the women they choose, they are rarely capable of participating in any form of fifty-fifty apportionment of roles. Horse men really believe they can do anything. And they can. But they know that if they wish to reach the summits of careers, their home time will be limited. So they choose wives the way generals choose lieutenants. It prevents the rapport from becoming competitive. The chain of command is established from the beginning.

I used to know a Paris Horse whose wife was totally incompetent at anything but listening to him and repeating his opinions in dinner parties. His name was Allan and his wife was called Jill.

For a start, Jill did not invent gunpowder. But she was sweet, good-natured, and a pretty addition to Allan's household. Though she never said much beyond echoing his thoughts, Jill kept a tidy and well-swept home. Allan, like Peter the Pumpkin-eater, had put Jill in a shell and there he intended to stash her forever.

Unfortunately for Allan the Horse, Jill grew up one day at about the age of twenty-five and said, "This jack-o-lantern is too confining, I'm going out into the world to seek my own fortune." Jill became a highly paid model for the House of Lanvin and was never heard from again.

Chagrined, Allan could not understand why Jill had left him. He used a lot of those "after all I've done for her" lines we have so often heard. I tried to explain. I told friend Allan that Jill was more than just a wife. She was a person. She needed some other stimulation besides his permanent gift of gab.

My words were no consolation to the jilted Horse. He went right out and found himself a replica of Jill. She was eighteen, beautiful, and dutiful. Three years later she ran away with the family doctor. She chose the only other man she had seen since her marriage to Allan and all our Horse could say was, "I never should have let him in the house."

Horses wish no interruptions would ever come snooping around their private lives. They are possessive and good-hearted toward their wives and children. But Horse men do like to have sway over their subjects. They work long and hard to provide amply for their families. In return, they demand utter fidelity and devotion.

The cruel truth is that Horse men sometimes wish they did not have to toil and struggle so much. Some of them dream of retiring at an early age and loafing about in some Mediterranean spa. But, much as they may aspire to a life of languor under a banana tree on a tropical isle, when you think about it, wouldn't a dapple gray look silly in a bathing suit?

CO-SIGNS

HORSE/Aries *(March 21—April 20)*

This is a double fire sign. No cooling element is present to calm the raging Horse temper. Angers will be febrile and frequent. A mass of projects and plans will surge from out this person's volcanic mind. Sentimental? Not for a nickel—but perhaps for two nickels. Aries Horses, when not enraged at the world, have a clear view of it. They can accomplish most any given task with efficiency and hustle. But Horses born in the sign of Aries are impatient. Rather than slog through a reluctant situation, they will drop it and start afresh somewhere else. When events turn in their favor, Aries Horses are jolly and full of fun. Yet, rather than blame themselves for mistakes, these

Horses rant on about how mistreated they have been. When this happens, your only recourse is a form-fitting nosebag.

HORSE/Taurus *(April 21—May 21)*

This Horse, though driven by fire, is deprived of some of his selfishness by a deep love of nature. Earth rules Taurus, a providential occurrence for the fiery Horse. The Taurean Horse will pull his equal share of any load with more grace than his counterparts born under less terrestrial signs. He will be materialistic, rather than intellectual, better with his hands than with his head. Wily, but not academic, the Horse/Taurus is longer on ego surrender than most. He is not absolutely sure if his facts are correct, so he gives in more readily than other Horses. You can bet on him to win. He's a plodder.

HORSE/Gemini *(May 22—June 21)*

Whip yourself up a bonfire and watch it dance and change shape in the night wind. Now you have seen what Gemini's air can do to the fire of Horse people. Ingenuity, even genius, reside within this multifarious creature. Gemini Horses crop up in the strangest places. Movies, the theater, music, art, politics, and other public careers attract their expansive natures. One small problem is that Horses born in the sign of the twins are periodically unsure what they really want to do with their lives. A Horse without personal mission is like a man without a country. Vacillation, mutability, indecision, and flightiness may beat this Horse to his own finish line. He rarely completes what he undertakes. And, if he does take a project to its end, he will be slow in getting down to the next one. Bored easily when not stimulated by success, the scatty Gemini Horse may be busily engaged in putting himself out to pasture before his time.

HORSE/Cancer *(June 22—July 23)*

Cancer's water does not extinguish the fire of Horse people. It controls it. The temper is softened, the ego trimmed to a manageable size. Because he feels confined, the Horse/Cancer will bog down easily. He is sensitive, moody, and more inward than his cohorts.

Good providers and sensuous lovers, Cancer Horses need the trappings of a solid home base. Material wealth and power attract them. They can apply their lives to a single project or career. With the proper amount of loving support from mate or friends, this Horse will go far. Not a circus Horse, nor a racing model, the Cancerian Horse is a clever puller of plows. He designs even rows and knows how to wait for the crop to grow before ego-satisfying harvests can be brought in.

HORSE/Leo *(July 24—August 23)*

Leos are ruled by fire. So are Horses. Leos are noble of stature. So are Horse people. Leos adore being applauded, respected, and revered. Horses enjoy the same pleasures. This Horse person will be a monster of egoism and a sure winner of any race he sets his fancy footwork to. Living with a Horse/Leo is a job for a broncobuster. If, by some chance, this Horse does not succeed in life, the blow to his pride will be too much for him to bear. Anger will ensue, then bitterness and self-pity. He will leave the paddock at a young age and gallop away to conquer the world. Don't try to stop him. Failure to achieve his goal could lead to mental breakdown. His ego is almost twice the size of his Horse sense.

HORSE/Virgo *(August 24—September 23)*

Nice Horsey, pretty Horsey. Virgo's pure mineral nature will do much to refine the Horse's febrility into solid energy. Virgo Horses are workers. They strive harder than any other people to achieve goals, as well as arrive at the summit of careers in the proper way. Virgos like to do things right. They will scarcely ever be tempted by chicanery or sham. Horses born in Virgo figure that if a job cannot be done efficiently, it should not be attempted in the first place. Sunny of disposition, sensual and bright, one problem does exist for the Virgo Horse. He is so attractive, so gifted and spirited that be may unwittingly seduce members of the opposite sex. Horsing around is to be expected. Curry him lovingly and take his shoes to the blacksmith for repair. Unshod Horses don't run away from home.

HORSE/Libra *(September 24—October 23)*

Here we see air and fire merge to create a mild chaos. Unlike the flighty Gemini, Libra's fresh air breathes eloquence to the tongue of this Horse. Libran Horses are harmony seekers. Injustice and wrong-doing are evils to be dealt with through fair exposition of facts and figures. Nobody is more talented for balancing right against wrong than the Horse born in Libra. He is a compulsive talker, an amusing entertainer, and a clever performer of myriad magics. In argument, though he will have strong opinions, he can see both sides. Because of this ability the Libran Horse can easily adapt to new situations, roles, and responsibilities. His indulgence of interlocutors is deceiving. He is a good listener. But don't think you have convinced or swayed him. The Libran Horse knows precisely what he is about. And he is usually about himself.

HORSE/Scorpio *(October 24—November 22)*

The Scorpio stands by, ready to chuck a pail of sensible water on the Horse's fire if it decides to rage out of control. This match is a solid one. Gibraltar never had it so good. Though you may perceive what you think are chinks in the armor of this fighter Horse, for him they are mere scratches. Oh, he can wax skittish and play the victim if he must, but don't be fooled. The Scorpio Horse knows exactly what he is doing. Sexuality counts, money mounts, and comfort abounds for the Scorpio Horse. Even a minor deviation from his path to victory will be well-calculated to insert itself discreetly into his plan of action. Unlike other horses, who can be toyed with and tamed by psychological connivance, the Scorpio Horse has no time for anything so impractical as untarnished virtue. If the right flank doesn't get them, then the left one will. And no shilly-shallying now! Hup! Two three four, ad infinitum.

HORSE/Sagittarian *(November 23—December 21)*

Volatile and idealistic, this noisy combination of fire signs will clang away hammer and tongs at whatever he chooses to conquer. Straightforward, honor-bound, and deeply motivated by the search for a mission, the Sagittarian Horse will either vanquish his enemies or die trying. Will and skill match forces herein to assist this Horse to triumphant photo finish. Once he has made up his mind to something, you can be certain the job will get done. The din may be deafening. Sagittarian Horses are wont to move heaven and earth aside in order to hitch their wagons to a star. These Horse people are loving and willing. Who could ask for anything more? A little less noise, perhaps?

HORSE/Capricorn *(December 22—January 20)*

So exceptional are the endowments of the Horse born under the sign of Capricorn, so sticklingly responsible to his mission is he, that life presents him with innumerable obstacles to success. The world will not likely stand in his way. But this Horse's emotions are like brittle pinions that break before they can mesh with those of a lover. Affection and tenderness may escape this Horse person altogether. He makes all the right motions. Why doesn't anyone take his rigor seriously? A weighty and mostly insoluble problem. Capricorn Horses resist learning new tricks in order to make love work for them. To the Horse born in this sign, a plan is a plan is a plan. He cannot understand deviation from order. He is confused by those who take advantage of his morality. Much of his romance will be hidden under a stern manner. I prescribe tickling, rolls in new-mown hay, and strokings with a fine-tooth comb.

HORSE/Aquarius *(January 21—February 19)*

Fire meets air in a flurry of mental communion. This Horse has inborn ability to outrun his competition. For a start, he sees beyond the moment in which he lives. He could find the finish line in his sleep. Trouble is, sometimes he tries to do just that. With all his gifts, the Aquarian Horse may be so preoccupied with promises of victory, he will neglect to saddle himself securely or even forget where the race is being held. He is mercurial and scatty, brilliant yet absent-minded. For this Horse, nothing matters but the end. He feels the means will take care of themselves. Emotionally, he thinks he needs no one but himself in order to walk away with the blue ribbon. Every Horse needs a jockey. He might do well to keep that minor detail written on a piece of paper inside his vest pocket. Better still, if you like this Horse, brand him with his name, address, and phone number. Somebody will lead him home.

HORSE/Pisces *(February 20—March 20)*

"If wishes were horses, beggars would ride," my Irish mother used to tell me. Some nice person ought to send all the Pisces Horses in the world a note to that effect. The fish's water quenches almost every flicker that the Horse brings to this alliance. Horses do like to scheme and plan. They spend large portions of their time inventing projects and plotting strategies. Pisces are the adaptable dreamers of this world. Together the Horse and his Pisces nature may spend a squalid life brewing up pain-killing elixirs or searching for fountains of youth. Easily influenced by almost any outside force, the Horse born in Pisces will go cantering blithely through life, so imbued with his own delusions of grandeur that he will not notice the Big Bad Wolf is hot on his tail. "Hello there, Mr. Horse. How about a little trot into the forest?" says the wolf. Off they go into the sunset, the Pisces Horse plunging through underbrush and hurdling scrub. When he gets home that night, the Pisces Horse may notice the bramble wounds, but he will have forgotten the stinging blows of the wolf's riding crop. He's too nice, you see, to ever regret any unseemliness. He prefers not to think about it. Maybe it will go away.

PRESCRIPTION FOR THE FUTURE

Hardy Horse, there, there now. Don't begin this exchange by trying to upstage me. I'm the soothsayer, remember? Yes, yes, I hear you. Of course, you know everything I am about to say. That's precisely what I wanted to discuss with you.

How is it, Horse human, that you persist in feeling your oats even when the chips are so demonstrably down? We do, of course, admire you. How could we dare not? That grandiloquent manner, that shiny, shiny coat and those amusing comments never cease to amaze and dazzle any and all of us who know you. When you think about it, don't you just want to hug yourself all over and whinny "Dixie"?

Well, I should think so! It is not just everybody who has the luck to be born in a Horse year. No runts of the litter here. Just pure-bred quality studs and mares, *n'est-ce pas*? Moreover, we can be sure that if you do not fall victim to some kind of parental infanticide, you will probably grow up strong and healthy as a Horse. And, even though it is your lot to put in long working hours and fall asleep on your feet, that seems a small price to pay for the winning ticket that is your birthright.

Feeling any better now? Is your ego sufficiently at ease for me to say what I ultimately must about how you might better use those multitudes of qualities with which you ambled into this greener pasture? Just for safekeeping, I will add a dollop of sweet whipped cream in the form of your most favorite compliment of all: Horse, you are a good-looker, a veritable showpiece of dapper and dash.

All right. No more horsing around. I'm about to take the plunge. Ready? Set? You are a selfish person. But we love you. You are egotistical. Yet, we honor you. You think the world was created for you alone. And we indulge you. Why all of this bittersweet homage? Well, you see, Horsie, if your best friends won't tell you, who will?

Your very appearance obliges us to spend some time idolizing you. There is no doubt your noble sign gives you automatic sway over the rest of us peons. You are eminently more talented than most. But you know it almost better than you should. There are a few things you might learn about getting along with intimates, pulling your weight (and no more) in a group effort, and allowing the spotlight to veer slightly toward someone equally worthy from time to time. We need you. You are our worker, our pet, our entertainer, our vehicle of competitive sport, our transport, and our Black Beauty. With all of those references, you ought to be the most employable person alive. And you are. There is nothing you cannot do.

The main rub in your character, however, is that streak of practicality in win-or-lose situations. I have noticed when a dicey or ambivalent crisis arises, you turn tail and make for the hills. For yourself, you are a fighter, a scrapper with perilous enemies, and a doer of monumental deeds. Over and over again, you run neck and neck with competitors for days, months, and years. You can lick illness, taxes, wolves at your door, and the devil himself, and do it with one leg broken and the other tied around your neck.

You are not ungenerous, you are simply crisis-shy. Despite your air of self-assuredness, you lack confidence. Anyone who has been close to you knows that. And you would prefer that they didn't. You hate to be told such truths. You like to believe that we are sold on the hail-fellow, well-met portrait you present to the world. But some of us have witnessed those moments of puerile purple rage that you can come up with. Those *sturim* and *drang* routines that you wish did not happen so frequently are our proof that beneath your silky mane are gears that don't always settle for turning obediently round and round. Sometimes they get off the track and you fly into a passionate fury of self-righteousness.

You must guard against losing all the Brownie points you so cleverly earn in good times. Those fits of temper can remove high marks for good behavior faster than you can run to make them up. People who see you in weaker moments may become suspicious of your ability to control yourself under stress. Go easy on the anger. You might hurt somebody, mainly yourself.

Finally, Horse, you should steer clear of shady deals. No matter how easy the money looks, it can never be yours for the asking. You have to work. You are a born striver. Don't be tempted by that tasty-looking carrot of ill-gotten gain. Keep those blinders on. Straight ahead is your goal. Wild horses should not be allowed to lure you from the path of your hot, yet chaste pursuit of the blue ribbon of happiness.

COMPATIBILITIES

Affairs of the Heart

The independent Horse is a possessive and sensual lover. Working assiduously at making his amorous alliance perfect is an integral part of the Horse's existence. Any hint of discord, threat of a sour note, or whiff of foul play can throw the nirvana-seeking Horse into a major tizzy of self-doubt. Horses are proud and powerful creatures who cannot only fall soundly in love with other people, but are also capable of going to pieces over love itself.

Horses who allow their driving ambition to take precedence over everything are usually safe from their own tendency to shatter or be shattered by a shaky love affair. For this self-drive to take over successfully and protect the Horse from emotional harm, the best-advised Horse would pick his mate from among Goats, Tigers, and Dogs. In the first case, Goat folks will be able to devote themselves to their artistry and dreaming while the Horse trots out into the world to seek their communal fortunes. Goat caprice does not offend the dignified Horse. He sees Goat peregrinations into the nether regions of the mind as endearing departures from otherwise ordinary planetary considerations. Goats amuse their Horse partners.

Tigers are those noble revolutionaries who think beyond the mundane vicissitudes of today and will fight for the rights of others. Horses respect Tigers. Since the Horse can give up everything for passion, he is well served in this area by the exciting Tiger. A Horse who loves a Tiger will keep himself busy during long periods of Tiger absence from home. When finally his tawny love reappears on the scene, the Horse will indulge the Tiger in torrid bouts of love-making and willingly stay up all night with his mate discussing new strategies for the Tiger's next foray into the public eye.

Like the Tiger, the Dog has an affinity for great causes. The difference here is that the Dog will obediently take up the mission of his Horse partner and aid him enormously in pursuing ambitious plans. In this relationship, the Horse will shoulder the eloquence, assisted by the acerbic-tempered Dog, who can spice the Horse's speeches with cynicism and wit.

Roosters will attract Horse people, too. The Rooster, with all his surface vivacity and curiosity about the unknown, piques the Horse's sense of adventure. The Horse will enjoy sporting a well-attired Rooster mate at social events. Their enthusiastic conversations may inspire the sometimes world-weary Horse. Over the long run, however, the Rooster's frank opinions may seem less edifying to the tired Horse, especially when familiarity begins to allow for some mutual criticism.

Horses and Rats are mutually appealing. But their struggle to survive over a long haul will be monumental. If they do keep things together, it will be the result of some serious compromise on the Horse's part.

With either a Pig or Ox person, the Horse will encounter problems. Horses manipulate Pigs. Oxen can out-toil even the strongest work Horse.

Above all, Horse lovers, steer clear of the Monkey. Our simian friends will madden you with their ruse and device. You don't mind applying an edge of sneak to your business life, but in love you want open forum, blunt truths, and straight dealing. Without honesty in a love relationship, you will feel all the passion seeping from your pores. Monkeys are too wily for your tender-hearted soul.

Social Affairs

The Horse is not a selfless, giving soul who gallops about giving handouts to the poor. Therefore, he must accept that unless he can adjust his egocentricity barometer a mite, certain friendships will be automatically prohibitive.

Horses get on swimmingly with Goats, Roosters, and Dogs. These creatures will follow a Horse chum almost anywhere. The Horse will instigate plans and fun that fascinate members of these signs. Horses also like Tigers and Cats. Both types intrigue the Horse and each in his own way will find the Horse's honesty and diligence pleasing. Much can be accomplished through associations of this kind.

Not so with Monkeys, Pigs, or Rats. The Monkey irks the Horse with all of his maneuverings and mannerism. Pigs, though they may be amused by Horses, find them overly loquacious and even more naïve than themselves. Rats are magnetized by Horses. But this pair suffers a surfeit of angular dispute over methods and means. Maybe they are too similarly driven by ambition to ever understand each other.

The Snake is a good pal to any Horse. Snakes are cool as cucumbers. Horses are revved up full-tilt at all times and their timing is not always adjusted correctly. The Snake can watch the Horse plunge along and rage at life without endangering even his superfluous second skin. Snakes are armored against the anger of others. And Heaven knows the Horse can make ire look frighteningly fierce.

Dragons are givers; Horses, not always. The Dragon is impatient with his Horse friend and usually does not hesitate to show it.

Business Affairs

Horses are good business people. Their instincts are often sound; they speculate wisely and they know how to turn a bad situation to its best advantage. But the Horse's choice of moment is not always apt.

For commerce to work, a Horse should either go it alone and build his clientele through cheerful personal dealings with customers, or he should associate himself with Tigers, Snakes, or Oxen. With any of these three subjects, the incidence of complete failure will be averted. You will recall that the Horse rarely enjoys conceding authority. Nor is he capable of recuperation from his own ruin. Tigers, Snakes, and Oxen will not allow the Horse the luxury of demise. They know how to leave him alone when he's off and running. And they also feel the critical moment of need for their intervention in his race. Tigers may kick him in the ribs and either spur him to hurry or slow his efforts at the correct time. Snakes will yawn and force him into a chair for a heart-to-heart. And Oxen will simply hoist the Horse off the race course and ploddingly take over where the Horse left off.

Dragons will work intermittently well with Horse partners. Short-lived deals and schemes between the two may be profitable. If they must see each other every day over a long period, the Dragon may try to explode all of the Horse's theories and soon the earnest Horse will begin to doubt himself.

If all the Horse wants is support in his organization, he can employ Dogs, Roosters, or Goats to assist him. He should never hire a Monkey or entertain the vaguest thought of a subordinate Horse twin. The Monkey will be critical of the Horse's tactics. A second Horse will steal all of his fire, want the glory for himself, and stop at nothing to provide his own ego with that much needed praise.

Family Affairs

As any child of any Horse knows, the household in which he lives only exists by virtue of the Horse parent's desire to make it work his way. The Horse is not your average blustery authority figure. He rules by walking tall and carrying a big riding crop. Don't worry, he will probably never use that whip on you. The Horse is too sentimental for the likes of corporal punishment.

Instead of bonking his children on the head, the Horse parent talks to his kids. Eloquence and cajolery find their way into almost everything the Horse attempts to prove to a child. And Horses are not above emotional blackmail of their children. They are sometimes guilty of the old "after all I've done for you" syndrome, which, if you think about it, is not all that ineffective.

Horse dads and moms fairly frolic along with Tiger, Dragon, and Cat offspring. None of these independents really get on the Horse's fiery nerves. Though the Horse may demand much of his kids, he does respect their integrity of spirit.

Dog, Pig, and Snake children will be exasperated and frustrated in the home of a Horse. No Dog or Pig can comprehend the Horse's selfish gropings for center stage. And in all that truculence, the Snake's silent opinion will often be ignored. Since Horses so excel at chatter, they should perhaps try to have a two-sided talk with their confused kidlets. No pontificating. Just a nice neck-and-neck discussion.

Monkey kids will do their all to avoid the Horse parent. Rats will argue with a haughty Horse, and often lose by default. Oxen may resent being left at the gate while the Horse parent incessantly gads about the world. The Ox prefers things to remain status quo around the house. Horses are not usually stay-at-homes.

A note here about the Fire Horse child/parent relationship. It is always troublesome for a Horse child to remain under the thumb of his family for long. He rears up against rules or else ignores their existence. He's deeply sentimental about filial affections. But he cannot tolerate much interference in his own business.

With the Fire Horse child, the best tack to adopt is no tack at all. He must be left very much to his own devices. Quiet time, solitary games, and many books should be provided. He will probably get on famously in his peer group. He will no doubt be respected and admired by teachers for his pluck, perseverance, and easy grasp of basic conceptual truths.

In the case of Fire Horse boys or girls, it often seems as though birth took place at age forty-six. Fire Horses, though they involve themselves in childish pursuits with vigor and vim, give one the impression they are merely waiting to be grown-up. They adhere only to rules that they deem efficient, all the while planning how they will arrange a campaign for their own presidency of the world. Cuddle and snuggle appeals to the Fire Horse child. Conflict can upset his equilibrium. If he is shuffled about or made to participate in trivial family arguments, he will balk and plan an early escape from the troubled nest.

THE GOAT

Goats Are:

*Elegant • Creative • Intelligent • Well-mannered
Sweet-natured • Tasteful • Inventive • Homespun • Persevering
Lovable • Delicate • Artistic • Amorous • Malleable
Altruistic • Peace-loving*

But They Can Also Be:

*Pessimistic • Fussbudgets • Dissatisfied
Capricious • Intrusive • Undisciplined • Dependent
Irresponsible • Unpunctual • Insecure*

GOATS I HAVE KNOWN AND LOVED

Goat People are renowned for their marked ability tò maintan an attitude of ingenuous naïveté in times of strife. When everyone else in the universe seems to be manning barricades, hurling rocks, and shooting bullets at enemies in the most bellicose fashion, you can count on at least one Goat to come bounding along, guitar in tow and peaceful expression on face, strumming a tune of lucid commentary on the events. Our friend the Goat is the ruminating minstrel of the Chinese zodiac.

Take Pete Seeger (Goat, 1919), for example. A past master of peaceful resistance to injustice, this soft spoken gentleman was responsible for many of the thought-shaping notions of the militant sixties. Wherever trouble brewed, over more than two decades, Pete Seeger and his Weavers were there to record incidents, sing us what they thought about them, and even risk censure for the sake of truth. Yet, when we reminisce about Seeger, we hardly think in terms of physical violence or hand-to-hand struggle. Instead, even well after the Weavers had disbanded, we can conjure the image of a one-man resistance movement, standing on a stage by himself, almost timid, belting out those protest songs of his in a quaveringly engaging voice. As momentum picked up, Seeger would ask his audience to join him in song. Little by little the volume waxed stronger. People sang along. The voice's quaver diminished. His public, his students of nonviolence as it were, adored Pete Seeger. They loved him for his shyness. They applauded him for his courage. He was their guru, their guide, and their tutor. Yet, strangely enough, when I remember seeing Pete Seeger on that stage under that single spotlight in a Greenwich Village club in the late fifties, what I recall most vividly is how deeply sorry I felt for him. As I reconsider the event, I truly think a large portion of the adoration I had for him was based on his vulnerability. Not that his songs weren't sweet and true to my adolescent ears. They were. But there was more to it than that. He looked like a lone tumbleweed up there. He made the scene so touching . . . one could not resist his diffident charm.

Goat subjects are best at doing what comes naturally. Routine, order, rigid schedules, and rules do not suit them. Whatever they do accomplish is rigorously founded on the foregone conclusion that they are not to be expected to do anything at all. Allow me, please, the luxury of further autobiography. My good father was born in a Goat year, 1907. Outwardly, my dad's act seemed wholly together. His office was neat as a pin; row upon row of pens and pencils lined his meticulously clean desk top. I always thought of him as Mr. Clean. Then one day, almost a year after his death, I was having a heart-to heart with my mother. "How could you stand it, Mom? All that ship-shape spruced-up businesslike organization of Dad's. It must have driven you crazy."

"What shipshape what-do-you-call-it? Your father was the most disorganized person alive. He was a darling. But he was far from neat," my mother informed me smilingly.

"But all those pencils and filing cabinets. I'm sure I remember that." I was dumfounded.

"Oh, that." My mom laughed. "That was just a cover. Your father couldn't remember from one day to the next if his head was screwed on or not. So he always hired tough-minded secretaries who kept everything in tiptop shape for him. The bossier the better. If he could have found her, he would have hired Mary Poppins to take care of him."

Disbelief was hardly the word. I honestly thought my mother

had gone senile on me overnight. "And what about those dresser drawers? And his closet? Daddy was a fanatic about such things. Wasn't he?"

"As long as I picked up after him and labeled the drawers and grumbled when he mixed up the socks with the undershirts, yes. Then he managed to appear more methodical than a computer. But I'm telling you he was not orderly by nature. He wanted things straight around him for fear he would get lost in the shuffle if they weren't. I loved him, you know that. But I wouldn't hesitate to tell you that your father was not a tidy person." She said this without malice, as though it were common knowledge.

What misconceptions we have about our parents. Very often until they are gone, we haven't the foggiest notion of who they really were. After that talk with my mom, I had to look up my father's animal sign. Sure enough, a Goat. How clouded is the child's view by blind faith in what seems to be authority. Because I had left home very young, I was ignorant of my father's true character. I wanted to know more. I questioned my elder siblings, who had not run off to Paris, as to what Dad was really like in adult life.

My eldest brother said, "Weak. Daddy was too loving and good to be truly strong. All that severity he spouted around the house and in the office? That was just a front. Under normal conditions, Daddy wouldn't have slapped at a mosquito. If you remember, he only scolded us when Mom told him to. He hated adversity. He was basically a peaceful man."

My sister? She told me this one: "Remember how be used to get us up in the middle of the night and take us on sneak picnics?" I nodded. Those excursions had been glorious fun. "Well, it used to make Mother furious. He never considered whether it was a school night or if we had measles or not. He just felt like taking us out. Mom used to fume about those days even after we were grown-up."

Those bits of family gossip set me to thinking. It was true. My father must have been perfect hell to live with. Under more specific questioning, my mother told me that she never knew from one year to the next whether or not she would have money to buy clothes for her five little school kids. And, just when she was about to run out of linens and sheets for the house, Dad would go out and buy her a new Cadillac. Then there was no money left for trifles like towels and pillowcases. I always wondered why we had to wear darned socks and mended jeans to school while my parents afforded themselves luxurious Hawaiian vacations. It somehow never jibed that my mother had two new fur coats even after my Dad's bankruptcy.

As it turns out, the whole thing makes infinite sense. Goats, loving and tenderly warm-hearted, are the most eccentric people around. Caprice is their middle name. One day they are buckling down to hard work, straining and drudging away so hard you feel sorry for them. And the next day? Well, they forgot to finish painting that fence or planting that row of beans. Would you mind terribly if they did it tomorrow? Goat are exasperatingly adorable, unflinchingly so. Don't try to nudge them into completing a task. And never imagine that you can request their services gently when they are not in the mood. It won't work. They will simply smile and flee to cloud number nine.

The only method I have found that works when dealing with dreamy Goats is blatant tyranny. Bark at them and nip at their ankles, all the while pushing them in the direction you wish them to go. To love them is to boss them. You have no other choice. They like to be told what to do. It doesn't even make them angry. As long as you offer the kind of security of affection they so fervently desire, they'll follow you anywhere.

Like mother, like daughter. Long before I knew that my own pater familias was a member of the brotherhood of Goats, I, myself, took up with one of their ranks. His name was Todd. I mentioned him in the introduction. The prince with the blue jeans, you remember him. Well, so do I. It was Paris, the sixties, the land of silk and honey and good red wine. How could I forget nirvana?

Sans grudge, I can safely say, Todd was the most appallingly idiosyncratic person I have ever had the pleasure of marrying. And, of course, he was born in 1931. Todd was the kind of airy vaporous soul whom nobody could ever bring him or herself to hate. Nothing ever seemed to faze him. I called him Mr. Rescue Squad. The name suited

him to a missing shirt button. At the precise moment when the baby
would begin to cry and the formula was boiling over on the stove, as
my own eyes filled with burning salty tears and the chimney caught on
fire, it was Todd to the rescue. Clean up, soothe, diaper, feed, extinguish. In a wink the curtain came down on tragic drama. Todd could
fix it. And fix it he did—calmly.

The rub? Unless there was a three-ring Greek tragedy going on,
Todd sat around placidly consulting his tarot cards. So, for five hectic
years of my early adult life, I made it my business to compete with
Sarah Bernhardt for front and center theatrics.

Being the champion of a Goat is tantamount to enjoying the
combination role of Florence Nightingale and Hider. It alternates, but
both elements must definitely be present in the person who succeeds in
getting along with Goats.

Here's a good example. About two years ago, I needed a baby-
sitter to replace my vacationing nanny over the summer. In France, we
call these mothers' helpers *au pair* girls. I never quite knew what it
meant but you get the idea. I met a young woman at the home of some
dear friends of mine who run an organic farm outside of Paris. She
was a distant cousin of the wife's former mother-in-law. She had what
we call references, plus which I liked her. Her name was Marie-
Antoinette. You can suppose this name is not common in France. It
doesn't exactly have the reputation for bringing luck to the person
who wears it. Anyway, Marie-Antoinette or, as I came to call her,
Marie-A, was about nineteen, plain of face, and voluptuous of figure.
She was a student of literature at the Sorbonne, the daughter of a pair
of dentists. She needed a summer job. I hired her.

Naïve I am sometimes. I didn't bother to ask her what year she
was born. Soon enough I found out she was not nineteen at all, but
seventeen (Goat, 1955). We were to spend the holidays in Ibiza. Ibiza
is an exquisite island of largely unwarranted ill repute, off the coast of
Barcelona, Spain. A poem in white beaches and unscrubbed ne'er-do-
wells, Ibiza has been my holiday stomping grounds for the past twelve
years. I was once a nether ne'er-do-well in Ibiza myself, but I had no
idea that taking a Goat to Ibiza is like hand-carrying kids to a sacrifi-

cial altar. I confess I didn't think about it. Marie-A was going to look after the kids and help out with the chores while I spent my summer vacation writing an overdue book.

For the first two weeks, life around the adobe in Ibiza's picturesque old town, was bliss. Marie-A hustled about the place scrubbing and cleaning, smiling all the while. She bugged me a bit about how things were supposed to be done and all that. But I chalked that up to the fact that I was not used to giving orders any more. The nanny I have in Paris is so efficient, she gives me orders. But, sad to say, I was miscalculating again.

One day, the kids came to me with earnest "we need to have a talk" looks in their eyes. In those breathy urgent tones for which little girls are so famous, first Daisy, then Autumn said, "Mommy, you have to send her away."

"Why's that?" I lit a cigarette to ease the angst. As you well know, a baby-sitter threatened is a baby-sitter lost.

Shuffled about from language to language, cultural shock to cultural shock, as they have been, my children almost never complain about anything so long as they have enough to eat. Daisy piped up then, "She forgets everything."

"Well, now, that isn't so serious is it? You forget a lot of things. So do I. What is so grave about Marie-A's forgetfullness?"

"Yesterday she forgot to give us lunch. The day before she forgot to turn off the hot dogs and burned them all up. And this morning she forgot to take us to the beach with her because she was drunk!" Her tone was urgent desperation.

I was not what you might call pleased to hear this latest bit of news. "Drunk!" I stood up to exclaim, "Where is she now?"

"We don't know. She went off and left us a note about two hours ago. Here it is." She handed me a scrap of brown paper with a penciled message on it: "My sweethearts," it said adoringly, "I am going to the beach with my darling Robin. I'll be back sometime tonight. Have a nice day. I love you, Marie-A."

"Who is this 'Darling Robin' creature?" I wondered aloud to the mystified pair of pixies at my side.

"He's a hippie," they agreed in unison. "He always bosses us around. He isn't as nice as Stevie was."

"And who then is Stevie?" I added.

"He's the one with the guitar who slept over last Wednesday. He was funny. He gave us a comic book each," said Autumn.

Then Daisy chimed in, "Yeah, you thought he was nice but all that jumping around he did in the next room making Marie-A giggle. That kept me awake. I didn't like him at all." She was adamant on the subject of old Stevie.

Now, as a single mother of two little cherubs, I consider myself open-minded with regard to sex and all the possible gory details that may surround same. Whenever the subject arises, I come up with those frank explanations we are supposed to supply. I am not, however, one of those ultra-libertine types who puts on sexhibitions for the kindergarten set in hopes they will grow up unthwarted. I was flabbergasted, annoyed, and worried sick that the girls might be marked for life by having been prematurely exposed to a surfeit of extraconjugal jostlings in the night. Also, I was thinking of Marie-A's parents. What would they think if they knew she was racing around the island of sin taking up with every available riffraff? I was reassured by the knowledge that the famous hoax charmer, Clifford Irving, was not in Ibiza that summer. At least he wouldn't have got at her yet.

That afternoon I took the girls to the beach myself And that very evening when Marie-A came trailing in all sun-struck and bleary-eyed, I had a quiet chat with her. I explained that her private life was her own business. That what she did on her off-hours did not concern me. Yet, she was a minor and I was responsible for her in a foreign land. Vis-à-vis her parents, I felt I must put my foot down. And vis-à-vis my kids, I was livid.

All the while I tiraded, Marie-Antoinette smiled and nodded and made like Saint Theresa's final act of contrition. I was right. She would never do it again. Why hadn't I told her before?

"You mean you have to be told not to drag home strays?" I chided. I should have told her earlier. She would never forget. And on and on. And for a few more days, Marie-A kissy-faced around the house with the kids and performed her duties as though she had invented work. It was more bliss. Then Jean-Claude came to dinner. Jean-Claude, the rake. Jean-Claude, the dirty old man. Jean-Claude, whom I scarcely allowed to peek into my children's room for fear he would jump them as they lay sleeping. He was a business acquaintance. A writer's agent. A lecherous old commercial genius.

You guessed it. Marie-A ran away with him in the night. Head in hands, I begged myself for some information on why I allowed myself to get into these messes. "I have been looking for you for seventy-two hours, young lady," I ranted. I hesitated to call the police. A Spanish jail is worse for a young girl than hiring her out to a brothel.

"You said you would introduce me to nice people. Jean-Claude is your friend, *non?*" sniffled the nubile creature.

"*Non. Non et non!* Jean-Claude is not my friend. He's someone I have to do business with. I invite him to dinner once a year out of sheer duty. I don't even like Jean-Claude!"

"You should have told me," whispered Marie-A. "I will never do that again."

Marie-Antoinette was the kind of person who had to be told everything. If you caught her crossing Main Street when you had strictly advised her not to cross Elm Street, she would look up at you innocently and say, "You didn't tell me not to cross this one."

In brief, I sent her home to her parents. She admitted she was happy to leave. "This place is not very fine for me. My mother never lets me go out with boys. My father is very strict. I live at home. I like it better there." Her parents had the right idea.

I am aware that it sounds as though I am unduly berating nanny Goats. I don't mean to. Goat people are some of the most creative and inventive individuals alive. They always think first of those who need them most. They are intelligent and sensitive. They are elegant and lovely to look at. They have many, many desirable qualities.

As long as life affords them a fertile pasture in which to browse, Goats can be expected to fare handsomely. Goat is a good sign for those of us who enjoy being dependent on others for our livelihood. Although I hesitate to say so, I do consider Goat an easier sign for a woman to live under. Men of this sign are often forced to struggle so hard against their capriciousness, that such routine careers as are traditionally thought to be theirs are nigh unto impossible for them to carry off.

Many people think Goat men are effeminate. Don't count on it. The billy Goat is, after all, one of the universal symbols of studhood. What we see as feminine traits in the Goat are nothing more than a delicacy of nature and a taste for the effete. Why society permits extra indulgence for whimsy in women is the real question. Yet, we cannot change that in a day.

Mick Jagger is a Goat (1943). Every time I see him in concert, the one thing that impresses me most about his presence is a manifestation of patent androgyny. He is undoubtedly one of the most flagrantly "sexy" humans one has the pleasure of surveying on a stage these days. He is decidedly a male. But in his aura, his dancing, his prancings up and down, there is a quality of the female which, albeit a bit shocking, is devastatingly appealing. Jagger is not the man's magazine idea of a good-looking hunk of male. But his sexuality reeks from off that stage. If you don't believe me, attend a concert and see for yourself. There is no denying he is "all man."

In the reverse, singer, songwriter, musician giant Joni Mitchell emanates a brand of earthy seductiveness peculiar to Goats. Another lone performer, standing on a stage singing songs of intricate poetical significance, that woman has the ability to light up the world with her poise. Her voice is almost pristine in its purity of tone. Her messages are never the simple rock thrusts of belting out a bawdy rhythmical tune. Oh, no. Joni Mitchell keeps her audience on its toes, mentally and physically. Her clear sounds ring out across an auditorium. Her range is remarkable. And what does she say? That is the most Goatlike thing about her. Joni Mitchell says what all the Goats I have ever rubbed shoulders with always say: "I shouldn't have got on this flight," "I miss my clean white linen and my fancy French cologne," and "I'm coming home to California," but first "Maybe I'll go to Amsterdam or maybe I'll go to Rome and rent me a grand piano and put some flowers round my room." Then she says she'll go back to her comfy California. If you are not conversant with these tunes, listen to her record called "Blue." It's worth the detour. It will also help you to understand Goat people.

Another stanza that brings it all home is this: "Went to a party down a red dirt road. There were lots o' pretty people there. Reading *Rolling Stone*, reading *Vogue*. They asked me how long can you stick around? I said a week. Maybe two. Just until my skin turns brown." That red dirt road is the rutted driveway of a friend of mine's farmhouse on the island of Ibiza. When Joni Mitchell was on the island, we did have a party and she came. Tall, willowy, strikingly beautiful, she gamboled when she walked. Her blond hair shiny clean, she had the scrubbed look of a Canadian Northwoods girl—not just any Canadian country girl but a star. And, when I heard that song later about the party down the red dirt road, I laughed to myself. She had captured the ambience of that soirée so perfectly. All the bored pretty people in Europe seemed to be there. They were sprawled about reading fashionable publications. And she did not stick around very long.

Goats never do. They are definitely not noted for their constancy. They seem instead to float in and out of situations in life, producing moods by their very presence in a place, and then floating back out. This quality is at the same time their strength and their weakness. It is a strange mixture of the two. On the one hand, because they can vary their attentions, devoting themselves first to one thing and then to another, they have an uncanny ability for diversification of talent. On the other hand, this versatility, if not controlled, can cause the very fiber of their lives to pull apart at the seams and fall into nothingness. I cannot stress enough, therefore, the importance of security in the life of a Goat subject. If he's comfortable and well looked after, he can remain happily tethered for a lifetime and will not pull at his leash. Without the insurance that he will be safe and cozy, he will soon begin sniffing about for greener pastures.

Goats give the most gorgeous parties. Ambience is their special talent. The lighting will be just right, the décor perfection, the food (providing he doesn't forget to hire the caterer) elegant and refined. In these instances, Goats don't miss a trick. They make remarkably fine hosts and hostesses. They seem to have a knack for setting up scenes that make their guests feel wanted. Too, since Goats are so often in the clouds, they have the ability to leave people alone and let them get on with enjoying themselves.

I said that Goats were persevering. I do not mean they are indomitable soliders who fight to the finish. Goats have a different way of sticking things out. I prefer to think of it in terms of self-possession. People born in the year of the Goat spend a large part of their time meandering around in search of a covenant, a pledge from one person or another, through which they feel their lives will somehow be protected from harm. What others may consider adventure, freedom from ties or independence, the Goat finds an untenable state of affairs. Their determination, then, is more directed toward finding this essential security in another human being. They honestly do need someone to depend upon. Mick Jagger sings about it: "We all need someone to lean on." Someone, that is, who will take care to see that our Goat gets up in the morning, puts on his clean shirt, and gets another day together. Goats are anything but self-sufficient. They like to live their lives through other people, they often see things better from out the eye sockets of a loved one, and they cannot be counted upon to change that part of their character.

Careers for Goats should be carefully chosen from the various arts. Anything from poetry to filmmaking or architecture can be considered. Education will help, but they will not always have a lot of respect for the sheepskin approach to job-finding. Goats are not the scholars of the world. They ramble and daydream in school. They gaze longingly out the window at the green grass and wish some strong sugar daddy or mommy would come dashing in to carry them off somewhere safe. In secure surroundings, they will think their thoughts, dawdle away hours over an idea for a painting or a novel, plan a new method of casting the future, or conjure up intricate ways to decorate a living room they have not yet found the funds to rent, much less refurbish.

Goats have practically no sense of time. They are invariably late or too early for appointments. My Goat husband used to ask me at least three times a day, "What day is this?" My friendly nanny Goat girl of whom I spoke so damningly was wont to request exactly one half-hour after the stores had closed, "What should I buy for dinner?" It became such a common occurrence, I found it endearingly infuriating. To dislike a Goat for this lackadaisical approach to schedules or any other of his vaporous attitudes is inconceivable. The best advice I can give you is to make-do with what they are.

One last marital anecdote will perhaps better illustrate why you cannot hate a Goat, even though they drive you to distraction with their eccentricities. At one dark point in the history of my life as a housewife, we lived in upstate New York where the Chamber of Commerce can tell you 1967 was a particularly frigid winter. We had a couple of toddling bear cubs to get out of bed in the morning, dress warmly, and drive to nursery school. Todd always stayed up late with his thoughts, while I went early to bed. One morning I rose about six to have the precious cup of solitary coffee all young mothers hold so dear. After a read of the paper and a quick toilette, I roused the babies and began the ritual feeding, dressing, changing, etc.

It was an ultra-cold day. I sent a sleepy Todd into the bathroom for his shower and began the slow process of bundling up two babies for facing the great outdoors. But where were their clothes? I couldn't find even one mitten or snowsuit. Being as orderly about such things as any exhausted working mother might hope to be, I knew I had put the children's outerwear in a closet before retiring. "But," I thought, "Maybe I really am crazy." I admit I had been having my doubts. So I hunted through dresser drawers and toy chests, thinking perhaps I had hung up the creative playthings and chucked the snowsuits in the toy box. But they were nowhere to be found. I called to Todd through the steam in the john, "Have you seen the kids' coats?"

He sang out gaily, "Did you look in the closet?"

Typical. I snorted impatiently. Didn't he think I knew enough to look for them where they were supposed to be? I slammed the bathroom door.

By the time Todd exited and dressed for work, I was unglued. It was getting precariously on toward eight o'clock and there were no clothes to put on the kids. Todd drank his coffee slowly. I begged him to hurry so he could help me run down the missing buntings. He gave me a knowing smile (by this time, not my favorite look). With a kid under each arm, I stood in the door of the kitchen and commanded, "Find those clothes! We will both be late for work."

Todd arose, finished his coffee, and took me lovingly around the waist. He guided me down the long hall to the front of the house, opened the outer door and said; "*Voila!*"

You won't believe this but it's true. I swear. There, standing on the front porch of my house were three of the most perfectly formed snow people ever built anywhere by human hand. There was Mama Snowman, Daisy Snowman, and Autumn Snowman, all holding hands in a row—and wearing our clothes. My raccoon coat was pertly topped off by a woolen hat I had knitted, the kids' snow costumes were intact as well. Impeccable likenesses, one and all. And written in the snow on the floor of the porch underneath these sculpted master-pieces were three words, "I LOVE YOU." I couldn't dress the kids that day so they wore blankets to the baby-sitting service. I put on my raincoat over three sweaters. But I could not get angry. Who could hate such an adorable madman?

This streak of lunacy in the Goat character should not be mis-construed. His apparent repeated absences of marbles are not of the frenzied raving variety. It is just that occasionally Goat people find themselves in the uneasy position of waking up after a delicious dream to face reality in the person of someone or something eminently more down-to-earth than themselves. During their lapses, they may be cook-ing up voluminous and intricate mosaics of artistic grandeur, which they dare not communicate, as an excuse for their disappearing act. It would seem foolish. Properly channeled, these periods wherein they seem to be hovering about three feet above their own heads can reap the most practical of benefits.

Moreover, the Goat's ability to acclimate himself equally well to both pragmatic and effete situations accords him an uncommon strength. Versatility, in this age of racing and changing images, can be a very desirable quality in a human being. Because the Goat mind can pick up and go just about anywhere it is summoned, Goat people are less emotionally destructible than many of us. Nothing shocks them, causes surprise, or clouds their view of a predicament. If you don't see what I mean, watch Barbara Walters (Goat, 1931) some early morning as she deftly interviews people on the "Today Show." She can turn an accused murderer, super con artist, or alleged embezzler of government funds into the most docile blabbermouth. She is the mother confessor par excellence of the video screen. Nothing ruffles her. No amount of guest circumlocution deters her from the goal she has set for herself.

Recently, I saw her talking to Julie Eisenhower. The former President's daughter was appearing on the "Today Show," ostensibly to plug a children's cookbook she had written. Ms. Walters kindly asked a few details about the recipes and methods of kiddie cuisine used in the book. Julie answered, "Well, I use a lot of strange ingredients like peanut butter and marshmallow with hot peppers between slices of brown bread" (or something to that effect). She smiled most winningly as though her father had never left the throne.

"I know you don't want to discuss Watergate," was Ms. Walters' next remark. "But let me ask you this. Is your father ever going to repent for his sins?"

"Clever lady," thought I.

As quick as a wink, from kitchen to confessional, Julie didn't know what hit her. She began blathering on about how her father recognized how wrong he had been and on and on, Barbara let her talk for a bit.

Then blam! "Yes, but how does he intend to make amends for what he did?" She wasn't letting up. There was a kind of gentle Colombo manner in her voice. "You know, Julie, I am sorry to bring up these dicey subjects, but all our viewers are so interested in your father. You and I have always been able to talk about just about anything." Behind her placid approach, lurked an immovable journalistic passion for truth at any cost. Julie didn't cough up much more than half-answers to the questions, but one had to admit that with Barbara's chumminess and likable way, it must have been very difficult to resist letting brother Rat (Nixon: Rat, January, 1913) out of the bag.

Goats are inventive, adaptable, and well-mannered. For the most part, they mean what they say. Dishonesty will only creep into the attitude of a Goat if his life style or source of income security is threatened. In these tight spots, he may flinch, quiver all over, become exceedingly angry, and ultimately break down. If he is clever, he never allows challenges of this sort to arise. He should watch his entourage carefully for eventual competition, and seek to control the threat before it grows too large to be peaceably handled. War is not healthy for Goats; strategy and peace talks are a wiser solution. The Goat is a good compromiser, a fine partner, and a superior team member.

MADAME GOAT

"Engaging" is the key word when describing Milady Goat. We know already that the Goat is a charmer. But until we begin examining the character references of the Goat woman, we haven't seen anything like how winning a Goat can really be. It must be the diffidence, or maybe it's the sleek, obtuse grin they assume when challenged. It could be the preoccupation with tasteful dress. But, quite honestly, I don't seem to be able to pin down one particular reason for this woman's superior ability to get herself married off to the right man.

If such a thing as Mr. Right exists at all any more, I suspect most of them are about to be gobbled up by all the Goat damsels in distress who remain shivering, eyelashes batting at twenty-eight frames a second, out there in Singles Land. You will recall that Goat people enjoy being taken care of. If you reckon yourself to be the solid, endurable type, find yourself a Goat wife. I can promise, however, that as soon as you give her license she will commence to support herself on your most available shoulder, lean on your hairy chest, and quickly make plans to accustom you to a life style of luxury beyond your wildest nightmare.

Goat women, not unlike their male counterparts, have a gift for spinning the most mundane of life's threads into voluptuous embroidered satin. No mistake, it will cost you plenty. But, for the proper man, such brilliant alchemy will be well worth it. Goat women are not afraid to spend money, especially other people's. They make excellent heiresses, marvelous rich widows, and uncommonly contented alimony collectors.

This voluptuous creature thrives on good times. Adversity, be it financial or emotional, does not suit the Goat woman. She is sensual and giving in her love-making. She will need to feel that your love for her is deep and lasting. No butterflies for her. It wouldn't be healthy. An unfaithful lover or husband would do her in—posthaste. A shaky bank account will render her the victim of a nervous breakdown in a matter of days. She makes it her business to build her nest on high ground or fertile sunlit plains. And, for her, this is the right fork in the road to choose.

When I insist that hardship does not please the Goat woman, I am not insinuating that she cannot take care of herself (and everybody else) in an emergency. I have an intense recollection of being stranded in an open boat with a Goat friend of mine off the Greek island of Corfu. We were five passengers. The craft was unsuitably small for such a crowd, yet the story was classic. When we left the shore, the weather gave no hint of change. About an hour later, a freak storm blew up. None of us was a seasoned sailor, least of all Elizabeth Stanislas (Goat, 1931). She had been raised in landlocked central Poland and had never so much as laid eyes on a sea until after the war ended. We were all novices. And we were all scared to death. In typical neophyte fashion, it was suddenly obvious that we were, all five, huddled together at one end of the boat. Safety in numbers? I can't really say. But, in any case, we were a panicky lot indeed.

Out of what seemed like nowhere, Liz crept to the other end of the rocking soup dish we were dependent on for survival and began barking out orders. "You, Florence, move over there." She pointed a finger starboard. Florence inched her way right. "Suzanne, stay where you are. Don't move!" I stayed. "Marco, move up here." Marco skittered toward her. "Pericles!" (In Greece, people are still called Pericles.) "left!" He crouched his way to the left. When true disaster was at hand, Liz came through. She redistributed all of us to balance the boat's precarious budget and then proceeded to order us all to

"Shift!" when the rocking seemed to move in one dangerous direction or the other.

That evening, as we dined on crunchy skewered lamb and woody retsina wine, away up in the mountains of idyllic Corfu, Pericles proposed a toast to our angel of mercy. "She is our saviour. We salute her. Our thanks are with her. May her house be safe from tigers. Etc., etc." (Greeks *do* go on.) As we raised our glasses high, we realized how foolish we looked. Elizabeth was nowhere to be found. She had been there a second ago. But we had got so involved in Pericles's speech, we hadn't noticed her departure.

After a woman-hunt of about ten minutes, we discovered Liz, sitting under an olive tree and watching the moon rise. "I have been noticing it changes faster in this season," was all she had to say on the subject of her absence. Lost to us for the duration, until perhaps the next disaster struck, Liz could not imagine why we were so relieved to find her. Who knew we would be making any toasts? What for? What had she done? Contritely, she returned to the table as though we had scolded her for disappearing.

Shamefacedness is another of the Goat woman's traits. She is always sorry. Why didn't you tell her you didn't want her to have the front bedroom painted? She was only trying to help. If only you had reminded her to do those dishes before the company came, she would have had enough clean spoons to go around. The Goat lady is not blaming her faults on you. She merely cannot understand why you did not come into the kitchen with big boots and a whip to order her to get that work done. She is not a self-starter. Nor is she an apt finisher. Her mind contains a fine network of involved receivers that, each in its turn regardless of importance, must be attended to. Tasks are not begun or terminated on time. Half the food is cold before the rest is ready to serve. She truly cannot remember to put the salt on the table every night. What do you take her for? Some kind of computer?

She regrets this scattiness in her character as well. Madame Goat longs to be everything she isn't. Nothing is ever the way she would have it. The button is missing from her blue slacks and the purple ones don't match the sky-blue blouse. Whatever will she do? She will lean on you. It's quite simple.

And speaking of my Goat friend Liz Stanislas, one last tidbit comes to mind. I met Liz one day in the center of her own living room, wearing two distinctly different types of earrings, one in each ear. I cracked up, fell apart laughing. "Liz, you nut case, you have on two different earrings." Then I really doubled over. She was not only wearing one gold hoop ring in the left ear and one silver dangle in the right, that is absolutely all she was wearing. Liz looked hurt. It wasn't fair of me to poke fun at her. But she did look terribly ludicrous standing there all nude in those garishly unmatched earrings. "I can't decide which ones to put on. What do you think?" she wondered.

"How can I tell? I mean, do you have any idea what you intend to wear with them? Or, are you going out to lunch like that?" I stifled my giggles for a minute. She was serious about this earth-shaking choice. What's more, we were already fifteen minutes late for a luncheon date.

"Come into my room. I can't quite tell. Is this shirt too gaudy to go with my orange pants?" She held up a mint-green Pucci number. "I can't see in this light."

Of course, it did not occur to Liz to carry the pants and shirt into the bright living room where she could better view the contrasting colors. She just doesn't think like that. And can you guess what she does for a living? Liz is a highly successful theatrical costume designer in Paris, France. How's that for a surprise?

MONSIEUR GOAT

Vested interest or not, I must endeavor to test my own objectivity when writing about male Goats. Far be it from me to wish make scapegoats of these vexingly lovable members of the opposite sex. Growing up, as I did, with nothing but their captivating kookyness upon which to base my image of what a man should be, I confess before I begin that I have a soft spot in my head when it comes to Goat men.

The best part of any Goat experience is the hors d'oeuvre.

Dalliances with Goat men are always a treat. The seduction consists of showering you with presents and unnecessary frippery for which you have no apparent need. This veritable debauch of generosity, when applied to the middle of the meal, manages to get somehow turned around backward. What was once a means of striving to make you love him more becomes a method of calming your ire when there is trouble afoot. If he uses your fingernail scissors to fix his electric razor, and finds you in a fury over same, the Goat mate will run right out to the nearest department store and purchase you a slew of the most expensive golden finger rings Tiffany sells. Of course, you won't be able to wear them until you get yourself a new nail scissors. That's part of life with the Goat.

Unless you are the type of lady who can manage to pay off the milkman with smiles instead of regular checks, don't get in too deep. Goat men tend never to get around to taking care of dull essentials. Though their adoration for your ability to cope in times of stress is without frontiers, it is, after all, you who are expected to do all that coping. My advice to the women who can't live without a Goat man is this: Take a cold shower, two valium, swallow a bottle of Chambolle-Musigny 1971, and lie down for an hour to think it over. Goat men make ever so much better lovers than husbands.

But there are compensations in being involved with a Goat man. He will never nag you. He may not in fact ever speak to you unless you speak first. He is usually a calm type, not easily angered nor aroused. But don't push him. Never ever ask a Goat man what he is thinking. Never press him for information about his inner self. He won't tell you. You can boss him all you want. He likes it. He'll find excuses, but basically he does not nind if you wear the pants. And, most of all, do not expect a Goat man to change. He will agree that he is difficult and hard to get through to and inscrutable most of the time. He may even come out of it for a time and help you with the chores once or twice to prove his good faith. But he doesn't mean it. The next day, he will forget where he put the broom and be terribly sorry that the steak for the children's dinner remained frozen solid. He will have taken them all to Howard Johnson's for ice cream. They'll have had a great old time. Please don't think that he's often getting your "goat." He means well. Just sit down and do the accounts. He'll bring you some stale tea and a dish of caviar.

CO-SIGNS

GOAT/Aries *(March 21—April 20)*

The Goat person born under the sign of the ram is a bit of a brawler. The agitation in question glows from within. The Goat, represented in the Chinese zodiac by "little fire," herein meets its "big fire" cohort. Aries are snappy warriors. Goat people tend to fight their battles with passive resistance. Conflicting points of view exist within the Aries Goat. He would do well to use the strategy of art or music to calm his bellicose nature. In such areas as this, he will shine. He can thus protest the injustices he sees around him in a peaceable manner. Goats, even strong Aries Goats, should not attempt politics or ply a military trade. The confrontations in store will appeal to them in the abstract, but when it comes to actually bonking some enemy on an unsuspecting head, the gentle Goat side of his nature will balk.

GOAT/Taurus *(April 21—May 21)*

The Goat's "little fire" flickers valiantly within this earthy subject. But, despite these rallies, it often falls victim to his heavy footed basic character. Taureans need that extra push of two hands clapping to urge them to succeed. Goats, as well, require regular benevolent prod-dings. This subject will make a fine employee. Executive responsibility does not suit him. An outsider, even a loving partner, must accept taking the reins. Over and over again, the tendency to lie back and wait for life's bounty to come his way will invade him. Just as you think he is on his way to sure success, he will decide that his choice of path was unwise, close himself off from you, and embark on new complex schemes that he believes are the real way he ought to behave. For the Taurean Goat, life is an endless series of uphill struggles. Hindered by his own inertia, when he fails he may pretend not to care. He can laugh it off, say it was someone else's fault. He has an excellent sense of humor—about everything except himself.

GOAT/Gemini *(May 22—June 21)*

The crackle of kindling can be heard over the roar of the crowd as gobs of Gemini oxygen feed the Goat's "little fire." Since caprice is rife among both of these signs, our subject must face the fact that he will spend much of his life attempting to survive the maelstrom of idiosyncrasies he was born with. Changeability can be a barrel of laughs. Flitting from flower to flower might be considered exciting by some. But settling down to one task or another from time to time is a more solid way of approaching real life. Goats born under the sign of Gemini can make the most dour old geezer smile. His talents are brilliant humor and an ability to mimic. Be he an actor, a writer, or a butcher, this character will need a serious guide by his side at all times. He is a self-starter whose first steps amaze and amuse. By the second day, he will be bored and begin craving yet another means of diverting himself from the job at hand. If he doesn't marry one, he should hire himself a professional taskmaster to assist in keeping his snout to the grindstone.

GOAT/Cancer *(June 22—July 23)*

Dampened spirits will hound the Cancer Goat. Deep waters and "little fire" may tend to slosh around a good bit. He will often wish it weren't all so murky. How to get out from under? Charity work will attract him. The subject would make a loving parent, an affectionate mate, and a perfectly charming dinner companion. As for his talents at leadership, they could be ample. Providing he does not allow doom and gloom to overcome him in the face of minor failure, the Cancer Goat should be a whiz at sticking to whatever he undertakes. The one inner hitch with this personality will be that both Cancer and Goats are easily bogged down by emotional hurts. A buoyant partner is indicated here to keep the atmosphere light and gay. Without this outside influence of enforced cheer, the subject may sink inside himself and spend valuable time licking wounds inflicted by those more unfeeling than himself.

GOAT/Leo *(July 24—August 23)*

Leos are, for the most part, strong, resilient, fiery types whose reputation for leadership precedes them wherever they go. Goats, as we know, do not suffer from this reputation. The influence of leonine fire on the Goat's infant blaze promises to ensure the Leo Goat stability and uncharacteristic will in the face of his favorite enemy, injustice. This person could be a fine lawyer, a worthy public servant, or a just-plain-terrific person. The sensitivity of the Goat may temper some of the categorical aggressiveness of his lion side. He will probably be more humane in his dealings with others than many Leos are wont. He is about the only Goat person who will not necessarily require a savvy partner in business or the home. His own inner strength should be his best cohort.

GOAT/Virgo *(August 24—September 23)*

The virgin's almost mineral purity will assist the giddy Goat nature in accepting some of life's inevitable grayness, Virgos are earthy and generally honorable souls. But, like Goats, they are naïve in the face of conmanship and treachery. A Virgo Goat will need a wily monkey or wise and helpful serpent partner to support him in times of disappointment. The Virgo Goat would do well to steer clear of unwieldy business schemes. He will be sure to win if he is protected by the bastions of a strong employer and/or an entourage of clever friends who are willing to lend him a bit of advice when he hesitates before making a decision. Without this assistance, his heart may be broken, along with his purse strings.

GOAT/Libra *(September 24—October 23)*

Once again we have air feeding the "little fire" of the Goat. Balance and a fervent desire to keep things on an even keel are Libran gifts. This Goat should be a good talker. He ought to know better than to let himself slip into characteristic Goat self-indulgence and pessimism. Libras are almost always emotionally dependent people. Goats don't relish being left on their own in high places. Both subjects adore beauty. The combination can be expected to flourish in luxury, wither in poverty. A Libran Goat should never be asked to manage in economically depressed situations. He needs the cushion of freedom from want in order to proceed with his life style of gentility. Abstinence does not make the heart of the Libran Goat grow fonder. Don't ask him to go to work as a file clerk until you have finished medical school and can give him what his heart desires. Neediness turns him off. Once grazing comfortably in a fertile field, however, this Goat will hang on for dear life. Don't try to push him aside, take his position away or even pull at his goatee in jest. He'll butt you right over the grandstand and out of the ball park.

GOAT/Scorpio *(October 24—November 22)*

Scorpio's water is fixed. The Goat's fire is small. Properly provided for, this Goat will not fizzle but blaze away. In times of disillusion, however, you may hear some very noisy hissing sounds coming from your Scorpio Goat person. These loud sounds could well take the form of scathing speeches or ponderous challenges. This Goat means business. Scorpios are vengeful and viper-tongued. This Goat does not take kindly to reversals of his desires. Never hit him when he is down. Don't flaunt power in his sensitive face. This Goat has devious and cunning methods of dealing death blows to enemies when the adversary least expects it. He can wait years. Then one *pow* out of nowhere, right in the chops, can level the unwary foe. The Scorpio Goat's a loving and loyal friend. He expects as much from his cronies as he does from himself. If you let him down, you will find out just how exigent this person can be.

GOAT/Sagittarius *(November 23—December 21)*

The double fire alliance possesses more will than most Goat persons. Although he will need a certain measure of sound guidance from without, he is idealistic enough to wish to carry through on projects he agrees to handle. Sagittarians are usually optimistic. This brighter view will open the Goat's eyes to a better method of handling trouble. Decision-making is not the forte of most Goats. This duo may surprise you. With a little help from his friends, the Sagittarian Goat will be a go-getter. He must be made to feel secure and cozy in order to exploit his own brilliance. Yet, hemming him in or attempting to hold him back from projects he feels strongly about would be disastrous. As his friend, one is advised to find the right balance of safety and freedom in which his talent for adventure can thrive.

GOAT/Capricorn *(December 22—January 20)*

Capricorns are rigid examples of durability and rock-hardness. Goats are not likely to be fighters unless they are struggling to keep their own fertile field free from poachers. Both signs have patience. They are both symbolized by the upright figure of a mountain goat. There is a nobility in the Capricorn Goat that sets him apart from other signs. He is not your common garden-variety grass-chomper on a rope. And he will not be satisfied to munch tin cans all day long. He will, however, have an ability to persevere even in times of need, which is not characteristic of the average Goat subject. Levelheadedness is the Capricorn gift to our Goat subject. The good Goat offers his conservative friend a fine share of caprice and fantasy. Given the proper hillside to conquer, he will be able to make excellent use of all those horns and hooves.

GOAT/Aquarius *(January 21—February 19)*

Nourished by the Aquarian surplus of airiness, the Goat's little fire will blaze brightly in all kinds of weird ways. Nobody is more idiosyncratic than our friendly Aquarian. Goats are not exactly boring, stolid plodders either. This union of signs should be expected to render its subjects either brilliant geniuses or raving madmen. There is a surplus of eccentricity herein that will have to be tempered by a firm guiding hand from the outside. Given this direction from without, the Aquarian Goat will shine more brightly than most. Poetics, films, music, social reform—if he applies himself—will assure him a more gentle slope to climb.

GOAT/Pisces *(February 20—March 20)*

Where other co-signs bring strength to the dependent Goat, the vacillating fish doesn't help at all. The Goat is influenceable, malleable, and artistic. So are the members of the Pisces family. Both are changeable and have a maverick mysteriousness about them that appeals to stronger souls. I suggest the Pisces Goat begin right about now to seek out that more forceful person who will take him in hand and help him direct all the talents he so obviously owns. Art, for this person, in whichever area he applies himself, should be an immediate pushover. It's the choosing of the area, the educational discipline, the final assertion of self over self that will defy him. Throughout his life, if he doesn't begin early to buckle down to work, he will be haunted by the inability to fix his imagination on a single pursuit. Surrounded with love and luck, he could become one of the giants of his time.

PRESCRIPTION FOR THE FUTURE

Gadabout Goat, now that I have botched my chances for ever going home again to any of the adoring Goats I have known or loved, I may as well proceed with the rest of this fiasco in the same earnestness. But before I place my foot too far into my mouth and garble the most important thing I have to tell you, let me say this: Regardless of how you may feel as you read what follows, please remember how much of my life I have willingly spent trying to sort you all out in my own head and heart. Not being much more than an interested soothsayer at this point, I trust you are aware that I now know there is no point in picking at sacrificial entrails through mere logic. Suffice it to confess I am cognizant of the fact that your charms and my perspicacity were destined from the beginning to lock horns. And, though we may understand one another a bit more in these, our adult years, it doesn't have to mean we are less fascinated nor bemused by the singular fact that persons such as myself will forever be drawn by those of your winsome ilk. I scrutinize you—and salute you.

Whew! And now a word from our common sense.

You Goats, above all, enjoy the comforts you are able to reap from the strength of those around you. Within the safety of a homelike framework, Goat types romp merrily through life without either a backward or forward glance. Your strength is your whimsy. Your appeal is your ability to love with a capital L. Your mission then ought to be simple. Find a way to protect yourself from open conflict. Do not engage in struggles that smell of deceit or call upon you to exercise guile. Craftier ones than yourselves are out there in the big, bad world, just longing for you to set a paw on their pasture. Danger does not agree with your sensitive nature.

You are by nature insecure. Every time you feel your magic carpet being pulled out from under you, remind yourself of this fact. It can help you to react positively to adversity. Wait it out. Don't allow your blood to boil. Simmer down.

"How can I?" you blast. "Why should I?" you repeat.

Because, if you do not, you will be the sole victim of your inverted anger. By virtue of your sometimes hurt looks and closed-mouth surly attitude toward those you feel have let you down, you often alienate people just when you need them most. If things are troubling you (and, trust me, they will), instead of clamming up speak out. Say what is in your heart precisely when you least want to.

Now, since you tend to take things to heart more readily than some, please do not misinterpret this advice of mine and go about suddenly shouting and thrashing at people who upset you. That will not solve your dilemma. There is, in all of this stuff of life, a happy emotional medium. It will definitely not do for you to begin self-righteously proclaiming that you are unnerved and bitter, and therefore have the right to pop somebody in the nose.

If you do get to feeling low, however, try to overcome your urge to pout it out. Experiment with communication in anxious times. Summon the courage up from your wounded depths and bring your problems to the surface by confronting a loved one or friend openly and candidly on the subject. Go ahead, spill the beans. It's easier than you think to approach the touchy side of life. Just walk right up to the chosen audience and say, "I am not feeling very sure of myself these days. Might we have a talk? Alone?"

As of now, begin to plan ahead. Make allowances for your eccentric nature by developing a rigorous, almost religious devotion to foresight. Look ahead. Don't get discouraged because it appears so complicated. Look again. Then say to yourself, "I can do it. I will be able to meet that deadline on Thursday, March 27, at three o'clock, providing I accomplish one part of the task at a time." Step by step (keeping in mind which day it is and how much time you need for each part of the job), hurdle by hurdle, you will be making your way toward a major victory over your own quirks of fancy.

During this time, if you feel like staying at a party until the hostess throws you out at five A.M., discipline yourself away from that temptation. Leave every alluringly wasteful situation just at the moment when you are having the most fun. Be strict with yourself. Tough it out. The profits will astound you. And the resultant strengthening of your character will please and astonish any and everybody who never gave you credit for being able to take care of yourself. Inch by inch, you will become your own shepherd. By hook or by crook, all of those whom you looked upon as obstacles in the course of your life will either applaud you or be insulted that you dared to fend for yourself. If they walk away in disgust, they weren't worth your intense admiration in the first place.

Goat people are often defenseless prey for the users of this world. They are easily shamed into giving when they should indeed be stashing their share of the taking. My advice to you is this: A helpless kid is a lovable addition to anyone's entourage. Youth becomes people born in Goat years. But can you imagine anyone buying a full-grown Goat to keep as a pet? What could be less attractive than a shaggy overgrown lawn mower bleating about one's backyard? Thus, if the funny little kidlet does not get wise and strike out on his own before maturity sets in, he is destined for somebody's tasty Goat's head soup. Don't let that happen to you.

COMPATIBILITIES

Affairs of the Heart

The emotions of the Goat are a delicate heartstring, often pulled too hard and easily broken by those who do not understand or take care to tread lightly. Needy of much unsolicited affection and peaceful surroundings free from want, the Goat lover can be destroyed in the wink of an eye by Oxen or Dogs. Neither of these signs is indicated as even a vague possibility for the Goat unless he has managed to achieve great success and is already in a position of self-assurance beyond that with which he was born. Dogs, although they respect the Goat's liberal views and charitable opinions, have little time for his seeming inability to go out and fight for his rights. Oxen just steam up their eyeballs at the very idea of the Goat, who is capable of meandering thoughts that take hours to evolve into actions.

Goats, except in crises, are placid and impractical dreamers. They just about never do the same thing twice in the same way. Goats get up every morning and create a new world. A rich and pragmatic Monkey, with his ability to see through the haze in the wink of an eye, will enjoy caring for the Goat's needs, advising him on how to see things more clearly and encouraging him to use his wiles wisely. Horses, too, will not mind helping the gentle Goat of their choice to deal with problems and processes.

The best bet for a Goat, however, is a Cat person. Affectionate, lucky in finance, and good at organizing diplomatically, the Cat can be counted on to make his Goat mate's life a better place to repose in. Besides, Cats are artistic and refined. The two can arrange their mutual existence in quite a lovely manner and never again be forced to deal with unappealing danger.

Pigs make good mates for Goats as they are always fortunate in money matters and will not mind sharing their wealth with so gracious a guest as the Goat. Two sweet natures like their own will be sure to have a special charm. If trouble does arise, Goats should leave it up to the Pig person to enter battle. Goats are easily trounced by strong enemies. Pigs, if angered, are winners every time.

Social Affairs

If I were a mild-mannered Goat, just about nobody would really offend my sense of self. Goats are easygoing where other people's foibles are concerned. They take things as they come and for the most part do not worry unduly about crises until they arise. Because Goats are so malleable, they are also extremely vulnerable to manipulative people.

The fact is, someone usually has to look after the Goat's best interests. Dragons and Horses will do this with pleasure. They recognize the Goat's sensitivities but do not mind giving a Goat a hand up the mountainside. Dragons and Horses can pep up Goat friends and sometimes cheer them into action.

Cats are good friends to Goats. So are patient Snakes and magical Monkeys. All of these will appreciate the Goat for the inventive person he is, and let him go about his business even if it is at their expense.

Conventional Roosters and meticulous Rats feel uncomfortable around Goats. All that dream and scheme without any sense of where it belongs in the real world make the very hackles of these two possible Goat chums rise in dismay.

Tigers and Oxen, though they may befriend the Goat, will soon become exasperated with his moonings and wish him gone from their sight.

Pigs know how to motivate Goats. Their conversations will be fruitful for the Goat and interesting to the Pig. It's a good old school-chum rapport.

With any of the other signs, the Goat will have to watch out for a tendency he is aware of, yet often tries to ignore. He will be capable of losing good friends in trite ways. Too often late for engagements, unmindful of the unspoken needs of friends, never bending to another's scale of priorities, and languishing too long over decisions, the Goat needs an exterior conscience to warn him when friends are becoming angry or impatient. Their temptation is to abandon hope of ever reaching the Goat who seems to them, seated on cloud nine. And the Goat is left bewildered as to where he has gone wrong.

Business Affairs

Business and Goats are two of the most incongruous words I have ever seen juxtaposed on a page. Goats are plainly too nice and generous and easygoing and foggy to purport to be commercially minded. As employees, they are often dutiful. They may be late to work every day, but tasks will be accomplished, anyway. Goats are terrific at overtimes and overnight stints of nonstop labor and can function under almost any duress. Their pattern of application is sketchy but they do persevere.

Partnership in business is quite another thing. Goat talents can be put to good use by those who do not try to routinize them. Monkeys, for example, are brilliant at divining the Goat's abilities and putting them to work for a mutual profit. The Pig, the Dragon, or the Cat will also be sensitive to the Goat's need for encouragement and constant direction.

The Tiger's hotheadedness and ability to charge forth into almost any crowd of dangerous enemies will appeal to the Goat's desire to be associated with someone stronger than himself. But Tigers are not even-tempered enough to battle it out with the Goat's unwillingness to fend for himself. Schism and even violence could ensue. The same holds true for the Ox partner. For a Goat, an Ox is a kind of scary big figure who tromps through the forest at night eating bear meat and growing ever more mean and powerful. If the Ox were not so adverse to giving directive aid, he could help the Goat succeed. But, after about two minutes of Goat gamboling hither and thither, the Ox loses patience and it is all over for that partnership.

Horses would rather eat a Goat than see him succeed. No self respecting Goat should team up with a Horse person. Even though the Horse is fully capable of aiding the Goat, he will be tempted to manipulate him. The generous, nonoriented Goat will lose face and funds in the bargain

Pigs find Goats more than useful. A Pig/Goat association will surely profit. You see, Pigs are scrupulous and honest to a fault. Goats, too, are a bit gullible. But the Pig is lucky. And the Goat has guile. Good things will result from this positive union of force and imagination.

Family Affairs

Here we have a basically indulgent, warm-hearted parent who may be overwhelmed at the amount of activity that childbearing and raising seems to involve. Will that baby never stop crying and grow up to be the parent Goat's companion? Sorry, Goat, that is not the way it works. Years of your precious dreamtime will perforce be spent walking floors and burping tiny bundles in the night.

You may not like these intrusions, but you do love your children. And, when you can, you provide admirably for their needs. The Goat is among the most soft-hearted persons alive. He will bestow time and money on his kids. But he could be disappointed to find that they do not always reciprocate.

With Monkey, Dog, or Cat children, the Goat parent will find common terrains of interest and discussion. Rats and Snakes find the Goat's shifts of routine hard to follow. But they are all amused by the Goat's fine sense of humor and ability to laugh at himself. Roosters and Oxen simply do not understand what all the fuss and constant change of rules is about.

Egocentric Dragon and Horse children, though they may love the Goat for his unorthodox ways and means, are often too demanding of the Goat's personal quiet time. A badgered Goat can be a very angry parent.

Tigers have no time for their Goat parents' wavering opinions. Avoidance measures will quickly be taken by the child born in a Tiger year. The Goat should be aided by a strong mate in the raising of this headstrong creature. Pig children indulge Goat parents in their peregrinations. Finally, it is the Pig child who appreciates his Goat mom or dad the most. He will always pay close attention to even an aging Goat parent. Pigs love romance. The romantic Goat supplies a Pig child with generous fairy tales for a lifetime.

THE MONKEY

THE YEARS OF THE MONKEY

February 2, 1908 to January 22, 1909
February 20, 1920 to February 8, 1921
February 6, 1932 to January 26, 1933
January 25, 1944 to February 13, 1945
February 12, 1956 to January 31, 1957
January 29, 1968 to February 16, 1969
February 16, 1980 to February 4, 1981
February 4, 1992 to January 22, 1993

MONKEYS ARE:

Acutely intelligent • Witty • Inventive • Affable
Problem-solvers • Independent • Skillful business people
Achievers • Enthusiastic • Lucid • Nimble • Passionate
Youthful • Fascinating • Clever

BUT THEY CAN ALSO BE:

Tricky tacticians • Vain • Dissimulators
Opportunistic • Long-winded • Not all that trustworthy
Unfaithful • Adolescent • Unscrupulous

MONKEYS I HAVE KNOWN AND LOVED

There is something indubitably wiry in the posture of this astute creature. Even portly monkeys such as Craig Claiborne, the food writer (a 1920 Monkey), and Elizabeth Taylor (a 1932 Monkey) seem to be more flexibly hung together than other corpulent types. Perhaps it is the eyes. You will recall the simian quality about the wise face of the famous Judge Learned Hand (an 1872 Monkey), and if you don't believe me, take a gander at a photo of Bella Abzug (a 1920 Monkey) or Melvin Van Peebles (a 1932 Monkey) when you have a chance.

Monkeys, you will find out as you discover which of your friends were born in those years, are generally remarkably bright. They also tend to be funny. I mean, fall-about-laughing, hilarious witty, and I also mean jab-stab, right-on-the-mark-sarcastic amusing. Either way, with a monkey in your entourage you are in for a lot of laughs.

I seem to have met jillions of Monkeys all over the world. Either they proliferate more than other people or they just happen to be on the lam much of the time. I say this only because one of the least attractive Monkey character traits is—I might as well say it—that they are not exactly the most honest people alive.

How can I put this so it doesn't sound as though all Monkeys are liars and cheaters and dissimulators? Frankly, folks, it isn't easy. But here goes.

There are two kinds of Monkey living inside each Monkey person. On the surface all Monkeys are affable, sociable, and loving individuals. But somewhere inside of every Monkey is the seed of deception. The Monkey's garden must be deftly weeded both by himself and those around him. Otherwise, he risks being hoist in his own petard.

Here's a good example of soundly applied Monkey deception. One day last year I drove to the suburbs of Paris to hunt for a low-priced antique couch. When a cup of coffee on a Paris café terrace costs one dollar plus tip, you can imagine the exorbitant price of antiques. One searches out low prices wherever they might find them. So off I went in my battered VW with my friend and fellow bargain hunter, Marie-Christine De La Rochefoucauld (Monkey, 1932).

Marie-Christine is one of the most comical women in the world today. She is one of those brilliant sorts who benefits from total recall of everything that has ever occurred in her own and everyone else's life. Every detail of every funny (and unfunny) event gets told and retold by Marie-Christine who has an uncanny ability for embroidery and satire in storytelling. In short, despite the fact that she talks a bit much, Marie-Christine is very good company.

After browsing through about six chic little antique "shoppes" on the main highway, we both realized that suburb or no suburb we were still over our heads money-wise. After looking at too many over-stuffed, over-priced monstrosities, Marie-Christine poked me in the ribs and suggested we try the Saint Vincent de Paul warehouse near St. Germain en Laye. This establishment is equivalent to our Salvation Army or Good Will Industries store. Unfortunately, though, French people are more conservative about throwing things away, so one doesn't expect to find a Louis XV buffet hiding in a corner, just dying to be snapped up for one franc. Occasionally there is a good deal to be had. And, knowing Marie-Christine, if there's a corner to be cut, she'll have her scissors ready.

Eureka! Right smack in the center of the heap of rickety furniture from the Early Concierge period stood a nineteenth-century love seat, the proportions of which were ideal for my pocket-hankie living

room. The people who set the prices of such castoffs are not as dumb
as they once were about the real worth of such pearls, but in any case,
forty dollars for an item I adored was better than two hundred for
something I hated. My purchase had a popped spring and spoiled a
jaunty tilt due to a cracked leg, but I knew I could fix that.

As I paid the little man at the cash register, I inquired as to the
days of delivery in the city. I'm glad you weren't there to see my face
when he told me, "I am desolate, madame, but Saint Vincent de Paul
does not deliver."

"Fie on Saint Vincent de Paul!" snapped Marie-Christine irreli-
giously. "Never mind. We'll find a way."

From a pay phone on the wall, I called at least ten local delivery
and moving services. All they could say was, "One small divan? Sorry,
madame. No go." And things like that. Discouraged, I told Marie-
Christine it would just have to wait until Saturday when I could have
my neighbor's Renault station wagon. I told the man at the cash register I would come back for my treasure on the weekend. "We are again
desolate," he lamented, "but we cannot hold merchandise for clients."

Verging on nervous collapse, I looked to Marie-Christine in
hopes she would at least say something to make me laugh off my
dilemma. Instead, she looked straight at the man in the booth and
said, "You keep that couch for one hour. We are going to find a
mover." Marie-Christine is from a noble family. Most of the time she
knows how to keep it to herself. But France is France and when
Marie-Christine feels the need she pulls her class out of her jeans
jacket and lobs it at whomever seems to need a dose. "*Oui, madame,*"
the guy said humbly. Proud almost to be put in his place by this suddenly haughty young woman, he ticketed the settee "Sold" and grumbled away to himself about "Les Parisiennes."

We giggled into the car. "Where are we going?" I asked.

"To the grungiest bar you can find. Step on it!" she replied.

Dingy is the word for the bar we found in a neighboring village, dingy and rundown. Sitting up to the bar, Marie-Christine told
me from out the side of her mouth, "I'll handle this. You keep
quiet." I kept quiet.

The proprietor wiped our bar space languidly with an antique rag and said, "What are you drinking?"

"Nice place you have here," smiled Marie-Christine as she surveyed the squalor around her. "So authentic."

"Yeah," he snorted disdainfully.

"That's some opening line," I snickered. "I'll have a kir, please, Not too much syrup."

Without convulsing even the slightest bit, Marie-Christine kept it up. "I'll have the same. How's business these days? A little slow with the inflation, I'll bet." She was valiant.

The bartender did not answer. He walked to the other end of the bar and picked up his racing form.

"Know anybody who has a pick-up truck around here?" she yelled at the top of her voice.

The owner only shook his head from side to side, wishing certainly that M-C would shut up and go back to the Champs Élysées where she so evidently came from.

But Marie-Christine was not about to give up her quest. Monkeys are inveterate problem-solvers. They like to see things through—on their own terms. She turned to the young man sitting next to her and began chatting him up. "Hello, my name is Marie Dubois, and this is Suzanne White. What's your name?" she inquired.

"Pierre," he muttered embarrassedly.

"Do you come here often?" An element of "What's a pretty girl like you doing in a place like this?" tinged her voice.

He smiled back at her. "Only when I'm not working."

"So you're on vacation then?" M-C nodded, raising her right eye brow. French vacations ordinarily do not take place in sordid suburban bars in mid-March.

"On strike," the man said, examining his beer dregs.

"Would you have a beer with us?" Good old M-C. Right in there when she's needed.

"That's nice of you. Sure will." He brightened immediately.

Marie-Christine ordered him a beer and excused herself to go to the 'toilettes.' I chatted with the man about hard times and how little the unions paid pickets. Marie-Christine cleverly returned when the man's beer was conveniently half drunk. The man clinked his glass against hers saying, "Here's to a *grande dame* who bought me a beer. Wait'll I tell my wife. Say, did I hear you say you were looking for somebody with a truck?"

I swear Marie-Christine is a miracle worker when it comes to hustle. I call her Madame Emergency.

Clinking her glass against his this time she gave him one of her specially conjured worried looks, "We sure do need a truck. We haven't got much money and we have to move a piece of furniture to Paris. You can't imagine how much movers charge for one trip to the city. It's insane. Since Giscard told them about the inflation, everybody's raising prices because they think it's good for France or something. Have you noticed the cost of food lately?"

Of course, this man had a truck. He was an out-of-work plumber with nothing else to do but move my couch thirty kilometers away. But he was also proud, a bit lazy, and not so sure he wanted to help out a couple of wise-guy girls from the city who bought him one measly beer.

"What are you doing this afternoon?" asked Marie-Christine, as she ordered him another beer.

"I'd like to watch the soccer match on TV, but my wife prefers the afternoon film, so I guess I'll watch that. Anyway, she doesn't like having me around all the time. I get in her way."

The "ah hah!" look in M-C's eye forced me to turn my head in shame. I knew just what she would do now.

She placed her hand on the man's shoulder in chumlike fashion. "Wehell, what a funny coincidence. Suzanne and I are avid soccer fans. We always watch the matches together at her house. It's better in color. I only have black and white. How about you?"

He only had a small black and white and he claimed that out there in the boondocks he did not get very good reception without an aerial.

"It's perfect, then. You come and watch the match with us this afternoon. I'll ride into town in your truck with you so we can find the house. That way, you get to see your game and Suzanne gets her couch moved."

How could he resist? Marie-Christine had plied him with every ploy known to man. Neither she nor myself had ever watched a soccer match in our lives, nor is her name Dubois, nor would she dream of owning a TV set, black and white or color.

The couch looks great now. I fixed the broken leg with epoxy and re-covered it in chintz. The spring shows through a bit but I keep a pillow over it when company comes.

Rather than calling it dissembling, I prefer to think of this twinge in the Monkey character as skill or inventiveness. When faced with an urgent puzzle, no means is too mischievous for a Monkey. He, in point of fact, takes great pleasure in pulling capers such as the one I just described. As long as the lies remain on the whiter side of gray, the Monkey should not have to leave town in a hurry.

Unlike the Tiger, who rushes in where Monkeys fear to tread, the Monkey's attitude toward challenge is one of clear-thinking lucidity. Faced with a complex situation, Monkeys sort things through. They weigh the pros and cons as they hop from foot to foot in front of the mirror (dandies, one and all). Then, and only after due consideration, they will either undertake to solve the problems at hand as quickly and cleverly as it can be done, or if they see a mountain before them and feel it is out of their mountain-climbing league, they are likely to drop the subject once and for all. They are not foolhardy and are usually well aware of their own limits.

One exceptional quality that Monkey people possess is their all-out enthusiasm for projects of vast scope. I wish you could have seen the "before" photographs of Yul Brynner's (Monkey, 1920) Norman-style manor house in the French countryside. Wooden beams going this way and that, crumbling stucco, immense rooms with sagging high ceilings, acres of overgrown shrubs literally crawling with weeds—the potential renovation job would have discouraged Tishman & Co. I swear Walt Disney (a 1901 Ox) would have balked at the idea of refurbishing such a palazzo. But not Yul Brynner. He just up and bought the whole shebang—lock, stock, and termites. For gossip's sake, I might add, those darling little shacks don't come cheap.

Mind you, if Yul Brynner were an idle millionaire and did not have twelve or fifteen scripts to read a week, a giant flock of homing pigeons to keep worldwide tabs on, a horde of dogs to breed, the odd TV series to act in, a feature film to make from time to time, an appropriately elegant French wife to love, a nine-year-old daughter to fly back and forth from Switzerland to school, and a brilliant prodigal grown son to sort out from time to time, such a project as he envisaged when he bought his country manor would not have seemed all that overwhelming to those of us who gasped as we were shown the packet of "before" photos.

"But, Rock," I felt obliged to tell his son as he carefully repacked the series of snapshots in his famous magic bag, "it looks as though it's about to cave in. Your father will be too old to live in it by the time the workmen even get around to replacing all the missing roof tiles."

"Not if he has anything to say about it, he won't be too old. You don't know my father yet. You cannot conceive of the brand of will he exhibits the face of such projects. All our houses have been like that. My dad is accustomed to transforming property. The worst sow's ears become sprawling, yet cozy homes when he gets his hands on them. That piercing stare of his cuts through the heart of the problem in no time. My illustrious father is no joke. He means business." Rock appeared worn-out at the very thought. He is a 1946 Dog and decidedly different from Yul. But more about that later.

In but a matter of months the aforementioned shambles was not only livable but it was metamorphasized. Orderly flower beds supplanted the vagrant vegetation; a new roof shone brick-red in the all-too-occasional Normandy sunshine; outbuildings, annexes, furniture, etc., were arranged in the best of taste. Yul Brynner's tumble-down white elephant had become a very spiffy residence worthy of its dignified master.

The day I saw the finished product, Brynner Sr. was not at home. "Where's your father these days?" I snooped at Rock, curious as always.

"He's in Vietnam today," Rock replied casually.

"Entertaining the troops?" was my only possible thought.

"No, silly. He's gone to pick up my sister."

"Stop mucking about, Rock. Your sister isn't in Vietnam. She's only nine years old and I happen to know she's in school in Switzerland." One of Rock's major talents is that of a raconteur par excellence—in four languages. I was dubious.

"Not that sister. The new one. He's adopted two Vietnamese orphans this year and he had to go there to be sure he could get the second one safely out of the country." Rock sighed with annoyance at my apparent naïveté where his father's latest comings and goings were concerned.

But, in his typically indulgent fashion, he dipped into the magic bag once again. "Would you like to see some photos of my baby sister? She's really smashingly cute."

And so she was. A China doll newborn whom Yul Brynner was winging single-handedly across thousands of miles to raise à l'Américaine in an old French chateau. I suppose for the average monkey c'est normal or something like that.

Although it is not altogether deplorable, there is one notable Monkey characteristic that can be vexing. Those born in Monkey years are wont to perform whatever deeds, good or bad, in the interest of self. Even the most seemingly charitable or helpful acts, when they come from a Monkey, are assuredly one form or another of means to an end. You may be astonished at this barb and hasten to point out to me that this could not apply to your Monkey friends, since the Monkey people you know are usually so willing to serve you, to care for your needs in troublesome situations, to be an indulgent listener (despite the fact that they generally prefer to do lots of the talking).

True enough, Monkeys make excellent companions and friends—for people from whom they want something. Not that going after something as decent as friendship or warmth or affection is a necessarily evil trait. It is just that because of the Monkey character, when dealing with Monkey people often, one should bear in mind that theirs is a peculiarly self-serving motivation. Otherwise, all those exhibits of self-denial, those long hours spent helping one dig out from under, those manifestations of apparent self-abnegation will fool you into thinking all Monkeys are striving to compete with Florence Nightingale (Dragon, 1820) for hero status.

The reason I bother to point this out to you at all is that it has been my experience as a long-time Monkey observer that they get away with rather more than their share of "looking-good" when the proverbial peanut butter has entered the electric ventilating machine. Perhaps I should explain.

For rather a lengthy period (for me) I was romantically involved with a wondrously sought-after Monkey gent who writes detective novels. From where he perches in his expensive and chicly under-heated little garret room overlooking the Seine River in the heart of the Latin Quarter, typing away and sighing impressive literary sighs all day, dreamily watching the smoke from his Gauloises rise and waft out into Paris's dappled skies, life just couldn't be all that bad. But for my friend, Jean-Valere, *la vie* is just a tiny bit too often an insufferable "drague." And, when he was my boyfriend, this untenable place he was forced to occupy off the most glorious part of the earth's face was all the more unlivable because of my overt insistence that it was entirely worrisome having to witness all those wistful gazings toward heaven he alleged were "nossing at all." I'm not the critical-type lady who picks and nags but obviously nobody wants to hang about someone else's life watching them dig themselves being miserable so much of the time. Especially when it was so obvious that Jean-Valere silently implied that the whole despicable ennui he had to put up with was all my fault.

So what did I do to try and cure the ill? Well, first of all, I wrote very fast. He was having such difficulty yanking even a syllable from out his IBM Selectric in a day's time that I began taking piles of work off his shoulders by toiling late into the early mornings at my own place on the ancient wreck of a typewriter Jean-Valere had so generously laid on me when he had received the hundred-thousand-franc advance on his latest book. Secondly, I might as well admit I wrote his book for him. He gave me some ideas a lot of the time, but since he can't stand to be *dérangé* at night, rather than phone him to ask how he wanted the killers to get caught or what gory aspect the gigolo's corpse ought to sport, I just began to make it up as I went along. It was good practice. Or, at least that's what I told myself as I slogged on through detail after detail, copying his style, and worrying he might not approve.

When I would arrive at his place with folders of bloodshed and chapters full of cops chatting in the back room about the facts of the case, Jean-Valere was always all over me with praise. I was so wonderful to him. He honestly thought he did not deserve me. No man was luckier than he. He gave me presents. He took me on trips. He showered me with fine wines and flowers. And in fact, for a time, he actually did less of that awful sighing.

It wasn't a bad life being the hired hand/mistress of a famous author. I am not attempting to imply it was. Six Paris months with Jean-Valere were glorious. He was a good lover and a fine friend. Besides, I was leaming. I had only written magazine articles in French before. I'd always wondered if I might be able to attempt a book in my adopted language. Doing his work had proven that I could.

When the book came out, the *editeurs* (that's the publisher in France) gave a *coquetale* (which is a stand-up drinking-party practice the French have adopted to add chic to their already overpleasant social customs) in honor of Jean-Valere. As we stood talking with my beau's editor, whiskey and ice tinkling away merrily in our gesticulating hands, I was asked the following question: "What do you do, mademoiselle?" French men have a winning habit of referring to ladies of all ages as mademoiselle to make them feel like nubile beauty queens, no matter how old or married they might appear.

I smiled. "I'm a writer."

"*Journaliste!*" Jean-Valere corrected me loudly. "You are only a journalist."

"Well, I do write things, don't I?" I winked at Jean-Valere, hoping for some show of complicity on his part about our recent "collaboration."

"You write magazine articles. In France, you are called a journalist." This was said as if being a mere journalist was like having full-time scabies from birth.

Tension was mounting. But so were my high horses. I certainly didn't want Jean-Valere to tell his editor that I was Mary McCarthy's gifted writer daughter who needed a ten-thousand-dollar advance right away in order to write her mother's biography. I simply wanted him personally, secretly even, to recognize and infer that I was not your average dumdum American fashion journalist running around Paris dashing off an occasional "Eye" for *Women's Wear Daily.*

So I nudged him. Then, addressing myself to his editor, I said, "I have done a lot of fiction ghostwriting in French this year. I am about to begin work on a novel of my own. I think I am about ready to do some serious work in French now."

"You are not French?" the editor commented, eyebrows raised.

Always delighted when people are fooled by my convincing Parisian accent, I poked Jean-Valere again and laughed. "You see, chéri, Monsieur Buffon didn't guess I am American." Then I explained I had lived in France since I was twenty-one and had struggled very long and hard to lose my accent.

"She has an accent." Jean-Valere was clearly losing his mind on the spot. I had never dreamed he could be so damning of me. He had always been my biggest booster, bolstering my ego and encouraging my writing efforts. I felt like pouring my drink on his left Gucci loafer.

While they spattered on about did I or didn't I have an accent, I stood there cooking up a scheme worthy of Catherine de Médicis on a nasty binge. When the proper pause came along, I lied through my teeth, in my most perfect French (avoiding the words I knew I might have trouble making absolutely authentic). "I have an outline for a detective novel I want to write. I have shown it to several editors. They are enthusiastic. I will come in and see you on Thursday at ten o'clock. *D'accord?*"

Jean-Valere choked on an olive. I went home to sulk with a good book.

This story could very well have been just another in a series of inflated male ego chauvinism or whatnot, were it not for the fact that the book I pouted over for the next two days was *Zelda,* by Nancy Milford. Out of curiosity, whenever I read about real people, I look up their Chinese signs. Scott Fitzgerald was born in September of 1896. Jean-Valere was born in 1932. That made a couple of apes out of both of them. And helped me to understand a lot more about the Monkey character.

Sublime, however, about Monkeys is their extravagant facility for being engaging. In all kinds of cunning ways, Monkey people exert their winsome personalities on even the most resistant of audiences. Gruff waitresses who chuck the food over diner counters all over the world, surly sales people in massive department stores who never even look your way as you shift from foot to tired foot at the underwear counter, hoping in vain for a receptive glance, tough-guy telephone operators who refuse to keep looking for your friend Charley's phone number in Podunk, Maine, where there is only one phone in the whole village and you don't know the name of the people from whom he is renting his house—all those ice-cube citizens we so cherish in our day-to-day—become sticky-sweet root-beer popsicles fairly dripping with cloy when wily Monkey goes into his seduction act.

Just for fun, I'll show you how it goes. You hop into a New York City taxicab's torn back seat, gun-shy plastic cubicle of a torrid tropical evening. You are from out of town and don't know Greenwich Village from Greenwich time zone. The driver (also of durable vinyl) doesn't understand you because you have an Ohio accent and you talk funny. You ask him to take you to Sheridan Square, which is only two blocks away. He groans and drives you down to Chinatown for a half-hour guided tour and runs up the meter so it shouldn't be a total loss for him. By the time you realize he is ripping you off, you get mad and threaten him with instant police action. He then shrieks some filth at you, which you can't comprehend, anyway, because he has a Brooklyn accent and he talks funny. In short, you have a row and you end up giving him your wrist watch in return for some peace of mind. End of scene with normal human being.

To a Monkey, this horror show would never happen. Monkeys are careful and clever, lucid, and inventive. A Monkey gets into a New York bullet-proof, hotbox taxicab of a blistering evening and says, "How far is it to Sheridan Square, please?"

"Couple o' blocks," murmurs the polyester hack inaudibly.

"I'm terribly sorry but I can't hear you. Could you speak up, please, Sir? I'm afraid this wall in front of me here is preventing me from hearing you correctly. I really am so sorry but would you mind repeating yourself?" It takes Monkeys a bit longer but they are effective.

"A COUPLE O' BLOCKS. I SAID TWO. ONE AND ONE AH TWO BLOCKS FROM HEEYAH! YOU DEAF ER SUMPMIN'?" Charm oozes from those altruistic souls who chauffeur one in Gotham. The cabby flicks open the clouded porthole, exasperatedly.

"I hate to ask you to do this. I realize it's a very short distance, but would you drive me there? It is raining so hard outside." The car starts rolling. "I can't see you very well, but your picture on that permit up there tells me you sure are a likable fellow. Is that an English name? I knew someone once in London who was called Lefkowitz. Just like you. He was a member of Parliament. Must be a distant cousin of yours or something." Chatter, chatter, ply, and ploy. The Monkey does go on. And with reason. The driver is so enticed astray by the interim Monkey business he is undergoing, he could not possibly refuse to run the two blocks quickly and efficiently and cheaply. Monkey wiles are like the worst (or the best) brand of feminine trumped-up subterfuge. It is not natural charm or magnetism that makes them win over the worst sorts of grumps to their side. Oh, no. It is real hard work, forethought, and malice of the top-drawer variety. It requires profuse quick-wittedness and a singular intelligence.

When the brains were handed out, Monkeys were at the head of the line. All the Monkeys that I know are smarties. Everything that has ever been fed into their mental computers has been recorded for life. Press the handy button located conveniently on the tip of the ringtail and Monkey people go into their spiels. If it was Sunday, the fourteenth of August, in 1934 when Rafe Hardy won his match against the world champion domino player in Helsinki, the Monkey will probably be able to tell you what the weather was like in Finland that day. They are the kind of people who finish crossword puzzles in five minutes while you're still erasing your first boo-boo from the down column, which ought to have been in the across squares. Their wisdom is not usually of the pithy academic ilk, either. They are impatient with heavy subjects such as philosophy or

Sanskrit. They would be more likely to know all about the exquisite table manners of Socrates than what he said in his writings. Their wits are snappy and nimble.

Monkey people should be given nonboring jobs. Ask a Monkey to be a file clerk for a living and see how long he lasts. It just wouldn't work—unless, of course, the files were in exceedingly bad shape and needed sorting through, reshaping, and revamping entirely. In two days he would have finished that heinous task and asked for something more to do. He likes to keep busy. He likes to deal with problems others cannot handle. But he is also rather easily discouraged if his task is too complex or unwieldy. Monkeys are anything but lazy, yet they will balk at too formidable a demand on their emotional time. Progress is their most important product. They must be made to feel they are advancing, improving, growing, as it were, within the confines of an employ. It is not necessary for them to be bosses, although they are often good at performing executive functions. Monkey people are capable of taking a back seat to someone they admire and look up to. They make superior journalists.

Emotionally, the Monkey is easily discouraged. One never knows all the tragic details of such untimely demises but Sylvia Plath (Monkey, 1932) must have found her acerbic writer's insight and image too Herculean a burden to be carried.

Marriage and family life will be complicated for most Monkeys. Fidelity is not their favorite sport. I mean, think about it for a minute. How would you like to be the long-suffering lifemate of Angela Davis (b. 1944)? Not that I am privy to whether or not Ms. Davis entertains more than one lover at a time. Such inferences would be presumptuous. But one must agree that her rather hectic life style is not exactly conducive to the "Hi, honey, I'm home" school of behavior. Monkeys are more than occasionally single. Or, they may just be between marriages. Multiple marriage is not uncommon among Monkey Year people. They are spurred by fantasy, drawn away from the ordinary more easily than most, and so enthusiastic about novelty that plain old meat-and-potatoes relationships don't manage to tickle their fancies for as long as they might.

MADAME MONKEY

Hark back, if you will, to your childhood. Do you remember some-body named Wendy? No, I don't mean the little girl with the pigtails who sat next to you in the second grade. I'm talking about Wendy Darling, the big sister of Michael and John. The bright little charmer who "oohed" and "ahhed" over a green fairy who flew in her window one day from off the label on a peanut butter jar. *That* Wendy.

Invented as she was by one of our most talented Monkey writers, J.M. Barrie (Monkey, 1860), clever Wendy is the arch-type Monkey lady. How many eleven-year-old girls do you know who would leave their happy homes, nannies, lullabies, comfort, and security to take off with an airborne nut case who refuses to grow up? At sixteen perhaps, but at eleven? If you give it some consideration, I think you will agree Barrie could not help but make his female star into something akin to himself. Wendy is somewhat softer and slightly more sensible and warm than your average knockabout male runaway dropout. (In those days women were not noted for pulling midnight splits on their fami-lies.) Still, she did take off without so much as permission from the control tower at London airport, hell-bent for an ephemeral destina-tion called Never Never Land. Child development specialists can tell you these are not the normal symptoms of prepubescent cold feet.

Granted, she did come back. She probably even grew up and had a baby and learned how to bake banana bread. For the purposes of Barrie's story, there was no other way for her to go.

Yet, who is to say that in the next installment—and we can only guess—another flight of fancy did not occur in the middle of some dark night? It could have been Zorro or the Little Prince who took her away. Fact is, Wendy is the kind of girl who does not at all mind being heisted from one situation to another so long as the kidnappers keep her amused.

One Monkey girl friend of mine in Paris is notorious for commit-ting such follies and befuddling me time after time with her elusiveness. When Kitty enters our inner sanctum writers' café in Montparnasse, cheers go up. She is invited to sit at everybody's table at once. "Where have you been? We missed you. What are you doing these days? We thought you moved to Africa? I heard you were on the Johnny Carson show last year. Is that true?" She smiles and inquires after this one's wife and that one's latest novel, oblivious to the fact that most of us really imagined her to be dead or spirited off somewhere.

If one succeeds in enticing Kathryn to one's table, an otherwise dull evening's writer conversation automatically turns into a one-woman show. Jokes, stories about far-out people in faraway places, eccentric events on trains and boats, the weensiest detail that nobody else would consider even vaguely amusing are transformed into a stand-up comic's best routine.

Is this marvel a writer? Is she a famous comedienne? Not at all. She's a free-lance secretary for famous people. With this, she runs about the world gathering tidbits of joy and bringing them back to her cronies at the café. Monkey women are not supposed to be personally ambitious. I would say Kitty is just about as typical as they come.

Monkey women have an endearing gaminlike aura about them. Maybe it is better expressed as jaundice-eyed innocence, or more simply as a Geraldine Chaplinesque funny-face look. In any case, they tend to be cute rather than ravishing beauties. They appeal to the big brother who lives in the heart of everyman. But watch out, messieurs, what looks like an ability to acclimatize in Monkey women, or a facility for adaptation, is once again not the whole picture. Within the confines of a sound marriage or family, fantasy will rear its clownish head day after day searching for distractions. Keep your Monkey entertained. Movies, parties, theater dates, all variety of media input are essential for Monkey ladies to even remotely consider accepting the role of stay-at-home. Sables? Luxury? Expensively decorated abodes? Ritzy cars? The Monkey couldn't care less. Data is what turns her on. Phones ringing and problems to solve are the very stuff of her life.

Interest in sex, for Monkey women, is less a purely physical pursuit than for those born in other years. Monkeys are cerebral. They have to be turned on upstairs before the lights flash in the basements of their souls. Tell a Monkey a good joke for her repertoire and she'll follow you anywhere. Remind her of her grandfather who spoke with a lilt in his voice and she will never forget you. And don't worry about her. I have seen Monkey girls make off in the night with men whose looks would startle you in a dark alley. Sinister types do not discourage the wily Monkey. Somehow, the viciousness you guess might be skulking behind that swarthy brow is never visited upon our heroine. She is the kind of girl who could live five years with a raving drunk who beats up sailors in bars for a lark and come out of it unscathed. Remember, she is flexible and she knows how to make lemonade out of sour apples in the wink of an eye.

More loyal than her male counterpart, the woman born in a Monkey Year is not by nature a gadfly. Too busy with her innumerable engagements and socializing, she prefers to remain faithful to one man rather than be forced out of her tree with what she considers the idle frippery of promiscuity for its own sake. If, however, her life with you is stultifying and she sees no light at the end of the tunnel, she will very possibly flee right out that bedroom window with someone jollier than thee.

This is not to say that Monkey women who run away with leprechauns are doing so because they don't like you any more. Not by a long shot. Monkeys like to keep their friends, smooth over old wounds, put Band-Aids on the injured psyche of a rejected suitor. Don't be surprised if she phones you up from Never Never Land and invites you to come for dinner and meet her new lover, the unemployed tap dancer who reminds her of her old boss and is laid up with a broken leg. She is neither vengeful nor does she feel remorse over your breakup. She hears no evil, sees no evil, and speaks with a forked tongue. It's anything but dull.

Finally, the best visual aid I can think of to help draw this picture of a Monkey woman is to tell you that Imogene Coca, the famous funny lady of live TV with the elastic face, was born in the Monkey Year 1908. Heaven knows, she got up to a lot of shenanigans in her day.

MONSIEUR MONKEY

How can I tell you? What words will describe this darling lunatic of a man? The thought of Monkey men conjures an image of Federico Fellini's (Monkey, 1920) maddest movies superimposed on Charlie Parker's (Monkey, 1920) most far-out chord changes, and somehow mysteriously jelled into a persona not unlike that outspoken curiosity seeker we all know as Howard Cosell (Monkey, 1920). It is not fair to say that they are all a little cuckoo, but that's about as close as I can come.

First of all, Monkey men invariably look as though they have been doing more laughing or crying than the rest of the population. Maybe they squint too much to put that gleam into their eye. Anyway, they always seem to be either convulsed or in deep despair. For a Monkey man there is no in-between emotion. The expression varies between comic and tragic. Take a peek at Milton Berle sometime (Monkey, 1920) and see if you don't agree.

For some reason they appear to have cornered the market on eternal youth. I guess that comes from a state of mind. Brynner has no hair, so it can't be that Monkey men don't lose theirs. My friend Jean Valere whom I wrote about earlier has deep furrows in his brow from heaving all those interminable sighs. So it is not that they don't take life seriously. The great Judge Learned Hand, though he looked like the meanest old man of the mountain when he scowled at crooks over a gavel, had a juvenile streak of "Monkeying around" in him that, according to one of his grandchildren, always disrupted Christmas and Thanksgiving dinners. What he did, among other merrymakings, was perform self-directed, produced, acted, sung, and danced versions of Gilbert and Sullivan operettas. Hopping about the room, Judge Hand would carouse and caper up a storm for the little ones whilst other grownups sat sedately in wing-back chairs talking of Michelangelo. I asked his granddaughter to what she attributed this kiddish behavior in the otherwise sage jurist. "Oh, Grandpa? He never took himself very seriously." That may be the clue we were looking for.

I think of one winter night in Montparnasse's fabled dining hall, La Coupole. It was approximately four years ago. In those days, one was still allowed to remain glued to the same chair in this railroad station of a restaurant for hours on end sipping the one drink you could afford and watching the world go by. It must have been midnight when I saw Melvin Van Peebles (Monkey, 1932), famed young black director/producer of *Sweet Badass*, etc., swagger down the middle aisle. He stopped at the odd table of fans, finally settling at the one I was sharing with a scenario writer friend. We had both known Melvin in the old days. The early sixties scene in Paris was crawling with geniuses who either ran away and sought their fortunes elsewhere or decided to stick it out until the prices went down.

After bussing him fondly on both checks (*á la Française*) and buying him a drink, my friend asked for the names of a couple of producers he might go and see about his film scripts.

"Call so-and-so at Warner Brothers here in Paris," said Melvin, smirking. "He'll try and put you off, but that's okay. He knows who you are. He's after his piece of the black movie market. He'll talk with you, anyway."

"Well, like what should I say? Can I say you have read my stuff and you think it's worth doing? I mean I sort of don't know how to approach it. If I could use your name—"

"Use my name??? Are you trying to do yourself in up front? I, man, am the pariah of all pariahs for those guys. I did it myself. Without their bread. I wouldn't advise you to even mention my name. But . . ." he sipped his drink, glowing with some inner glee, and added, "if one of them does bring up my name, tell them you think I'm crazy. Tell them you have always considered me to be totally nuts. That's what they want to hear. How do you think they feel knowing I'm out here laughing all the way to the bank? Not too well-disposed, man, not too well-disposed."

What struck me about these remarks was their obvious absence of self-aggrandizement. Humility is a superior form of strength. Monkeys have lots of that.

If you meet a Monkey man in a party, he won't tell you he is the president of Standard Oil when he's really a ditch digger. Nor will he tell you he is the president of Standard Oil if he is. He'll probably think up something silly to say to put you off your question. He wants first to be liked for himself, for his personality and ability to amuse and beguile you. He, in fact, worries about whether he is liked or not. It would never be enough if you simply told him you "loved him to pieces." He needs to be your friend, too. He wants someone to chat with.

Exchanging ideas and opinions is far more important to the Monkey male than whether or not he gets you into bed on the first date. Although he is sexual beyond belief, he is not one to share his wild oats with just anybody. Foreplay and afterglow, to him, are the best part of love-making. He wants to play. Conquests for the sake of themselves bore him to tears. It's too easy. Monkey men like girls with pep, girls who speak up and do things on their own. Don't lean on him. He'll trip you and giggle when you fall down.

Who could say it better than J.M. Barrie? Peter Pan was a Monkey man/boy. What he cared for more than anything was that permanent boarding pass to get him on the fantasy-land express. As he flew across the stage in the Broadway production singing, "Ah, the cleverness of me," and taught his boys to repeat after him, "I won't grow up. I won't grow up. I don't want to go to school," who didn't want to hug him, to agree with him, and to enter his wonderland—if only for a moment? Titillate the fantasies of your Monkey man. Find out what turns him on in his head. I guarantee he will teach you how to fly.

CO-SIGNS

MONKEY/Aries *(March 21—April 20)*

Fire and metal combine to make Aries people born in Monkey years possessed of a will of iron and nerves of steel. Aries subjects will benefit from being born Monkeys. Forging ahead on a hundred and one projects at once, they will profit from monkey lucidity, caution, and forethought. Howard Cosell is an Aries Monkey. You can see that he doesn't let any grass grow under his feet.

MONKEY/Taurus *(April 21—May 21)*

This time Monkey metal joins forces with earth. A gold mine? . . . Very likely. Since Taureans are slow to arouse, phlegmatic, and langorous, they would be lucky Monkeys indeed. The quick-witted Monkey infuses the surly bull with a much-needed sense of humor about himself. Monkeys are nice guys. Taureans can use a bit of that affability. There ought not to be much worry about money here. Both signs are lucky in finance. The Monkey side of this character, however, will push to spend it more flagrantly than his Taurus half. If you spot any unusually jolly toros in your entourage, find out what year they were born.

MONKEY/Gemini *(May 22—June 21)*

One of the Chinese astrologers I spoke to in my hunt for this data wrote down some of the characteristics I should look for in the Monkey people I was writing about, saying, "Monkey is for me like Gemini to you." It was one of the few cross references he mentioned specifically. It is patently true. Monkey people do resemble Geminis. This air and metal combination takes off in so many directions at once you may think you are standing in the middle of the main runway at O'Hare Airport when he taxis into your life. Geminis are supertalkers. Monkeys never stop chattering. Geminis are flighty of spirit, fanciful, and unpredictable. Monkeys never do anything the same way twice if they can help it. Mercurial as fifteen Rhodes scholars with jet engines tied to their ankles, Gemini Monkeys will need constant watching lest they go into orbit and never come back.

MONKEY/Cancer *(June 22—July 23)*

I see a brilliant nugget of highly polished gold resisting the rushing advances of a mountain torrent. Or, maybe it is a rare gold coin in the bottom of a wishing well. But whatever it is, the Monkey side of this Cancer will be doing all the hustling. Cancers born in Monkey years may feel discomfited by all the levity in their souls. Monkeys are so distracting. Cancers hate being diverted from their comfy routines. You can expect a warm-hearted, motherlike person with a mind like a steel trap. But you might find instead a highly strung grump. Extra effectiveness can be derived from this product by placing one knee mid-stomach on prone subject and tickling until it says uncle. Ponder the glare of Yul Brynner if one put him in this position. See what I'm getting at?

MONKEY/Leo *(July 24—August 23)*

More fire and metal. This blast furnace of a person ought really to cease all that heroic stopping of locomotives with a single hand. Try and tell one of them to cool it once. All those hot sparks . . . Oooohhh . . . That doesn't tickle. How about Bella Abzug in a strait jacket? Perhaps you can better see what the results would be. Monkey/Leos will make you laugh harder, seethe with a brighter rage, and cry more tears of exasperation than a flotilla of failed love affairs. Pyrotechnics . . . The human dynamo . . . You name it. These people just don't quit with the power trip until they are satisfied the enemy is six feet under. Befriend it. Enemies of this persuasion are not advisable.

MONKEY/Virgo *(August 24—September 23)*

A finely honed scissors of forged Sheffield steel. This character is useful, to himself and others. Virgo naïveté tempered by the Monkey's sharp wits. I think of a song we used to sing in Girl Scouts: "Make new friends but keep the old. One is silver and the other gold." Friendships with either of these signs promise to enrich anyone's life. We have a very nice person here, a bit on the fastidious side perhaps, but pleasant in the extreme. One danger: Each of these characters tends to be easily discouraged. Too much pressure could cause them to crack neatly into millions of spangled flakes of emotional breakdown. Take it easy on them. They deserve it.

MONKEY/Libra *(September 24—October 23)*

If I had one of these people around the house all the time, I'd buy a lifetime "Interbanana" subscription for regular deliveries of squishy ripe fruit with which to muffle the constant stream of gabble and froth emanating incessantly from such a companion. But some people like a lot of company around the house. With this duo, you've got it! You'll never be lonely again. Libran Monkeys should be smarter than most Monkeys about how to find equilibrium in a raging battle. They will have extensive wardrobes of finery, beautifully decorated homes, money to burn (hide the matches), and a compromising nature, the likes of which you have never seen. Their unparalleled sense of gallantry may save the day. This person will have oodles of charm.

MONKEY/Scorpio *(October 24—November 22)*

I would rather not have to discuss it but since you asked, Scorpio Monkeys risk finding themselves committing suicide by default. It is not an easy alliance. Put self-destructiveness on top of easy dejection and stand back to watch the action. A Scorpio with a Monkey on his back will be well-advised to keep it light. There is room for all kinds of fun and games, providing the ambience is cheerful. Too many obstacles will derail the sensitive creature. Art, music, lots of love, and plenty of money to spend are a fine remedy for almost anybody's ills. Those elements are particularly recommended in this case. A highly developed sexuality, complex fantasy life, and some very sound deep thinking could result from this combination. Creativity reigns within. Boost morale every night and call me in the morning.

MONKEY/Sagittarius *(November 23—December 21)*

I would vote for this person. Neither truth nor intelligence are missing. Idealism toned down by common sense ought to give excellent results. This person may never marry. Not that he would choose celibacy, but he may opt for bachelorhood. If there is anything to this Peter Pan business, one should expect to find it here. Neither Monkeys nor Sagittarians are particularly drawn to accepting the facts of maturity. Although affable and easy to get on with in company, this subject will probably enjoy the spotlight a mite too much. If he isn't careful, he could end up being the fourth monkey on those old triple monkey paperweights—the one with the foot in his mouth.

MONKEY/Capricorn *(December 22—January 20)*

If this were a novel, my main character might well be a Monkey/ Capricorn. There's enough conflict, Heaven knows, to fill three anxious volumes. Yet, there is also plenty of down-to-earth plodding and slogging, honesty and ambition, wisdom and pluck. I am not certain how the story would end because of all the fighting. Those knockdown drag-outs would be difficult to conclude. Capricorns are rigid so much of the time that an injection of Monkey business might serve them well. A fearsome leader with a twinkle in his eye is a pleasant-enough thought. The elements are metal and earth again. The tunnels are deeper than in most mines, but the yield ought to be worth your trouble.

MONKEYI/Aquarius *(January 21—February 19)*

Again, society will be served by this union of characteristics. Our old friend Learned Hand was an Aquarius and so is Ms. Angela Davis. I would not stay up waiting for this person to come home every night. I wouldn't even bother to leave the light on so he can find his keys. You'll be wasting energy. With all those smarts and social conscience, this anybody is sure to be much too busy becoming "somebody" to bother with trivialities like whether or not the dinner is cold or baby needs new shoes. It is a promising union of high-mindedness and wit. It will not do to argue over small things. Your Monkey/Aquarian won't listen. Don't pick on him. He means well.

MONKEY/Pisces *(February 20—March 20)*

A silver fish slithering here and there, adapting to one environment after the other, brewing fanciful creations for the world to behold, is this amiable soul. Pisceans will gain strength and independence from being born in a Monkey year. Since art and sensitivity belong to the fish, anyway, the addition of the Monkey's wit and ability to cut through the proverbial red tape of complexity insures a good balance. Often overly soulful, Pisceans complemented by monkeyshines and a bit of the zany will be saved all that mooning about they are so famous for.

PRESCRIPTION FOR THE FUTURE

Monkey mine, why is it that such an inventive person as yourself consistently allows himself to wonder, "Am I liked? Will I appeal? Have I made another *faux pas*? Isn't anybody annoyed with me?" Chances are, most times when you are pulling out your own hair with self-doubt, the people you think may not adore you as much as they did two seconds ago still feel exactly as they did then. But, still, you want some sign, some reassurance, a smile or a wink to tell you nobody is put out with you. Frankly, my little Monkey, the more of that precious recognition we give you, the more you crave. The more recklessly you pour forth your affections, try to make us laugh, try to be a good kid and keep everything together and everyone amused, the more exasperating it is to the other guy. Take it easy. We love you.

Born as you are with the gift of shrewdness, it is fairly difficult for those of us who surround you to figure out why you cannot work out a way to halt this flow of emotional overkill. Always giving too much of your time and self the way you do is sure to backfire. Your outpourings of selflessness tend to draw profiteers to your side. Soon, if you allow them to, they will be raiding your refrigerator and usurping your favorite armchair.

You are funny and delightful and sweet and willing and good at everything you do. Everybody loves your wit. We are always touting your qualities of charm and pleasantry. You are the one who goes around kicking yourself in the teeth. Is there no way we can prove to you that entertaining the troops is not your only role in life? Why don't you try this? Instead of escaping into your readings and scrubbings of your inner floors and walls until they shine, when you feel discouraged take stock of your inner blessings. Realize how superior you are as a collaborator. Remember all the nice things you have been doing for us all these years. We, of all people, have scarce forgotten. Take a course in some subject you have always wished you knew more about. Become a sky diver or learn to build things from scratch. Perhaps that way, through your own achievements, you will begin to believe in yourself.

The trouble with you all in the first place is that you know how superior you are. Secretly you may even feel nobody or nothing under the sun is good enough for you. Meanwhile, you chalk up to experience all the time you waste hurrying about looking for the right atmosphere in which to feel accepted. This same conflict goes on within. Despite all you do for others, regardless of how many sacrifices you make, you still can't believe you're really even good enough for yourself. Rather than tearing at your insides, go after something you want. Be objective. You're not likely to win the nomination for President of the United States, but you may learn to accept yourself for what you are.

And what are you then? Certainly not the Rock of Gibraltar, the Rock of Ages, or any equally dull pillar of permanence. You, Monkey-face, are as mutable as the seasons. Your strength lies in your ability to adapt, to change your ways, to deal with each ensuing dilemma with needlelike precision. Your facial expression is the very barometer of your mood. It won't be easy to fool all of the people all of the time with those forced smiles or hurt looks. Yours is not a static nature. That much we can deal with.

The tendency to extremes of emotional heights and depths is not necessarily a problem. The rub only comes along when you imagine that others, stronger than yourself, are supposed to be models of behavior. Not so. Brute force is not everything in life. For a person like yourself, the essential is to cultivate your potential for riding out crises, rolling with the punches, waiting for the moment to strike. That, if you look at it positively, is called timing. Of that precious commodity you have more than your share.

My advice? Don't let them fence you in. Beyond your capacity for adaptation, you must always insist on room for adjustment. Request of any given situation that the person in charge turn on the light at the end of the tunnel. Then take each avenue, one at a time. Solve the problems along the way, slay the dragons big or small, and come up smiling. Meanwhile, try not to think about the long run. Don't plan too far ahead. Leave the long-term projects to those more perseverant than yourself. Live with your mercurial disposition rather than against it. Take stock often. My guess is, the hefty amount of small victories you have accomplished will stack up favorably against anybody else's single large-scale conquest.

COMPATIBILITIES

Affairs of the Heart

The Monkey is an inveterate child. He doesn't really ever want to grow up and settle down to raise a family. Yet, Monkeys notoriously produce large broods of children upon whom they shower attention and with whom they share a multiplicity of likes. Perhaps it is best to say that the Monkey lover, despite himself, usually grows up, but never quite settles down to raise that family.

Monkey emotions seem to be all over the map at one time. One minute, Monkeys are enthralled by a blonde dreamboat who talks with a lisp, and the next second, they have found a brunette pussycat of a gentleman friend who tells funny, funny stories all night long. They seem to have no preference for size or color, shape or intention. Monkeys simply love to be amused and amusing.

Best equipped to serve the Monkey's tastes for diversion is the delightful Dragon. With a Dragon to love, the Monkey person will never ever be bored. Moreover, even the most smitten Dragon manages to maintain an air of indifference that spurs the Monkey's desire for challenge and keeps his imagination alive. Also, Monkeys are the only people who know how to best a Dragon at his own game. The affair will be intriguing.

Second on the list of preference for Monkey lovers should be the restive Rat. Again, the Rat will know how to amuse and entertain the Monkey. Besides, Rats always adore Monkeys. No matter what the Monkey thinks up next, the Rat will stand in awe. The two will drum up some wonderful party ideas and can share many a giggle of complicity in their love lives. Tigers go well with Monkeys as long as the Tiger is too busy and elsewhere occupied to indulge the sometimes devious Monkey mate in his shady schemes. Tigers are honorable souls. To avoid being duped by the clever Monkey, they should remain independent of him. The Tiger's frequent absences may leave the Monkey's need for physical love unsatisfied. But even the most sporadic Tiger excites the Monkey's passion to such a degree that infidelity loses its attraction.

Monkeys get along fairly well with many other signs. If a Monkey person is of good will, he can adapt his life style to suit a Snake, a Goat, or even an accomplice Monkey person. With lucky Pigs, too, the Monkey thrives. Of course, duping a Pig is as easy as swinging from a tree. But the Monkey is not all trickster, he is also exceedingly bright. Any intelligent human being knows it's child's play to fool the innocents of this world. So the Monkey abstains from doing Pigs in. If there are no tough stakes to be gambled on, the Monkey doesn't bother to place a bet.

The Ox will suffer at the hands of the agile Monkey. There may be passion at the outset but once the Ox has children, he sometimes gives up that verve of youthful desire and favors his offspring instead. The meretricious Monkey may be driven elsewhere for some vital pleasure.

Dogs and Monkeys are too mutually cynical to make their lives together. It would be best to nip such a relationship in the bud or else find plenty of money to close the gaps and avert defeatist attitudes.

Horses, because they are so often jealous of the Monkey's ease in gaining fortunes and tricking the world, do not covet Monkeys as love objects. A Horse with a Monkey spouse is nothing but a beast burdened by a Monkey on his back.

Social Affairs

Monkeys are such fascinatingly witty creatures that almost everybody wishes to have at least one in his entourage. Resisting the charms of a merry Monkey is a chore in itself. Always ready with a laugh, full of vim and enthusiasm, and lucidly aware of his own worst failings, the Monkey is an easy companion to have around.

Horses, Snakes, and Roosters are most likely to find conversation with the Monkey little more than a joust or sparring match. None of the three have much time for the magical Monkey's youthful flair, and in some cases are even slightly envious of his achievements.

The Monkey's skill in problem-solving should be of much use to those who admire him. Dragons, Tigers, and Cats usually find Monkeys make superior friends and wily advisers. These three are wont to meet up with crises or emotional setbacks, but the resilient Monkey will shoulder them through in the wink of an eye. What's more, even though Dragons and Tigers know very well that the Monkey can twist them around his finger, they figure it's all in the game of life and take a certain pleasure in fending off his inventive ploys.

Rats always adore Monkeys. Any mutual attachment between these folks will be durable. The Rat may merely be enchanted by the nimble-witted Monkey's seeming ability to listen to and laugh at his jokes. But, as long as the Monkey pays minor attention to his Rat friend, the relationship will last.

Monkeys, in their turn, respect and admire the gifts of Pigs and Oxen. Both of these signs are possible victims of many less moral than themselves. But, remember, the Monkey is always after bigger game. He does not meddle with the emotions of straight-dealing souls. Monkeys prefer outwitting those who seriously challenge their wiles. The gentle Goat does not pique the Monkey's spirit of dissimulation.

Other Monkeys, too, make excellent lifelong accomplices.

Business Affairs

With his natural bent for finding practical solutions to weighty problems, the Monkey would make a sterling business associate for anyone whom he decided never to outmaneuver. But, as we already know, the Monkey is a manipulator. He must be challenged and provoked by his entourage or else he will not be efficient.

Due to the Monkey's penchant for daring opportunity everywhere, their best allies are to be found among Tigers, Dragons, or Pigs. The Tiger couples his force with the Monkey's guile; the Dragon infuses him with his snappy force; and the Pig brings the Monkey luck and understanding.

A business partnership or work alliance with Horses, Cats, or other Monkeys would surely lead to much ado about nothing. The clever Monkey can feign subordination to a Horse, but the Horse never believes in him. Cats are not particularly creative in themselves and Monkeys are better critics than inventors. Their business would stagnate. And another Monkey, though he would understand his partner, would vie for the position of "trickier than thou" and little would be accomplished.

All other signs are here warned that a Monkey can make a silk purse out of your left ear and a bundle of cash from your right one. Unless you have your thinking cap on night and day, a Monkey business partner could end up being your favorite enemy.

And, above all, Rats must be wary of the Monkey. Whatever Rats undertake with Monkeys will be interesting. But Rats are so blindly willing to serve a Monkey pal, they may never be able to see him for what he is—unscrupulously adorable.

Family Affairs

Monkeys like children. Unless they find it too difficult to give up the role of child themselves, Monkey people usually breed great bunches of little ones. Children, for a Monkey parent, are like playmates. No matter how dignified the Monkey parent, his kids will usually be able to entice him to participate in their fun. Monkeys revel in the innocent laughter and affection of small things. They usually like animals and will take time to train and nurture things weaker than themselves.

Monkeyshines are at their best when the Monkey parent has a Rat, Tiger, or Dragon child to amuse. Too, all of these kidlets will listen to their Monkey parents' stories and never mind heeding their lucid advice.

Horse children will find the Monkey a bit light of heart for their taste. Dogs and Roosters will be baffled by all the fun and games, which strike them as vain methods of amusement for amusement's sake. And the Monkey will have trouble with an Ox child. Monkeys do not always learn to respect hard work for what the Ox thinks it is.

If he gives the Ox tips on how to get around this or that rule, the Ox will lose respect for his Monkey parent.

Two Monkeys in a house should pep things up radically. And a Rat child will spend most of his youth trailing about after the Monkey parent, demanding to be talked to, played with, and loved to pieces.

THE ROOSTER

THE YEARS OF THE ROOSTER

January 22, 1909 to February 10, 1910
February 8, 1921 to January 28, 1922
January 26, 1933 to February 14, 1934
February 13, 1945 to February 2, 1946
January 31, 1957 to February 16, 1958
February 17, 1969 to February 5, 1970
February 5, 1981 to January 24, 1982
January 23, 1993 to February 9, 1994

ROOSTERS ARE:

Frank • Vivacious • Courageous • Resourceful
Attractive • Talented • Generous • Sincere • Enthusiastic
Conservative • Industrious • Stylish • Amusing • Contemplative
Popular • Adventurous • Self-assured

BUT THEY CAN ALSO BE:

Nit-pickers • Braggarts • Quixotic
Mistrusful • Acerb • Short-sighted • Didactic
Pompous • Pedantic • Spendthrift • Brazen

283

―――――――――――   ―――   ―――――――――――

ROOSTERS I HAVE KNOWN AND LOVED

Childlike enthusiasm for novelty lives within the heart of every Rooster born. They never lack for diversion. Every part of life intrigues and amuses them. They love to travel, to discover untrammeled places, to learn how to cope and deal with implacable forces, and to practice new life styles.

In all of them, male and female alike, we find a bit of the banty. Strutting about from dawn until dusk, pecking at pretty-colored stones in an effort to uncover some profit or entertainment, Roosters are the sort of individuals who enjoy treating each day as though it were the first and last of their lives.

When confronted with routine tasks that might stultify even the most plodding among us, Roosters manage to uncover fresh and novel ways of accomplishing them. Because of this unusual outlook, our Rooster friends are often misunderstood. Hierarchies, chains of command, and requisition slips literally baffle them. They work best on their own time, at their own speed, and are happiest in situations that do not require conformity to tired sets of rules and regulations that Roosters, by nature, consider are only made to be broken.

The Rooster is often at odds with established authority. Owing to self-assuredness and a vast capacity for personal achievement, this subject many times reacts too vehemently to even the most well-intentioned criticism. Peace and prosperity do not come easily to Roosters. They must scratch away all of their lives in search of virgin ground and new sources of income. Nobody is better equipped to eke blood from a turnip, and just about nobody has to work at it so hard.

Ups and downs are the norm for Roosters. Put them on an even keel and they become bored. Although one may constantly hear them wishing aloud for greener grass, longing for a more settled environment or fastuous harvest, deep down, Roosters prefer to have their creativity challenged by adversity, even if it hurts.

For the past eight years, I have had the honor to be acquainted with an enchantingly picaresque Rooster gentleman/linguist/world traveler/gourmet/*bon vivant*/accomplished musician/expert chef, whose professional hobby among hobbies is opthamological surgery. Valentine Armani (even his name is roguish) was born in 1945. At the age of nineteen, from out the boondocks of upstate New York's industrial wasteland, this young vagabond genius first set forth into the heartland of his parents' native Europe in search of a summer's adventure, culture, change of scene, and a few good laughs.

What he found there, as he so aptly puts it, was "A new world!" I never wanted to dampen his spirits by reminding him that he had come from the new world. So instead, I listened.

"In Parma," he exclaimed, "where my grandparents were born, they have real Parmesan cheese! They grate it right in front of you in the shops!" Val never states facts. He expounds them. "And, in Verona, there is a restaurant where you can eat heaps of broiled freshwater crayfish on skewers! You wouldn't believe it. It's so cheap. They practically give it away. And they have a special kind of mustard there. It's so delicious, you can eat it on bread. Next time I go to Italy, I'll visit the town where it's made and try and wheedle the recipe out of them. I sensed they had used a bit of coriander, but I can't be sure if they mix in a touch dill as well."

As he recounted his maiden voyage to me, we were comfortably seated in front of the fireplace in my Paris house. I had no idea then that in years to follow, Val would return to Europe so many times, travel to so many exotic places, and always bring me equally exciting and baroque tales of his escapades as he passed through my adoptive city. From Hungary, he brought records of Gypsy music. He had learned five of the songs by heart in Hungarian. From Morocco, he returned bearing gifts of embroidered djellabah robes for me and the kids and kept us up for two straight days and nights, telling stories of desert wonders and Arab soukh markets. In England, he learned how to make Yorkshire pudding and to affect a Cockney accent. Just last year, he came roaring into my Parisian living room at three in the morning, on his way back from two weeks in Sicily. As I dragged myself from bed to answer the door, I thought, "It's Val. He must be on his way to Normandy for some of that sweet butter he likes to use in his chocolate mousse." I made us some coffee.

Val began to recite: "Stromboli is the most fantastic sight in the world. It's an active volcano. People live right beneath it. They aren't even afraid it will erupt. I talked to them in their dialect. Do you know what the Sicilian patois for Grandmother is. . . ???" He paced as he spoke, brandishing his demi-tasse cup. Then, abruptly, he turned to face me. "Aren't you using a bit too much chicory in your coffee these days?"

With Rooster friends like Val, the most puzzling aspect is their innate talent for jumping from subject to subject within the same breath. Plunk in the middle of a conversation about the inner workings of the eyeball, Val will suddenly remark that he really thinks we ought to put our roller skates on and go to a baker in the heart of Paris where they still cook over a wood fire. "If we hurry, we can stop by the Lyonnais restaurant in la rue du Faubourg Saint Honoré and have lunch. In this year's Michelin Guide, they received another star," he extols as he fastens his skates tightly. "Can you change some Deutschmarks into francs for me?"

With all of these dashings about, you may have begun to imagine that Rooster people are not serious or hard-working in their professional lives. Nothing could be further from the truth. People born in Rooster years, if clever enough to have chosen careers wherein they are more or less their own bosses, are infinitely more diligent than they seem. Because of a superficial preoccupation with finery and an avid interest in almost any subject that comes their way, Roosters often appear less profound than they really are.

James Jones, author of *From Here to Eternity* and long-time expatriate resident in Paris, is a prime example of Roosterness in full swing. When first I met Jim, he was holding forth on about four different subjects at once and presiding over a heavy poker party in his sumptuous Ile Saint Louis mansionette parlor. In rather strong and self-assertive tones, Jones was instructing his pal James Baldwin that living in the south of France was for the birds. In the next breath, he reminded Sidney Chaplin (eldest son of Charlie) not to walk on the new carpet with shoes on. Then, as he bet another hand of cards, he greeted me warmly, shook the hand of my escort, and wondered aloud if anyone's drinks needed freshening.

Roosters like to feel they are doing right by everyone. When he lived in Paris, one of Jim Jones's favorite pastimes was playing Sunday night host to slews of local friends and passers through town. In his Roosterly manner, Jim was always at his garrulous best during these weekly bashes. Here and there around the celebrity-dotted room, one overheard Françoise Sagan discussing the season at Deauville with Irwin Shaw's wife, and as well caught snatches of the conversations of less well-known people whom James Jones just happened to like. Paris people who were not acquainted with the Joneses always imagined their parties to be snobbish shows of wealth and fame. This was really not the case. Jones is a popular figure and a celebrated author. He always liked to spend money, but then he always earned plenty.

Yet, this prestigious life style has never hindered him from befriending struggling young writers or painters or musicians in whom he believed. Like all his fellow Roosters, Jim loves the role of teacher. Whenever a lesser writer or simply an acquaintance requests his aid or advice, Jones will bring himself up proudly and begin to talk about his cherished profession, the early days, his Army experiences, or a dazzling trip he took once where he saw a church that left an indelible impression on his soul. Sometimes, this banter of his smacks of preaching. But what people mistake for sermonizing is often little more than eagerness about the topic that is being elucidated.

Enthusiasm is a Rooster trait. A-swagger with their own zeal, these people often mistake another's polite curiosity for a cue to launch into a two-hour discourse on the glories of Egyptian tombs. They are opinionated and often brutally aggressive in speech. And, no matter how jocular their comments may seem, when a Rooster crows a resounding sarcastic remark at an interlocutor, he means every word. Your Rooster friend may try to laugh off a smart snipe with a shrug or a giggle, but underneath that grin, when he teasingly said that he thought you were putting on a little weight, he meant, "Go on a diet! You are fat as a pig!" It is practically impossible for Roosters not to say what they think.

Rooster people are cocky. Their lives are packed with adventures that they take great pride in recounting to friends. When they know things that others do not, they rejoice in tutoring the latter. They have great difficulty hiding their opinions. Diplomacy and tact flee out the nearest exit when a Rooster person is in any manner threatened or annoyed.

Moreover, Roosters are finicky folk. If anything is out of place or missing from their orderly surroundings, they begin to act as though the end of the world was on the immediate horizon. Dramas are played out in the lives of Roosters over what the rest of us might consider to be the most picayune trifles. One of my male friends who was born in a Rooster Year abandoned me precipitously during a friendly lunch, proclaiming out of nowhere that he absolutely had to rush one of his three underwater deep-sea-fishing watches to the jeweler before three o'clock that day, or the repairman would never have the calendar feature fixed by the following Saturday.

"Oh," I remarked casually. "Are you going diving over the weekend?"

"Not in the dead of winter." He laughed snidely at my question. "I just don't like things lying about that aren't in working order."

I admit it occurred to me that the exact date was probably one of the last things I would need to know if I were spending any time underwater. "Do you honestly need that date thing on your watch when you're swimming?" I asked candidly.

"You never know," was his acid reply.

Suddenly I saw a mental image of Jacques Cousteau (Pig, 1910) meandering gracefully along beneath some southerly sea on December 23 and glancing nervously at his submersible watch, only to realize to his horror that there were only two more shopping days until Christmas. I found the whole idea absurd. But that is the type of punctiliousness for which Roosters are famous.

One Rooster woman whom we all revere for her stylish flair and overall appeal is Katharine Hepburn (b. 1909). Is there anything about Ms. Hepburn's public image that needs brushing up? Would you feel free to point an accusing finger at her to say, "Ha Ha. Kate Hepburn's slip is showing!" Not on your life. If Katharine Hepburn's petticoats are apparent, it's because she means them to be fluffily attractive. Even a rumpled coiffure and smudges of black dirt look good on her classical face.

Hardly a sex kitten or character actress, Katharine Hepburn's appeal is dignity. Her tone is warmth with a bite. She sports her own brand of elegance, cleverly muted by that smiling Irish eye. The glow that emanates from that sparkling glance is irresistibly Rooster all the way.

Something about these people makes us wonder what would happen if we stripped them of their stately reserve. Would Kate Hepburn come apart if she was suddenly forced to exhibit her well-turned calves to the press? How would she respond to an indiscreet question or pushy journalistic query?

Well, at first she might snap at the person who would dare impose on her Roosterly pride. Ms. Hepburn is not above airing a concise opinion.

Nor is she noted for chewing her words before uttering them. But, if an acerbic comment did not work, Katharine Hepburn might resort to some unusual tactics of self-defense such as I witnessed her using on a recklessly curious photographer during a Paris press conference.

I spoke of this event in the Tiger chapter. But what I did not tell you is how effectively Ms. Hepburn dealt with one particularly zealous scoop-seeker on that day.

The journalists had been forewarned that Katharine Hepburn was not very comfortable about being interviewed in French. Her grasp of that language is quasi-perfect. Yet, she had some reservations. Perhaps her fluency in French was rusty and she feared being misconstrued or falsely quoted. The queries were being delivered slowly by a group of international journalists who stood some six feet from Ms. Hepburn's raised podium.

With her customary grace and charm, Ms. Hepburn answered question after question in careful grammatical French. All at once a slack-suited camera lady pushed her way through the crowd and onto the dais, and literally thrust her 35 mm camera into the face of Katharine Hepburn. The gesture was shocking, pure *paparazzo*!

With a black box poised three inches from her face as though it were a menacing weapon, the star of stars did not lose a syllable, but went on speaking until she had finished her sentence. Then, she turned and spoke directly into the lens, saying, "Really! Do you mind?"

The shutterbug, undaunted by Ms. Hepburn's remark, moved in even closer on her target. The elegant Kate, still smiling and nodding to the reporters down in front, raised her arm as though to shield her face from the probing camera and hauled off and pushed the newsmonger, apparatus and all, down three steps and back where she belonged.

Frankly, for a moment, nobody seemed more shocked at what Ms. Hepburn had done than Katharine herself. Rash acts of physical aggression are obviously not one of her hobbies. But, when threatened, her normally superior dignity did not go all to pieces. Hepburn neither called for help nor did she burst into tears. Instead, she simply, forthrightly, and bravely decided to put some proper distance between her assailant and her beautiful self.

Roosters, you see, can take care of themselves. Surely, they prefer to be surrounded and loved by friends and associates. But, if Roosters must be alone, handle adversity by themselves, and fend off danger single-handedly, they are never afraid. Failure, disappointment, and declared enemies do not send Roosters into traumas or plummet them to emotional depths from which they bewail their misfortunes. The Rooster is a resilient and resourceful character.

Too, hidden beneath a somewhat banty, off-the-cuff manner is the Rooster's deep sincerity of feeling for his fellow-man, woman, or child. Helpless creatures, though he may refuse to enter into their morasses of disability, inspire the Rooster to help them. I have a Rooster brother named George (b. 1933). He's all of the things that Roosters are purported to be and then some.

Whenever I need a loan, a means of transportation, a smile, or a wink of reassurance, George is there to help. Reserved and unable to really share in my woe, this brother is not the sort who holds my hand and listens far into the night. On the surface, George is Mr. Cool and Collected. Unruffled, he goes about the world calmly and smooths out wrinkles both for himself and those he loves by extending checks, money orders, airline tickets, cheerful comments, and pats on the head. But, with all of this generosity, the one thing George prefers never to be forced to do is "involve himself" in trouble.

Before I knew about Rooster traits, I thought George was simply "chicken" where his and my emotions were concerned. Now I know better. The Rooster that he is feels so profoundly for others, he cannot allow himself the luxury of commiserating. When pressed to discuss the past, our childhood, an illness or death in the family, Rooster George's feathers gum up and prevent him from flying a straight course. With him, as with all the Roosters I know, outward shows of emotion are difficult, if not impossible.

Because Roosters are seemingly stolid souls and hide many of their truly sympathetic sorrows or woes under an air of strut and pride, they are sometimes misunderstood by those who love them. The many compassionate gestures that they do make in a material way are actually their method of showing love. Even if they chuck you under the chin and say, "Come on now. Cheer up. Don't get all mushy," what they are thinking may be more like, "Oh how sorry I feel for you. I wish I could cry with you. But I must appear strong."

Roosters think a lot. But they are not introverts. Perhaps one ought to call them schemers or even dreamers. Forever hatching complicated plots whereby they reckon on earning a quick fortune, producing the best movie of the decade, or somehow striking it rich or famous overnight, these people are prodigiously inventive. Unfortunately, many times their projects fail as rapidly as they were cooked up. But never mind. Roosters are accustomed to playing a close game with Lady Luck. They have extraordinary powers of recovery, endless personal resources, and temerity in the face of fiasco that never ceases to astonish their friends and enemies.

Bankruptcy, broken hearts, and aborted projects are nothing new to the Rooster. You can pull the magic carpet of idealism out from under this person with impunity. It won't faze him. He can always move out of town, start afresh, find new friends and associates, and refashion a life in the most arid of territories.

This "here today gone tomorrow" attitude on the part of Roosters imbues them with tremendous strength vis-a-vis their own emotional letdowns. Despite all their kind attentions and generosity toward lovers or friends, if those same folks suddenly betray them, Roosters are always ready and able to pick up from where they left off and make a go of life alone.

They thrive on compliments. Roosters give and take praise and approval with ease and grace. You will rarely find a Rooster person who enjoys solely the company of members of his own sex. Men and women of this sign seek out their opposites. The very ambience of attraction or possible conquest spices life sufficiently for them. The opportunity to parade themselves, the chance to please the eye of a beholder, or perchance hear a laudatory word said about their attire or coiffure are but a few of the motivations for this Rooster attachment to coed situations.

The vivacious Rooster is a popular party guest, a fine host, and a willing conversationalist. He delights in amusing others with his adventuresome ideas and takes a pixieish pleasure in teasing those he feels he can titillate with his witty remarks. Those born in the Year of the Rooster are proud as peacocks and only show off their finest feathers in assembled companies.

Under the cover of brillant plumage and hiding their heads among those brightly hued feathers, Rooster types are sometimes bewildered. Often, their crowings result in hurt feelings. Frequently, nobody is more surprised than they are. It is safe to say here that their cock-a-doodle-doos are much worse than their pecking orders.

Though a Rooster may strut and spew forth his dissatisfaction with life's imperfections, he really doesn't mean to offend anyone. He is, in truth, so often disappointed in himself, annoyed by his own miscalculations of delicate situations, and deeply sorry to have once again put his foot in it, that he suffers extreme personal doubt. He could kick himself around the block for having told his mother-in-law that her new hair color looked like laundry bluing. But he cannot prevent himself from being explicit where discretion might have been the better part of valor.

The Rooster's life, though it may be riddled with near-misses, minor catastrophes, and slips 'twixt cup and lip, appears to him but a series of joyful highs and lows. If he is down in the dumps, don't stand around waiting from him to come to you for support and chitchat. He sincerely likes to sort out his own quandaries in his inimitably personalized fashion. Once he has come through the tunnel and found stability waiting in the sunshine of success, the Rooster will delight in recounting his victory in detail. This after-the-fact tale-telling on himself is one way the Rooster protects himself from criticism.

Finally, though your Rooster friends or lovers may always act as though they have been sitting on top of the world forever and a day, you can try to recall that they too have feelings. Their occasional jibes and blatant comments are nothing more than fleeting statements of impressions that they cannot hide. Their erstwhile boastings are really sincere efforts to communicate their enthusiasms. They are at home with disappointment, valorous in the face of setbacks or failures, and capable of enormous devotion and loyalty in friendship. They may not always be able to share outrageous attitudes or commit themselves to unorthodox views. But, no matter how bizarre they may think radical ways and means are for themselves, Roosters are most tolerant of the zany in others.

MADAME ROOSTER

Lady Roosters make the most intriguing partners for their gentlemen friends. They are at the same time motherly (as all good hens should be) and self-propelled extroverts who like to get things done in the outside world. Usually, these cocky ladies resist becoming overly dependent in a financial way on their men friends or husbands. They like to do their own thing within the framework of a marriage or ongoing love relationship.

Because Rooster women are able to achieve a certain notoriety or greatness on their own terms, they can be testy and difficult to live with. For a start, they cannot abide inefficiency or tolerate a messy household. They truly believe in the old adage that one is best served when one serves one's self. Compromise is not their favorite method of problem-solving. To give orders and lectures seems to them a natural means of creating order out of chaos.

If you are the companion of a Rooster woman, the best advice I can give you is this: Keep your clothes picked up, your car interior shipshape, and your feet on the straight and narrow. Any deviation from patterns (which you can count on her to establish early in your relationship) could cause her to commit at least temporary mayhem around the nest.

I speak from some experience on this subject since my niece Pamela is a very self-assertive and accomplished young lady who was born in a Rooster Year (1957). No matter how much parental or educational pressure Pam received, she always gave her family the impression that she had every intention of living life in the fashion that suited her best. As a child, although reasonable where standard disciplines such as going to bed on time and cleaning up her plate were concerned, Pamela always sported the oddest of quirks. If her mother asked her to clean up her room, she would try to invent new ways of using the vacuum cleaner attachments. Sometimes this chore, which other children despised, would take Pamela an entire Saturday to accomplish. She claimed she did not mind using her playtime for work, as long as she was allowed to play with what she called "grown-up toys."

Recently, when my sister returned to her own oil-painting career, she told her daughter that she would have to take over some of the duties around the house. Hiring help to assist with the work was out of the question. Pam, who is a senior student of pre-law at the local university and a part-time bank clerk, agreed to share the cooking and shopping during the week and save the heavy cleaning tasks until weekends, when she and her mother could go through the house together. This arrangement lasted exactly one week. By Friday, the two women were arguing about whether it was quicker to use cake mixes or start from scratch. They fought over whose spaghetti sauce was more delicious and bickered constantly about every detail of how work should be most efficiently accomplished. Pam claimed to know better how to boil her father's eggs in the morning. My sister was certain her way was faster.

My sister despaired. How would she ever be able to pursue her own interests if her daughter refused to cooperate with her? She wrote to me: "Suzanne, you have always understood Pam. I don't know if your Chinese astrology charts will help out this time, but I am willing to give it a try. She is so bossy. It's driving me bats. She knows how to do everything better than me. You know how efficient she is. Should I let her tell me how to run my own house?"

Luckily for my pocketbook, the letter did not reach me in Paris. From New York City, I made a quick long-distance call to advise my anguished sibling, "I don't see why you just don't accept the facts about your gifted child. She can do everything more quickly and competently than you. For that matter, she's more capable than anyone else I know. Her methods are not the most orthodox, but as long as the work gets done, why do you fight it? Cooperate with her and she will take over all the jobs you have always hated so much. Buck her system and you've had it. She'll end up moving out of the house."

I heard the old familiar maternal sigh through the phone. "Sometimes I think I've raised a monster. She's only eighteen. And she is two years ahead of herself in school. I'm worried about her. If she takes on all that extra work, she's bound to get sick on me. You cannot imagine the homework she does. She stays up until all hours reading. Then she plans meals and makes shopping lists. Sometimes I get up in the morning and find she's already ironed her father's shirts before leaving for an eight o'clock class. It's positively eerie!"

What could I say? My sister always thought I was a bit on the eerie side myself so I hesitated to tell her that, as a Rooster person, her beloved progeny could probably run General Motors if she was allowed to do it at her own speed. So instead, I reminded her that Pamela was and still is a remarkably capable young woman who never minded working as long as other people kept their sticks out of her spokes. I suggested that my sister sit back and enjoy the ride. "Pamela is as strong as the Kremlin. Leave her to her work. Put your energies into what you can do and let her run the show her way."

It took a few more weeks of unsuccessful sharing before my sister finally gave in and devoted herself entirely to her abstract expressionism. Until she did, the battles were monumental. Pamela told her mother that she didn't know how to get the creases out of shirt collars, and if she would only watch how she herself pressed shirts, she would learn a thing or two. Pam's cooking pleased her father and younger brother so much they made snide remarks about how the service had improved around the kitchen. My sister's pride was taking a dreadful beating. Then, the inevitable occurred. Pamela threatened to move out. She said her mother was sabotaging her vegetable soup and meddling in her affairs by cleaning the stove behind her back. Her words were cutting and Roosterly, "Stay out of my business and I'll stay out of yours!"

Since business was what my sister had in mind when she went back to painting, she finally consented to quit the stalling and let Pam get on with the serious business of running her household. When she phoned to tell me about it, she said, "As long as we keep our things picked up and don't forget to scour the bathtub after each use, she doesn't scold much. I sure hope you were right about her health. The girl next door came down with mononucleosis last week and she doesn't even do her own hair!"

That was six months ago and Pam is still going strong. She is a straight A student, still earns pocket money working at the bank, and is currently teaching herself how to make a fluffier soufflé au Grand Marnier.

Rooster women are effective. They are also models of "the studied casual" in dress and personal grooming. Katharine Hepburn has worn the same uniform ensemble of basic black pants and shirt for thirty-five years. And she always looks smashing. Jacqueline Susann, the actress/novelist who passed away not long ago, always appeared dressed in her own comfortably elegant style without much ornamentation. Rooster women have a kind of natural elegance. Carly Simon (b. 1945), singer and wife of James Taylor (Rat, 1948), is a good example of this. Her presence alone, tall, head held high, long sleek hair blowing loosely yet neatly about her face, is awesomely dignified.

If you have a Rooster lady in your entourage, please remember that she needs more approval and applause than most people. Try not to get in the way of her personal progress. Do not take offense when she seems authoritarian or preachy. And, most of all, be jolly in her presence. Keep her laughing, both at life and at herself. She suffers most from the fact that she takes herself much too seriously.

MONSIEUR ROOSTER

For a man, the Rooster sign is a combination burden/trump card. Incumbent upon his very existence from beginning to end is the dichotomy of interest between his family and all the wonderful adventures, both amorous and secular, that life might be able to offer him. Often, he desires fervently to be a good husband and provider. He sincerely wishes he were a more attentive spouse. Yet, he constantly feels the pull of the outside world, beckoning him away from routine. Maintaining love alliances is more difficult for him than it sometimes appears. Roosters are, after all, what their name implies. They like to flirt, to please women, to attract attention to themselves.

Unfortunately, Rooster men are by nature conservative. Extracurricular love affairs tend to get in the way of the Rooster's idea of propriety. That streak of perfectionism in their heart of hearts will almost always win out. Remember that although the Rooster likes being in the limelight, he wants that spotlight to focus on his better points. He really cannot tolerate the idea of looking bad.

Among Rooster men whom we have all observed are such supermales as Errol Flynn (b. 1909), Roman Polanski (b. 1933), and Philip Roth (b. 1933). The reputations of these three gentlemen for repeated sexual conquest and ensuing publicity are nothing to be sneezed at. However, on the same list figure such talented and reputedly sensible men as James Jones (b. 1921), George Segal (b. 1933/4), Steve Allen (b. 1921), and William Faulkner (b. 1897). These last members of the Rooster clan adhere to the one-woman man school of thought. They have plied their trades through thick and thin, reaching amazing heights and suffering giant setbacks, and most of them have stayed dutifully married to the same woman for many years.

The latter group of one-woman Roosters is definitely the wiser. Roosters, even though they may strut through every one of life's barnyards with a different chick on their arm, are rarely completely happy with such arrangements. They do dream of settling down, of establishing roots like all their more serious friends, and of pipes and slippers by the hearth. Trouble is, they find it bard to resist the travel urge.

George Segal, the handsome actor and sometimes talkshow replacement host, was in Paris a few years ago working on a film at the time I was trying to pay my bills by working as a dress shop manager. The shop was located around the corner from Segal's hotel. George knew Vicky Tiel, the shop's designer, through her business partners, Elizabeth Taylor and Richard Burton. They had worked together on *Who's Afraid of Virginia Wolfe*. One day, George came striding into the shop's office looking for Vicky and politely introduced himself. "Hi!" He shook my hand and chirped gaily, "How are you? My name is George Segal."

Not having been in the States for quite some time, I did not immediately recognize George as an actor. He could have been a sales representative as far as I knew. I shook his hand warmly, saying, "And my name is Suzanne White. How do you do?"

One of the ladies in the office whispered at me as I went to fetch a drink for the visitor, "That's George Segal, the famous actor."

One always tries not to show awe when meeting celebrated figures, so I acted as though it was normal for me to serve whiskeys at two o'clock in the afternoon to members of the coveted profession of movie star. "What do you do?" I inquired of my guest, as if I didn't know.

"I'm an actor," he smiled engagingly to reply. "I'm shooting a film here. Just thought I'd pop by and say hello to Vicky. I'm staying at L'Hotel, that tiny place around the comer. If she won't be in soon, I can always stop back later."

"Oh, she'll be along in a few minutes. She just stepped out for coffee." I bade him sit and make himself comfortable. We chatted amiably about this and that for a few minutes. Soon, the door opened to admit two charmingly pretty little girls of about nine or ten. "Daddy," they clambered up to George to announce. "Mommy's ready. She says you better come back right away. We have to go shopping."

Mr. Segal promptly presented his two daughters to me and rose to leave saying, "Please tell Vicky that I came by. I have to run now. My wife is waiting for me."

When Vicky returned, I gave her George's message. Her face lit up. "Did he bring Patty with him? I haven't seen them in years. Where are they staying?"

A few hours later, George came back to the shop, Vicky was all over him with "How are you and how are the kids and Patty?" They gossiped away for a while and then he left.

Vicky came over to my desk after his departure. She looked worried. "George doesn't smile any more. He used to be so funny. I wonder what's wrong. I hope he's all right. I'd better call Patty and talk to her. Maybe something with his career. . . ."

Not being acquainted with the Segals, I had no reason to imagine George was ever anything but the way I had met him. Pleasant in the extreme, a bit taciturn, and nervously chatty.

That evening about midnight, I got in my car to perform the nightly Parisian expatriate American ritual of going to the Latin Quarter to pick up the early edition of the *International Herald Tribune*. As I was driving down a small street near the Place Saint-Germain des Pres, I noticed a hunched figure slouching along the sidewalk. I glanced at him. Then looked away and suddenly right back again. The dejected man I had seen was George Segal. He was so hunched over that his otherwise tall stature had diminished by about half. The sight was alarming. I stopped the car and leaned out the window to call his name, "George? Is that you?" I wondered.

Astonished to hear some lady beckoning him from an automobile in a Paris street, he only half-looked at me. Then, recognizing me, he straightened slightly and shrugged, "Oh, hi, Suzanne. Yeah, it's me."

I don't ordinarily ride around the Paris streets at night hunting for dejected movie stars, but frankly, his demeanor was so obviously one of misery in the extreme, I thought perhaps he needed some company. So I said, "Are you all right?" He was patently neither drunk nor in any other falsely induced state of intoxication. He just looked sad.

"I'm not feeling too cheerful, if that's what you mean." He strolled over to the car. "I have a cold and the movie's not going as smoothly as I had expected. The kids love Paris and I'd like to be able to spend more time with them. But I'm so busy with work and preoccupied with my own problems. I guess I'm just depressed."

"Do you want to have a drink?" My gesture was one of simple humane charity. "Maybe you need to talk about it." George did not exactly tell me in so many words that if he had a drink with me his wife would murder him, but the implication was there. "No. Thanks, anyway, but I've been out too long already. Just walking around trying to get my head together. Patty will worry."

I never saw George again after that encounter, but I did have a talk with Vicky about him the next day. She told me it was not uncommon for him to have these depressions. His wife, she said, was the most patient of women. Vicky called it his artistic temperament. I was not surprised to find out his Chinese Chance was that of a Rooster person.

The next time I saw George Segal, I was on the home side of a TV set in New York City and he was smiling at me from Los Angeles, across Johnny Carson's desk. George was singing a funny song and playing a ukelele. Cocksure and having a whale of a time, George

Segal looked as though he had never suffered a moment's sadness in all his born days.

Highs and lows in the extreme are not the exception but the rule with Rooster men. Their enthusiasm for life and their eagerness about everything that surrounds them often place a falsified plus value on the reality of any given situation. Because they fly so high so often, they are easily disappointed when an experience does not live up to the image they have built around it.

When dealing with Roosters, try to remember that their moods change rapidly. When they are down, grumpy, sad and woebegone, remind yourself that the next day they may very well be on top of the world. Take two aspirins and go to bed with a book. Left to their own devices, Roosters always work things out for themselves. No amount of chatting or chiding will assist them. Activity sometimes helps. Social intercourse may cheer them up. Keep the applause meter turned up loud. It's about the only solution from the outside that Rooster men respond to in any real way.

CO-SIGNS

ROOSTER/Aries (March 21—April 20)

Aries is a fire sign. Rooster is represented by metal. The two signs together in one human being produce a product similar to burnished gold. This is a positive match. Both Aries and Rooster people are self directed. Neither enjoys being dominated. I am not certain I would enjoy sharing a one-room apartment with a member of this cerebral race. Aries Rooster people are likely to be garrulous in the extreme and busy, busy, busy almost all of the time. Getting things done will be the mission of such a person. The emotional barometer will rise and fall with typical Aries Rooster enthusiasm. They will be gobbling consumers of life's good things. Sex is of uppermost importance to them. Nature in all its forms will fascinate and occupy this bustling soul. Overall, they retain a quality of naïveté and candor that can prove endearing as long as the new projects they are attacking are neither wars nor domestic crises. Witty and fleet of foot and mind, this subject will never be a bore.

ROOSTER/Taurus *(April 21—May 21)*

This combination of cock and bull is anything but what it seems by virtue of its name. Earnest of character and studious in the extreme, this union of earth and metal is a gold mine of wisdom. Dauntless, in their own quiet way, these careful people will undertake to administrate those less organized than themselves with uncommon zeal and gusto. They work harder than anybody else when it comes to accomplishing thankless tasks. As a result of this industry, they cannot put up with inefficiency from those around them. Always wary of friends and acquaintances, the Taurean Rooster often has to accept his lot as a loner. Apparently, he will take up with underdogs and seem willing to aid those less fortunate than himself, but he quickly loses patience with charity for its own sake. He must guard against the temptation to surround himself with people who take from him. Because he is so capable and independent, he may be easy prey for those who cannot fend for themselves.

ROOSTER/Gemini *(May 22—June 21)*

Talk about ups and downs! This person will be a veritable thermometer of mercurial rise and fall. Air has the unfortunate tendency to rust unprotected metal. Since Geminis are two-sided, anyway, the alliance of the explosive Rooster with their sign may produce complexities of personality. What some might call sensitivity in this subject could also be interpreted as weakness of will and instability of character. This person could aspire to a career as an actor. Theatrics will give him an outlet for his eccentric emotions. Frequently, Geminis born under the sign of the Rooster gain much from working with others. They are themselves gifted for development of new ideas. They are innovative and enthusiastic. But when it comes to long-term realization of a project, they may bog down. I advise anyone born under these signs to take a strong partner along when embarking on any new plan of action. This subject will be a fine starter and a less successful finisher.

ROOSTER/Cancer *(June 22—July 23)*

Cancerian water can gnaw away at this Rooster's shiny metallic make-up. This subject is a grudge bearer. He must struggle harder than other Roosters to achieve success. Born as he is in the fiery summertime, he must resist distraction in order to maintain the rigidity necessary for hard work. He may sometimes appear to be lazy or shiftless. Let him be. He's thinking or plotting some new scheme. This person is neither perky nor energetic by nature. But he can be peckish, and at times, weary of his uphill battle against the elements. With application, the Rooster/Cancer can accomplish big things. The power is there. He needs much outside encouragement and affection from loved ones.

ROOSTER/Leo *(July 24—August 23)*

This human alloy of metal and fire will not be the kind of person who enjoys taking "no" for an answer. Pride beams from out his very eyes. He wants power and will know how to go after it with much charm and wit. Like most Roosters, he is quick-tempered, but because he is also a Lion, there can be much more than froth behind that roar. The Leo Rooster is bound to be attractive and socially popular. Men flock around women born under these auspices. This subject's faults are a tendency toward wishy-washiness and inability to make up his emotional mind. Roosterly eccentricity is strongest among those born under the sign of Leo. They love to dress garishly and perform outrageous feats of daring, which they hope will impress onlookers. The main virtue of these people is open-mindedness. There is less of that cocky conservatism present here than in other Roosters.

ROOSTER/Virgo *(August 24—September 23)*

The Rock of Ages was cleft for this Rooster/Virgo subject. Above all, he stands fast for his beliefs. While many Roosters are somewhat less than virtuous and given to vacillation, the Virgo streak of purity of heart in this person will inject his character with untold individuality and strength of character. Though not always lucky with money, Virgos born into this sign will know better how to save than other members of the Rooster family. Watch out for that temper. The measliest little bone of contention could lead to all-out war. The nature of this subject is a brittle one. Firm, solid, and yet rather too delicately honed for much heavy-duty elbow grease, the Virgo Rooster will find much peace in being self-employed. He is not lazy, but he doesn't take pleasure in working for others.

ROOSTER/Libra *(September 24—October 23)*

Here air and metal seem to stand shimmering side by side, each wondering in his own way whether or not any action should be taken. This character is two-sided. Back and forth, up and down, and around goes this Rooster in an attempt to find equilibrium. Libras make excellent diplomats. Roosters are usually unable to hold their tongues. The two signs are at odds over this problem. The Libran Rooster woman may have business acumen and a healthy supply of luck. Her male counterpart, because he is less able to get away with capricious remarks and employ himself at trades that mostly require a gift for tasteful dress and beauty, often has to work very hard before he arrives at the top of his field. Many dashed hopes and failed schemes will pepper the life of this subject. Courage!

ROOSTER/Scorpio *(October 24—November 22)*

This combination of metal and mettle will always seem to make great strides even when he is doing little more than putting in an appearance. The Scorpio Rooster speaks better than he acts. He is generally talented for discourse and has a reputation for "talking a big story." Too, unlike most Scorpios, these subjects have a juvenile streak in them that never clears up until they die. Even as mature adults, they react to life in a childish manner. Easy to anger and often vengeful, these cocky people possess a viperous tongue. When criticized, they don't hesitate to use it. Because of this defensive quality, Scorpio Roosters do put others in a difficult position. Often, to avoid disappointment, they strike first and pick up the pieces later. Doubly mistrustful of others, Scorpio Roosters find it hard to depend on friends or loved ones for strength or security. Their sexuality is often repressed and misdirected. Because they are afraid to show their true colors, profound emotional involvement is often taboo. Or, perhaps they are just simpler than the rest of us. In any case, complication annoys them.

ROOSTER/Sagittarius *(November 23—December 21)*

Breezier and more easygoing than other Roosters, people born under the sign of Sagittarius do not resist parasitic relationships in which they can feed off the spoils of others' hard work. They might devote their lives to what they consider idealism. It would not be surprising for persons of this group to flee to Africa and become missionaries or neocolonialists. Any challenge that bids them apply high-flown objectives to profitable gain will suit their somewhat selfish purposes. As a mate, the Sagittarian Rooster will not be easy to pin down. Freedom and independence are his first goals. Secondly, he wishes to avail himself of culturally enriching travels. Family and home, though he may yearn to establish and nurture them the way he feels he should, come last on his list of objectives. As a young person, he will almost never be near his place of birth. With age, he may mellow. If you are thinking of capturing one of these volatile persons, you will have to settle for at least part-time celibacy until your loved one is too old to get on a plane.

ROOSTER/Capricorn *(December 22—January 20)*

This person will correspond nicely with the "snow on the roof, fire in the hearth" dictum. On the surface, he appears cool, and even though he may be intensely wounded over an unrequited love, he will rarely show his feelings. In a purely social way, Roosters born in the sign of Capricorn are exceedingly well-liked. What struttings and preenings they do are neither offensive nor pedantic. When they launch into a speech on a favorite subject, they usually know what they are talking about and have a clever way of presenting their thoughts. Smartly dressed and well-spoken, these people make excellent lawyers and politicians. Still diplomacy as a career is better left untouched by Roosters of any sign. Capricorn Roosters are sometimes foolhardy with money and overly generous with their hospitality. Early in life, they will be attracted to foreign places. One never quite knows with these subjects if they are dissatisfied with their own existence or simply intrigued by those of others. In any case, they find it difficult to sit still or stay in one place for long.

ROOSTERS/Aquarius *(January 21—February 19)*

Not the most reliable of the human race, this person is nonetheless one of the most lovable. Generosity is his middle name. He always wants to pay the way for anyone who will love him. Perhaps he can see no other reason for people to love him. He is not very sure of himself and demonstrates this by means of interested questioning of people with whom he wants to ingratiate himself. This Rooster is the complimentary type who can make you feel as though he has never before met anyone so enchanting as yourself. Women of this sign have good luck in love. They are rather more soft and gentle than other Rooster women. And they are jealous. Rooster/Aquarians are not always faithful themselves, but they have a selfish way of expecting their mates not to stray from the roost. One must not expect serenity in a life shared with this Rooster. His successes will be many, but his mistakes will run a close second.

ROOSTER/Pisces *(February 20—March 20)*

Both the Rooster and the fish are eminently adaptable. In many cases, this adaptability could be positive. Socially, for instance, this subject ought to be successful. However, in business dealings or administrative positions, he will not always enjoy victory. Better at appreciating art or music than he is at decision-making or commanding respect from underlings, the Rooster/Pisces should be encouraged to steer clear of any negotiations that require more than just charm and affability. Under the best of auspices, Roosters are easily discouraged and will jump at the chance to feel sorry for themselves. Piscean Roosters are the most common victims of self-deprecation and doubt. They can be heard to lament, "Ah me, I have done it again. Where have I gone wrong?" over and over throughout their checkered lives. As far as they can see, any slip-ups that may occur in their experience have been someone else's fault. Often this is true. But, even if it is, you can be certain that much of the regret that issues forth from the Piscean Rooster is part of a pattern to which he has become comfortably accustomed. Instead of feeling so bad about it all, he would do better to take a lesson from his errors and be more wary of those in whom he places his trust.

PRESCRIPTION FOR THE FUTURE

Reserved Rooster, though I could call you a rascal, you are really just a scamp. Sometimes you are a mite rash, but you're always loving and giving of your possessions and money to those less fortunate than yourself.

I will bet that you are often accused of arrogance. People who do not know you well, in the face of your reticence to discuss your own deepest feelings, have a way of misjudging your basically kind nature. Because they cannot see beneath your veneer of cocky self-assuredness, strangers often think you are not humble enough for their tastes.

In order to live down this false reputation, one bit of advice may serve you well. Hold your tongue for three seconds before saying what you think. Turn your words around in your head and consult for a second or two with your heart. Perhaps it would be better not to make that drastic comment. Maybe you should save that biting remark for later. Instead, when you want to say something, give the people what they need to hear. Turn your criticism into a compliment. The result may be worth your moment's hesitation.

There is no doubt you have many friends. Roosters are always popular among those who know them well. You can, in fact, count on getting along in most any company. You are garrulous and witty in purely superficial conversation or small talk. But you do not risk talking about what you consider touchy subjects, and perchance you are right. Engaging ourselves in deeply emotional chats can sometimes get us into hot water.

But are you not missing something? Would it not be more edifying if once in a while you took those plunges that others offer through their honest displays of affection? A public kiss, a wanton hug in the street, a smootch in the car, or a good mutual cry cannot hurt your image. Those who love you long for a bit more of the tenderness that is inside of you to be allowed to surface when they are with you.

Your lust for life is commendable. Your varnished exterior amazes us. But, just for fun, why don't you let your hair down from time to time? Mess yourself up a bit. Let us see your true colors on those days when you have forgotten to shave or put on make-up. Relaxation can be very good for the soul.

You may protest, tell me how conservative you are about politics, love, child-rearing, and all. This makes you feel uncomfortable, doesn't it? But I mean no harm. I just long to see you come out of yourself for a few minutes, without the stringent rules you impose on yourself.

Proud Rooster, we hail your valiant efforts at preserving order. We admire your strength in the face of adversity. But can't we just sit down, take off our socks, and have a good old gab session tonight? I'm a bit tired of seeing you at your "best."

COMPATIBILITIES

Affairs of the Heart

Rooster people work as hard at love as in their professional lives to prove themselves worthy of the esteem of others. When they find love and tenderness, they wisely hold onto what they have. Roosters do not uncover new sources of affection gladly. They love their homes, and even when travel seems to take precedence over same, are the types of lovers and mates who ring up every night to remind their loved ones of their warm feelings. Should they find the person to whom they give all of this time and thought lacking in the ability to reciprocate, Roosters at first may seem panicky and ill at ease. But, once he gets his thoughts together and realizes he is being duped or used, the Rooster is capable of stalking away from a former love and washing his hands of the whole shebang. Regrets? Perhaps. But the Rooster can always break new ground and does not fear the unknown.

Roosters get on well with the faithful Ox. Both are equally conservative. They care much for home and family. And the Ox will plod away lovingly for the Rooster while he travels to far-off places.

Intellectually, the Snake and Rooster are well-matched. Both enjoy the study of ideas and can hold brilliant metaphysical discussions. They will probably be a beautifully attired couple. However, if the Rooster is unlucky in business from time to time, the spendthrift Snake may have trouble adjusting its belt.

Dragons bring amazing good fortune to the Rooster person they choose to love. The Rooster is a worker bee. He will never mind taking a back seat to the Dragon's swashbuckling and should be proud to boast of his Dragon's achievements in society.

Roosters, though they worry the disquiet Dog with their endless pursuit of novelty, can get along well with a Dog if much passion is present between the two. Rats make good partners for the busy Rooster person who travels a lot. Rats are faithful to lovers they hold in high regard and can give up their own excitement for the sake of a loved one's happiness.

Roosters and Cats do not usually manage to find *détente* from their differences. Unless the Cat can learn to ignore the sharp tongue of the Rooster, sparks are inevitable.

And Roosters deplore the very co-existence of other Roosters. They neither enjoy the competition nor do they admire mutual faults that they may see mirror imaged in their twins. It is not a possible long term affair.

Social Affairs

Society is the Rooster's favorite place to evolve his theories, strut his stuff, and appear attractive and cheerful to one and all. But the Rooster is not always as comfortable as he looks in public. Finally, though, his image becomes the reality of this character. He is certainly capable of enormous anxiety underneath all that flash and flair, but he never lets us see it. Can you imagine a flustered Katharine Hepburn? And, if so, certainly not in public.

Roosters make their best friends among Horses (who like parading alongside their Rooster pals), Oxen (who find the Rooster imaginative enough for both of them), Snakes (whose intellectual opinions they share), and Rats (who deal with Roosters adroitly and know when to don kid gloves).

Two Roosters are likely to scrap at each other without any result other than more scrapping. Pigs are not usually good friends for Roosters because they are a bit on the timid side and find Roosters frightfully brazen. Goats are so unconventional, they upset the conservative Rooster's basically earthy psyche. Monkeys tease the rigorous Rooster into a permanent snit.

Dragons find Roosters make superior sidekicks. Tigers feel about the same way. And Cats arch their backs at the vivacity and forthrightness of a Rooster crony. The Cat finds the Rooster too openly pedantic possibly because they themselves are so quietly pedantic.

Business Affairs

The Rooster makes an excellent military officer. He can function well where his personal order is not disarranged by meddling minorities. Roosters can be courageous and work well alone. They are fine professional people and even teachers. Their philosophies are not always far-sighted nor are Rooster gains retained in custody for long. The Rooster is a flinger about of cash. He is penny-wise and pound foolish, generous in spurts, and aghast when the money has run once again out through the holes in his bankbook.

As he is so often sociable and able to meet new people with ease, the Rooster could conceivably run a restaurant or even a shop. But he should arrange to be seconded by a wise Dragon or Tiger person who will keep the Rooster's spending in check, and clamp a comradely hand over his mouth if he gets cheeky with customers.

The Rooster person is so often at odds with his luck that any other subjects who enter business partnerships with him may find the ups and downs exasperating and most unfunny. As we know, the Rooster is not overly concerned with full-time security. The more responsible Cats, Dogs, Pigs, etc., who involve themselves with his schemes will be made to suffer occasional dips in their own finances. A Monkey would not mind all this perilous peregrination, but the Rooster may take exception to being ripped off by his Monkey manager.

Roosters can make it through almost any business crisis. But they cannot expect such a cavalier attitude toward income to please a full-time associate. Roosters always muddle through best on their own. With a good education in hand, they can do just about any job for as long as it interests them.

Family Affairs

A Rooster parent is cocky and authoritarian. Roosters like things kept shipshape. Any child who has the misfortune of being shrug-shouldered vis-à-vis his Rooster parent's neatness will not be comfortable under his roof. Obedient children are kings in the home of the Rooster parent. The Rooster feels that order must be established so that things can get done, run smoothly, and bring well-being to all. His kids usually took scrubbed and are well-dressed. He is a no nonsense, yet deeply affectionate parent.

If a Rooster gives birth to another Rooster, Chinese legend says something will have to give. These two not only struggle with each other's well-developed egos, they actually work against each other to destroy their mirror image. No peace will be theirs until one of them moves from the house. Unless, of course, there is a firm handed Dragon around to keep strife to a dull roar.

Dog children sometimes find their Rooster mom or dad a bit on the flashy side for their quiet tastes. The same holds true for Cat kids. Snake and Oxen offspring will listen and obey their Rooster parent dutifully. There is much to be gained on both sides.

Roosters allow their Monkey and Goat children as much scope as they want, but are often disappointed by their idleness. It is strange how the human mind works. What the Rooster fears most in himself is laziness. Any smack of lassitude around the house will set him on edge.

Tiger and Pig children will feign subordination in order to make it through their youth without a scratch. And, finally, the Rooster's firm hand will not harm them a bit.

A Rat child may flare up at his Rooster parent. But he is a lovable person and will eventually concede that the Rooster is king.

THE DOG

The Years of the Dog

February 10, 1910 to January 30, 1911
January 28, 1922 to February 16, 1923
February 14, 1934 to February 4, 1935
February 2, 1946 to January 22, 1947
February 16, 1958 to February 8, 1959
February 6, 1970 to January 26, 1971
January 25, 1982 to February 12, 1983
February 10, 1994 to January 30, 1995

Dogs are.

Magnanimous • Courageous • Noble • Loyal
Devoted • Attentive • Selfless • Faithful • Modest
Altruistic • Prosperous • Philosophical • Respectable
Discreet • Dutiful • Lucid • Intelligent

But they can also be:

Disquiet • Guarded • Introverted
Defensive • Critical • Pessimistic • Forbidding
Cynical • Stubborn • Moralizing

DOGS I HAVE KNOWN AND LOVED

Every dog has his day. Or, so it is said. But, before that proverbial day arrives, people born in Dog years must often accept to lead a dog's life.

Dogs are uneasy. As though the very act of being born were tantamount to receiving perpetual guard duty, they are watchful, disquiet, sharp of ear, and keen of eye. Sentinels for the world at large, these people feel they were put on earth to safeguard integrity. Should they appear overtly suspicious or mistrustful, you can be sure their motives are ultimately honorable. Dogs are almost never self-seeking. If they look askance at life, it is because they are searching for a loophole, a trouble spot, or a weak link that will afford them the opportunity to repair some damage or hurt. Not satisfied merely to scout out evil, Dogs sincerely want to do something about it.

Hypocrisy and ill will offend the fiber of a Dog's noble soul. Profiteering or misuse of human life can incite a Dog to brave acts of self-abnegation. People born in the year of the Dog never hesitate to stick their necks out for what they believe fair and just. Trouble is, this risky habit of laying themselves on the line for others sometimes leads to their own defeat.

I have three brothers. The eldest, a Rooster, always lends me money if I am in need. Then he politely requests that I not call him again until the emotional coast is clearer. Sharing strife is not his forte. The youngest, a Tiger, will cook me a dinner, tell me how wonderful I am, or commiserate with me for hours. But most of the time my younger brother is nowhere to be found. Tigers move around a lot. John is no exception. The middle brother, Peter, was born in 1946 and is therefore most irreparably a Dog.

If I am in any kind of moral anguish that hinges on a particular circumstance or person, Peter will almost never lend me any cash, invite me to his tiny apartment for a meal, or request that I phone him only after the crisis is through. Peter, my Dog brother, will take the next plane to where I am and give me any reasonable amount of money. This done, he rolls up his sleeves in preparation for stalkingout of my house to punch whom or whatever might be at the root of my problem squarely in the snout, his own reputation be damned. Peter's safety really doesn't matter to him. He is neither violent nor hotheaded. Peter just doesn't like people who get in the way of what he feels is right.

A sweet anecdote may show more specifically how Dogs behave when they feel injustice is afoot. Peter had a veritable army of childhood playmates. One of these was a fat little boy named Bunny. Bunny's parents were too old and too selfish to respect the fact that nicknaming a boy Bunny, proceeding to overstuff him with candy and cake until he looked like a curly-topped feather pillow, and then sending him out to play in the cruel world of normally tough street boys, was a rank unkindness and constituted a real danger to the child's welfare.

Everyone in the neighborhood found time to taunt Bunny. His appearance on any baseball lot, playground, or backyard game of hide 'n seek was always accompanied by jeers and sneers from other children. "Get out of here, you old sissy. My father says you're gonna grow up and be a pansy. Yer mother wears Army shoes. Yer father is a drunk. Etc., etc." Poor Bunny. He just stood there, thumb in mouth, and took it. Running away would have been more trying than his chubby little six-year-old legs could take.

Peter, on the other hand, was a large muscular five-year-old who could ride a two-wheeler when he was three and always played well with kids of any age or strength. He was not mean, but Peter was tough.

One fine summer day, at about six P.M., I was sent out to find Peter and bring him home for seven o'clock dinner. After having scoured the sand lots and prowled the playgrounds for about half an hour, I thought to look for my brother in the wooded vacant lot down the block. And there I found him.

Engaged in kicking and biting his way out of a crowd of approximately fourteen boys and girls ranging in age from four years to twelve, I saw our Peter. His face streaming with sweat, his crew-cut soaked and gleaming in the late afternoon sunlight, my little brother was single-handedly attempting to beat the pants off an army of chanting, screaming meemies.

"Bunny sucks his thu-umb! Bunny sucks his thu-umb!" they jumped up and down and sang mockingly.

Intrepid Peter, as he bashed first one, then another kid in the stomach, shouted, "Stop that! Stop it right now!" But naturally the band played on. The odds were not exactly in my brother's favor. Details like that have never daunted a Dog.

In the middle of the angry troop of nasties, tied securely to a huge elm, was a stricken lump of pale pink flesh whom I eventually recognized as Bunny. Tears gushed from his terrified eyes. I was baffled. But soon my father, who had been sent out looking for us, untied bloated Bunny and admonished the oldest children severely with, "You ought to know better than that." Peter kept up his own final reproofs. All the way home, dragged along by my dad's hand, Peter huffed and puffed, "I told 'em, Daddy. I kept telling 'em. His name is not Bunny. His name is Eldridge. They could call him Eldridge, couldn't they, Daddy? Couldn't they call him Eldridge?"

Peter was scolded for fighting. We were both sent to bed early for not getting home on time for supper. After things quieted down below stairs, I sneaked into Pete's room, sat down on his bed, and administered a few hugs. He was sound asleep. My interventions only roused him slightly. Peter took my hand and said sleepily, "His name is Eldridge, Susie. I told 'em. His name is Eldridge." I tiptoed out, proud to be the big sister of an unsung hero.

For a Dog person, no amount of social disapproval is reason sufficient to hinder his flailings at wrongdoing. Ralph Nader (b. 1934), a most famous figure of virtue, was born in a Dog year. For many years now, Nader has been seeking (and sometimes finding) flaws in our consumer goods, abuses of pollution laws, and ways and means to rectify some of these. What motivates a man like Nader? Is it desire for national renown? Ambition for power? Delight in bucking the system? Money? Obviously none of these.

If Nader had wanted acclaim or applause or even material gain from his crusades against commercial foul play, I expect we would have seen him appearing on late-night talk shows, endorsing so-called "natural" products, and asking to be paid for his good deeds in the bargain.

But, however I turn it around in my head, I cannot imagine that Dog Ralph Nader collects hush monies from companies who pay him to keep his curious nose out of their products and processes.

Weather, temperatures, atmospheric conditions, and ambience are what cause the emotional barometer of Dogs to shift. Placed in a rich social climate where the mood is full of gaiety and mirth, Dogs can wax suddenly jolly, join in the fun, and even perform tricks for their companions. Dump them in a boondock where the company is boring, the landscape uninteresting, and the media lacking in inspiration, and Dog people become dull. A Dog's perspective is limited by the amount of input he receives from without.

Humans born under the sign of the Dog are apt to choose mates and partners whose appearance, manners, life styles, or causes appeal to them. The Dog person enjoys adapting his energies to another's mission. Dogs make perfect helpmates for politicians, union leaders, and other such socially involved people. They sincerely want to champion causes, but because they prefer the wings to the spotlight, Dogs will sometimes agree to do what we call other people's dirty work. However famous they are, no matter how often required to appear before audiences, Dog people are basically unsure of themselves, suffer from stage freight, and worry that their performances will not be up to snuff.

Partially, this self-doubt is based on a kind of disdain that Dogs feel for taking the easy way out. No amount of application, attention to detail, preparation, rehearsal, rewriting, practice, or general "woodshedding" (should he choose to perfect his product) will deter a Dog. He will work overtime, stay awake for days, push himself to the very brink of collapse until satisfied with the result. Moreover, presentation is as important to him as the quality of his handiwork. Dogs are not the sorts who, after painting a lovely series of seascapes and arranging to exhibit them in a chic art gallery, would spoil the aesthetics by arriving at the opening of their one-man show in paint-spattered tatters.

The temptation to say that Dogs approach both work and play with Dogged determination is difficult to resist. Dogs' social and business events are meticulously planned. From food to music and proper lighting effects, entertainment offered by a person born in a Dog year will be well-prepared and efficiently run. Sometimes, Dogs pay so much attention to detail, they tend to find themselves drowning in it. This is particularly noticeable in their conversation, where they may employ a clipped or sharp tone. When asked about a specific subject, Dog people sometimes launch into accounts of all the infinitesimal minutiae that surround the central point of discussion. The original question somehow gets lost in the shuffle.

Also, Dogs always appear to be more in command of a situation than they actually are. Whenever you see a Dog whose carriage and demeanor are almost offensively stiff or controlled, you can be sure that underneath he is saying to himself, "I hope they like me. I wouldn't want to offend anyone. If only I don't make some terrible *faux pas.*" Despite a sometimes cool exterior, Dogs are sensitive, warm-hearted, and affectionate. Like their animal counterparts, they may growl and bark as you near the door of their home. But, if you ply them with a few soothing words, "There, there, now, nice Doggie. Down, boy," and extend your hand in a peaceful gesture, Dog people will melt at your touch, shimmy all over with pleasure, and wag their tails for joy.

My first meeting with Rockwell Brynner (a 1948 Dog) was at the quay-side home of mutual friends in Paris. Balancing on his haunches, he kissed me on both cheeks, and introduced himself. "My name is Rock."

I confess I had never before met anyone named Rock. It sounded like a name for a prizefighter or, at the very least, a Chicago gangster. But this Rock had shaved his head and wore one gold earring. From his spangly garb, I guessed he was neither a boxer nor a tough guy. His hairdo and jewelry led me to think Rock was a hippie freak trying to look like an Eastern potentate. His unctuous Indian perfume stung my nostrils, but he seemed so gallant and cheerful that I stayed right there and had a chat with him.

What Rockwell Brynner had to say in ten short pre-dinner minutes meant two things to me. First, he was bright, well-informed, articulate, and funny. Secondly, his conversation was peppered with "And so I said to Yul" and "Liza thinks I'm in love with her but really I'm not"; and, moreover, he told me a daring story about the time he saw Princess Margaret smoke a marijuana cigarette at a London party. I was convinced that this odiferous flower child was a rank snob, a dreadful name dropper. Did he think that I really believed that wild tale about Princess Meg? And how did he get off talking about Yul Brynner as though he was his best friend. "Liza," I supposed, was Minelli, but that exaggerated business about being in love with her I found annoying.

Snottily, I said, "Excuse me. I don't wish to be indiscreet, but why have you shaved your head? Did you have ringworm?"

"That, my dear young woman, is what psychiatrists like to call an outward manifestation of the eminent father syndrome. I had a very bad case of that disease for a while. So I shaved my head and bought an earring." Rock got up to escort me to the dining room.

Luckily, I twigged to this last hint. "Just who is your father? Why the problems?"

Pretending to speak into a microphone, Rock announced, "My father is the great, the outstanding, the fabulous machismo star of stage and screen, Yul Brynner!" I was amused.

Rock Brynner is so many things at one time, I fear that by

attempting to describe him I may omit something important. Let's just settle on the fact that Rock is a finite example of Dogism.

When one first meets him, Rock's almost aloof debonair manner belies the fact that much of his life has been spent searching for an affectionate muse. As the son of a celebrated talent, Rock suffered almost all his childhood days, half-wishing to emulate Yul Brynner. How simple life would have been if only his father was a simple shopkeeper from Indiana. Of course, Rock is proud to be the genius son of a genius. But, at the same time, the burden of trying to live up to his strong-minded sophisticated father has caused Rock much pain and self-doubt. Born as he was in a Dog year, Rock came into the world more naturally susceptible and vulnerable than most. Though courageous, Rock now and again lacks the ability to know exactly where or how to apply his bravery.

This sensitive young man arrived on earth with a generous portion of self-doubt clenched between a silver spoon and his heartstrings. Probably, it would have been facility itself for Rock to enter the movie business. But, rather than accept gratuitous aid from all the powerful, influential people whom he had known all his life, Rock preferred to approach a theatrical career as though obliged to start at the bottom. Independent of pressures from Hollywood and handouts from the studios, Rock wanted to use his talents and wits in his own way, in his own time.

Dog people are more conscious of the fact that this is a dog-eat-dog world than they ought to be. When things don't quite jibe, if situations appear too gray and contain an insufficient number of blacks and whites, Dog subjects will be the first to notice. This aptitude for analysis can cause Dogs to fall prey to cynicism. Even people who know them well are at times afraid of the Dog's acerbic commentary and biting remarks. Just when everything is moving along swimmingly, Dame Lucidity shines her laser beam from out the private eye of a Dog, and before you can wink back the tears, he will bark, "That cake you made tastes of baking soda!" or "Your bathroom wallpaper looks like a chicken got loose in there."

Dogs are offended by a misplaced detail or even an excess of zeal.

They seem unable to choke back snappy observations that would be better left unsaid. Unfortunately, Dogs dish out these rabid tidbits with considerably more ease than they accept them. So tender-hearted are Dogs that it requires little snipe in order to hurt their feelings, make them scuttle to a corner, lie down, and whimper. What they say and what they mean are frequently vastly opposed, even in their own minds. That chicken-scratch wallpaper remark may have been meant in jest. But somehow it didn't come out that way. Dogs find subtlety mystifying. While young, they should endeavor to master the trick of tasting their words before drooling them so flagrantly about.

Dogs warily avoid the unknown, the avant-garde, and the untried. Unless a method of operation has proven itself efficient for their purposes, Dog people will usually prefer to wait and see if it appears to work for others. However, once an idea or theory is firmly established as a means to an end, Dogs will pick said notion until every shred of meat is consumed. Then, just to be on the safe side, they bury the bones. Dogs never know when an old friend will need that castoff jacket or worn-out electric razor.

Though not frugal or stingy, Dogs are cautious when spending money. Similar to their habit of dispensing time and energy for the missions of others, Dogs would rather buy things for those they admire and love than acquire material goods for themselves. Part of this seeming lack of acquisitiveness is due to the Dog's unwillingness to commit himself to any pursuit or full-time occupation that is not beneficial to someone outside himself. Also, he is naturally pessimistic and unsure of himself. This quality can hinder decision-making in shopping, as the Dog hesitates before obtaining things. He feels they may displease, not match what he already owns or clash with the existing color scheme. Dogs are those people who stand for hours in front of department store dressing-room mirrors, hemming and hawing, consulting the sales force, and asking to see the buyer. Finally in extremis, as the shop is about to shut its doors for the weekend, Dogs will notice that the garment they have chosen is missing a button or has a seam out of line, and decide against buying it.

In the end, when Dog people do apply their talents and critical eye to a career, forget their uncertainties, cease vacillating, and get down to the business of succeeding for themselves, this seeming change of heart is usually based on their acceptance of support, encouragement, and patronage from someone else. The enthusiasm of others can be contagious. People born in Dog years thrive on it. Give them an inspirational kick in the hindquarters from time to time, and Dogs will follow you anywhere.

This may not mean that every Dog needs a stern master, but it is indicative that Dog people would do well to hitch themselves to a wagon that does a bit of the pulling itself. On their own, Dogs fluctuate and shilly-shally. When well seconded (or should I say "firsted"?), their gifts can bring great reward. This third-party cure for the Dog's self-doubt features one insidious side effect. Because he so needs the underpinnings of a helping hand in order to charge ahead and accomplish things, this same hand may be capable of exploiting the Dog. Abuse of his good nature and courageous efforts will most surely disillusion and depress him to the very depths of his soul. The Dog will probably not viciously strike out at an enemy or even sue a person guilty of alienating funds or affections. No. A victimized Dog would rather just up and die of a broken heart, drown his sorrows in some addiction, or even be driven to suicide.

A rapid perusal of celebrities born in Dog years may further explain some of the facts we already know about our loyal subjects. In 1922, Judy Garland, Helen Gurley Brown, and Zsa Zsa Gabor entered the scene. You may find this an unlikely trio. The public images of all three of these women conceal some very important private information. Only parts of it are available to us.

Judy Garland, of course, died so young that we are now, privy to her inside story. Biographies abound. Each gives us a slightly different slant. They all bespeak tragedy. Judy Garland was a talented musical star whose entire career was built on a strength of character about as sturdy as a warped stilt. From the age of two, Judy's mother forced her to perform. And perform she did for her driven stage mother.

Judy Garland hated her self-image. All through school, she wanted to be as beautiful as her classmate, Lana Turner. At the MGM studio, she longed to be appreciated for her sex appeal. Judy's figure was that of a fattish adolescent meadowlark. Too fat. Mayer ordered her to take diet pills and eat only chicken broth for months at a time. She would emerge from that regime nervous, scrawny, and wan. To reinforce her own idea of a sexually attractive woman, Judy tried to shake her dependence on diet pills. She would return to normal eating and again become over-weight. Back she would go on the pills and soup. A truly great performer, she was. A pillar of strength, she most decidedly was not!

All I can tell you about Zsa Zsa is that her forceful mother pushed her to become a star. In many cases, that is all it takes.

From what Helen Gurley Brown says about herself, she performs good works for the sake of her needful readers and is spiritually sustained by her wise and loving husband who encourages every step she takes. *Cosmopolitan* magazine, under her able patronage, became America's best-selling women's magazine. Ms. Brown made its success her personal mission. Rumor has it, Ms. Brown sets an example for her employees by working harder than anyone in the *Cosmo* office. That is certainly typical of the diligent Dog.

The famous Dogs born in 1922 are also a characteristic lot. Pierre Cardin, Norman Mailer, and Kurt Vonnegut are some of them. Cardin designs (by European standards) very conservative clothes for men and women. Mailer has never been noted for his placid optimism. Loopholes and acerb commentary are his life's blood. And Vonnegut . . the retiring, diffident Vonnegut appears only in his own books, never in public.

Vonnegut, the master of fanciful social commentary, the brilliant sticker of pins in our precious national mythologies. Have you ever seen Kurt Vonnegut on TV? Or, for that matter, have you ever even heard of this magnificent writer's books? Take a gander sometime. I think you'll see why he was born in 1922.

Next comes 1934. If you do not see the similarity between Brigitte Bardot, Carol Burnett, Shirley Maclaine, and Kate Millett right off, I'll forgive you. It's easy enough to see that the two comediennes Burnett and Maclaine might fit into the Dog category. There is something of the Garland syndrome in both. But Bardot and Millett? Yes, of course, now I remember. Diffident Brigitte Bardot never comes out of her Saint-Tropez house except to visit friends. She lives surrounded by her foundling animals and has spent most of her film earnings on the promotion and building of animal shelters all over France. Bardot is a fine Dog person. Kate Millett's book, *Sexual Politics*, if you recall, made a lot of feminist noise. In a very scholarly way, Ms. Millett said much to support the cause of less gifted vocal innovators such as Ms. Gloria (Pig, 1935) Steinem and Co. That's what Dogs do. Crusaders one and all, they fight other people's battles.

As for 1934's male crop, we have Alan Arkin, Leonard Cohen, Gene Wilder, and "Elvis the Pelvis" Presley. Rather than go into a lengthy description of their Doggish traits, I only suggest you take a look at their most obvious mutual physical characteristic, that adorable hangdog expression. Their stock in trade, their very image, depends on that canine look of candid pessimistic puppy dog vulnerability.

One last fame flash. Liza Minelli was born to twenty-four-year-old Judy Garland in 1946. That makes Liza a Dog as well. Perhaps a more sensible woman than her departed mother, Liza should nonetheless be on perpetual guard against exploitation.

Having covered the major pitfalls and strengths, I will only reiterate that Dogs make excellent friends. They are fine, upright citizens. Their pessimism, their apparent lack of enthusiasm, their self-doubt should be indulged. Dogs need constant reassurance and morale boosting. In the long run, be they lap Dogs or watch Dogs, they are truly man's best friends.

MADAME DOG

Where her own advancement is in question, Dame Dog is compulsively circumspect. At every turn, she asks herself whether or not such an inept, inarticulate, not-so-sexy lady as herself has a right to enter the competition. Nonetheless, what happens when you invite a Dog woman to express her opinions regarding the essence of her own character may surprise you. She could well blurt, "I am a very ambitious person."

From my experience, aspiration among Dog females is not accompanied by enough healthy selfishness or driving ego to properly qualify for the title, ambition. Rather, what does gnaw at the innards of such women is a kind of coveting of power. Dog ladies keenly wish they were on top of that mountain that they so hungrily eye. They take little vicarious pleasure in witnessing others climb those peaks. Yet, without receiving impetus from respected friends or loved ones, they know they are condemned to the ignominious role of envious spectator.

Earlier, I said that Dogs are dependent on their environment. Placed in a desert, their minds dry up. In a stimulating friendly atmosphere that challenges them, Dogs seem to sprout wings. Suddenly, former obstacles to their achievement and self-realization lose their forbidding quality. Women of this sign are directly affected by this pattern. An arid partner, dull surroundings, and/or witless colleagues will sap the very strength from a Dog lady. Whatever brilliance she may be hiding inside, unless piqued by inspirational circumstances, will remain forever hidden. Dog women prefer to have their scripts written for them. They will be able to interpret, edit, revise, make corrections and improvements with style and intelligence. But they must not be asked to innovate without the comfy crutch of something to go on.

There is in my acquaintance a charming Dog lady whose prudent vigilance is second only to her passionate yearning for self-expression. Her name is Marie-Laure Castellan. Though of French parentage, Marie-Laure (b. 1946) and her American physician husband have moved back and forth between continents so many times, she no longer knows to which country she lends more allegiance. Marie-Laure has lived in Spain, France, Italy, and Germany. At present, because her husband's work demands it, Marie-Laure lives in (of all places) Buffalo, New York.

Buffalo is my home town. With all of its polluting industrial clamor and mixed ethnicity, I still love it. Marie-Laure, try as she might, has not been able to catch my nostalgic disease. Each day of her sojourn slows and depresses her energies further. The gloom cast by the very act of rising to shine every morning in Buffalo's grayness makes Marie-Laure's blood pressure plummet.

The reason I know all of this is that I had to go to Buffalo early last year for some long overdue divorce proceedings. In order to obtain a divorce judgment in New York State, one must provide the court with a witness. My sister Linda lives in Buffalo. She is a Pig (b. 1935) and Pigs don't like legal entanglements. When I could not convince Linda to tell the judge what she knew about my long-dead marriage, I hastily dialed Marie-Laure's number from New York City.

Marie-Laure answered the phone. Privately, I thanked Zeus that she was home. Then I rattled off my plan. "Marie-Laure, listen. It's me, Suzanne, I'm arriving tonight on the eight o'clock plane. I'm finally going to get that divorce. It's on the docket for tomorrow morning. Can you possibly meet me at my lawyer's office at nine? He'll tell us what to say."

"Us?" Marie-Laure interjected timidly.

"Oh, yes . . ." I went on talking. "I nearly forgot. I need you to serve as a witness for me. Can you? Will you? Pleeease. . . ."

"Oh, sure." Marie-Laure sounded ecstatic. "Finally you will put some adventure in my life."

Court was two minutes of nothing. All the nice judge wanted to know from Marie-Laure was "Yes or no." Did she corroborate the story my lawyer had told him? She was a bit disappointed. She was itching to recite a speech she had prepared on the subject of my failed marriage. The judge addressed Marie-Laure on the stand and asked, "Do you believe the aforesaid information to be factual?" Marie-Laure (though the lawyer had warned her not to waste time and only to answer in monosyllables) stood up on her hind legs and said huffily, "Well! I most certainly do. It's criminal what that poor woman went through to raise her sweet children. Why, do you know that she has had no support from her husband in years? We don't even know where he is. She's had to do it alone. All alone." I swear there were tears in her voice.

Luckily, before Marie-Laure got herself too deeply embroiled in details, the attorney suggested she step down from the witness box. The judge awarded me the formality of a no-contest divorce and we left the courtroom.

Pink in the cheek from her efforts, outside the building, Marie-Laure hugged the lawyer, she hugged me, jumped up and down, lost her hat in the shuffle, and said, "Oh, thank you. Thank you both for such a good time. That is the most fun I've had in years." My attorney, a dignified young gentleman whose professional interest in my complicated international case was the only reason he had agreed to represent me, looked at Marie-Laure and said, "You know, you really should go to law school. You were incredible up there. I would have let you continue but I could tell the judge was pressed for time."

A week later, Marie-Laure applied to law school. She said she had often thought about doing something with her talent for public speaking. But she added, "You know how I am, Suzanne, I need someone to inspire me. I'm a receiver. Sometimes I can even be an amplifier. But I'm not a generator. You, on the other hand, you're a generator.".

Flattering though her remarks were, I could only say, "Maybe, in time, if you do study law and go into practice, you'll gain some confidence of your own. I am older than you. I used to be shy. You'll see. Just give yourself time." Though I had promised this, in the back of my head a little voice insisted, "She's a Dog. Remember, she'll always seek her inspiration from outside."

Law, medicine, missionary, or social work make excellent careers for Dog women. They are not likely to want to stay home and raise kids all of the time. Women born in Dog years are doers. They care not for flower arranging and afternoon teas. They need a cause upon which to focus their activity. Armed with any mission, Dog women will take over from there. And, when they do, watch out for flying fur.

Love a Dog woman? Then nurture her courage. Build her ego. Tell her pretty lies that boost her morale. If you are gruff and silent, even though you may love her in your own quiet way, the Dog woman will surely retreat inside herself. She, like all Dogs, needs many a tender pat on the head, loving hugs, warm words of reassurance, and lots of playful romps in the woods in order to be happy. Throw the stick as far as you can. Urge her on with encouraging words. Lady Dog is an ace retriever. She'll always come, wagging her tail, back to the side of a loving master.

MONSIEUR DOG

The male Dog is a wary beast. Permanently ingrained in his furry little head is the idea that he must forever watch out, be careful, stay abreast of the news, keep his eyes peeled for danger, and not let himself be misused. For a cohort, lover, or pal, the Dog man will extend almost any service. For his own ends, he will often be afraid to step outside the gate.

Marco is Rock Brynner's ex-schoolmate from Yale. Like his favorite crony, Marco was born in 1946. He is at once a farmer, a writer, a songster-minstrel, and a gentle, faithful friend of mine. As a youngster, his parents moved him from the States to Milan, where he mastered public school Italian. Back at Yale, he studied French, which he speaks and writes with flair and excellence. What Marco does for a living alternates between hard farm labor around his small property in the French countryside, and using his trilingual expertise in the development of screenplays and dialogue.

Marco's last name is Prince. At one point in my budding writing career, Marco and I established a small business, from which we hoped to gain our daily breads by writing advertising copy in French and in English. The company title was The White Prince. After committing a few heinous commercial crimes for ITT and beefing up some languid soap ads for the Common Market distribution of an abrasive chemical detergent, Marco was called away to Rome to work for Alain Delon on a film about Zorro, and I involved myself in the composition of my first novel. The White Prince went the way of all white princes. It rode in on a shimmering stallion, reared up for a fleeting glorious moment, and vanished in its own dust. We lost interest.

Marco, who writes poetical songs worthy of rendition by the gods, is playful as a puppy, loyal as a Labrador, and dogmatically dedicated to the proposition that the world may be coming to an end at two o'clock this afternoon. Although he would never do so in a century of wheedling and persuasion, if by some miracle Marco decided to become a professional singer of his own works, I am certain he would outrock Jagger, outprotest Dylan, and outseduce any crooner alive. Tall, dark, handsome, and suave, Marco is a natural-born genius.

But he is, as well, a Dog person. If anyone wanted to sing Marco's songs in public, he would probably give them away for nothing. But, since he so rarely trots them out of their guitar-case hiding place, scarcely anybody even knows that Marco owns any songs. Among the hundreds of people who know him, only about four of us have heard even so much as a note or lyric of Marco's masterpieces. Why? Well you see, Marco doesn't really trust anyone not to poke fun at him for writing the romantico-cynical music that he does. Too, he is fearful that someone might commercialize his glorious tunes and thereby expose him for what he is, a gifted writer. Then, of course, he would have to write more songs about what he thinks and open himself to more imagined criticism. So, rather than make himself vulnerable to abuse from the nit-picking public, Marco keeps his creative talents a deep, dark secret.

However, should Marco be requested to share in the writing of something that a less talented writer has badly botched, his long-lashed eyes brighten. He sits down and types out brilliantly, fastidiously, amusingly perfect pieces of fine literature. Because he is not about to agree that he is a fantastic writer, he is fast becoming a professional Mr. Fixit of crippled composition. He's the best in his field.

Yet, Marco is not at all content with his lot. Often, he has confessed to us intimates, "Wouldn't it be great if somebody wanted to do one of my songs on a record?" All of us nod away, urge him to send them to this agent or that, offer to show them here and there to the right people. At this point, Marco puts down his old guitar, lights a cigarette, and sighs "Yeah, but then they might become all electronic. Some jerk would arrange them all wrong. I would hate that."

Marco's problem is a Dog problem, magnified because he is more clever than most. Within his willing spirit exists a raging conflict of interests. Brilliance plays a losing battle against self-doubt. People like myself yearn to put a firecracker under people like Marco. But one bomb would never do the trick. Those fuses would have to be lurking everywhere—about his studio, in his bathtub, under his pillow—each with a note attached saying, "You are wonderful! You can do it! We're with you, baby! Sign this contract on the dotted line," and the like.

For many people, this form of encouragement would do the trick. Armed with the courage of friends and the pluck of cheers from admirers, lots of us would go out and lick the world. But this is unlikely to be the case with Dog people. Men born under the sign of the Dog might very well consider such urgings to be intrusions on their privacy. Too much applause may merely render a Dog suspicious of his audience. In Marco's career, as in the careers of all Dogs, an excess of outside interference angers him.

To love a Dog mate well is to know how not to push him too far. Each day, you lead him to the very brink of accomplishment, then back off and hope for the best. All you really need be steadily aware of with a Dog gentleman is that, nourished with the proper inspiring confidence and pluck he so urgently requires of you, he will never bite the hand while it feeds him.

CO-SIGNS

DOG/Aries *(March 21—April 20)*

When Aries' fire touches the metal element that symbolizes the Dog years, it will warm the ingot with some difficulty. The unbending, cool-headed Dog is a tough crusader. Aries people possess an undeniably soldierlike quality. In combat, this Dog subject will find his true calling. Be it a battle for human rights or favors of a loved one, the Aries Dog will exhibit uncommon valor. The hitch is, a Dog born in the sign of Aries may be tempted to advance on his enemies in the dark. Strategies must be worked out carefully. Otherwise, he may charge before he thinks. His excessive confidence is based more on the importance of his mission than on his true ability to conquer.

DOG/Taurus *(April 21—May 21)*

More conviction and rigor than other Dogs enjoy can make this earth/metal subject into a veritable gold mine of talent and execution.

Taureans are sensitive from the inside out. Dogs tend to be the opposite. It's a lucky combination of signs. Nothing can discourage a determined Taurus. The diffident Dog will benefit from this injection of resolve. Taureans are sensual, they love a bawdy joke, revel in a good time. The Dog's cool exterior may take on a warmer glow. Never actually outgoing and bold, but more so than if he were not endowed with the Taurean's ribaldry, this Dog subject will not be as critical of "foolishness" as his kennelmates.

DOG/Gemini *(May 22—June 21)*

Air and metal fail to mesh into any kind of orderly pattern. In order for the Gemini Dog to succeed at a given task, he will need a firmly entrenched magnetic force to keep him from blowing away. This Dog seems to be everywhere at once. At times, he is confidently up. Then, again, the dumps will not seem a lowly enough place in which to be down. The mercurial Gemini will cause the disquiet Dog to suffer from overthink about his possible failings and faults. Good-hearted and altruistic beyond measure, this Dog subject's bank account should be frequently checked for wasted capital. Gifts to friends, squanderings on members of the opposite sex, and indulgence in pound foolishness are to be expected. Early training in self-discipline is advised. This Dog wags his tail for almost any approaching stranger. He should be taught to put some bite in that bark.

DOG/Cancer *(June 22—July 23)*

Deeply emotional and sensitive, the Dog/Cancer, represented by water and metal, has a soul of purest old gold. Cancers do suffer more than their share of sentimental chagrin. Dogs are not exactly towers of might and strength. The Cancerian born in a Dog year will be self-sacrificing for family, job, and country. He wants to believe in good, but something tells him there is a lot of bad out there. If not encouraged to go and see for himself, the Dog born in Cancer may in hermit fashion hole up and allow the victories that are rightfully his to be won by one less worthy. As a parent, he will excel. In love, the Dog/Cancer will realize his talents. In war, he will feel too sorry for his enemy to really destroy him. He'd rather reason out conflicts than be obliged to use force. However, don't be fooled by his sweetness. There is a well-controlled temper in there. Don't tempt him to use it.

DOG/Leo *(July 24—August 23)*

The leader of the pack. If this fiery metallic fuel tank ever allows himself to be sent into orbit, the game is over for everyone else. Nothing should stand in the way of a Leo Dog in motion, except perhaps lack of sufficient motivation and pride. Without enough fuel, this Dog subject may be too feisty to deign request an extra gallon of gas from the reserve tank. No doubt about it, the Dog born under Leo wants to rule. At least, he talks about it often enough. But, unfortunately, sometimes he can't fend off adversaries with loud noises. If he succeeds, the achievement will be brilliant. He must be wary of over extending himself. Even though he is a limitless Leo, he is also a doubting Dog.

DOG/Virgo *(August 24—September 23)*

The purest metals lie locked in the bowels of the earth. Both Dogs and Virgos refuse to tolerate the alloys that life may try to impose on their sterling spirits. Much time and effort will be spent removing people, objects, and invading forces that threaten to dilute the Virgo Dog's unsullied surroundings. Meticulous attention to detail, profound idealism, and extreme modesty characterize this virtuous subject. The Dog born under the sign of Virgo will prefer country life to the clankings of city existence. Urban living heightens the insecurities that, no matter how he tries to protect himself, peer out at him from every doorway and dark alley.

DOG/Libra *(September 24—October 23)*

Again, air brushes shining metal. This time, rather than creating storm warnings, the combination should produce a balance-seeking Dog whose ability to forgive and forget provides him with numerous friends and acquaintances who love and understand him. There is more danger of exploitation for Libras born in Dog years. They are almost too malleable and insecure to know when the enemy is manipulating them. This Dog is the one who takes two friends along when he buys a new suit, asks the opinions of fifteen sales persons and four fashion buyers before deciding on a purchase. Because he seems to require the presence of so many extraneous people about him, one-to-one relationships are discouraged. Madame or Monsieur Dog/Libra may always drag along a pal on dates, bring home a co-worker for dinner, and spend a goodly amount of time. "out with the boys." Almost entirely other-oriented, this subject is the soul of altruistic behavior. He wants not only to have people like him, he wants to show them how far he will go in risking his life and limb for them.

DOG/Scorpio *(October 24—November 22)*

I would not wish to be smack in the path of this PT boat of a person. Endowed with superior abilities for combating his enemies and routing out trouble spots, the Dog/Scorpio will make short work of anyone who tries to hurt a person he loves. Endowed with a rabid desire to change the world, the Dog born in Scorpio both can and will try his best to do so. Cynical, acid-tongued, and often humorously inclined, this Dog gives the impression of being able to see through walls. So lacking is he in trust, so wary of possible adversaries and competition, the Dog/Scorpio bites first and barks later. If you see him engaged in a fight, I suggest that you make no effort to disentangle the melee. He spares no means to his end.

DOG/Sagittarius *(November 23—December 21)*

A veritable blast furnace of energy and idealism drives this humanitarian to champion causes. Too much, however, is still too much. The Dog/Sagittarius is sometimes more energetic than realistic. Causticity and straightforward remarks will cut even those who love him most to the very quick. To accomplish his crusades, this subject may have to accept some degree of compromise. This is difficult for such a heady and bold knight in shining armor. Sagittarians want action. Dogs are restive and uneasy. The match portends much conflict and inner turmoil. He may want to prevent the world from self-destruction. Born with the ability to stop at nothing, if anybody can aspire to assuring the salvation of our planet, the Sagittarian Dog should get first bite.

DOG/Capricorn *(December 22—January 20)*

Generous and tender-hearted beneath that cool exterior, the Dog/ Capricorn marries metal with mettle. Here is a friend you can count on, an adviser you can trust. For his own purposes, he will not wish to enter into much competition. For the sake of what he believes in, the Dog/Capricorn will dedicate his life to the rigors of any contest. This subject is an ascetic. Physical comforts do not tempt him, material wealth offends his socialist spirit. The Dog/Capricorn watches over those he loves with the astute ear of a German shepherd dog. He has a nose for evil and ill will that astonishes the modest Dog side of his character. Vicious only when necessary, but vicious all the same.

DOG/Aquarius *(January 21—February 19)*

What a pair! May his house be safe from Tigers. An Aquarian Dog is the busy combination of liberal social worker and crusader for good causes. He will probably have a taste for culture, bordering on pure intellectualism. The works of the philosophers will offer this Dog much in the way of food for thought and grist for his mill of alchemical notions about changing Bad to Good. Because often the Dog is overly concerned with the feelings of others, he will be fortunate to be born under the sign of Aquarius. As we know, although Aquarians love their fellow-man, they often forget to nurture the affections of their closest family and friends. The match is a positive one. Much fine social reform could ensue if this Dog subject puts his snout to the grindstone.

DOG/Pisces *(February 20—March 20)*

There is a wealth of imagination present in the character of this person. He may know how to take a simple thought and turn it into a poem or painting. Dogs, though disquiet and unsure of themselves, are strongest when they confront a weaker soul. A Pisces can use all the force of character he can get. Dogs are eminently charitable and generous. Instead of withholding their energies and refusing to aid the

Pisces side of their natures, Dogs born in the sign of the fish will be likely to urge vague creativity into a solid career. Early in life, this Dog should learn to perform in front of others. Otherwise he may lack the ability to express his thoughts articulately. Extol those early poetic efforts, rave over his attempts at story writing and recitation. He needs all the ego-building encouragement he can get. A late start in any career pursuit may be disastrous. A ten- or twelve-year jump on the competition will protect him from oversensitivity when the grown-up fighting begins.

PRESCRIPTION FOR THE FUTURE

Doubtful Dog, I number you among the saints of our Chinese zodiac. For little or no return, you devote such grand portions of your time and thought to doing for others who call on you for assistance in need. Truly a self-sacrificing soul, you deserve a hearty round of applause for willingness, cheerfully taking up our burdens, hard work in the cause of injustice, and just plain love of your fellow-man. Even if sometimes your bark pierces us with its too-direct irony, we still love you very much.

Please do not shrink away in fear that I am about to deride you for your blurted comments about how much you like that stain on my new couch, or how becoming you think that bit of gray in my hair is to my aging face. I forgive you for your lack of subtlety. I might even go so far as to say I think your tactlessness is endearing. You do not contrive to hurt us with your blatant ingenuousness. It's part of your charm.

But what is most exasperating about you, Doggy dear, is that your bottomless pit of selflessness sometimes allows other people to misuse and hurt you. Now, if you were content with the status quo of professional victimhood, I promise you we would not utter a further syllable. But, over and over again, you cry yourself to sleep at night wondering why you allowed this or that injurious person to enter your life and hurt you.

It is a strange twist of fate that you should always appear to be on the defensive, and yet so often end up the loser in your fervent battlings against enemies who sneak up on you unawares. In all honesty, you look like you know what you're doing. Although we would sometimes like to advise you against those too-charitable undertakings, your aura of sure-footedness and history of truly brave deeds lead us to think you have the situation under control. What I mean is, you don't look half so diffident as you may feel.

That proud gait, those earnest sharp eyes and ears dupe us into believing that you have enough courage and strength for all of us. You rarely come to us when you feel so nervous that you are sleeping with one ear cocked in readiness for the attack. When you need us, why don't you call? Perhaps the sharing of some of those psychic burdens would ease your load.

You may answer, "Well, why don't you ask?"

Fact is, we'll be Dog-goned if we know! Is it your forbidding attitude? Your cool, collected exterior? Your philosophical policy of taking everything in stride? What is it that keeps us from walking right up to you and saying, "Hey, pal, how about one of those good old heart to hearts?" That approach somehow doesn't seem feasible. We're afraid you'll just make some clever cynical comment or tell us to get back to herding our own sheep.

You need encouragement from us. That much we know. But what troubles us is that when we need you, it's as though you have a presentiment or vibration. You are always Johnny on the spot. As for us, must we play a guessing game with your poker-faced appearance just to earn the right to lend you a hand?

Speak up, old faithful, whine a bit more loudly when you see the horizon clouding over. Do not always accept to lie down and whimper sadly after it's too late. I know you are stubbornly self-possessed and able to leap tall fences at a single bound, but you are not Superdog. You are only human. Even the most private of people needs an occasional shoulder to cry on.

And, while I'm at it, I might as well tell you that what you fear to be the worst about yourself is rarely if ever half as bad as you imagine. Are you in debt? How much do you need? Have you hurt someone's feelings? Perhaps we can help you make amends. You do tend to take both others and yourselves too seriously. With that combination of group spirit and cynicism, in time, you could forget how to laugh and cry altogether.

Listen, Doggy, if I can be my old big-mouth soothsayer self for a moment, I'll just tell you this: Maybe you are more timid and willing to do for others than you feel like. Now, by that, I do not mean that your gestures of good will toward those you love are false. But you must admit that on the rare occasions when we do get to have those soulful late-night chats, the one secret thought that repeatedly creeps from without your depths is a masked, but still earnest desire to make something of yourself.

It begins something like this: "Well, you know, Suzanne, I have often thought that if it weren't for the fact that I got such a late start in the profession, I might be a great figure skater by now." Or, even worse, it goes as follows: "You know, I would love to have been an actress. But having the kids and the dogs and Jerry to wait on hand and foot, there really never was much time for me to take lessons or even join a little theater group." Or, maybe you just block all roads for yourself by saying this: "Look, I'm really too old to break into TV in New York. I probably could begin in Iowa somewhere. But I don't like halfway measures. If I can't be broadcast from New York, I don't want to do it."

Sound familiar? I guess so.

Far be it from me to accuse you of laziness. I know how industrious you are. But let me be the first to tell you that if you weren't so patently a Dog, I might want to dub you a C H-I-C-K-E-N.

Come on now, pal. Let's have one of our heart to hearts.

COMPATABILITIES

Affairs of the Heart

The Dog is a loyal and attentive watcher of both his own and the steps of those he loves. No one could ask for a better companion or more affectionate mate. The Dog is a true sidekick, shoulder to cry on, helpmate, and booster of egos. Because a Dog basically believes everybody more capable of generating energy than himself, the Dog will usually agree to stay in the shadow of a lover's progress and keep the home fires alive in his absence. Dogs, though pessimistic for themselves, are usually able to infuse a love partner's depleted morale with much-needed optimism.

The Horse, in exchange for his independence, will give the Dog a much-needed sense of security and well-being. Horses can cajole a loved one out of almost any despair. Even though they don't always share them, Horses admire the Dog's liberal views.

A Dog with a Tiger mate is a very contented Dog, indeed. Tigers are rebellious and strong. Dogs are rebellious but worried. As the object of a Tiger's affection, the Dog will bask in some of the victories he so dreams of winning for humanity's sake. The intemperate Tiger can use the Dog's good counsel. Also, Tigers need passion, tenderness, and loads of the fidelity that Dogs are so famous for.

Cats and Dogs get on beautifully. Theirs will be a calm, intellectual rapport. The Dog inspires confidence. The Cat likes his Dog partner's quiet diffidence and makes much of Dog causes in a silent supportive way.

Goats are a bit whimsical for Dogs. They sometimes add to his nervousness. Though they may love each other passionately, the gentle Goat and the anxious Dog are not always a productive pair.

Dragons, much as they admire the Dog's high principles, are anxious souls. If these two get together, the Dog's pessimism may inhibit the proud Dragon. A double dose of caution could be debilitating to both parties.

Social Affairs

If a Dog has to choose anything carefully, it is his friends. Since he is not naturally optimistic, the Dog needs companions around him who will urge him ever onward to accomplishment. As for his own loyalty and true ability to behave as a good friend, there is no problem at all. Once a Dog subject has decided to pick a pal, his constancy is incorruptible.

The watchful Dog can team up nicely with members of the following signs: The Cat, who serves as an excellent and honest confidante for his earnest opinions; the Horse, who admires the Dog's policies and can use all of his dash to encourage his Dog friend; the cheerful Monkey, who jollies the Dog along and doesn't try his tricks on the likes of dutiful Dogs; and the virtuous Pig, who knows how to spur the Dog to let his guard down and have a good fling. Two Dog people can be excellent comrades-in-arms. But the pair will be almost too wary for their own mutual good.

Rats are not as nobly ambitious as Dogs. Conflict is unavoidable between the two. Dragons are not realistic enough to please Dogs for long. Goats and Roosters discomfit the Dog with their hazy notions and adventuresome ideas. Snakes are a mite too elegant for the earthy Dog to join in more than a socializing relationship.

But Tigers . . . Tigers are the Dog's best bet. No more adoring or durable camaraderie exists in the Chinese zodiac than that which Dogs and Tigers feel for each other.

Business Affairs

The business world is not the Dog's bailiwick. He is better suited for the professions or for political pursuits than for commerce. Dogs are not very materialistic. And, even when they do manage to dabble in money-making schemes and find that they can make money, Dogs tend to spend profits too generously on others. Dogs can be infinitely happier as professors, doctors, lawyers, or social workers than if embroiled in the business rat race.

Of course, some Dogs will become business people. Through the wise choice of associates, they can be taught to make intelligent financial decisions and may learn how to deal with all manner of negotiation. For the best mutual understanding to evolve from a business partnership, Dogs should associate themselves with Horses. The Horse can wean the diffident Dog slowly but surely out of his self-doubts and into the big time. Cats are good co-workers for Dogs, as well. They rarely argue and the Dog trusts the Cat's sensible judgment in touchy situations.

Tigers and Dogs, though well-adapted to each other's ideals, are not particularly apt when coupled as wheeler-dealers. They both prefer politicking to money-making.

All other business colleagues will be too hasty, plodding, or insufficiently motivated to undertake the apprenticeship of a Dog in the world of finance. Dogs should either avoid these possible allies, or plan on some sleepless nights.

Family Affairs

Dog parents are worriers. Surely the Dog has a very well-developed sense of duty and will always be loyal and faithful in dealings with children. But, goodness, how he frets!

The Tiger child learns much from his Dog parent. Their complicity is total. The Dog will be proud of his Tiger child's strength and sense of humanity. Horses get along better with Dog parents than might be expected. Problems may arise from the disappointment that the Dog parent feels in regard to the Horse's excessive selfishness. Nonetheless, the Dog respects his Horse child's cherished independence.

Cat children delight their Dog moms and dads. The Cat's brand of quiet charm and intelligence makes sense to the doubting Dog. And Dog children are a fine addition to the Dog parent's entourage. There may be an excess of mutual admiration. But Dogs play together nicely.

In most other cases, the parent Dog's watchful eye will impose more responsibility on the child than he may like. In dealing with a Dog parent, the child must spend energy reassuring the parent that he is well-adjusted, sufficiently fed, and dressed. In short, the child of a Dog parent must remove some of the burden from the anxious mother or father's shoulders.

Since all children will be extremely well-provided for by a dutiful Dog parent, it is most unlikely that a child of any sign could have much to complain about.

THE PIG

THE YEARS OF THE PIG

January 30, 1911 to February 18, 1912
February 16, 1923 to February 5, 1924
February 4, 1935 to January 24, 1936
January 22, 1947 to February 10, 1948
February 8, 1959 to January 28, 1960
January 27, 1971 to February 14, 1972
February 13, 1983 to February 1, 1994
January 31, 1995 to February 18, 1996

PIGS ARE

Obliging • Loyal • Scrupulous • Indulgent • Truthful
Impartial • Intelligent • Sincere • Sociable • Thorough • Cultured
Sensual • Decisive • Peaceable • Loving • Profound • Sensitive

BUT THEY CAN ALSO BE:

Naïve • Defenseless • Insecure • Sardonic • Epicurean
Noncompetitive • Willful • Gullible • Earthy • Easy prey

PIGS I HAVE KNOWN AND LOVED

Endearing and gallant, gentle, yet strong of will, those who are born under the sign of the Pig are the vanguard of purity and good. Nothing is too much to ask of a Pig. No secret will escape his lips, no disappointment daunt his loyalty nor scar his belief in the basic worth of humankind. Though he may falter and stumble in the face of treachery and ill will, the Pig usually emerges clean as a whistle, brandishing the banner of humanitarianism and charity.

All the Pig people I have ever known were made to suffer undue strife throughout their lives. Whether or not any part of these struggles were their own doing remains a moot point. Perhaps if I recount some of their stories, you will begin to agree with me that whatever haunts the very footsteps of Pigs is both an elusive and malevolent force. If any responsibility for frequent demise lies with the unwary Pig, it is only partly his fault.

It seems like last week that I was growing up with my three brothers and sister Linda in apple-pie normal American surroundings. In the old days, I found plenty of puerile reasons to call Linda a "Pig." Little did I know then that her 1935 birth date would turn my sibling insults into fact.

Linda was always too good to be true. She was the kind of older sister who does everything right. I was the kind of little sister who prided myself on doing most things backward. Linda rarely, if ever, got scolded. I, on the other hand, spent many a long evening lying on an empty stomach and staring at the flowered coverlet of my bed. Recently, while discussing our idyllic childhood with my beloved sister, she told me of a few very chilling subconscious thoughts that she had entertained way back then.

Tossing her long-haired pageboy with characteristic flair, pretty Linda confided, "I loved it when you other kids got into trouble. Not that I enjoyed the scenes. You know how I hate fights. But I always tried to be a good kid. The rest of you always got away with so much murder, it made me feel victorious if Mom and Dad caught you disobeying." Smiling, Linda sipped at a long-stemmed glass of thick sherry.

"Ah hah!" I laughed lovingly. "Now I remember how you used to stand by while I was punished. You never sneaked me goodies when I was sent to bed without supper. You never lied for me when Daddy caught me roller-skating in that forbidden busy street."

Linda looked suddenly dismayed and hurt. "I couldn't do that, Suzanne. To this day I don't know how to lie with a straight face. Daddy always told me my eyes would turn green if I told a lie. Somewhere in the back of my mind I still worry about that."

Pigs can never utter an untruth without fearing the worst. Their good deportment and will to behave are not based on cunning or a desire to get more than their share of applause and attention. They just don't believe there is any other way.

I venture to hope that everybody knows at least one Pig whom he or she considers a friend. Pig people are among the most likable, respectable, and upstanding citizens of this planet. When they decide to befriend someone, they take the alliance seriously. I'll even bet that most of the willing souls who drive long hours to and from airports, picking up traveling friends and family members so they won't be obliged to take buses or taxis into cities, were born in Pig years.

In sickness and in health, Pig people are always there to fetch juices and hot water bottles for those they love. Coincidentally, my own mother was also born under the sign of the Pig. Since I was not only a knock-kneed chatterbox pain-in-the-neck girl child, but also of the sickly anemic variety, Mother had thousands of chances to prove her worth as an enduring, indulgent parent. Being ill in our house was next door to heaven. I had a brass dinner bell with a turtle on the handle with which I could summon my sweet mommy to my bedside at any moment of the day or night. Two years of a serious illness that my siblings always called Beditis could very well have driven any other mother crazy with both worry and supplementary travail. There were five children to be fed and laundered, sent off to school, scolded, and loved. For many years after growing up, I used to wonder how in the name of Zeus my mother ever did it all. I don't recall that she yelled or screamed very much. I was spanked only for serious offenses like trying to commit suicide by hitching free slides on the rear bumpers of cars in snowy weather. Mainly, as my lyrical Irish mother herself so aptly stated not long ago, my childhood was "a forerunner of Disneyland."

Pigs are not much on the use of their tongues for thinking purposes. They do not function brilliantly in circumstances where negotiation requires quick on-their-feet volleys of words. Rather, where language is a factor, Pigs are better advised to let others do their business talking. Yet, when Pig people are in comfortable social situations wherein they do not feel threatened, they can literally take the floor for an entire evening of storytelling, banter, and jokes. Often, Pigs enjoy turning a tale with a spicy or risqué flavor. They are extremely sensual (even a bit shockingly so from time to time) and emotionally dependent on sex and all that goes with it. A Pig without a mate or lover is a woebegone Pig indeed.

Most Pig people are intellectuals. To remove books and cultural events from their lives would be both cruel and foolish. Since they are sensitive as well as emotive, what they gather from reading and attending plays, concerts, art openings, and the like feeds the Pig soul and has a stabilizing effect on their sometimes tormented spirit. Because they are neither showy nor flashy in dress or demeanor, these creatures of habit and docility often go unnoticed in crowds. Please don't think for a minute that because they appear shy or retiring in a group, this position of relative ignominy does not bother them. On the contrary, it troubles them deeply and causes them to feel insecure and unworthy. Pigs always wish they were not so vulnerable. But their timid natures are uncooperative in this regard.

Sadness is an emotion with which the Pig feels at home. He is rarely guilty of self-pity, but he will suffer for the woes of others. Disappointment hounds Pig people throughout their days. People, jobs, children, the weather, and God constantly let them down, hurting their feelings and stepping on their piggies. Try as they might to live in fantasy towers of security, ever building up bastions of wisdom and safe harbor, Pig people unwittingly find themselves in jeopardy.

"Fat Jim," a young man I know rather well, was born under the sign of the Pig (1935). For years, he was a successful stockbroker in Wall Street and provided handsomely for his wife and fine family of four children. Then, a few years ago, when the market appeared to be dangerously shaky, Jim very wisely captured the last of his failing assets and moved his family away from New York's chic Upper East Side to Martha's Vineyard in Massachusetts. There, Jim opened a restaurant and with Piglike determination, began putting his talents as a chef to some very tasty use. The first year, Jim lost money. But then everybody knows about first-season losses in new business ventures. The second year, Jim broke even. With nothing showing in the red column, Jim was ecstatic. He had escaped the ranks of stockbroker unemployment and was managing to live, comfortably self-employed at a trade he adored.

During this third season at the Vineyard, Jim decided to invite a few old friends and ex-cronies from New York to come up and visit his place for a free meal and some sorely missed erudite conversation. If there was one thing he did not love about island living, it was the lack of culture and pals with whom he could play bridge and rap. Being a Pig, Jim does not make new friends easily. He needed the company of old cohorts. He owned a gourmet restaurant and so felt that by extending his hospitality, people might be enticed to pay him a visit or two.

What Jim did not reckon on, however, was what all of us less naïvely warm-hearted types instinctively feel. An open invitation to one's summer place can very well cause an outbreak of vacation fever among overheated, underhoused city dwellers who need free room and board in order to offer their families a vacation. Friends (and some acquaintances whom Jim never cared if he ever saw again) began thronging Jim's already busy establishment. At first, he was delighted by this response to his generosity. But by the time June turned into what might have been a very profitable July, almost half of the restaurant's clientele was composed of Jim's free-loading "friends."

I called Jim at the restaurant to ask him what he intended doing about the problem.

"Simple," said Jim. "I raised the prices. A little here, a little there. It's hardly noticeable."

Naturally, the tourist trade at Jim's seaside eat-in came to a grinding halt. By the end of August, things began to look grim. Jim's landlord had come to dine there with his wife. The prices were so exorbitant and all the tables so full, the proprietor of the building thought Jim must be making a veritable killing with his cookery. So he raised Jim's rent by fifty dollars a month.

In a panic, the good Jim opened up his heart to those of his friends who had stayed late one evening for a bridge game. "I'm going broke. I'm really sorry, fellows, but it looks like I'll have to ask you if I can borrow some cash to get up the rent for the winter months."

But one by one Jim's "friends" began to find reasons for departing the premises and the island.

By October, the resaurant was lost to Jim. He couldn't make the rent. Sandra had to take a job as a waitress. Jim stays home now and watches the kids while she works. Once in a while he does a little private catering to keep his hand in. But mostly Jim just spends a lot of time drinking and wishing he weren't such a nice guy.

Jim's story is typical of Pigs in commerce. They work very hard, put in long hours, and struggle valiantly against all odds, only to lose their shirts because they are often much too kind-hearted to say "No" to a customer who needs credit or a discount.

There are some extraordinary Pig-tales of industrial or business wizards who have more than "made it through the winter." There is, in fact, a branch of the Pig family that is known for its diligence as well as its brilliant successes. A sampling of names will surely surprise you. William Randolph Hearst, the newspaper tycoon, was born in 1863; Al Capone, the heartless gangster and his co-Pigs Ernest Hemingway and Humphrey Bogart were born in 1899. In 1911, Aly Khan came along, accompanied by Lucille Ball. Henry Kissinger, Prince Rainier, Peter Lawford, and photographer Richard Avedon were all born in 1923. 1935 gave us Woody Allen, Julie Andrews, Diahann Carroll, Eldridge Cleaver, and European cinema stars Alain Delon and Bibi Anderson. Elton John was born in England in 1947 and he certainly isn't starving.

It is difficult perhaps for anyone to see similarities among the members of this group. But then, we don't know them personally. A public image is always slightly false. Who, except Nancy Kissinger, actually knows whether Henry Kissinger cried his heart out when Gerald Ford (a 1913 Ox) upbraided him for committing a grievous international bungle? How many people do we speak to who could testify that Al Capone never gave his stolen monies to the poor? We know from the movie, *Citizen Kane*, that W.R. Hearst was a blubbering fool when it came to women. He built them fabulous palaces in exchange for a smile. The Aly Khan was a womanizing loser and he never had to earn any money because the entire Arab populace awarded him his weight in gold every year just for breathing in and out regularly. Bogart? He worked for his money. But he died of that work, as well. And I honestly cannot tell you how many nights he may have spent weeping limply in the arms of Lauren Bacall because he hated his tough-guy movie image.

Let us take a quick look at Ernest Hemingway. "Papa," as he was known to intimates, always wrote stories and books about his own super machismo and bravery in the face of danger. While he was alive and for a time after his death, public opinion had it that Hemingway was the very soul of masculine courage and strength. In his writings there were no anti-heros such as we see emerging today. It seemed that to "Hem," a man was a man was a man.

But remember what Willie Shakespeare told us about those characters on the stage of life who "protest too much." He warned us to be on the lookout for any person who raved too fervently about or against a given subject. Thanks to Shakespeare, we know that if a woman seems excessively resistant to a man's advances and pays a lot of lip service to insulting and berating him, it is probably a sign that she is attracted to him. So much for Shakespeare.

After rereading Hemingway's last published novel, *A Moveable Feast*, I did a bit of ruminating about just what sort of private man the bearded burly writer must have been. The small book I had just read was about Hemingway's early years with his first wife and baby "Bumby" in Paris. *Moveable Feast* is one of the most touchingly sentimental pieces of literature I have ever read. I looked up the sign of our "Uncle Ernie" and found out he was born in a Pig year. This discovery at first surprised me. But then I reconsidered. Hemingway probably felt obliged to write all that heroic baloney about soldiering and heroism. For a start, effete esoterica was most unpopular in his day. Tearjerking books of flowery prose would never have sold. Secondly, his exhibitions of bravado with everything from women to rampaging bulls were most likely a cover for the fact that Ernest Hemingway was a deeply sensitive and gentle man.

Whether as a means of concealing their shyness or simply because they enjoy it, Pigs often perform for their friends. They make excellent actors and actresses and fine singers and dancers. Fred Astaire is an 1899 Pig. There is a natural incisiveness in their humor. Pigs, though sometimes duped and tricked by life, have an innate ability to see experience for what it is worth. They are among those who can easily say, "I knew I was making a fool of myself by buying that fur coat. I suppose I deserved to find out it was fake." A twinkly Pig smile turns easily into a guffaw—and many times the laugh is on him.

People born in Pig years are not adverse to bearing the brunt of teasings or practical jokes. As the saying goes, "They can roll with the punches." Unluckily, this good-naturedness on the part of Pigs renders the task of victimizing them almost too easy. Pigs are not fools, nor are they slow-witted and dull. In their work, Pigs are almost invariably gifted. Be it the arts or plain hard labor, Pigs always accomplish what they begin and pay close attention to detail. What is it then that causes them to fall prey to those less moral and benevolent than themselves?

Pigs lack judgment about other people. Because they adhere so fervently to the theory of the "Noble Savage," it is next to impossible for them to lend credence to the regrettable truth that many times "people are no damned good!"

In Paris about three years ago I met a couple at a small dinner party. The husband, Yves (b. 1935), was seated next to me at table. During the meal we had a long chat about painting. Yves, it turned out, is a very successful art dealer. He buys and sells eighteenth-century prints about which he knows literally thousands of interesting facts. Yves's wife, Martha, is an American girl from California. Blonde and statuesque, Martha is rather more thin than pretty. She is the kind of woman who wears clothes well but spoils the effect by intermittently squinching her mouth into a pout while speaking. Still, I so enjoyed the company of her scholarly husband that I asked them if they would like to come to dinner at my house later that week. Screwing up her mouth in a most unattractive manner, Martha answered for both of them. "I suppose we could come. Where do you live?"

I gave her my address and set about mentally planning a dinner for some of my most art-oriented friends. I knew Yves would like to meet my great pal, Marie, who is an abstract painter of no little talent. Marie loves to discuss art history and has a fund of knowledge about same. Ticking off a few more names in my head, I assured myself the get-together would be a jolly one. We would be eight. I decided to make *boeuf bourguignon* and serve chocolate mousse for dessert. Yves was a portly fellow, whose *gourmandise* at dinner had left no doubt in my mind regarding his taste for rich foods.

Though I had enjoyed the planning of my dinner party, the event itself left much to be desired. Yves's wife, Martha, turned out to be a Class A bore. She did nothing but nag her poor husband from the apéritif through the dessert (which she could not eat because of her liver condition). To me, Martha said little or nothing throughout the evening. But to Yves she had plenty to recount. "Your eating disgusts me" came up during the main course and pleased all in attendance no end. After my guests squirmed through that remark, Martha said, "Yves, I think I'm going to be sick." That pleasant dinnertime tidbit was followed by a trip to the bathroom and all of its incumbent wretchings and flurry. When Martha and Yves returned from her bout with nausea, I was asked if it would be all right to remove the Roquefort cheese from the table. Its odor offended Martha's sensitivities. And P.S.: "Could she have a peanut butter and jelly sandwich?"

After interminably careful preparations for facing the night air were made for Martha's delicate self, Yves bade one and all a cherry *Bon Soir* and took her blessedly away before I served the cognac and coffee around the fireplace.

Charlotte, who had given the earlier soiree at which I had made Yves's and Martha's acquaintance, heaved a sigh of relief at their departure and said, "That woman is a monster. She has no children to look after. Stacks of money to spend. And too much time to think up ways of torturing her husband."

Since Yves had been so raptly attentive to his wife's every whim and repeated snipe, I asked Charlotte if her friend Yves had always been so lenient with losers.

Charlotte gave me the inside scoop. "It's the story of his life. We can find it amusing or not. Sometimes it makes me sad. Yves is a wonderful, talented man. He has everything to offer a woman. Yet, his experiences with people, male or female, are always borderline mistakes. For years, he has supported a couple of do-nothing painters here in town, because he thinks they are talented. They take advantage of him. They never do much work, nor do they repay his kindness with so much as a dinner invitation. Too, he's been known to lend women money, because he thinks that will make them like him better. I suppose you might say that Yves is insecure, although I see no reason why he should feel that way. On the odd occasion, when he does take up with nice people, they accept him just as easily as all the ne'er-do-wells he likes to pick up. I mean, if you want a concise description of Yves De La Barre, I would say he is the kind of man who would give money to a cirrhotic alcoholic who told him he was dying for a drink."

My faithful friend Marie had been listening to this story, eyes filled with pity. She said, "The poor man. I reckon I shall have to call him tomorrow at his office and ask him to lunch. He could use a friend like me."

We all laughed at Marie's left-handed concern for Yves's welfare. Yet, I remembered that she too is a Pig, and Pigs are hard to stop when they are about the job of helping someone less fortunate than themselves.

As I said earlier, whatever it is that hounds the Pig and causes him so often to lose, when he ought to be winning, is still a mystery to me. When I look at the lives of all the sweet Piggies I know, I always wish I were able to infuse them with some healthy selfishness or at least give them somewhat more of a mistrustful attitude toward people who may try to hurt them. But, then, if we didn't have any gullible Pigs around us, who would take up the slack in the benefactor department?

If there is one Pig character trait that might be considered a fault, that characteristic is stubborn unwillingness to heed the advice of others. Though Pig people are good listeners and fine friends, they have very little real regard for the opinions of others. The stubborn way Pigs resist the truth about themselves is uncanny. Just try to advise one of these creatures and you will see what I mean. They find ways around every possible suggestion that might set them on the right path. It's almost as though they want to fail.

Pigs, through use of their talents and the help of adoring friends, sometimes do perform great feats. But more frequently they don't seem to care enough to push their careers over the top. Real worldwide renown or notoriety seem to frighten the Pig. In his dreams he may wish for fame and fortune, but the upward road in any given domain will surely involve much compromise, perhaps even a bit of pandering, and certainly the confrontation of new contacts. Such entanglement is foreign to the Pig's nature. Remember, he does not like to tell fibs or even so much as skirt the truth by omission. The road to that pinnacle that others may term triumph is much too arduous for the honorable Pig.

What Pigs fear most is incrimination. If in any way they are enticed into dubious situations where their respectability is questioned, Pigs can become dangerously enraged, both at themselves and at the party who seduced them into the hated position. It is for this reason that the Pig's mental stability can sometimes be fragile. Although he tolerates almost any honestly induced setback or blow to his ego, the Pig cannot live through any experience wherein his integrity might be jeopardized. The possible disapprobation of his fellow-man strikes terror in his heart. If a Pig does allow himself to be lured into a shady deal, or is persuaded to commit a crime, it will cause him eternal suffering. From that point onward, his life will change. The Pig's guard will be up, his mind full of torment, his timorous manner that of a beaten animal. Either the transgressed Pig will thenceforth lead a life of virtue, trying to live down his error, or else he will flounder and wallow in the muck of his misdeed. Excess of any kind threatens the Pig, which is probably why so many of them are overweight. Temptation lurks behind everything the Pig encounters. He is strong of mind but weak of spirit.

You will find Pigs in all professional walks. They thrive in the arts, do well at industry, and are even capable of the hardest slave labor. They make charming acquaintances and fast friends. Pigs never really have to worry about being rich enough. They are so well-liked and respected that people bring them goods and food. A grave danger to Pig well-being exists, however. While generosity abounds in his very backyard and manna seems to fall from the skies to fill larders and feed children, the Pig nonetheless must always question the source of such bounty. It could just be that those he thinks are philanthropic souls are merely showering him with donations in order to fatten Mr. Piggy for market.

MADAME PIG

When my exasperated mother used to ask me to shovel debris from out my filthy bedroom, she often said this: "How can you stand to live in this pigsty?" Had I only known that because both my elder sister and my darling mother were born in Pig years (1935 and 1911 respectively), our house was truly just that—a Pigsty! I might have come up with some characteristically (for me) smart remark. But per-

haps it is better that I had not yet studied Chinese Chance. Pig or no
Pig, my earnest mother would never have put up with what she liked
to call backtalk.

Having spent my first seventeen years in the above mentioned
Pigpen, I can assure you that Pig ladies are anything but piggy. Our
house was as clean as a pig's whistle at all times. Without resorting to
even minor blasphemy, I can tell you that my Pig of a mother spent all
her precious youth cleaning up after me and my sibling rivalries in
patient adherence to the hopeful ideal that someday we would probably
grow up and learn to stay clean. She was right. Thanks to her fine example, her progeny turned out to be maniacally, squeakily clean adults.

But besides winning the Good Housekeeping medal for cleanliness,
there are a ton of fine qualities in my mother's kit bag. Like all other
Pigs I know, Elva (that's what we now call Mother around the barnyard) is loyal, honest, and naïve to a fault. She often tells stories on herself. The impact of my dad's brand of biting British humor depended
entirely on the intentional placement of one person or another into a
position of ridicule. Until there were enough of us children around the
house for my papa to practice his so-called wit upon, Elva bore the sin
gle-minded burden of playing victim to her husband's jibes.

Not too many months ago, I phoned my mater familias from a
faraway American city to ask her one small question. As always, we
ended up chattering at each other for over an hour. During this
marathon of girl talk, I divulged her Chinese astrological sign. Elva tit-
tered in her ladylike fashion and asked, "A Pig? Whatever does that
mean? Am I supposed to roll in the mud or something?"

"Not at all," I reassured her. "It just means you are gullible and
sweet and too good for this big, bad world."

Verily, Elva riposted, "I'm gullible, all right. Did I ever tell you
what your father and his poker cronies used to do to me when we
were courting?"

Ever the curious sooth-seeker, I begged my mother to retell all.
She reminded me of at least ten funny stories, all of which my taunting
father presented as facts during their courtship. Elva admitted that
until four or five years ago, she believed most of them to be patently

true. I retained only the three best ones, which I hasten to impart as prime examples of Piggish credulity:

1. My mother was told that it was a common parking practice among motorists to hitch their cars to the paw of a giant stone lion that sits menacingly in the city square of Buffalo, New York. My father informed her that in order to insure a vehicle's safety one merely walked up to the lion's huge mouth, stuck a head bravely inside, took a numbered padlock from the gullet of the beast, and left a nickel in its place. Elva believed that one until she began driving her own car some twenty years later and tried this unique parking method for herself.

2. Niagara Falls lie some twenty miles to the northwest of Buffalo. As a young woman, my mother had no idea of local distances. She was neither born in those parts, nor was she the type who bothered to look at maps. So my father told her that, if she so desired, one night they would get on an overnight train and travel to the falls in style. Now my mother was never a stupid person. But she believed in that luxury sleeper train until a very short time ago. She knew full well that one might drive to Niagara Falls in less than an hour. But it never occurred to her that a sleeper train might not have needed to exist. "It seemed such a nice idea," she giggled.

3. This, to me, is the topper. Have you ever noticed the Indian-head symbol on old Pontiac car hoods? Well, if you have not, believe me, it was very much there when Elva was younger. One day, having seen the emblem while strolling with my father and one of his friends, she remarked on its attractive lines. Always eager to tease, my dad said, "Oh, yes, it is an excellent likeness of old Joe."

"Joe who?" wondered my mother.

"Joe Pontiac. The chap from the Indian reservation out in Tonawanda. We know him (wink, wink over Elva's head), don't we, Jim?" Jim nodded his accord. Once more, my mother took what they had said as gospel. She had no personal reason to resist.

Pig ladies are just plain wonderful people. They are neither aggressive nor harping toward their mates or families. They seek little or no glory for their kind deeds and words. Yet, in later years, they often regret not having been more daring or selfish. Harboring long-term frustrations is always very much with women of this sign. Many times, they grow bitter and sorrowful in middle years because of the hard knocks life deals them. As long as they are safely married and securely cared for, Pig women don't think very much about the outside world. But, if suddenly widowed or stricken by illness or depression over children fleeing the nest, coping with sadness becomes their major pursuit.

If you love a woman who was born under the sign of the Pig, you will have to make two pacts with yourself before embarking on any prolonged relationships with her: For a start, you must realize that you will be her main source of security. The Pig lady is by nature a leaner and a dependent. With this in mind, you must entrust her to your careful custody. Nurture her. Comfort her. And don't tell her any lies!

Secondly, even though she prefers to hide her head in the sands of time and plant her feet firmly on the path of least resistance, you must encourage—nay, force—your beloved Pig mate to get out into the world at an early age. Patiently, you must teach her to fend for herself. Show her the ropes of life. Shower her with gifts if you must, spoil her indulgently with loads of love and sex and more love. But, please—oh, please, kind sir—do not allow her to sink into the morass of her own unwillingness to face facts.

The Pig woman's entire existence is crowded with enemies. She must learn to fend them off, to fib a little in tight spots, to cultivate that streak of eventual vengeance inside herself by expressing anger or sorrow or fears as they come along. Otherwise, unless she is lovingly cajoled into interpreting truth and justice for what they are (rather than as she would like them), as your pet Pig approaches middle age, you may begin to notice that you have a very disappointed and crazy lady on your hands.

MONSIEUR PIG

Goodness appeals to the Pig male. Evil causes him to bristle, seethe, and sometimes drives him to destructive excesses. It would be foolish to suppose that there are no malevolent forces at play within the Pig's heart. We all know that Al Capone and William Randolph Hearst were far from namby-pamby or wishy-washy benefactors of humankind.

Yet, much of what these despotic beasts are famous for, if interpreted according to their own set of values, was perpetrated under the guise of doing good for those they believed should inherit the earth. Just as Hearst thought the world should be willed to tyrannical reactionaries like himself, it is conceivable that Capone committed his crimes in hopes that the gangsters would take over a troubled America.

Most Pig men are malleable, loving providers of warmth and material wealth for wives and families. The notion of infidelity, which automatically infers hypocrisy, is distasteful to the average Pig. If provided with sufficient affection, a Pig mate tries to do his best by everybody who lives under his wing. Take away the ardor, remove the sympathy, strip away the romantic trappings of a relationship, and the Pig male will shrink inside himself, eat too much, drink outrageous amounts, and suffer in silence. Though he is hurt and saddened by what he considers his own failure at making things work, the Pig is not likely to show any emotion beyond glum.

Now, Pig men are not fools. They are intelligent and usually extremely cultivated people. Gifted for social rapport with almost any person of their own or other signs, Pigs give smashing parties, wait on their guests, and tell amusing stories in company. They are generally well constituted for earning more than adequate incomes. And, too, Pigs are lucky in business.

But in love situations. . . .

Pig men are so often so good that they end up standing at the altar alone. They have difficulty understanding that some women like conflict, a spirit of competition and challenge. Instead of contesting, when Pig males get hurt or are sent an inevitable "Dear John" letter, they shake their weary heads and wonder why.

Pig gentlemen are so winning, so loving, so direct and honest and sensual, it's enough to make me want to run to the farthest corners of the earth to escape the coax of their male wiles.

Should you have the luck to be courted by a Pig, remember to take him seriously. Never dally with a Pig man's sentiments. That is not by way of warning you that he will break your door down or employ some hideous revenge tactic upon you if you do such a thing. Oh, no, it is you who will be doing the breaking of his tender and trusting heart.

So, my sisters, take it easy on the Pigs. If you consider yourself to be a trustworthy and strong lady who can handle recurring pessimism, lamentation, and a surfeit of love in the form of too much attention and sentimental surrender of emotion, marry yourself to a Pig man. For this match to work, you must be buoyant, brimming with gaiety, honest in the extreme, and truly giving of your sound advice for his frequent bouts with melancholia.

If, for any reason, you fear that your own nature will not permit you to indulge your Pig in such overlove, please do me the favor of bowing out while the bowing is good. I don't know how you feel about it, but in a very old-fashioned way, it breaks my heart to see a man weep.

CO-SIGNS

PIG/Aries *(March 21—April 20)*

Here fire meets with the element of mitigated water. A geyserlike Pig character is born of this union. A trifle more volatile than most, the Pig/Aries will fight more for what he thinks is right than Pigs are wont. Snap judgments and too-quick jumping to conclusions are the least attractive traits of his character. Above all, Pigs born in the sign of Aries are talented for the arts. They seem, in one lifetime, to be able to attack at least three or four different forms of artistic endeavor with equal gusto. Their private accomplishments may grow into public achievements, providing they are willing to accept the assistance of patrons and/or the advice of those more cunning than themselves. Endowed with plenty of energy, what the Pig/Aries lacks is ruse.

PIG/Taurus *(April 21—May 21)*

This body of apparently still waters will most probably contain an undertow of hidden rage at the world. Because the Pig/Taurus has trouble expressing himself except through deed, all that artless sensuality may bottle itself inside his head. Without proper outlet for his earthy power, an inner struggle for victory over ingenuousness will ensure. Art, literature, culture in all of its forms will intrigue and delight the Taurean born under the sign of the Pig. Perhaps he should endeavor to learn to sing and dance in order to lighten his ponderous presentation of self. Pigs cling stubbornly to purity. Taureans are obstinate on almost any subject. Both signs enjoy material comforts and the pleasure of the table. If these subjects are not able to check their tendency for excess, they can become fat as pigs and pig-headedly stuck in a rut.

PIG/Gemini *(May 22—June 21)*

As the light-headed air of Gemini brushes over the stillness of water, this Pig's approach to life may gain in levity what it loses in calm. In an unsophisticated, yet intelligent manner, this Pig subject will be born with the gift of diplomacy and tact. He is able to shift his viewpoint with the wind. Yet, he is not in danger of becoming wishy-washy, as he is mercurial enough to be well-spoken and therefore able to express his wishes eloquently. Properly channeled, this porcine character's mental agility will win him much acclaim. Albeit that as a Pig he may desire to shrink from ambitious careers in the limelight, he will be saved by his innate Gemini desire to perform. *En garde*! Pig/Gemini. Those who applaud you now may be feeding your ego for their own purposes. If you suddenly get a whiff of the smell of fresh blood, it could very well be your own sweet juices escaping through a tiny hole in your jugular. Enemies abound.

PIG/Cancer *(June 22—July 23)*

Too much still water is likely to run very much too deep for the Cancerian Pig's own good. Frustrations will oppress this person. No matter what he tries to accomplish in the world, he will meet with opposition from within. Instinctively, this subject defends himself before being attacked. He leads with a strong arm to avoid being hurt. He is overly sensitive, profoundly emotional, and often troubled with sorrow and pity for those less fortunate than himself. Because of this love of humanity, our Pig/Cancer may become superficially surly. He is frightened that his sentimental feelings may surface and be visible to any and all enemies who he knows are lurking, out there behind every tree and bush. So he squelches the urge to be jolly and easygoing. The Pig/Cancer hides his innocence behind a mask of strength. You need not be fooled by this disguise. Scratch the surface of a Pig born under the sign of Cancer and you will find a Santa Claus, all crinkly-eyed and jolly. Privacy is imperative to his survival.

PIG/Leo *(July 24—August 23)*

This subject is aboil with a sanely jaundiced view of the world. Bubbling over with the urge to trot out his sardonic opinions, the Pig/Leo is well-equipped to handle the rigors of public display. The fires of Leo heat his limpid waters into a pleasant stew of jocularity. Twinkly and full of fun, the Pig born in Leo may hope for greater spotlighting of his talents than those born under other signs. Leo gives him verve, adds fuel to his tank of talents, and lends him aggressiveness. The Pig's influence on Leo is a calming one. The alliance is both positive and destined for success. Watch out for self-indulgence. How would such a gifted person look under those studio lights with a paunch and a hangover? Not so pretty, I'm afraid. Go easy on the desserts and drink a lot of water. Thin is beautiful.

PIG/Virgo *(August 24—September 23)*

Herein we find a gemstone, washed and polished to perfection by the loving waters of time. Unless someone plucks this pearl from out erosion's path, he may simply disappear and never be heard from again. Virgos are so like Pigs (and vice versa) that one is tempted to encourage them to run and jump and roll in the nearest mud pile for a bit of comic relief from virtue. In every way—sensuousness, purity of thought, meticulous attention to detail, and rank naïveté—the two signs resemble each other. For this subject to erase some of the clean, I suggest much education, an enormous variety of experience, travel, and even an occasional taste of the seedier side of life. Even with all of this, our Pig/Virgo may continue to wish the world would get off his back and let him wallow in the simple life. At all costs, he will always veer from success and back onto what he considers the path of righteousness. The Pig/Virgo could do with a scheming manager to crack the whip of bitter truth at him daily.

PIG/Libra *(September 24—October 23)*

Caught between the heavens and the deep blue sea, this subject can just about never decide upon which foot he prefers to dance. Yes, he is willing to do that errand for you. Certainly he longs to sit by your sickbed holding your hand. But why doesn't anyone ever want to do the same for him? Libras are characteristically nonaggressive. They never want to rock the boat. Pigs adore peaceable solutions and recoil in horror from scenes. Shilly-shallying is the natural enemy of the Pig/Libra. If he is nice to people, he is too nice. So he will decide to be horrid for a while. That doesn't work either because then he has to settle for being disliked by at least one or two outsiders. This Pig cannot tolerate disapproval. He longs only to please and keep things on an even keel. Unfortunately, reality always rears its ugly head. Inevitably, he must peer beyond those blinders of luxury and material wealth that he had specially constructed to keep out the devil. What he categorically refuses to see is that old Satan resides comfortably and in style right inside his own head. Somewhere, some way, the old geezer will insist on being heard from. His apparitions could be disastrous. Libran Pigs must be made to get out there and fight from an early age. Otherwise their comeuppance will be visited upon them in bitter ways.

PIG/Scorpio *(October 24—November 22)*

If I had to be a Pig, I would choose this brand. Scorpio, although a water sign, is at ease with power and comfortable with intrigue. Pigs need this injection of murk. No person born under the sign of the Pig can ever expect to be 100 percent free of innocence. But the Pig/Scorpio borders on the acceptance of trickery and wile. Not that he will be Machiavellian or evil, but this Pig may know better how to handle subterfuge than other members of his family. Sex will always play an important role in the life of a Pig/Scorpio. Sensuality holds great sway over his life. Warning! Preoccupation with lasciviousness can be destructive. The Pig/Scorpio must keep those trotters firmly placed in reality and not be tempted away from the straight and narrow. Delvings into seamy depths would condemn this subject to remain stuck therein forever.

PIG/Sagittarius *(November 23—December 21)*

Once this combination of signs gets up a good head of steam, he ought to be dauntless in any area of endeavor. Because by virtue of his outrageous idealism this Pig will often be disappointed and may falter in early years, he should not be expected to begin reaping the benefits of his efforts until middle age. Love, for the Sagittarian Pig, is testy ground. He gives too much credence to the power of affection as a solver of problems. The strength to fight it out with the world must come from within. It is never found in romantic tiltings at windmills. This subject must spend much time building and plotting his own fate. Those around him will not be able to resist manipulating him. Although they may recognize his talents, they may try and make use of him for their own self-aggrandizement.

PIG/Capricorn *(December 22—January 20)*

Capricorn's rigor will lend grit to the waters of the Pig. He will probably be defensive and slightly abrasive in his dealings with others. Since he is gifted with natural virtues such as willingness to work and a desire to do the right thing, this Pig/Capricorn person should have no difficulty succeeding at whatever he undertakes. Pigs are sometimes stubbornly bossy (especially when they feel threatened) and wildly sophomoric. In his attempt to get to the top of that mountain, the Pig born in Capricorn may forge almost too blindly ahead. There are two possibilities: He may fall and break a leg. Or else he may commit an error of judgement that will plummet him to the depths of chicanery, never to return.

PIG/Aquarius *(January 21—February 19)*

A veritable whirlpool of activity, the Aquarian Pig draws himself downward into oblivion, unless some outside influence takes the reins. Aquarians are heady people. They care little for the here and now. Pigs are terrestrial souls. Careless whimsy not only frightens them, it offends their sense of what is right. Much pushing and pulling will be present in this personality. The Pig enjoys long-standing intimate relationships. Although Aquarians are friendly, they are often thought to be more interested in superficial contacts than in more demanding deep friendships. Indeed, this union of signs is a fascinating one. If ever they get their heads together, Aquarian Pigs would have enough combined intelligence and strength of character to rule the world. It's an unlikely possibility, but a possibility all the same.

PIG/Pisces *(February 20—March 20)*

A soggy duo, to say the least. The pliable Pisces and the pacific Pig forever entwined in each others' sentimental arms. Probably, the one true defense that this Pig has against deception and disappointment is to adopt an attitude of shrug-shouldered indifference to pain. For this reason, you may find the more successful of Pig/Pisces both blustery and vain. Although they may be obliged not to admit it, Piscean Pigs are among the most faint-hearted souls ever conceived. Mostly scared of their own shadows, they must cling like obstinate old grandmothers to whatever measure of security they have found in life. Old songs, classical paintings, traditional literature are among their favorite playthings.

This combination of signs represents the final influence in the Chinese cycle of Rat to Pig. By the time the earth's water gets around to allowing this fish to swim in it, the depths are very murky indeed. Perhaps we might say that the twelve-year cycle is weary of all this changing. Pig/Pisces people have to work harder than anyone else to make even a tiny scratch upon the surface of the earth. The wisdom of twelve years of mitigating circumstances is upon them. And so is the weight of all the sorrow and complexity that the other signs have managed to stir up.

Following the appearance of the Pig/Pisces, the aggressive Rat arrives anew to cavort and prattle like a freshly spoiled child. Pigs born under the sign of the fish have not been given an easy row to hoe.

PRESCRIPTION FOR THE FUTURE

Pristine Pig, never you fear, I am not about to embark on any disparaging sermons where your honor will be threatened. Rather, I would enjoy the privilege of revealing my sentiments about just how admirable I think you are. If your integrity is still intact, your virtue spruced in its Sunday best, and you can screw up the courage to believe me, perhaps you might gain a pace or two on all of those beasties who repeatedly beat you out in the rat race.

Prancing Piglet to hefty Hog, one and all of you is far too obliging. For reasons that none of us understands fully, you insist on bearing the brunt of criticism with porcine placability. The dreadful things you allow people to say to your face, the way you put up with tension in order to avoid scenes, the giant portions of love that you serve up gratis for no particular return—all of these apparently noble qualities are ironically your worst faults.

A wise man once told me, "Nobody loves a benefactor." What he meant by that cryptic remark may seem to you harsh and even unacceptable, but his statement was based on brutal fact. Well-meaning beneficence is rarely appreciated by those who receive it unless they are eventually forced to return the charity in kind. I am aware that you find this shocking. I can almost hear you mumbling, "Cynic. Who does she think she is, trying to disenchant my silver soul?" Buck up! I promise you that I am Piggishly sincere in my private aid mission to save your pure and loving soul.

Truth is, Piggy wig, you can do absolutely anything to which you set your intelligent mind. That much you probably already know. Whether given the agreeable task of decorating a ten-room house or the less appealing one of cleaning out said house's cluttered closets, you will go at your job with equal diligence, application, and intelligence. Where there is work to be done, you are never the last to the finish line. Even when no one will help you, when cooperation from others is nil and you are left holding the bag, you accept the state of affairs at hand and go about your business as though monumental single-handed chores were your favorite thing to do.

"Oh, never mind about me," you may want to tell me. "I'm doing all right just as I am"; or, "Actually, I prefer to do it myself because the result is better." And you are probably correct. Surely nobody is more thorough and scrupulous than a Pig. But Pig o' my heart, if you find listening to my ravings less than melodious, perhaps you ought to listen to yourself. Your willingness to go it alone and roll with the punches may be fine for you.

Yet, all the Pig people I know well have confided to me at one time or another, in weak moments, that they would dearly love to be recognized. Among them are my mother, who always wanted to be a movie star, and my friend Jim, who has drunkenly confessed that he really wanted his restaurant to become the meeting place of the stars. Both of them would love to step right into that spotlight lickety-split. "I'm a star!"

Like my friend Marie, who always wishes some clever agent would come along someday and scoop up her canvasses for a one-woman show in Paris. Magical Marie, you forever ask me why talent and hard work are insufficient for success. And over and over again I tell you that sometimes in order to gain the upper hand, you must accept that the under-hand will be hard at work performing magical tricks of sleight.

Forget about your integrity for one minute. Paint that blue paint-

ing for the banker's wife, even though you hate blue. Do the best job
you know how. Set a high price on your custom-made masterpiece. You
can be certain the nice lady will hang your canvas smack in the middle
of her living room wall. All of her friends will wonder who the painter
is. Soon, one of them may call you to ask if they might buy your work.
Or, better still, maybe the woman knows a gallery owner. The most
unusual gifts surge from the strangest places. But you must know how
to step outside the ivory tower of principles for the sake of principle.
One blue painting more or less is not going to stain your reputation with
the label "commercial." Blue paintings can in fact be very nice.

"Well!" you may protest, "I'm not going to take that chance.
Anyway, I'm not really all that ambitious. How do I even know if I'm
that good?"

Methinks, Pig, you doth protest too much. If you don't really give
a damn about achieving success, then why do you get so excited every
time somebody wants to buy something you have made? What is so
important about recognition if you don't even care to be recognized?

Maybe someday, dear Pig, when you are long gone, your children will be going through your effects. I can hear it now: "Hey, look,
did you know that Dad could write? Look at all these diaries. The
prose is exquisite. Hey, dig this poetry. Boy, Mom could really turn
out those verses." Bewildered, they will scratch their mutual heads and
carefully place your thoughts back inside your memorabilia trunk. Is
that what you want? Posthumous glory among your offspring?

Come on, get with it. Compromise with reality doesn't hurt a
bit. Why don't you give it a try? Face the music while you can still cut
the mustard, and dance yourself up and over those hot coals of treachery. You can do it. One foot in front of the other. Head up! Eyes
front! Now, MARCH!

COMPATIBILITIES

Affairs of the Heart

Pigs are far from weak. In love affairs (as in business and pleasure) the Pig is a hardy, yet peaceable soul. Because a Pig would never commit a crime or even step on a toe in an elevator if he thought it would make him subject to recrimination, his dealings with lovers are generally open-handed and plain-speaking. Pigs are usually devoted to their mates and often overly generous with a loved one's foibles and inadequacies.

The kind of discretion that Pigs exhibit in their private lives sometimes belies the fact that they are enormously sensual and even a wee bit bawdy. A Pig's love is uncomplicated. He needs no complex fantasies or trite notions of sin to make love enjoyable.

Cats make the best mates for Pigs. Slightly puritanical and even prissy at times, the Cat may be shocked by the Pig's Rabelaisian wit. But, in the long run, Cats gain a hearty sense of earthy pleasure from a patient Pig spouse.

If the Dragon is kindly and well-intentioned, love between a Pig and a Dragon subject can be enduring and mutually beneficial. The Pig will not mind looking after a Dragon's domestic needs and the Dragon will protect the Pig from worldly harm. The Dragon is often tempted to fib to a gullible Pig mate. Lying to a Pig can be simplicity itself. But picking yourself up off the floor when he finds out he has been made a fool of is a shade less easy. The Pig's motto is "Peace at any price" except at the cost of his honor.

In a large sense, Pigs indulge just about everybody's faults. He never holds grudges for long and is rarely guilty of cavalier behavior toward a mate.

There are no further signs, however, that risk making any intellectual, scrupulous, lucky Pig turn back flips of passion. The Pig has a good grip on the rudiments of self-esteem and is not about to let himself be manipulated for long. Roosters, Snakes, and Goats may try to gain a Pig's affection. But he sees them as rather too unsettled for his sensitive tastes.

Even the humane Dog and the high-minded Tiger are tempted to take advantage of the pig's good nature. Pigs are aware of this fact. They do not often make unwise choices.

Social Affairs

Friendship for the Pig is serious business. It is unusual for Pig persons to cultivate scads of intimates. Aware of their good-natured reputation as easy prey for beguiling abusers, Pigs avoid too much close contact in social situations. They are charming and cheerful. But they normally stay away from promiscuous friendships.

A Pig's really top choices for companions should be made among those born in Rat, Monkey, Dog, or Pig Years. These signs have much in common with the Pig and are never shocked by his superficially low-brow approach.

Second-best friends could come from either a Cat or a Goat Year. Though the Cat is initially somewhat taken aback by the Pig's rakishness and may prefer not to attend elegant social functions with a Pig chum, their private rapport is excellent. Besides, the Pig is not a dandy and could not care less if he ever attended an urbane gala. Goats and Pigs understand each other. The Pig can take care of the Goat's basic financial needs with grace and ease. The Goat brings much imagination into the Pig's existence.

Dragons and Tigers can befriend Pigs. But the Pig will never quite trust their good will. The Pig is so susceptible to the force exerted by these creatures, he never feels quite at home in their auras. Roosters and Pigs just get along on the surface. They have little to discuss that doesn't cause conflict. Snakes do not excite the Pig, either. The Snake is too preoccupied with sagacities and elegance to please the rustic Pig.

Business Affairs

Pig people, though neither wily nor willing to employ underhanded methods, are almost invariably successful at earning money. According to Chinese legend, a Pig is the luckiest business person. Through thick and thin, the peace-loving Pig will endure consequences that others, less profound, might consider reason for ruin. After each debacle the pig comes up smiling, valiant, and ready to face another season of worthy endeavor.

The predilection for naïveté that Pigs display from time to time is pointed up by associations with Rat people or those born under the signs of Rooster or Horse. In business, these three have different ideas from the Pig. Easily deceived Pigs are incapable of ever abandoning their policy of straight-dealing for its own sake.

Oxen, Dragons, and Cats are the best partners for the prosperous Pig. All are gifted for hard work and will add just enough guile to the Pig's managerial talents to avoid the Pig becoming enmired.

Tigers and Dogs are too glibly generous with money for the Pig to endure long association with either. Monkeys and Goats perceive the lucky Pig's need for imaginative schemes and can be very useful to him.

And one of the most fortunate unions of all is that of one Pig with another. Their mutual good fortune is undeniable.

Family Affairs

Pig parents are wonderful people. Parenthood is to the Pig what over-throwing a government is to a revolutionary anarchist. Victory! A chance to stay home, away from the madding crowd, out of the line of fire, and cozily ensconced as head of his own household.

Now, due to this feeling of parental well-being, once the Pig subject becomes a parent, he does tend to cling a bit too much to his children. In some cases, the hovering parent syndrome is well-received by the off-spring in question. In others, the Pig risks being hurt.

Snake children, for example, can enslave a too indulgent Pig mom or dad. Snakes need more and more and more attention. And the good Pig cannot refuse. Horse and Cat children do not meet the Pig's smoth-erings with as much *élan* as they might. Both Horses and Cats are slightly indifferent to their parent's wishes. The Pig may find this apa-thy hard to tolerate.

All other signs can be happy with a Pig parent. The Pig parent is self-denial itself. The child who wishes to enjoy a peaceful youth, devoid of scenes and dispute, should only be fortunate enough to be born into a Pig's home. Pig parents make childhood a snap, adolescence a veritable well of comprehension, and will lavish attention on even the most grown-up of their children until death do them part.

THE CHINESE YEARS

What They Tell About Your Future

THE YEAR OF THE RAT

(1900, 1912, 1924, 1936, 1948, 1960, 1972, 1984, 1996, 2008, 2020)

Rat years are full of surprises. A time to invest or preserve existing finances. Though these years sometimes appear full of wealth and bounty, such harvest is merely the calm before possible storms of future poverty. Open savings accounts, start a vegetable garden, put that gold jewelry under your mattress. Rainy days may be ahead. Children born in these years are luckier if their birthday comes in summer. They will not have to dig through the snow for provisions and can benefit from seasonal sunshine to make the hay they will so need during those long winters.

RAT. These years are yours alone. Profit from every possible angle you see before you. It won't be long before your sign comes under some straining influences. Lay in stores.

OX. Rat years favor the Ox. Albeit he is rarely wasteful with money, in Rat years he can count on stashing some extra income.

TIGER Tigers find Rat years uninteresting. They, like everyone else, should not let their boredom blind their sense of economy. Save, scrimp, and tighten your stripes.

CAT. In Rat years, things do not always go well for Cat people. Basic trusts can be broken. *En garde!*

DRAGON. All is well for the Dragon. Rats revere these extroverted fire-eaters. Dragons should invest their fortunes, both monetary and emotional, in Rat years.

SNAKE. Snakes may be ill at ease in the flurry of Rat activity. But they like Rats, and Rats are good to them. Put away that checkbook, Snake. The following year you may need a hefty balance to get you through.

HORSE. Rats do not take kindly to the proud Horse's air of superiority. One of them will give much of himself in the Rat year. Horses should take care in both business and love.

GOAT. Goats had best keep their expenses in check in Rat years. Even other people's money can become scarce if it isn't carefully tended.

MONKEY. A good year for the Monkey subject. Success in every facet of life. If the Monkey is fortunate enough to be in love with a Rat, rapport will reach uncommon heights.

ROOSTER. Watch out for those fragile savings you have worked so hard to build up. Don't count on the Rat for support. He likes you, but has little time for you.

DOG. The Rat year is bereft of the idealism necessary to spur Dogs into action. They find these years superficial and tritely material.

PIG. If I must say so myself, this is an excellent vintage. Have fun, Pig. It's all yours to enjoy when the Rat is running the show.

THE YEAR OF THE OX
(1901, 1913, 1925, 1937, 1949, 1961, 1973, 1985, 1997, 2009, 2021)

In these years, everybody has to buckle down and tote those barges. For those who resist work, Ox years can be disastrously infertile. Dictators flourish in the Ox years. Watch how you vote in those committee meetings.

Ox years are benevolent for farmers. Harvests are usually not attacked by beetle, flood, drought, or marauding animals. For once, the Ox himself is not at odds with his security.

Oxen born in winter are safe from harm and tend to have more jolly dispositions than those who enter the world in summer's season of laborious cultivation.

RAT. For Rats, the Ox year is not prosperous. Remember that Rats like to live off the fat of the land. The Ox does not take kindly to poachers.

OX. Naturally, since he gets to do all the bossing, the Ox should be happiest in his own year. He can make his best decisions when his authority is unquestioned.

TIGER. Tigers do not benefit from the good will of Oxen. Tigers should sit tight and wait until better things roll their way, as all enterprise is ill-advised for the Tiger during Ox years.

CAT. Though the Ox does not directly threaten the Cat's equilibrium, he is not very indulgent with his prissy ways. If I were you, Cat, I'd smooth out any wrinkles. Use your charms while you can. The next year is not going to improve things much.

DRAGON. Not much in the way of authority seriously affects the dauntless Dragon. Still, these will not be his happiest years. Oxen think Dragons are false gods. They do little to make a Dragon's life easier.

SNAKE. Slow to react, the Snake will seem to ignore the Ox's authority. Sit this one out, Snake. Oxen don't give away prizes for beauty while they are on the throne.

HORSE. Work, for the Horse, will be profitable in Ox years. But love will dry up and blow away. Beware of irrational decisions based on emotional letdowns. The next year will be more your cup of tea.

GOAT. The worst. Pity the Goat who loves to pasture in repose. The Ox will come along with his plow and turn over all the sweetest clover.

MONKEY. Whatever the year, the Monkey usually manages to find a way. He is happy in the Ox's reign. Court jesters are useful to the grave Ox king.

ROOSTER. When he has to, the Rooster can pull his own weight. An Ox year will make or break the Rooster. If he applies himself, much profit lies in store.

DOG. Not your best years, my friend. Though you may try to play your greatest deeds, the Ox will find you out. Don't jeopardize your position. Better luck the next year.

PIG. In Ox years, Pigs will have to adjust to the intemperate climate of hard work and stodging. Not his worst years, but perhaps his least amusing.

THE YEAR OF THE TIGER

(1902, 1914, 1926, 1938, 1950, 1962, 1974, 1986, 1998, 2010, 2022)

Tiger years are notoriously turbulent. Political unrest, coups d'états, and catastrophes often strike during these action-packed years.

Prudence is advised in all new undertakings. During a Tiger year, nobody should leap before he examines a venture or adventure. The Tiger, though noble and honorable, endows his years with uncertainty and danger. Tigers never know where they might place their next paw. In Tiger years it sometimes is incumbent upon the rest of us to face head-on collisions with our own enemies. When we least expect that calamity, it surges out of nowhere. Much strength is required of us during these testy times.

A Tiger child born in the daylight hours will be better armed to meet with the almost inevitable perils of a Tiger life.

RAT. Tiger years do not bring Rats that essential security they are always seeking. They should stay out of ubiquitous situations. The Tiger does not take kindly to meddlers.

OX. One year under the influence of a Tiger is enough to infuriate the cantankerous Ox. Prudence and nonviolence should be his watchwords.

TIGER. For a Tiger, nothing could be better than life in a Tiger year. Whatever large-scale projects he envisages, now is the time to formulate a plan of action. He can't miss.

CAT. Tiger years are disquieting to the comfy Cat. He hates to modify his thinking or life style. Nonetheless, the Tiger demands that the Cat do some rethinking. It's never easy to be a Cat in a Tiger year.

DRAGON. The Tiger may just put his Dragon crony up to some daring bravado in his year. Dragons should have no trouble being noticed, which is what they love best.

SNAKE. Snakes find Tiger years exhausting. So much hustle and bustle. Perhaps the Snake will learn some small lesson as uninvolved spectator.

HORSE. Horses can make big decisions in Tiger years. They will find no resistance from the Tiger. Changes are in order for the Horse.

GOAT. Not the happiest years for the Goat. He should take advantage of the fact that nobody is watching and prepare his next coup.

MONKEY. Though the Monkey may feel left out, he will not suffer from the Tiger's influence. Perhaps he should just sit back and watch the show.

ROOSTER. Tiger years are tiring for the Rooster. He will need a rest after one.

DOG. All Tiger causes interest the earnest Dog. He, too, will have a chance to shine in Tiger years.

PIG. The Pig admires the good deeds of the Tiger. He will participate willingly in the fray.

THE YEAR OF THE CAT

(1903, 1915, 1927, 1939, 1951, 1963, 1975, 1987, 1999, 2011, 2023)

Look forward to some big world-wide changes. Meanwhile, we can sit back and enjoy ourselves. Parties, teas, receptions of all kinds are favored for Cat years. Intellectual activity will be rich and durable. Take a course, learn to paint, write, or sew.

Justice is everywhere. Nobody escapes the long arm of the law in Cat years. Stay away from clandestine activity.

Cat children are better off born in summer months. Winter is not kind to the delicate Cat nature.

RAT. If I were a Rat in a Cat year, I would simply hole up somewhere warm and wait until next January. Cats can't wait to get their paws on you. Maintain a low profile.

OX. Things are improving. But Oxen are not yet in their element. The Cat smiles on him from a distance, but prefers not to soil his hands in all that drudgery.

TIGER. Tigers will not be brilliant shining stars of acclaim in Cat years. They might as well wait them out. Patience. The next year is a doozie.

CAT. Good business. Good pleasure. What more could a Cat ask for?

DRAGON. Dragons amuse Cats. And Cats don't have any reason to hurt their Dragon pals. No alarms go off. The applause meters are set very low. Wait, dramatic Dragon, next turn is yours.

SNAKE. It's a successful influence for Snakes. Cats and Snakes have much in common. Taste and finery everywhere cannot help but encourage the Snake to keep on with his mission.

HORSE. Horses have a profitable time. From all angles—amorous, professional, and social—Horses are allowed to shine.

GOAT. Aren't you glad, Goat? These are delicious years for you. Parties, travel, excellent work results will come your way under the Cat's benevolent influence.

MONKEY. Business opportunities are all around, Monkey. Keep smiling. All is well.

ROOSTER. Take this year to recuperate quietly. Keep your eye on the future. Next year things improve immeasureably.

DOG. Cat years relax and delight the Dog. For once, someone else is on the *qui vive* in his place. Go ahead Dog, enjoy yourself. You are protected.

PIG. Is someone trying to get at you? If so, just avoid them. Stay away and don't listen, even if the trouble is coming from within. The only way to fight back is "No!" Your refusal to cooperate will bring you luck.

THE YEAR OF THE DRAGON
(1904, 1916, 1928, 1940, 1952, 1964, 1976, 1988, 2000, 2012, 2024)

Dragon years often give rise to celebrations or festivals. These years are meant for those who dream of vast success and brilliant victory over adversity.

Because of the essentially mythical nature of Dragons, any gains reaped during his year may be fleeting and largely unreal. Much work is ahead for the person who benefits during these years of extravaganza. It's one thing to get to the top, another to stay there.

A child born in the Dragon year is blessed by the forces of magnanimity and good fortune—unless there is a storm on his birthday. In that case, he will require the observation of a watchful parental eye.

RAT. These years appeal to the Rats' sense of panache and flourish. Dragons take kindly to Rats. You may be chosen to lead the parade.

OX. Despite what appears to be an easy and plentiful harvest for the Ox in the Year of the Dragon, it would be wise to keep that yoke tightly harnessed to the plow.

TIGER. Tigers can expect the best. Dragon years are powerful and spectacular. Tigers who start new projects or are involved in old ones will prosper under the Dragon's influence.

CAT. Fulfillment, perhaps even recognition for past efforts, will come your way in the Year of the Dragon. Cats can climb discreetly on the bandwagon, but may prefer their own flaming hearth as refuge from the extravaganza.

DRAGON. The storms have passed. You have every right to promenade your smashing self along the avenues of success. Plan carefully, think things through, and then strike up the band and send yourself some flowers. It's your year!

SNAKE. Snakes thrive in Dragon years. They are fond of grandeur and pageantry. The Dragon smiles down from on high. The Serpent stands by, a willing spectator.

HORSE. Dandy years for Horses. What gregarious Horse could resist such jubilant ceremonies? Head high, go forth into the crowd. Your efforts will be recognized.

GOAT. Goats gain ground in Dragon years. The happy goings-on please the Goat's rampant imagination. The Dragon urges you to join him in prosperity.

MONKEY. The reigning Dragon can always use a helping Monkey hand. When the Dragon is up, so is the Monkey. Enjoy!

ROOSTER. It's fine weather for Roosters all Dragon year long. Dragons deem Roosters inventive and sensible. If big decisions are in the offing, make them now.

DOG. You may not be at ease with the Dragon's showiness and wonder why he celebrates himself. Though Dragon speeches seem trivial, they may just hold some surprising news for you.

PIG. The Dragon year's festivities may smack of too much ado over nothing. Watch from a distance if you must, Pig. But do watch. That Dragon pomp and circumstance are not as empty as they seem.

THE YEAR OF THE SNAKE
(1905, 1917, 1929, 1941, 1953, 1965, 1977, 1989, 2001, 2013, 2025)

Snake years have often engendered cataclysmic events. Revolutions, financial depression, and general upheaval resulting from treachery or flagrant spending may occur in these years.

These are the best years for occupying one's self with physical appearance or beginning new romances. There is sensuality in the very air during Snake years. Studies, too, are favored during Snake years. Sign up for that course you have always wanted to take.

Children born in Snake years will be happiest if the day of their birth is warm and balmy. Snakes do not thrive in cold weather.

RAT. Finances may be a bit tight in Snake years for the Rat. A good time to take off on that long-desired trip or read those overdue library books. Don't consume all those stored-up supplies yet, Rat. Try to smile and keep your nose to the grindstone.

OX. Insecurity is the most threatening of feelings for you. In Snake years, you will have more than your share of self-doubt to deal with. Take your time. Think positively. It will all be over soon.

TIGER. Mind your Ps and Qs, Tiger. And please don't stick around waiting for things to get more lively. Go places. It's your hope for some distraction.

CAT. So much thinking to do. Cats can spend the entire Snake year meditating in front of the fire. The Serpent's influence shines luck on him.

DRAGON. Not quite so brilliant as the year before. But, then, the Dragon is no longer totally in charge of his destiny. The Serpent wishes you no ill. Keep on with your success by applying yourself just that whit more.

SNAKE. Plan, fair Snake, for a year of repose and *l'amour, toujours l'amour*. In your year, no evil can befall you. Besides, this truce with trouble is not all that boring. Or, is it?

HORSE. Don't leave your spouse in a Snake year, harried Horse. The next year is yours to do with what you like. Give yourself one more chance. It may simply be a difficult period.

GOAT. You are in no danger now, gallant Goat. For once you will not have to watch out for disaster or misfortune. The Snake protects you.

MONKEY. Don't let down those barriers yet, Monkey mine. Smile the while you work and drive for success. No use missing out on all that Snake voluptuousness by pulling a long face.

ROOSTER. Something could be troubling you that you are tempted to solve by abandoning it altogether. Slog on through, Rooster dear. Things are looking up around the barnyard.

DOG. The Snake year finds you busily engaged in intellectual forays. Snakes have no bone to pick with you. Relax your guard for a while.

PIG. As usual, you will be making money grow on the trees in your backyard. But there may not be such a prosperous harvest in your heart. You feel constricted. Try to say "No" more often. You may have been far too nice already.

THE YEAR OF THE HORSE
(1906,* 1918, 1930, 1942, 1954, 1966, 1978, 1990, 2002, 2014, 2026)

These are the years when all of us are called upon to shift into first gear and make it over the next hill. An all-out flurry of industry and social gathering will surge from out the woodwork. Build, rebuild, make friends, leave old ones behind, change your image, clean up the existing picture of your life.

Activity is everywhere. Join in, or go home and lock your door against those busy, busy Horse people who may trot up and knock, saying, "We would like to invite you, or ask you to participate, or give you a medal. . . ." For the energetic soul, Horse years are trump cards. For those addicted to lassitude, a Calvary!

Horse children born in winter will fare better than those who first see the light of day in a hot climate.

RATS. Rats, it's true, are vibrant souls. But Horses tend to get in their way. If a Rat spends all of his time worrying about these unfriendly vibes, he'll lose a bit of ground for himself. Ignore the frenzy and go about your work. It's the only method of survival.

OX. Workers to the fore. You will gain much from the diligent Horse's influence.

TIGER. Tigers should take Horse years seriously. They must strive to discover new ways to attack adversaries. You had last year off. Remember?

CAT. Though Cats do not take kindly to excessive activity, a Horse year is full of promise from a social angle. Go places. Luck is on your side.

DRAGON. Nothing stands in the way of Dragons, except perhaps an excess of pizzaz. Take it a wee bit slower. Horses can't quite fly as fast as yourselves.

SNAKE. An excess of passionate pleasure-seeking could smite a Horse year with emotional ups and downs. Certainly, you can count on a busy social life. Falling in love again and again and again.

HORSE. If there has been a catastrophe lying in wait for the Horse, it may now break wide open. Keep a watchful eye on finances and a curb on emotions. Your year is never the best one for you, especially if you are a Fire Horse.

GOAT. Goats are comforted to know that so many are so busy. It probably means the harvest will be rich.

MONKEY. Monkey people will perforce remain in the wings. They can work well under the Horse's influence, but do better to keep out of the spotlight.

ROOSTER. Horse highs and lows do not endanger the Rooster's welfare. He can go wandering about in relative security, if he can find the necessary funds.

DOG. Nervous as usual, the Dog finds Horse years inspiring but anxious-making. He may take a perilous plunge if he doesn't think before he barks during the Horse's reign.

PIG. Emotional trauma still hangs heavy. But things have been worse, and are on the brink of improvement.

THE YEAR OF THE GOAT

(1907, 1919, 1931, 1943, 1955, 1967, 1979, 1991, 2003, 2015, 2027)

Albeit Goat years usually witness some extraordinary political and financial ups and downs, just as things appear to be on the precipice of disaster, a gallant savior rides up and whisks us from the edge of total calamity. In Goat years, there is room for the unexpected to happen. And a good time can be had by those who do not mind dealing with improvisation.

Art, music, and theater should flourish during Goat years. All the Goat's favorite pastimes are indulged when he is in power. Indulge yourself in the unpredictable. There is little else one can do. And the Goat likes it just that way. Goat children are more certain to achieve their goals if they are born on a clement day. Foul weather is not conducive to making those friends essential to a Goat's welfare.

RAT. You see, things are looking up. Throw yourself a party. Send some roses to your own house. And dig out that last bottle of cognac. There will soon be more where that came from.

OX. Oxen do not function in their usual plodding fashion during Goat years. Incertitude befuddles the sensible Ox. He doesn't tolerate caprice. But he might be able to learn something by watching the gallant Goat function so stylishly in disaster.

TIGER. Once again, it's time for travel. Tiger, you will be bored stiff as a stay-at-home this year. The Goat wishes you away. He hates being spied upon.

CAT. A happy time for Cats. Goat years favor all the arts. Cats revel in such an atmosphere. They can relax.

DRAGON. A wise Dragon should not involve himself in such lighthearted frippery, but he might do so out of love. The Goat diverts the Dragon's attention from himself.

SNAKE. It doesn't look very secure, does it, silent Snake? Well, stop worrying and join the fun. The Goat wishes you no harm.

HORSE. Your future looks as good as your present. Now is your chance to make up for lost time. Work will benefit you, slowly but surely. Rejoin the race.

GOAT. This is your life, gentle Goat. How does it feel to be on top of the world? After all the struggles of recent years, you are back on your feet. Plan ahead.

MONKEY. All the unexpected things that happen are grist for your mill. Ideas everywhere. Take a good look before you leap. But do leap.

ROOSTER. The Rooster is a conservative. Goats are so easygoing, it may make the Rooster person anxious. He will worry unnecessarily.

DOG. Oh, Dog, I am sorry things are not in better order. You are such a loyal subject, but the Goat doesn't recognize your form of devotion. If you can just relax a bit, it will all soon be over.

PIG. You have enough money. Love is settling down to normal again. Hope springs eternal. You are back on your emotional feet.

THE YEAR OF THE MONKEY
(1908, 1920, 1932, 1944, 1956, 1968, 1980, 1992, 2004, 2016, 2028)

In a Monkey year, there is no use planning, one's life, storing up goods, or waiting until things blow over before taking a plunge. In Monkey years, anything can happen.

The Monkey's influence puts everybody into orbit at one time. Things do get accomplished, but they are often the result of individual or personal efforts. No major political upheaval or revolution ordinarily finds its way to the top of the heap during these years. If Monkey years are anything at all, they are most decidedly not boring.

Go ahead with your life. Make strides, move ahead, jump hurdles. It is a time of opportunity for risky business and unplanned success. If you have a new idea, now is the time to act on it. Don't look back. You're likely to land on both feet.

Monkey children born in the summer season are favored by nature, fair of face, and clever as the dickens.

RAT. This is the time you have been waiting for. Do things. Go out and find fun. All of your efforts pay off now. The Monkey is your friend.

OX. You are not at home with improvisation. The Monkey's shenanigans trouble you. Take a deep breath. Muddle through, and smile.

TIGER. Tiger, take that dive. Go ahead and move those barriers out of the way. You must keep busy this year. And watch the Monkey's activities. There may be some unhappy surprises in store.

CAT. Coy Cat, if you think you can escape the *sturm* and *drang* by swatting at it with your right paw, watch for what the left one is about. Nothing is sacred during a Monkey year.

DRAGON. You will probably commit some rash act. It may profit you, then again it may do you in. Monkeys are not always kind to Dragons.

SNAKE. All the Monkey's business intrigues you. But you find it perhaps a bit offensive? Go ahead. Leave your thinking behind. It won't do you any good, anyway.

HORSE. Keep your eyes peeled for ruse. But do things. Take steps. Make speeches. Gain ground. The Monkey wishes you no harm.

GOAT. It is not going to be easy for Goat people to escape bewilderment now. Everything is happening so fast. And Goats have no time to ponder.

MONKEY. Have fun. But don't stick your neck out all the way. This is your time. But you could get carried away if you are not careful.

ROOSTER. It's all right to cry, Rooster. Sometimes things just get a little out of hand. Think up ways of reorganizing. You'll need them. Courage!

DOG. Your dander may be up. That's good for your shy spirit. This period will not seem easy. But you'll exit from it victorious if you dare.

PIG. This is a fine place for you to evolve your new theories. Monkeys bring you the guile you so often lack. Luck is with you. And your heart is in harmony with your head.

YEAR OF THE ROOSTER
(1909, 1921, 1933, 1957, 1969, 1981, 1993, 2005, 2017, 2029)

Rooster years are those in which we all must go back to our desks, tools, and fields. The Rooster is a resourceful person. He wants everyone to think his way. Inventions and creative living projects are favored in this year. If you ever wanted to get back to the soil, now's the time to buy that broken-down house in the country.

Disorder will be righted. Military successes may cloud the horizon with bloodshed. Generals will be decorated for valor.

A spring Rooster will be less defensive than one born under winter's duress.

RAT. Put your cellars in some kind of shape. The Rooster will be around to inspect them. You have nothing to fear from this, however. The Rooster king protects his Rat subjects.

OX. You love being alive when things begin to form patterns once again. Take advantage of orderly Rooster years to get back under the yoke of hard work.

TIGER. If ever you wanted to revolt against authority, it will be possible in the Year of the Rooster. That revolution may just have its day. Fight it out. And good luck.

CAT. You pacifists will not take kindly to imposed order. Keep that profile lower than low. And thread unnoticed through the melee until things settle down a bit.

DRAGON. You are in a good position to shine. Roosters need strong fellows like yourselves around them. But put your liberal notions in your back pocket. Save them for the next year. They'll come in handy.

SNAKE. It is all moving a bit too quickly for you, fair Serpent. Your best bet now is to fight depression any way you know how. Smile a lot. Take heart. Read a lot. And stay off the streets.

HORSE. You, wise Horse, are most likely perpared for the events at hand. Your work is protected. Keep your nose to the grindstone.

GOAT. You will probably be obliged to take to the hills. Live as well as you can off the land and don't let the Rooster's influence get you down. Appearances are deceiving. This pause may be most refreshing.

MONKEY. As usual, there is not really any danger to your adaptable self. Keep grinning and make light of it. The Rooster finds you amusing.

ROOSTER. Things are back in perspective for you. But still you must continue to work hard for what you want. There is no rest for the weary.

DOG. Go underground with those bones of the free-thinker era! Wait it out patiently. Don't be discouraged. The next year is your turn.

PIG. You always work hard, anyway. But since you like things in order and are not a trail-blazing rebel, the Rooster year appeals to your sense of industry.

THE YEAR OF THE DOG
(1910, 1922, 1934, 1946, 1958, 1970, 1982, 1994, 2006, 2018, 2031)

If, in the Dog years, we do not all feel perfectly confident that our future will be bright, there is compensation to be taken in the form of a general sentiment of good will and generosity.

Politicking will reach an all-time high of liberal idealism. Those who have felt themselves oppressed will have a chance to speak out. Socialism may rear its little pink nose. Everyone is imbued with giving. Taking is on the decline. Dog children take more time away from guard duty if they are born in the daylight hours. A Dog born at night will be restless and doubly wary.

RAT. The Dog year will be favorable to your business endeavors. Keep your emotional life on an even keel. These are years of progress in work.

OX. You, Ox, do not have much time for those youthful liberals who line the pavements crying for more power to the people. There is much good being accomplished. Keep on with your work. It's only a stage they are going through.

TIGER. You get ahead during Dog years. Despite an overall air of disquietude, you can charge ahead with your plans.

CAT. You don't feel secure. But, remember, the Dog is your friend. For once, you can count on someone else to assist you.

DRAGON. You are not afraid. And there is nothing to fear. Keep your good sense about you. Others may need your advice.

SNAKE. Go after your highest aspirations. And don't be afraid of failure. You are protected.

HORSE. Though this politicking is not your brand, it is always fun for you when the speeches commence. Stay right in there and fight for what you believe.

GOAT. Perhaps you feel abandoned by the masses of people who are too busy getting attention to have much time left for you. Patience. Virtue is at work.

MONKEY. Financially these are not your best years. But then you have probably already taken measures to preserve your fortune. Keep your wits about you.

ROOSTER. Where did the money go? It looks like you may have to get back to work. But you never minded that, did you?

DOG. Step by step you have arrived at your own pinnacle of success. Don't just shrug and say "shucks." Your influence is positive and humanity will benefit.

PIG. Peace has come in the form of virtues you always extolled. Relax your drive a bit. Take time out for some study.

THE YEAR OF THE PIG
(1911, 1923, 1935, 1947, 1959, 1971, 1983, 1995, 2007, 2019, 2031)

Pig Years make everybody feel that life is not so bad, after all. You will recall that the Pig is indulgent with others. He sincerely loves humanity. He believes in the basic goodness of mankind. His influence can only be rich and joyful.

Money and academic matters will be favored during the Year of the Pig. As the final Chinese Chance sign, the Pig represents all the bounty that has built up over twelve years. He embodies not only the good times, but carries with him the sorrows and failures of the dozen-year cycle that his own year concludes. Those Pig children born near the end of the year are blessed. The closer a Pig birthday falls to the Oriental New Year, the better. Otherwise, legend has it that the Pig fattened from the beginning of the year is more likely to be consumed during New Year festivities.

RAT. Nothing to fear. Your life is full of promise.

OX. The Pig year offers you almost too much opportunity. Do not tire yourself.

TIGER. The more temerity, the better. You will be assured of success if you dare. Take chances.

CAT. Security is in style for Cats now. You can go about your business in safety.

DRAGON. A veritable fireworks of occasions to shine. Follow your lucky star with characteristic skill and application.

SNAKE. Things never seem quite perfect enough for you, fair Snake. But these are one of the best years for you. Wisdom is all the rage.

HORSE. You have done fine work in the past. Now you should begin to spoil yourself a bit. Feel your oats!

GOAT. Much good will come your way. Pigs understand Goat people, and shower them with gifts.

MONKEY. Go to it, Monkey! Not that you don't usually, but this is a very good time for one and all. Profit while the irons are hot.

ROOSTER. You would do well to drop some of those barriers of conservatism. The goodies are all around you. Take while you can. Your sign is favored.

DOG. Always looking out for others, you can now relax your guard a tiny bit. Smile. The Pig comes in peace.

PIG. If you have a rich uncle, it is now his turn to leave it all to you. The Midas touch is with you. Love and luck are yours for the asking.

Suzanne White, an American, is a longtime resident of France. Her colorful career includes stints as a high-fashion model and manager of a Paris couture house owned by Elizabeth Taylor. Intrigued by the degree to which famous and influential people she met reflected the characters associated with their birth years, she began earnestly to study Chinese horoscope casting and today is recognized worldwide as an expert in the field.